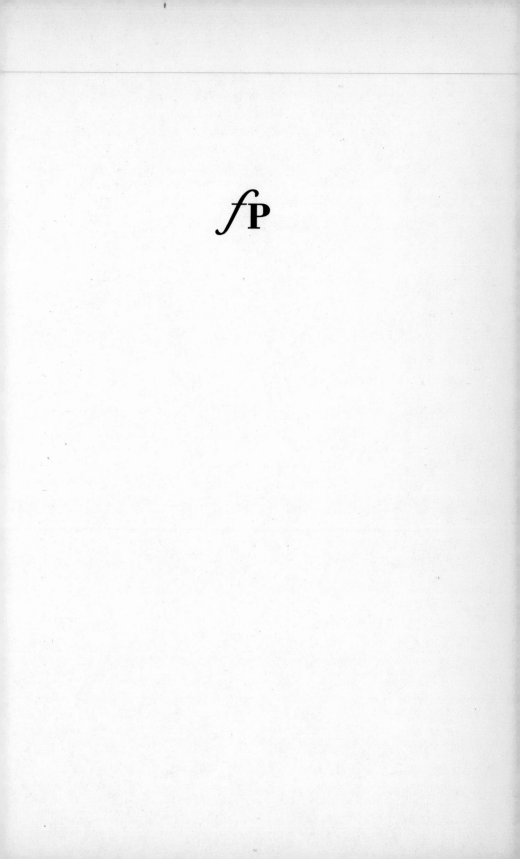

ALSO BY DOMINIC GREEN

The Double Life of Doctor Lopez:
Spies, Shakespeare & the Plot to Poison Elizabeth I

Three Empires on the Nile

THE VICTORIAN JIHAD,
1869–1899

DOMINIC GREEN

Free Press
New York London Toronto Sydney

*f*P
FREE PRESS
A Division of Simon & Schuster, Inc.
1230 Avenue of the Americas
New York, NY 10020

Copyright © 2007 by Dominic Green
All rights reserved,
including the right of reproduction
in whole or in part in any form.

FREE PRESS and colophon are trademarks of Simon & Schuster, Inc.

For information about special discounts for bulk purchases,
please contact Simon & Schuster Special Sales:
1-800-456-6798 or business@simonandschuster.com

Book design by Ellen R. Sasahara

Manufactured in the United States of America

1   3   5   7   9   10   8   6   4   2

Library of Congress Control Number: 2006049669

ISBN-13: 978-0-7432-8071-6
ISBN-10: 0-7432-8071-7

All photos are from the author's collection except:
16, 17: Taken by Italian photographers L. Fiorillo and P. Sebah immediately after the
bombardment (Album 331, Vol. 31 of the Lady Anna Brassey Collection); reproduced by
permission of Huntington Library Archives, San Marino, California
18, 32, 36: From the Sudan Archive, Durham University
25: Courtesy of Leeds City Art Gallery
33: From the Hulton Archive, reproduced by permission of Getty Images

All maps courtesy of Chris Robinson

To my aunt and uncle, Roberta and Terence Conoley,
who first sparked my interest in Egypt.

Contents

Cast of Characters

—— ⌘ ——

Abbas II	Teenage puppet ruler of Lord Cromer's Egypt
Abbas Pasha	Xenophobic son of Mehmet Ali
Abdu, Mohammed	Radical Egyptian cleric
Abdul Aziz	Sultan of Ottoman Turkey from 1861 to 1876
Abdul Hamid II	Abdul Aziz's heir as sultan of Turkey
Al-Afghani, Jamal ed-Din	Founder of Islamism
Al-Barudi, Mahmoud Sami	Egyptian politician, Urabi's patron
Anti-Slavery Society	Influential London-based lobby group
Baker, Sir Samuel	Hunter, explorer, and authority on Nile affairs
Baker, Valentine	A convicted sex attacker, later Egyptian police chief
Baring, Sir Evelyn (Lord Cromer)	British administrator in Egypt
Blunt, Wilfrid	Radical poet and lover of Islam
Chamberlain, Joseph	Radical politician and convinced imperialist
Colvin, Sir Auckland	British commissioner of the Egyptian Debt
Delcassé, Théophile	French statesman and *colonialiste*
Dilke, Sir Charles	Radical member of Gladstone's cabinet

Gladstone, William	Liberal prime minister and aging colossus
Gordon, Augusta	"Chinese" Gordon's evangelical sister
Gordon, Charles George "Chinese"	Soldier, explorer, mercenary, and mystic
Gordon, Henry	Officer and brother of "Chinese" Gordon
Gordon, William "Monkey"	Son of Henry Gordon, nephew of "Chinese" Gordon
Granville, Lord "Pussy"	Gladstone's foreign secretary, a Whig aristocrat
Hanotaux, Gabriel	French prime minister
Hartington, Lord "Harty-Tarty"	Gladstone's secretary of state for war
Hicks Pasha, Colonel William	Retired but ambitious soldier
Ismail, Khedive	Visionary modernizer and reckless speculator
Ismail Ayoub Pasha	Corrupt Kurdish governor of Khartoum
Ismail Sadyk Pasha	Egyptian finance minister, murdered by the Khedive
Khalifa Abdullahi	The Mahdi's Baggara general and eventual heir
Kitchener, General Sir Herbert	Admirer of Gordon, creator of the Egyptian army
Leopold II, King	Creator of Belgium's African empire
Lesseps, Ferdinand de	French engineer, creator of the Suez Canal
MacDonald, Major General Hector	Tough Scottish general

Mahmoud Ahmed	Abdullahi's nephew, a Mahdist general
Marchand, Jean-Baptiste	French soldier and *colonialiste*
Mehmet Ali	Albanian warlord, founder of the khedivial dynasty and its Sudanese empire
Mehmet Said Pasha	Effete heir to Abbas Pasha
Menelik of Abyssinia	Tribal chief and French ally
Mohammed Ahmed	Dongola mystic who declared himself the Mahdi
Nubar Pasha	Corrupt Egyptian politician of Armenian Christian origin
Osman Digna	Hadendowa slaver and Mahdist ally
Power, Frank	London *Times'* correspondent at Khartoum
Riaz Pasha, Mustapha	Authoritarian "Mountain Jew" in the Egyptian government
Rosebery, Lord	Ambitious Liberal imperialist
Salisbury, Lord	Three-times Conservative prime minister
Sharif Pasha, Mohammed	Grand, mildly reformist Turk in the Egyptian government
Stewart, Colonel John Donald	Intelligence officer, Gordon's companion
Stewart, General Sir Herbert	Wolseley's general, leader of the Desert Column
Tawfik, Khedive	Ismail's son, a weak and devious puppet
Urabi, Colonel Ahmed	Egyptian officer, leader of the nationalist revolt of 1881

Wilson, Sir Charles	Wolseley's chief intelligence officer
Wolseley, General Sir Garnet	Ambitious and brilliant general
Zubair Rahmat	Master slaver and Egyptian pasha

IN A MAJOR ARAB NATION, A SECULAR TYRANNY is toppled by Western intervention, but an Islamic backlash turns the liberators into occupiers.

Caught between interventionists at home and radical Islam abroad, a prime minister flounders. His ministers betray him, his alliances fall apart, and a runaway general makes policy in the field. As the media accuse Western soldiers of barbarity and a region slides into chaos, the Armies of God clash on an ancient river, and an accidental empire arises.

This is not the Middle East in the twenty-first century.

It is Africa in the nineteenth century, when the River Nile became the setting for the first major encounter between the West and Islam in the modern era. This human and religious drama shaped our world, and prefigured the crises of our time.

In an extraordinary collision between Europeans, Arabs, and Africans, three empires rose in the space of thirty years.

The first, the plaything of an Egyptian tyrant, fell to European meddling and Arab nationalism. The second, an apocalyptic Islamic fantasy led by a Muslim messiah, fell to European expansion in Africa. The third, the British Empire, arrived in a flurry of humanitarian concern, but endured through brutal force

Three Empires on the Nile

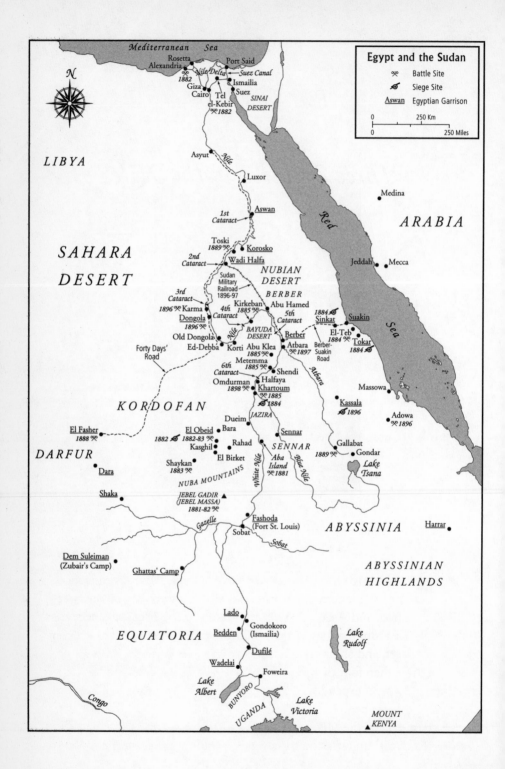

Mediterranean Sea

Port Said
Rosetta
Alexandria
1882
Nile Delta
Suez Canal
Ismailia
Giza
Cairo
Suez
Tel
el-Kebir
1882
SINAI
DESERT

N

LIBYA

Asyut
Nile

Luxor

SAHARA
DESERT

Aswan
1st
Cataract

Toski
1889
2nd
Cataract
Wadi Halfa
Korosko

NUBIAN
DESERT

Red Sea

ARABIA

Medina

Jeddah   Mecca

Sudan
Military
Railroad
1896-97
3rd
Cataract
1896   Karma
4th
Cataract
Kirkeban
1885
Abu Hamed
BERBER

Dongola
1896
Old Dongola
Nile
5th
Cataract
1884
Sinkat
Suakin

Forty Days'
Road
Ed-Debba
BAYUDA
DESERT
Korti   Abu Klea
1885
Metemma
1885
Berber
Atbara
1897
El-Teb
1884   Tokar
1884
Berber-
Suakin
Road

6th
Cataract
Omdurman
1898
Halfaya
Khartoum
1885
1884
Shendi

Atbara

Massowa

KORDOFAN
Dueim
JAZIRA

Kassala
1896

Adowa
1896

El Fasher
1888
El Obeid
1882   1882-83
Kasghil
Bara

Rahad
El Birket

Sennar

SENNAR

Gallabat
1889
Gondar

Lake
Tsana

DARFUR
Dara

Shaykan
1883

NUBA MOUNTAINS
White Nile
Aba
Island
1881
Blue Nile

Shaka

JEBEL GADIR
(JEBEL MASSA)
1881-82

Gazelle

Fashoda
(Fort St. Louis)
Sobat

ABYSSINIA

Harrar

Dem Suleiman
(Zubair's Camp)

Ghattas' Camp

Sobat

ABYSSINIAN
HIGHLANDS

EQUATORIA
Lado
Bedden
Gondokoro
(Ismailia)
Dufilé

Lake
Rudolf

Wadelai
Foweira

Congo
Lake
Albert
BUNYORO

UGANDA
Lake
Victoria

MOUNT
KENYA

Egypt and the Sudan

Battle Site
Siege Site
Aswan   Egyptian Garrison

0   250 Km
0   250 Miles

Port Said, 1869

—⌀—

From the pier of Port Said, a forty-foot statue of
Ferdinand de Lesseps directs shipping into the Suez Canal.

O N THE MORNING OF November 17, 1869, Africa became an island. A modern waterway severed the sandy isthmus between
Africa and Asia, mingling the waters of the Mediterranean and
the Red Sea. From that day, maps would show that the two continents lay
250 feet apart, and shipping schedules would announce that Britain had
moved more than four thousand miles closer to India. With fanfares, fireworks, and a great expenditure of borrowed money and Egyptian lives, the
Suez Canal was open.

At Port Said on the Mediterranean, sixty ships from over a dozen nations
sheltered in the largest artificial harbor yet built, waiting for the signal to

enter the Canal. To the triumphal piping of military bands, the guests of honor took their seats in the viewing stands: the host, Khedive Ismail of Egypt, and his guest of honor, Empress Eugenie of France; the bishop of Jerusalem and the sharif of Mecca; the emperor of Austria-Hungary and the prince of Prussia; the empress's Catholic confessor and the sheikh of al-Azhar, the Islamic world's premier university; and all flanked by complementary battalions of European consuls and Egyptian ministers.

A sea of smaller fry washed around the feet of the stands. In the scrum on the quayside, the Turkish fez mingled with the spiked Prussian helmet, the frock coat with the *jellaba,* the veil with the parasol. French financiers elbowed for room with the international crust of the Ottoman Empire— Greek, Armenian, and Jewish businessmen from Alexandria, Turkish cotton magnates, Coptic army officers—and the mute extras of Egyptian society, the Arab peasant farmers and African slaves who in the chaos wandered onto center stage.

The French engineer Ferdinand de Lesseps waited amid the robes, plumes, and uniforms in his dark business suit. This was the culmination of his fifteen years' struggle against sand, politicians, and bankers. No obstacle of diplomacy or geology had been too great for de Lesseps's calm mania. He had burrowed around or dynamited through every obstacle. Displacing the opposition of the Turkish sultan and the British prime minister like so much wet sand and bedrock, he raised diplomatic support and funding in France, romancing Emperor Napoleon III with a mirage of empire, and the French public with a share flotation that promised a stake in the global economy to the smallest investor. He had supervised every detail, devising elaborate financing deals that tied both France and the Egyptian government to his Suez Canal Company, designing mechanical diggers when the shovels of his Egyptian laborers proved useless against the water table, even planning the guest lists and firework displays for the opening festivities.

Now he waited fretfully. The bottom of the Canal was only seventy-two feet deep and twenty-six feet wide. Protocol dictated that the first ship to enter should be the *Eagle,* Empress Eugenie's broad and ungainly yacht, sixty feet in the beam and three hundred feet long. In a trial run the previous day, a sprightlier vessel from the Egyptian navy had run aground. To remove it before the guests arrived, de Lesseps had blown it up. An accident now meant economic and diplomatic catastrophe. The eyes of the world were on the Suez Canal.

AT THE JUNCTION of Europe, Asia, and Africa, the Canal was intended as a unifier of civilizations, a conduit for the modern obsessions of trade and transit. In the third quarter of the nineteenth century, the global economy boomed. In Europe and America, new machines and mass production created an unstoppable, uncontrollable economic revolution that turned rural peasants into urban factory hands. A machine pulse raced across the world, girdling the seas with coal-fired, iron-hulled steamers, crossing continents and borders with smelted rivulets of railway tracks, bounding immensities of land and water with the electric cables of the telegraph. It created a global civilization, based on Western technology and speaking English or French. "We are capable of doing anything," Queen Victoria marveled after visiting the Crystal Palace at the Great Exhibition of 1851.[1]

This was the spirit of the age: industrial potency and runaway optimism. In France, the Saint-Simonians, a utopian group of technological cultists whose adherents included Ferdinand de Lesseps, prophesied that the convergence of technology, trade, and communication must culminate in the triumph of liberal, mercantile civilization. Free Trade, the British ideologue Richard Cobden had predicted, was "God's diplomacy," its mutual dependencies the best guarantee against war. Between the Great Exhibition of 1851 and the opening of the Suez Canal, this vision leaped into reality. Innovation in transport and communications opened new sources of raw materials, and new markets for finished factory goods. In 1840 the major nations of the world had exchanged annually 20 million tons of seaborne merchandise; by 1869 the figure had more than quadrupled to 88 million tons. The volume of coal shipped rose from 1.4 million to 31 million tons; of iron from 1 million to 6 million tons; of grain from 2 million to 11 million tons; with a further 1.4 million tons shipped of a commodity new to international trade, petroleum.

Britain, the most industrialized economy, saw a manifold increase in its exchanges with the rest of the world. Its earnings from exports to the Ottoman and Persian empires rose from £3.5 million in 1848 to £15 million in 1869. Integrating India into the global economy through the construction of a domestic railway system that allowed the export of cash crops and the distribution of imported goods, Britain's exports to its most profitable possession grew from £5 million in 1848 to over £20 million.[2]

As communication and travel accelerated, the world shrank. In 1869 the telegraphic system between Britain and India generated nearly half a million telegrams. Earlier that year, American engineers had connected the coasts of America with the completion of the Transcontinental Railroad. Now the path to the East was open. Optimism and share prices ran high, and expectation rippled out from Suez. The European economies had to reach abroad to the south and east in order to grow. The Canal would allow the raw materials of the East to flow more quickly and cheaply to the factories of Europe, whose finished goods would wash back east in a great tide of civilization and profit. Just as the flooding of the Nile had fed ancient Egypt, so the transit tolls of the Canal would be the commercial artery of modern Egypt. Progress, the presiding deity of the age, would follow in the wake of the ships taking the Suez shortcut.[3]

On the quayside at Port Said the military bands segued into a three-part harmony of religious platitudes. First a Muslim imam claimed the Canal for a new, modern Egypt. Then the bishop of Jerusalem bestowed the blessings of Greek Orthodoxy on the Canal's commercial aspirations. Lastly Father Marie-Bernard Bauer, Catholic confessor to the Empress Eugenie, closed the service with the hope that Christianity and Islam, two faiths with common roots and a history of violent competition, might be reconciled in the Canal's union of "splendid Orient and marvellous Occident."

"Today, two worlds are made one," he announced. "Today is a great festival for all of humanity. Bless this new highway. Make of this Canal not only a passage to universal prosperity, but make it a royal road of peace and justice; of the light, and the eternal truth."[4]

The international flotilla anchored beyond the breakwater issued a thunderous broadside and lined up behind Empress Eugenie's *Eagle* and Khedive Ismail's *Mahroussah*. Edging into the Canal without accident, they began their lurid progress. Narrow and shallow but perfectly executed, the Canal ran south from the new city of Port Said, down through the desert to the Bitter Lakes and another new city, Ismailia, and into the Red Sea at the port of Suez.

Halfway down the Canal, the fleet paused at Ismailia for a wild carnival. Fire-eaters and acrobats vied with the "Whirling Dervish" dances of Sufi ecstatics and the horseback shooting competitions of the thousands of curious Bedouin who had camped outside the city. That night the flicker of Chinese lanterns lit the sandy road to the khedive's new palace. The invited and uninvited elbowed for room at the buffet, admired a midnight firework display, and watched the khedive and empress waltz to *Leaving for Syria*, a romantic legacy of the Napoleonic age.

The fleet left for Suez the next day, where its triumphal arrival fired off another round of theatricals and pyrotechnics. It took days for the stragglers to return north. Those who could not squeeze onto the express train to

Cairo were left stranded by the Red Sea, and missed a final ball at Cairo and horse races at the Pyramids. Khedive Ismail paid for everything. The hawkers handing out Turkish coffee to rally the flagging revellers, the café proprietors offering honeyed tobacco and *nargila* pipes when they had to sit down, and the hoteliers in whose rooms they collapsed, all sent their invoices to Ismail's Coptic accountants at Cairo.

The Canal opened for business. De Lesseps married a woman a third his age and started work on his idea for a canal at Panama. The guests returned to the courts and counting houses of Europe, aware that as geography had changed, politics must follow. The Canal was a new artery for the global economy, but would it bring peace and prosperity? Would the religious harmony and internationalist optimism of its opening ceremonies fade with the fanfares? And what would happen when the new age of nation-states and technological innovation met the old order of faith and autocracy?

FROM HIS PALACE on the Bosphorus, Sultan Abdul Aziz ruled over a million square miles of Africa, Europe, and Asia: from Cairo in the west to Baghdad in the east, from the Balkan foothills in the north to the rocky coasts of the Arabian peninsula in the south. Thirty-third in a lineage of Ottoman autocrats, warriors, and maniacs that reached back six centuries, Abdul Aziz was also the twenty-sixth Ottoman *khalifa*, the "successor" of Allah and his Prophet. In the Islamic blend of temporal and religious authority, the sultan was the Commander of the Faithful, the spiritual leader of the world's Muslims, and the guardian of the Arabian holy places of Mecca and Medina.

He was also the world's largest absentee landlord. Rotten with corruption, conservatism, and xenophobia, his empire crumbled like a neglected summer palace. European exports besieged his ports, European weapons battered his armies, European loans mortgaged his future, and the European virus of nationalism nibbled at his borders. In 1683, a Turkish army had laid siege to the gates of Vienna, and been repulsed by a European coalition using modern arms and logistics. Now, less than two centuries later, another European coalition had carved a gate to the East through the geographic center of the Ottoman Empire, and at the invitation of the rebellious khedive of Ottoman Egypt.

The sultan was powerless to resist. The emperor whose motto was "The Ever Victorious," whose forebears had terrorized half of Europe, was reduced to junior membership of the Great Powers, as the Europeans now styled themselves. They still addressed him as the Sublime Porte—after the building that housed his foreign ministry—but this was an exotic sham. Among themselves, they called Turkey the Sick Man of Europe, and his treatment the "Eastern Question": to keep him alive for profit or to finish him off for his legacy?

The Russians, first to diagnose his condition, wanted to kill him for a warm-water port on the Black Sea and access to the Mediterranean. The Austrians and the Italians wanted to preserve him, mainly to block the Russians. The French, who had precipitated his terminal illness, sustained him in order to be the sole beneficiaries of his will. And the British, whose "Overland Route" to their Indian empire passed through Turkish territory, appointed themselves the guardians of his sickbed. To Abdul Aziz, the Suez Canal was a Western bridgehead in the heart of his empire, but it was also an opportunity. If he played the Europeans against each other, he might yet recover Egypt.

IT WAS IN EGYPT that the encounter between rising West and declining East would play out with the most spectacular results. In 1798, Napoleon had broken the Ottoman hold on Egypt. British and Turkish troops swiftly displaced him, but the cultural impact endured. The Napoleonic blueprint for the modern state remained in Egypt: an army, a bureaucracy, and the printing press that Napoleon had stolen from the Vatican. Exploiting the chaos, Mehmet Ali, an Albanian tobacco dealer turned Turkish mercenary, forced the sultan to appoint him *pasha* of Egypt. Encouraged by France, Ali set up an efficient despotism. He massacred the Mameluke aristocracy, imported French technical experts, and sent batches of his subjects to Paris for training.

Ali needed men and money for his struggle against the sultan. So he turned south to *Bilad al-Sudan,* the "Land of the Blacks." The black animists of the Sudan had always been Egypt's reservoir of human material, a resource to be exploited like gold, ivory, and ostrich feathers. In the pattern of his twin inheritances, Ali combined the Ottoman model of military slavery with the European model of industrial slavery. Sudanese slaves labored on his cotton plantations, campaigned in his army, and passed through the giant slave market at Cairo.

When Ali's troops reached the Turkish border, the Great Powers pushed him back. His consolation was the hereditary governorship of Egypt. He had the dynasty he wanted, but not the empire he desired. Increasingly senile, and haunted in his clear moments by the ghosts of his victims, he faded with his dreams. When European tourists visited Ali at the Cairo Citadel, they found him sitting in dingy candlelight like a mangy lion, one eye "incessantly rolling about."[5]

Ali's heirs struggled to escape the cage of international consensus. The first, Abbas Pasha, was a portly, paranoid xenophobe who hid in a palace outside Cairo with a menagerie of dogs, horses, peacocks, and bodyguards, entertaining himself with mad tyrannies. It was rumored that when he caught a harem slave smoking, he had her lips sewn together, that he buried men alive in the brickwork of his palace, and that he was "notoriously addicted" to "filthy sensualities." When Gustave Flaubert visited Abbas's palace in 1850, he found the coffee "execrable," the bodyguards dressed like "servants supplied by a caterer," and Abbas "a moron, almost a mental case." In his French-run military hospital, an entire ward was filled with syphilitic bodyguards. "Several have it in the arse."[6]

In 1854, two of Abbas's eunuchs strangled him in his sleep. His uncle Mehmet Said succeeded him. Said had been educated in Europe. French became the language of the court, the frock coat replaced the kaftan, and dinner ended with brandy and cigars. He was so tame to European interests that he trembled in the presence of the French consul. To oblige British travelers en route to India, he built a railway between Alexandria and Suez. To oblige the French, he agreed to de Lesseps's Suez Canal proposal at ruinous terms. Egypt would provide the labor, but it would receive only 15 percent of the profits, and would cede the land on the Canal's banks; irrigated by the Canal, these sand dunes would soon become some of the most expensive agricultural land in the world. To oblige Britain and France, Said took huge loans from foreign banks. In 1863, he bequeathed to his nephew Ismail a 40 percent stake in an unfinished Canal, a revenue of £3.5 million, and a debt of £9 million.[7]

While the French saw the Canal as an opportunity to recover lost influence in Egypt, the British saw it as a threat. Their foreign policy centered on the defense of India, and the Canal complicated the picture. Britain already had an impregnable "India Route": around the coast of Africa. She also had the "Overland Route" through Turkey and Persia. Why divert British shipping through a narrow canal that could be easily blockaded?

The Conservative premier Lord Palmerston derided de Lesseps as a con artist, tricking "small people into buying small shares." All Britain wanted from Egypt, said Palmerston, was "mutton chops and post horses" along the road to India. A patriot to the wisps of his sideburns, Palmerston believed in Free Trade and gunboat diplomacy, not territorial conquest. He saw the Canal as a French conspiracy, "founded on intentions hostile to British views," and a step toward "the future severance of Egypt from Turkey."[8]

As if to confirm Palmerston's suspicions, the French emperor Louis Napoleon stepped in as the Canal's patron. When the first shovels of sand turned in 1859, Britain realized that its greatest rival would soon sit astride the fastest route to the East. This forced a sudden revision of strategy: For the sake of British India and the balance of trade, Egypt and the Suez Canal must be prevented from falling under hostile influence, Arab or European. In turn, this produced a second strategic creep. As in ancient times, Egypt's stability rested on the annual Nile flood. Therefore, the River Nile was integral to the security of the Canal. So were its sources, although it was not yet clear where exactly in central Africa they lay.

APART FROM BEING MEDITERRANEAN, Egypt was also an African country, and in 1869 Britain had no African policy. It had strands of interest—strategic, moral, and economic—and a sweeping ignorance. Britain possessed several ports on the African coast, but they all faced outward; they were stations on the India Route, or bases for the interdiction of slavery. Luxuries from the African hinterland arrived through Arab intermediaries. For centuries, Europeans had found this arrangement so congenial, and the climate so terrible, that they showed little interest in the African interior.

Three factors disturbed this casual arrangement. The first was strategic: the Canal, Egypt, and the India Route. The second was moral. Britain had turned from one of Atlantic slavery's most enthusiastic practitioners to its most earnest scourge. The Royal Navy blocked the Atlantic trade so successfully that in 1868, the court established at Cape Town for the trial of slaver captains closed for lack of business. Having triumphed over the Christian-run trade from West Africa, British abolitionists turned on the other great slave trade, the Muslim-run trade from East and North Africa.

The abolitionists were overwhelmingly Evangelical. They attributed Africa's poverty, ignorance, and slavery to the "degraded" state of the Africans and the "false religions" of paganism and Islam. The answer was the "Three Cs": Christianity, Commerce, and Civilization. British history showed that an economy geared to slavery could be redeemed by a simple appeal to self-interest. Once the Africans had been converted, clothed, and incorporated into Britain's global economy, slaving would naturally give way to "legitimate trade." The abolition of slavery, and its sister cause, the conversion of Africa, would be enabled by Free Trade.

The third factor blended economic optimism and Evangelical urgency with another aspect of the Victorian mentality. Africa was a mystery, and this, the age of Darwin, Sherlock Holmes, and the crossword puzzle, was the great age of problem solving. Even the Africans had no idea how many Great Lakes their continent contained, which mountain was the highest, which river the longest. This blankness was an affront to science. For, apart from being the age of popular religion, this was also an age of popular science.

Pious explorers walked into the steaming forests and disappeared for years. They emerged skeletal wrecks, bearing the tablets of a national drama: tales of months lost to fever dreams, of native porters evangelized in forest clearings, of natural wonders never seen by a white man. They also reported the devastation of slavery: children chained like animals in convoy for the coast, highways littered with bleached bones, the weak dying by the road.

Each report caused a fresh burst of interest and outrage. Never before had a public been so literate, so deluged in newsprint, so connected to the outside world. Britain's industrial and military power already reached around the globe. Now its citizens took part in the march of civilization without leaving their armchairs. The adventurers and evangelists became a familiar cast of favorites, their names coupled like music hall double acts: Burton and Speke, who argued in public about who discovered what; Sam and Florence Baker, who most certainly did not; Henry Stanley, the American self-publicist, and David Livingstone, his Scottish straight man.

When the hero returned, a further burst of glory awaited: the packed lecture at the Royal Geographical Society, the newspaper editorial calling for more money and more discoveries, and the private audience with an admiring Queen Victoria. Then came the apotheosis of Victorian celebrity, akin to the raising of a monolith among the ancients: the book. Great bricks of memoir clad in red pigskin, they mixed flora and fauna with God and geography. Every reader could share the first sight of a new Great Lake. Folding out the soft linen map, he could trace the paths of slavery, the hut where the burning chill of malaria first struck and, discreetly, the village where batches of underdressed native girls had been offered as brides. In the 1850s, a bestseller sold 10,000 copies; in 1853, Dickens's *Bleak House* sold 35,000 in its first year. In 1857 alone, Livingstone's *Missionary Travels and Explorations* sold 70,000.[9]

The missionaries and explorers agreed that a strong dose of the "Three Cs" would cure Africa. The values seemed universal, the debate limited to deciding how vigorously the light should be poured onto the Dark Continent. No one consulted the Africans.

This was Britain's interest in Africa: abolitionism and mapmaking, Evangelism and strategy, the coastal ports and the India Route, the ivory that Britain coveted for the piano keys in the parlor and the billiard balls at the club, the slavery that it abhorred. Little seemed urgent, unless to evangelists accounting souls lost and saved, and little seemed significant, until the Canal arrived, and securing the Canal, and with it Egypt and the Nile, became so crucial. After 1869, these African threads began to tangle and knot, until they could cause the dispatch of armies and the death of a hero, the rise of a messiah and the fall of a government, the spread of the British pink across the map of the world and an arms race that threatened the peace of Europe, a Scramble for Africa and the subjection of millions of African Muslims to a Christian empire.

It was a long way from Port Said to Lake Victoria.

1

Ismail's Dream
1869–73

Ismail, Khedive of Egypt.

Meanwhile it is singular how long the rotten will hold together, provided you do not handle it roughly. . . . Rash enthusiast of change, beware! Hast thou well considered all that Habit does in this life of ours?

—Thomas Carlyle, *History of the French Revolution* (1837)[1]

THE KHEDIVE'S RECEPTION ROOM was more the office of a secretary than a prince. Pink cotton curtains blocked the Cairo sun, muffling the sound of soldiers drilling on the parade ground below. The same material covered a divan floating on a Persian rug, and the family of chairs bobbing around it. The walls were bare but for half a dozen fine crystal sconces, trophies of hunting expeditions in the shops of Paris. In the rosy haze, Khedive Ismail, gourmet and visionary, sat behind a small gilt table like a dozing bear.[2]

Short, broad, and corpulent, Ismail wore the hybrid costume of a progressive Turk, a *stambouli* frock coat topped with a fez. His thick eyebrows, afterthought of a nose, and small mouth rested in a face soft with fat; his barber carved him a close-cut beard in memory of the jaw somewhere beneath his jowls. He spoke an elegant French, low and sonorous, and when he delivered his salon courtesies, his round mouth formed an ingratiating smile. His eyelids drooped. Sometimes his left eye closed entirely, leaving his dull, brown right eye on solitary duty. Now and then, both eyes would widen and focus on his interlocutor, shooting a sharp stare like a python considering a mouse. His admirers compared him to the Sphinx.[3]

Ismail's days were a taxing routine of paperwork, audiences, and fine wines. Rising early, at eight he received his sons, known to the public as the ministers of works, finances, and war, then passed the morning behind his gilt table receiving a stream of consuls-general, concession-seekers, and cronies foreign and domestic. At the firing of a noonday cannon from the ramparts of the Cairo Citadel, he broke for a light lunch, returning to his desk until early evening. Sometimes he left Egypt to look after itself for the afternoon. He took his constitutional in a modest two-horse carriage, identifiable as a monarch only by the doffed hats of European pedestrians, the slight royal wave with which he replied, and the dozen cavalrymen in crisp chocolate-brown uniforms who escorted him. Dinner was at seven, a blend of family supper and state banquet. His guests ate French food from silver plate, and drank Veuve Cliquot and Chateau Yquem from gold-rimmed crystal goblets monogrammed with a golden "I." "The wines are abundant," reported the American consul, "and of superior quality." After the feast, Ismail repaired to a balcony for cigars and brandy. Then he returned to his office, to work until midnight.

He was back at the gilt table the next morning, thirteen hours a day for three hundred days a year, a cross between a delinquent prince and a diligent clerk. Nothing escaped his notice. Nothing happened without his permission, from negotiating a foreign loan to fixing the price of wheat or planning the path of an irrigation canal. An autocrat in the twin tradition of Napoleon and Mehmet Ali, a bureaucrat on a golden tread wheel, and the first of the modern African kleptocrats, Ismail was a man possessed.[4]

———

KHEDIVE ISMAIL had a dream of Egypt. A great land had run to waste, and he would restore it. As in ancient times, the Nile Valley would be the spine of an Egyptian empire in Africa, and he would be its pharaoh, from the Mediterranean to the Mountains of the Moon. Ismail had been educated in Paris and Vienna. He admired the elegance and dynamism of Europe's industrial cities, their manicured parks, grand boulevards, and smoking factories. He saw the machinery of technical civilization at work, and how the wealth it generated gave power to its owners. Intoxicated by the brute power of the machine age, he determined to import to Egypt the exotic European model of the industrial city at the heart of the nation-state. A potent, westernized Egypt could shake off the Ottoman sultan and claim its place among the Great Powers.

Ismail had also witnessed the failed liberal revolutions of 1848, and he feared the volatility of modern industrial society. He wanted the machines and their promise of economic vitality, but rejected their other creation, a meritocratic middle class who might want to turn their wealth into political power. He decided to import technical civilization selectively: Free Trade without the freedom. Modernity aside, Ismail was still the grandson of Mehmet Ali.

Ismail never expected to be khedive. A second son, until his twenty-eighth year his life was one of private wealth and country estates. Like the rest of the ruling family, he made an unlikely Egyptian. A Francophone "Turk" of Albanian extraction, he grew up in European hotels and returned to Egypt at nineteen with French tastes. Ostensibly Muslim, he prayed rarely, ate ham, and maintained an extensive cellar. During the reign of his uncle Said Pasha, he stayed out of politics and concentrated on getting rich. Inheriting vast estates, he used their revenues to buy further acreage, becoming the largest landowner in Egypt. As a member of the royal family, he diverted irrigation canals through his estates, used forced labor to dig them, and bought Sudanese slaves to work the fields. This variation on modern farming methods, combined with open intimidation of his rivals, ensured that Ismail's wheat, cotton, and sugar commanded the highest market prices. The liberalization of government monopolies did not benefit the ordinary Egyptian *fellah*.

All this changed on May 15, 1858, one of the few occasions that Ismail had been known to miss a party. To mark the end of Ramadan, Said Pasha organized a lavish festivity at the Ras el-Tin palace in Alexandria. Ismail's older and younger brothers, the princes Ahmet and Halim, attended, but Ismail was unwell, apparently on his mother's advice. After the party, the two princes chartered a private train to carry them and their retinues back to Cairo. Midway, the railway crossed the Nile at Karf ez-Zayat, where a bridge was under construction; in the meantime, each carriage was pushed onto a barge and pulled across by tugboats. A crowd of loyal subjects gathered to push the carriages. The stationmaster neglected to close the gate leading down to the barges; three carriages slid down onto one barge; it capsized, tipping the carriages and their passengers into the Nile. The "fat and clumsy" Ahmet drowned with his aides. Only sprightly Halim survived, leaping clear as the train went under and swimming several hundred yards before escaping the current and crawling ashore.[5]

Ismail, overlooked and underestimated, was now the next pasha of Egypt. When he overcame his grief, he promoted the stationmaster of Karf ez-Zayat to a government ministry.

ISMAIL INHERITED A kingdom of paradox. Egypt was neither an Ottoman province nor an independent state, but somewhere in between. The heirs of Mehmet Ali observed technical fealty to the sultan, each year sending £320,000 to Istanbul to prove it, but worked energetically to break that bond. Socially, Egypt suffered from the Ottoman legacy of sharp division between rulers and ruled. The rulers came from the international elite of soldiers and administrators who ran the Ottoman Empire, the mixture of Turks, Circassians, and Albanians known as "Turks." Ruling from Cairo, they spoke Turkish, French, and English and carved up government concessions with their partners, the European businessmen and investors. Ismail's three closest advisers were "Turks." Nubar Pasha, a sad-eyed Armenian Christian with an herbaceous mustache, was an ambitious diplomat and adroitly corrupt financier. Mustapha Riad Pasha, his authoritarian protégé in the Ministry of Justice, was a "Mountain Jew" from the Caucasus. Nubar's rival Mohammed Sharif Pasha was an elegant graduate of Mehmet Ali's military academy who affected the manner of a retired French colonel and spent more time at his billiard table than his desk.

The most productive element of Egyptian society paid no tax. The urban middle class that made Alexandria the economic hub of Egypt were mostly Greek, Italian, or Maltese Christians. Even after the Ottoman sultans had reconciled themselves to the necessary evil of trade with infidel Europe, they had wished to exclude European influence. Under a series of treaties with European states known as the Capitulations, the Ottomans had allowed foreigners to reside and trade in their territories as resident aliens, subject to the laws of their native countries. This suited the traders, too: Apart from giving them tax exemption, it allowed them to evade Islamic social law, under which they were *dhimmis*, second-class citizens liable to extra taxation and random exploitation. In Egypt, the Europeans existed in parallel to native society, cohabiting profitably with the Turkish elite, while contributing little.

The majority of the population lived outside the cities. The *fellahin* were the real Egyptians: Arabic-speaking peasants, traditional farmers whose precarious methods—the waterwheel powered by a cow or donkey, irrigation through the annual Nile flood—had changed little since pharaonic times. A few of their most promising sons benefited from the educational and military innovations of Mehmet Ali, but all of them had to carry Egypt's tax burden, and work in the *Corvée*, the rotating army of forced laborers who built state projects, including the Suez Canal.

At the bottom of Egyptian society were the substantial minority who did much of the work: black slaves from Sudan. Even the most humble urban home had its female slave. As much as a third of Cairo's population was an invisible army of slave porters, janitors, cooks, cleaners, eunuchs, and concubines.

AT HIS ACCESSION in 1863, Ismail had no debts or mortgages, an income of £160,000, a dilettante's expertise in the micromanagement of his farms, and no experience of the governmental and fiscal systems that drove a modern economy. On the second day of his reign, he summoned Egypt's foreign consuls and businessmen to a reception at the Cairo Citadel.[6]

"Gentlemen," he announced, "I am firmly resolved to devote to the prosperity of the country which I am called upon to govern all the perseverance and energy of which I am capable. The basis of all good governance is order and economy in the finances."

He listed his reforms. Egypt would have a constitution and a parliament, the Council of Deputies. Instead of dipping into the treasury, he would take a salary like any other civil servant. Government contracts would be opened to public bidding. The *fellahin* would receive free education, and fair courts to judge their complaints. The *Corvée* would be abolished. A modern and productive Egypt promised "greater facility in the relations of Egypt with the Western powers."[7]

His program was timely. In 1863, the Egyptian economy was beginning a spectacular boom. With American ports blockaded during the Civil War, the price of cotton quadrupled from £65 per ton in 1862 to £270 per ton in 1864. Egypt's cotton exports more than trebled, from 25,000 tons to 87,500 tons. Egypt became Britain's prime source of raw cotton; in 1864, cotton alone brought in £23,625,000, ten times the total revenue for 1862. So much money washed into Egypt that some even trickled out of the hands of the elite and down to the *fellahin,* who began to buy their own slaves.[8]

With the economy soaring and Ismail promising economic and political liberalization, foreign cash poured into Egypt like a Nile flood. Ismail used the money to remake Egypt in the French image. Cairo became a modern city almost overnight. Ismail hired Jean-Pierre Barillet-Deschamps, official *jardinier* to Baron Haussmann's Paris, to create the Ezbekiyyeh Gardens, a twenty-acre pastiche of Paris' Park Monceau, complete with grottoes, artificial lakes, cafés, and a bandstand. Grand hotels and Gallic apartment buildings lined the road from the Ezbekiyyeh to Ismail's seat at the Abdin Palace, which squatted behind a wide parade ground modeled on the Champ de Mars at Paris. Plots worth two thousand pounds were offered for free, creating a leafy suburb of modern mansions—called, naturally, Ismailia—where Turkish ministers and Levantine bankers rubbed shoulders with "Franks" like "Mr. Remington, the well-known arms manufacturer, who has armed the khedive's troops," and the duke of Sutherland, one of whose developments became the home of the English club. The European quarters of Cairo and Alexandria had better sanitation and street lighting than most European capitals.[9]

A new infrastructure appeared: train stations, railways, telegraph cables, roads, ports, lighthouses, bridges, post offices, museums, libraries, hospitals, opera houses, and palaces. The countryside of the Nile Delta became crosshatched with irrigation canals, cotton plantations, and sugar mills. Steamships sporting Ismail's livery appeared on the Nile. Productivity and life expectancy increased, and the state planned the education of all children, girls included. The government welcomed European engineers and businessmen to the new suburbs, and soon the "Franks" composed a quarter of Alexandria's population. Egypt became a giant building site, a modern state in the making, and an investor's paradise.

"SHADES OF THE PHARAOHS!" trilled the *Levant Herald* when the Council of Deputies assembled. "From Khartoum to Damietta constitutional rights are to be enjoyed by all, and a Parliament of seventy members, sitting under the shadow of the Great Pyramid, is henceforth to ensure to

Copt, *fellah* and Bedouin liberty to an extent and with guarantees never before dreamt of in the East."[10]

At the council's first meeting, the Speaker explained to the Turkish landowners and aristocrats on its benches that European practice required them to divide into two factions, one for Ismail's government, another against it. The entire council gathered on the progovernment benches. They met twice more before Ismail tired of demonstrating that his whim was identical to the national will. The parliament had served its purpose as an advertisement of progress. He gave it a more potent name, the Chamber of Notables, and then mothballed it.

The revolution had been Ismail's idea, and he intended to steer it. To rework Egypt in the modern image was hard enough. Industrialization drew labor from the villages to the city. The growth of local government and its network of tax collectors devalued the traditional dignity of the village headman and the local sheikh. Foreign money and culture antagonized the Islamic clergy, and a peasantry hostile to its Turkish masters. Ismail could do without the complications of "constitutionalism" and mass enfranchisement. Building up the army and the bureaucracy, he concentrated on control. Like Haussmann, who planned the boulevards of Paris as a shooting gallery against the mob, Ismail fortified the state against its subjects.

In 1865, the cotton boom slowed as America resumed its exports. The bubble had been pricked, but Ismail used loans from French, British, and German banks to keep it from deflating. Egypt's modern facade enticed European investors to buy stock in the loans: If wild building was caused by wild growth, then fat dividends must follow. Ismail and his ministers ensured that Europeans received little accurate information about Egypt. Nubar Pasha gave European consuls and journalists preferential access to the government's business initiatives, effectively putting them on the payroll. The Reuters news agency clarified its perspective with the help of an annual secret payment of one thousand pounds. One key source for investors, the correspondent of the London *Times,* was an intimate of Ismail and his ministers who earned more from his investments than his journalism. He promoted Ismail as "a thrifty saving landlord who looked after every *piaster.*"[11]

Not all the foreign money went on canals and bridges. Corruption was systematic, the partition between state treasury and Ismail's pocket hypothetical. Ismail and Nubar Pasha devised a scheme to divert millions of pounds into his campaigns for independence from the Ottoman sultan and the Suez Canal Company. The government set up a company, mostly funded by European bankers, but with enough of Ismail's private cash to imply his personal interest in the company's success. The government—Ismail again—engaged the company to perform services advantageous to the economy. When the company issued orders for material from Europe, its European directors received private commissions. In return for the monopoly and the kickbacks, the European banks allowed Ismail to borrow on open credit. Ismail guaranteed repayment from his earnings as a shareholder and from the revenues of the Egyptian treasury, which meant the same thing. By borrowing on open credit, he avoided commitments to fixed schedules of repayment and interest, and by doing it privately, he did not need the sultan's permission. As Ismail both licensed the companies and held substantial shares as a private investor, he could control them and prevent them from becoming the instruments of his French and British partners. When the companies foundered, Ismail wound them up, selling their assets for cash and passing their bad debts to the Egyptian taxpayer.

They began with the Sudan Company, which proposed to launch river steamers and railways into Upper Egypt and the Sudan. The prominent Alexandria bankers Henry Oppenheim and Edouard Dervieu raised most of its £2 million capital, and both received seats on the board. Suddenly, its name changed to the Egyptian Trading & Commercial Company, lending money at high interest to the farmers of the Delta against the value of their crops.

Then came the Agricultural Society, which imported and rented irrigation pumps to farmers, until Ismail, Oppenheim, and Dervieu took it over and turned it into a fund for speculating in urban real estate. Through Nubar Pasha, members of the society's board privately obtained contracts for urban developments, then sold the contracts to the society at inflated prices, taking colossal profits.

Next Ismail took to the high seas. Having inherited a batch of inactive steamers from one of Said Pasha's failed ventures, he set up an Egyptian Steam Navigation Company, put his sons on the board, and sold it his steamers. The company cast off on the money of investors tempted by images of Egyptian steamers ferrying goods and businessmen around the Mediterranean, and Ismail's promise of a 6 percent dividend on every share. When the company hit the rocks, the government paid the dividends and bought back the shares.[12]

With the cash rolling in, Ismail sent Nubar Pasha to Paris and Constantinople to buy his independence. Or so he thought.

"I AM MORE *canaliste* than Monsieur de Lesseps," Ismail had promised the French consul in 1863. "I believe that no work is so grand, none will be so productive for Egypt. But at the present moment its bases are uncertain and badly defined. I will affirm them and then, surpassing my predecessor, I will push the works to their completion."[13]

Although Britain had become Egypt's main export market and source of investment, France had more influence there. Said Pasha's deal with the Canal Company made Egypt the junior partner of a French-run project. Said's folly became more apparent as the Canal progressed southward. Said had committed Egypt to maintain a rotating workforce of twenty thousand forced laborers. Most came from the *fellahin* of the Nile Delta, whose agriculture suffered in their absence. Yet though Egyptian labor dug the Canal and its subsidiary irrigation channels, the Canal Company owned the two hundred thousand acres of lush agricultural land that the irrigation created. French investors stood to take all the profit. Ismail decided to reduce French influence in Egypt by switching to British patronage and playing the two countries against each other.

Ismail chose the *Corvée* as the pivot of his European policy. Nubar Pasha went to see the most influential foreigner at Constantinople, British ambassador Sir Henry Bulwer. How, asked Nubar, would the Palmerston government react if the progressive Ismail banned the *Corvée*, and the French tried to force him to keep it in order to finish the Canal as planned?

The *Corvée* had always attracted humanitarian disgust in Britain; now France was forcing Egypt to enslave its own people. Moreover, the Canal threatened to create a web of financial dependency that would turn Egypt into a French colony and split the Ottoman Empire. Palmerston, presented with a scenario he relished—devious foreigners undermining the road to India—pressured Sultan Abdul Aziz, whose foreign minister duly wrote to Ismail, to protest the *Corvée*.

Next, Nubar Pasha went to Paris and denounced the Canal Company's unworkable contract. The company's shares fell, its directors sued Nubar for libel, and Nubar countersued. Egypt's divorce from the Canal Company was under way. A French court ruled that Ismail should pay £3.5 million to buy Egypt out of the contract, including £1.5 million for abandoning the *Corvée* and £1.2 million to recover 150,000 acres of irrigated land. The total figure happened to approximate the value of Ismail's shares in the company; de Lesseps had suggested that, presented with the bill, Ismail would prefer to lose paper shares rather than pay hard cash. But Ismail preferred to buy his liberty.[14]

Next Nubar returned to Constantinople, whose sultan-caliph was the greatest obstacle to Ismail's dream of Egypt as the nexus of East and West. Abdul Aziz understood Ismail's rebellious intentions but, deeply indebted to European banks, he was prepared to sell the elements of Egyptian sovereignty to Ismail. Abdul Aziz predicted that the British policy of holding together the Ottoman Empire at all costs would keep Ismail from full independence.

Nubar Pasha became a regular visitor to Constantinople, dispensing cash to Abdul Aziz and his ministers. In 1863, a bribe of £50,000 bought Ismail the right to choose his own heir, effectively confirming his dynasty. In 1866, he doubled his annual tribute to £670,000, obtaining the title to the Sudanese territory south of Wadi Halfa, and the Red Sea ports essential for Sudanese trade. In 1867, further bribes allowed Ismail to conclude economic treaties with foreign governments and granted him the royal title he coveted. Ismail could not tolerate being a mere pasha, an honorific granted to any senior Ottoman administrator, but Abdul Aziz refused to dub Ismail a sultan or king. So he dusted off a mutually agreeable title from Persian history. In 1867, Ismail became the khedive of Egypt.

When the khedive took his new title on an image-boosting European tour, his hosts lauded him as the foremost pupil among the sultans, emirs, maharajahs, and nabobs who had cut deals with Europe and opened their economies to its exports. *Ismail le Magnifique* was praised as a liberal constitutionalist, a modern industrialist, a beneficent visionary. With easy money waiting for the bold investor, the eccentricity of Egypt's finances could be excused as a growing pain, curable by the march of progress. Egypt's image in Europe acquired the slick gloss of a stockjobber's prospectus.

ISMAIL NEEDED MANPOWER for his factories and farms, money for his dreams and debts, and prestige to buttress Egypt against the sultan and the Great Powers. Imperial ambition and financial necessity drove Ismail south, where Egypt had an uncontested claim to the resources of the Sudan: ivory, rubber, hardwood, and, most valuably, slaves.

The skeleton of Egyptian rule in the "Land of the Blacks" already existed. In 1820, Mehmet Ali had sent south a party of soldiers and French and British miners in search of Nubian gold and conscripts for his army. They found little gold, but plentiful ivory and slaves. In 1838, Ali established a capital for his colony among a handful of fishermen's shacks on a proboscis of land at the junction of the Blue Nile and the White Nile, its name derived from its fancied resemblance to an elephant's trunk: Khartoum. This settlement, whose low-built mud-brick houses flooded when the river rose, became the heart of Egypt's exploitation of the Sudan.[15]

Sudanese slavery was ancient, entrenched, and endorsed by local custom and Islamic law. The first Europeans to venture upriver in the early nineteenth century found a society of Muslim masters and pagan or Christian slaves, and an economy distorted by cheap manpower and the profits of the transit trade. The economic life of the independent sultanate of Darfur consisted of little else. Its sultan licensed up to seventy slaving raids a year, partitioned his terrain between raiding parties, gathered their booty at a central camp, and took commissions from their sales. His neighbors the cattle-herding Baggara, who scorned manual labor as the province of inferior settled peoples, were almost outnumbered by their slaves. In a crude precursor of plantation slavery, the Baggara enslaved entire tribes, holding between twenty and two hundred male fieldworkers per farm, plus extensive collections of domestic female slaves. Among the settled agriculturalists of the Nile Valley, a quarter of the population were slaves. Along the caravan routes, town dwellers lived comfortably from the trade. In 1813, visiting the centers of the trade disguised as a Syrian sheikh, the Swiss pioneer Jean-Louis Burckhardt reported, "At Berber or Shendi there is scarcely a house which does not possess one or two slaves, and five or six are frequently seen in the same family; the great people and chiefs keep them by the dozens."[16]

The trade was run by Muslims and regulated by Islamic law. The Sudan was a frontier land, the border between *Dar al-Islam*, the Land of Islam, and *Dar al-Harb*, the House of War. Under sharia, a Muslim could not enslave a fellow Muslim, but he could enslave an infidel captured in *jihad* to expand *Dar al-Islam*. So the slavers concentrated their operations on the pagans of the southwest, the Nubians of the southeast, and the Christians of Abyssinia, whose women were prized for their light skins and purported sexual appetite. The slavers justified their depredations by forcing their slaves to convert to Islam, and they masked their greed by using the Koranic term *ghazwa* to describe their raids, after the early battles of the Prophet Mohammed, who had taken slaves and concubines from the defeated non-Muslims of Arabia.

The result was abduction, rape, mutilation, and murder on a gigantic scale. Raising private militias, the slavers would attack a village, killing those who resisted and enslaving the rest. Chained, whipped, and deprived of food and water, only the fittest survived the march to the markets. The elderly were left to die by the road, and infants too young to walk were simply thrown aside. The slavers prostituted their women prisoners at the towns they passed, and genitally mutilated prepubescent girls to raise their market value. Every year, each of the thirty thousand slaves sold at the coast represented as many as nine others who had been massacred in a *ghazwa* or abandoned on the road. In the early 1820s, the British explorers Dixon Denham and Hugh Clapperton found the caravan routes of the western Sudan "lined on either side by human remains," with the ground around the wells "covered with whitened bones" and the desiccated corpses of children. "They were only blacks," their Arab guides explained.[17]

Like rain, the distribution of slaves divided between the watershed of the White and Blue Niles. Two caravan routes served the export trade. The White Nile trade pooled at El Fasher in Darfur. From there, the Forty Days' Road, a thousand-mile trek through the desert, shadowed the west bank of the Nile north to Egypt, terminating at Asyut, where dealers sailed their cargo down the Nile to Cairo. Also at Asyut, two Coptic monks "said to excel all their predecessors in dexterity" prepared the eunuchs prized by Muslim potentates as gifts and harem guardians. Caucasian eunuchs were left with partial and occasionally functional genitals, but Africans were believed to have a higher libido that necessitated total excision. The monks cut off the entire genitalia at the abdomen and cauterized the wound with boiling butter. In 1815, Mehmet Ali sent the Turkish sultan a gift of 150 Sudanese eunuchs.[18]

The Blue Nile trade collected at Sennar, then moved downstream via Khartoum to Shendi and Berber. Caravans then walked three hundred miles to the Red Sea ports of Suakin and Massowa, where they were shipped across the Red Sea to the giant Arabian slave market at Jeddah. From Cairo and Jeddah, Sudanese slaves were traded across the Islamic world. The most valuable slaves were whites from the Caucasus, eunuchs, and girls in their early teens.

Demand was constant. Unlike the industrial societies served by the Atlantic trade, the preindustrial societies served by the Islamic world ran on domestic slaves: cooks, concubines, eunuchs, and cleaners. In Egypt, some 80 percent of slaves were female. The average slave survived ten to twelve years, dying in her midtwenties, a mortality rate that her masters attributed to the humid Delta climate, not the miseries of her servitude. Forcibly converted to Islam, she was kept in isolation from the smaller male slave population, with any unwanted infants who beat the odds deliberately neglected by her master. If she became pregnant by him, the child was born a free Muslim.[19]

UNLIKE EUROPEAN IMPERIALISTS, Mehmet Ali and his heirs did not intend to turn Sudan into a stable partner for "legitimate trade," by encouraging agriculture in order to sell finished goods. Egypt had little to offer its empire other than garrisons and governors, and it needed raw materials to prop up its balance of trade. It came only to exploit the Sudan by seizing its goods and people. If the Turkish elite considered the darker-skinned Egyptians to be their ethnic inferiors, they considered the black pagans of Sudan to be an expendable resource, like the hard *sant* wood that Egypt used for the butts of its soldiers' rifles. The government became a major supplier and customer in the slave trade, indistinguishable from the disorder it purported to replace.

The Sudanese called the Egyptian system the Turkiyya, the rule of the Turks. Levying implausible taxes on the Sudanese, local administrators ruled through the *kourbash*, a long hippo-hide whip applied to the soles of the feet. Local government and military officers partnered with the slavers and shared their profits. When the tribes could not pay their excessive taxes, the local officials forced them to surrender their children to the slavers and took commissions on the proceeds. All ranks used slaves as currency and concubines. In the Nile Delta, thousands served on the sugar and cotton estates of the Turkish elite. Sudanese conscripts became Egypt's cannon fodder. At the infantry school at Aswan, they received a calico vest, vaccinations, and basic Islamic instruction. Of the first thirty thousand conscripts abducted by Mehmet Ali, three thousand survived.[20]

THE TRADE MUTATED through the economic and ethical assault of European traders and missionaries. In 1838, Britain obliged the sultan to cancel all government monopolies, opening the entire Ottoman Empire to Free Trade. Sudan was remote enough for the pashas of Egypt to ignore this attack on their business, but by the late 1840s the European appetite for African ivory produced European demands for open access to the Sudan. A trickle of European adventurers joined the Arab and Turkish traders in the shabby settlement at Khartoum: Andrea Debono, a Maltese merchant following his goods to their source; Alexandre Vaudey, a French clerk in the Egyptian government; Bruno Rollet, who began working for a French slaver and branched out alone; and John Petherick, a Welsh engineer who came looking for gold and stayed for the gum trade. Misfits of indeterminate morality, they came to the end of the earth in search of oblivion and wealth, abandoning European costume and custom to dress like Arab traders and take Abyssinian concubines.[21]

The traders worked constantly to break the Egyptian monopoly on the White Nile and open the river to free navigation, and their governments supported them, appointing them as local consuls. In the Sudan, the flag followed trade. And the trade boomed: Between 1840 and 1870, the quantity of ivory imported to London doubled, but demand was so great that the price doubled, too. In 1851, the Khartoum merchants sent 12 boats downriver carrying 20 tons of ivory; in 1863, they sent 240 boats and 100 tons. Each ton represented the deaths of at least ten mature bull elephants or fifty females, or even more immature males and females. Stocks collapsed in the slaughter.[22]

As the elephant herds shrank, the traders copied their Arab partners and used slaving to underwrite their ventures. Importing high-powered rifles, they exacerbated tribal disputes, enlisted private militias of local collaborators, and launched brutal attacks on native villages, enslaving the survivors and paying their local helpers in slaves and low-grade "Manchester goods": rough cotton, baubles, and glassware. They bribed the Egyptian authorities, and launched joint *ghazwas* against "hostile tribes."[23]

The opening of the Nile to European trade and exploration also opened it to missionaries and humanitarians. The Anti-Slavery Society lobbied the British government, which pressured the pashas of Egypt, laying the steps of a diplomatic dance in which the pashas made placatory gestures toward the abolitionists, while deepening their dependence on the trade. In 1857 Britain forced Sultan Abdul Aziz's predecessor Abdul Mejid to ban the trade in African slaves throughout the Ottoman Empire. Two provinces were exempt. At Mecca, the affront to business interests and religious conservatism set off a jihad against the Ottoman authorities, who backed off and permitted slaving in the Hejaz. In Sudan, the trade was too distant and too lucrative to control, and Abbas Pasha simply ignored the ban and continued enslaving adult males into the Egyptian army. Under British pressure, his heir Said Pasha announced the ban and ordered his governors to intercept slave caravans. This convinced the British consul that "his desire to suppress slavery was a genuine one." Shortly afterward, Said treated himself to a new bodyguard of five hundred Sudanese slaves.[24]

A combination of European pressure, Egyptian decrees, and diminishing ivory stocks pushed the slave trade south. Khartoum, now a sleazy boomtown of thirty thousand shady inhabitants, became the financial and logistical base, providing boats, mercenaries, supplies, rifles, and money at 100 percent interest. The *ghazwas* moved beyond the law to the Gazelle River region, a patchwork of forest and White Nile tributaries opened up by two of the Khartoum consuls, Britain's John Petherick and Sardinia's Bruno Rollet. An irruption of Egyptian soldiers, Arab slavers, and European traders took over the district. Their massacres and round-ups left a trail of dead bodies and burned villages. Leaving the youngest and oldest to starve, they added the fittest males to their militias and enslaved the rest. The traders paid their militiamen one slave for every three months' service and allowed them unlimited wives and concubines. They used children as slave porters and soldiers. They partitioned the region among themselves like medieval warlords. Each kingdom had its complement of Egyptian soldiery and slaver militias, and its capital at a central *zariba,* the fortified camp where slaves and ivory gathered for shipment. The Gazelle River district became a giant factory of death.[25]

Occasionally a European government made inquiries in response to rumors that its Khartoum consul had been raiding on the Gazelle River, at which the consuls denounced each other as wicked slavers, but there were no real investigations. In 1859 the British Foreign Office appointed John Petherick full consul. Emboldened, Petherick attempted to set up a private army. Claiming he was "amongst turbulent and warlike tribes," Petherick asked the Foreign Office to license the importation of five hundred muskets, eighty elephant guns, and two tons of lead for bullets. At the same time, the British consul at Cairo received a report from the Austrian representative at Khartoum that a British resident was involved in slaving. Apart from Mrs. Petherick, there could be no other suspect. But the foreign secretary, Lord Russell, was more amused than alarmed.

"Mr. Petherick has a wild Arab sort of manner, fitter for those districts than St. James's," noted Russell, issuing Petherick with a fraction of his shopping list. "A fourth of the number should suffice."[26]

The complicity of Egyptians and Europeans in the slaughter on the Gazelle River came to light through a series of expeditions funded by Britain's Royal Geographical Society, with the aim of mapping Africa's system of Great Lakes, key to the sources of the Nile. In February 1858, John Hanning Speke, having discovered Lake Tanganyika with the orientalist Richard Burton, pushed on alone to find a "beautiful sheet of water." Identifying it as the fabled Lake Nyasa, source of the White Nile, he renamed it Lake Victoria. In 1862, Speke returned with James Grant to map it. When they vanished in the forests, Consul and Mrs. Petherick set out to find them. They, too, disappeared, so the society engaged the big game hunter Samuel Baker. In February 1863, as Baker worked south from Khartoum, he ran into Speke and Grant, who had located the falls on the north of the lake where the waters of the White Nile began their three-month, four-thousand-mile journey to the Mediterranean. By calculating water volumes, they had inferred that the White Nile had a second source somewhere to its northwest. In March 1864, Baker found it, a "sea of quicksilver" that he named Lake Albert for Victoria's recently deceased Prince Consort.[27]

Baker's *Albert Nyanza, Great Basin of the Nile* recounted in detail the terrain, tribes, and untrammeled slaving of the territory between Khartoum and the Great Lakes. Baker received a knighthood and the gold medal of the Royal Geographical Society. John Petherick was dismissed and his consulate abolished. British moral outrage fixed on the Sudanese slave trade as an affront to humanity comparable to the East African trade, and on Khedive Ismail as its ally against evil.

ISMAIL WAS MORE WORRIED about money than morality. Even during the cotton boom he had borrowed large sums from European banks to subsidize his lavish ambitions and the £9 million debt inherited from Said Pasha. In 1864, he took £5.7 million from the London bank of Fruhling & Goschen to pay off the Suez Canal indemnity, and in 1865 a further £3.3 million from the Anglo-Egyptian Bank. As the economy slowed and his sham companies collapsed, the borrowing accelerated. In 1866, he borrowed £3 million more from Fruhling & Goschen to cover the bankruptcy of the Egyptian Trading & Commercial Company; in 1867, £2 million from the Imperial Ottoman Bank; and in 1868, when revenue was £7,277,785, a colossal £11 million from his friend Henry Oppenheim. The loans were issued at 7 percent interest—9 percent on the 1867 loan—and after commissions licit and illicit, as little as half the money reached Ismail, with a corresponding smaller fraction passed on to the state. Tame journalists might point to the frenzy of public works, the gas lamps in the streets, and the sewage pipes beneath them as evidence of Egypt's stability, but by 1869 Ismail's kingdom ran on credit, and the £2 million tab for the opening of the Suez Canal was a mere fraction of his debt. In the weeks that de Lesseps planned his guest lists, Ismail's Agricultural Society and his steamship line both went bankrupt, leaving the Egyptian government to buy up £3.3 million in shares.[28]

The arrival of Victorian moralists in Ismail's empire placed him in a quandary. Repressing the slave trade meant losing one of Egypt's most productive sectors. Contrary to humanitarian theory, Egypt's appetite for slaves had only increased with the growth of "legitimate trade": A growing economy created new wealth and new customers. At the British Consulate in Cairo, the register recording the names of slaves who had escaped and claimed their freedom contained a parallel column listing the names of their erstwhile owners. The list was a transection of Egyptian society: governors, judges, bankers, merchants, civil servants, policemen, butchers, and *fellahin* who, indentured to their own government by the *Corvée,* sent their slaves to the Suez Canal works as substitute laborers. The government used slaves on its public works projects. Ismail personally held nearly three thousand agricultural slaves, and thousands more staffed his palace as bodyguards, servants, eunuchs, and concubines.

Slavery was the unacknowledged pillar of Egypt's export and domestic economies. The sultan's antislavery decree of 1857 made little difference. When the British consul bought the liberty of escaped slaves, he passed them to the Egyptian police, who gave them to the army, who sent them back to the Sudan in uniform, slaves again in all but rank. A decade after the 1857 ban, the British consul found over three thousand slaves for sale in covert markets at Cairo, and a further two thousand on open show at the Delta agricultural town of Tanta. Even after the cotton crash of 1866, it remained "a matter of public notoriety" that Egypt exported at least thirty thousand slaves a year from the Sudan, an atrocity equivalent in size and misery to the notorious East African trade.[29]

Ismail could not fall back on the gestures and promises of his forebears, washing his hands of the trade in Cairo while quietly profiting from it upriver. As a vassal of the Turkish sultan, and a modernizer with an image to maintain, he must appear to implement the 1857 ban. Nor, under the Turkish antimonopoly edict of 1838, could he keep European merchants and missionaries out of the Sudan. These two Turkish concessions to British pressure would crush him in an economic pincer. He had to turn them into assets. If the growth of his African empire rested on British approval, then that was how it must grow: He would ride the British obsessions with open markets and abolitionism all the way to the equator.

In the spring of 1869, when Edward, the playboy Prince of Wales, visited the Suez Canal works, he took with him Sir Samuel Baker as Arabic interpreter, and as tutor in the art of crocodile hunting. At a masked ball at his new palace at Ismailia, the khedive asked the prince if Britain might spare Sir Samuel for an expedition to suppress the White Nile slave trade and open the Nile to peaceful commerce from the sea to the Great Lakes. While the prince went on to Constantinople as the guest of Sultan Abdul Aziz, Baker left for England to collect his medicine chest and rifles. He would operate with the approval of the British government, but as an employee of the Egyptian government. He would not be the last British mercenary in Africa, but he was the first to wear a Turkish uniform.

On Baker's return, Ismail gave him a salary of ten thousand pounds, the ranks of Ottoman pasha and major general in the Egyptian army, a Turkish uniform that made him look like a patriotic cartoonist's idea of the Russian bear, and a *firman* granting him "absolute and supreme power, even that of death" over a space in the map between the terminus of Egyptian control at Gondokoro, five degrees north of the equator, and the Great Lakes, a vacuum of ninety thousand miles square now dubbed Equatoria. Considering "the savage condition of the tribes which inhabit the Nile basin," that they had "neither government, nor laws, nor security," that "humanity enforces the suppression of the slave-hunters," and that "the establishment of legitimate commerce throughout those countries will be a great stride towards future civilisation," Baker was to "subdue" the territory, introduce "regular commerce"; open the Great Lakes to navigation; and establish "a chain of military stations and commercial depots" between Gondokoro and Lake Victoria.[30]

A fierce, angry giant who had rescued his wife Florence from a Turkish harem, Baker was a hunter, not a diplomat, and he planned a military campaign. Stocking up on enough beads, cotton, and agricultural seed to draw the Equatorians into legitimate trade, and an arsenal of mountain guns and rocket launchers should they resist, he ordered six iron-hulled steamers, constructed in sections so they could be hauled over the Nile cataracts and assembled on the Lakes. Then he, the indomitable Florence, a thousand Egyptian soldiers, and a further thousand native bearers went to war.

Baker faced two enemies, the Nile and the slavers, and his tenure divided into two battles. The first was exploratory: hacking his way through the Sudd, the mass of floating, rotten vegetation that blocked the Nile south of Khartoum, taking anthropological notes, and hunting his dinner. Already a legend for slaughtering swaths of Indian and African fauna, Baker's fascination for what he might kill helped him stay sane as his expedition foundered for a whole year in the Sudd's watery labyrinth. Up to their necks in the water, many of his men died from heatstroke and disease as they labored to cut their boats free. Even the expedition's doctor was sent back to Khartoum. But the Bakers ploughed on, Samuel plotting their slow progress in his notebooks and devising a type of dum-dum bullet that took half the skull off a hippopotamus at thirty yards, Florence supervising the laundry and devising new ways of cooking hippo.

In April 1871 the survivors floated free of the Sudd and down to Gondokoro, a riverside clearing marked by a ruined Austrian mission. They built some huts, sowed some maize, and renamed it Ismailia, almost in parody of the modern suburb at Cairo and the palace by the Suez Canal. On May 26, 1871, Baker paraded his entire force in dress uniform, ran the Turkish flag up an eighty-foot flagpole, and informed his audience of naked, perplexed Bari tribesmen that they had been annexed to Egypt. Then he ordered a celebratory dinner of roast beef, Christmas pudding, and rum.

The Bari, having seen the interlopers raise the flag of the slavers' ally, began nightly raids on the camp. These ceremonials in the middle of nowhere marked the beginning of Baker's second battle, the "pacification." They also marked the limit of his resources and strategy.

Baker made war on an entire society and its economy. Some fifteen thousand Arabs worked in the Sudanese slave trade, and in close harmony with the Egyptian government. One of the major slavers on the Gazelle River, a Copt named Ghattas, was father-in-law to Ismail Ayoub Pasha, the Kurdish governor of Khartoum, who extorted an unofficial duty of two pounds per slave from every caravan his men intercepted. The slavers' private armies far outnumbered Baker's Egyptian troops. And as Baker wore the uniform of the Turkiyya and marched with Egyptian troops—dubbed by Baker "The Forty Thieves" for their picaresque way with Sudanese property—the tribes he had come to liberate judged him merely another Egyptian official come to hunt, kill, and enslave. When Baker responded to the Bari's poisoned arrows by dipping into his fifty thousand rounds of ammunition and blasting the tribesmen with Snider rifles, he drove them into an alliance with the Arab slavers. This obliged Baker to raid the surrounding countryside for cattle, just as the slavers did. A mission of liberation became a war of attrition against people who refused to be liberated.

As Baker pushed south to establish his chain of bases, the devastation of slavery, and the evidence of Egyptian complicity, surrounded him. At Fatiko, the outpost of 1864 had mushroomed into a thirty-acre slaver compound, where parents sold their children and a young girl was valued at an elephant's tusk, one new shirt, or thirteen English sewing needles. South of there, in May 1872 he announced the annexation of the Kingdom of Bunyoro, without asking Kabarega, its angry cannibal king. A farcical, brutal encounter followed, dignified by Baker as the Battle of Bunyoro. Kabarega's warriors had no chance, even though they had the starting advantage of having disabled many of the Forty Thieves with a batch of poisoned cider. As thousands of armed tribesmen charged down on his camp from the tall grass, Baker massacred them with rifles, mountain guns, and rocket launchers. His men went on to Kabarega's capital and burned it down, killing anyone they found. The dead were so numerous and spread over such a large area that an accurate body count was impossible. Baker lost four men.

Kabarega did not give up. Avoiding the fatal imbalance of battle, the Bunyoro harassed Baker from the tall grass and cut him off from food and water, forcing him to retreat through swamps and ambush. Instead of becoming the storehouses from which Equatoria might receive the light of legitimate trade, Baker's chain of forts became his redoubts from the enraged Equatorians. When his contract with Ismail expired in April 1873, it came as a relief.

The Bakers returned to Cairo for six weeks of chilled Bass's Pale Ale, clean sheets, and celebratory dinners. In the autumn, they took ship for England, where Samuel received an ovation from the Royal Geographical Society and the personal congratulations of the Prince of Wales. Pressed by allegations that he had killed more natives than he had liberated, Baker wrote up his journals for another blockbuster wedge of exotic savagery and English grit, *Ismailia: A Narrative of the Expedition to Central Africa for the Suppression of the Slave Trade*, although he appended to that title *Organised by Ismail, Khedive of Egypt*, in case the suppression did not turn out to be as total as he claimed.

"In the end," Baker claimed, "every opposition was overcome; hatred and insubordination yielded to discipline and order. A paternal government extended its protection through lands hitherto a field for anarchy and slavery. . . . The White Nile, for a distance of 1,600 miles from Khartoum to Central Africa, was cleansed from the abomination of a traffic which had hitherto sullied its waters. Every cloud had passed away, and the term of my office expired in peace and sunshine. In this result I humbly trade God's blessing."[31]

Claiming total victory, Baker then admitted his utter failure to create more than a skein of forts in the wilderness. "I was most thoroughly disgusted and sick at heart," he confessed, helpless before the obvious truth that the slavers relied on "some high authority behind the scenes." Their vessels plied the White Nile "in triumph and defiance before the wind, with flags flying the crescent and star, above a horrible cargo of pest-smitten humanity, in open contempt for my authority." Like the floating morass of the

Sudd, the slavers had parted where Baker hacked a path and silently closed behind him. The policing of the White Nile only forced the slave caravans onto remote, waterless overland paths. From Cairo, Alexandria, Massowa, and Suakin, Egyptian smugglers continued to trade Sudanese slaves across the Islamic world. Ismail had found a bargain in Baker. Thirty thousand pounds of borrowed money had bought a new province.[32]

With Ismail's salary Baker bought a country seat in the shires, its hall and billiard room decorated with the taxidermist's catalogue that constituted Samuel's souvenirs. In the garden, Florence designed an avenue of cypresses that led to an African "palaver hut" giving expansive vistas over the Devonshire fields, should Sam develop a late taste for negotiation. From retirement, he fired periodic elephant gun invectives at the Letters Page of the *Times*. The Egyptians, he warned, could not be trusted, the Africans were incorrigibly idle and superstitious, and the humanitarian pieties of trade and prayer would never stop the slave trade. A clash of civilizations was brewing on the Nile between Muslim custom and Western ambition, and Khedive Ismail's client state was part of the problem.

"The first thing that must be done to civilise a savage country," Baker fumed, "is to annex it."[33]

2

The Engineer
1873–79

Charles George Gordon, Governor General of the Sudan, 1879.

I will take divine aid from any of those who may be dispensing it.
—Colonel Charles Gordon, R.E., 1881[1]

A T AN EMBASSY PARTY in Constantinople, Nubar Pasha met a certain colonel in the Royal Engineers. His current duties—reporting on the free passage of shipping on the Danube and inspecting the British war graves of the Crimea—suggested a career on the sidelines of the Eastern Question. Nubar asked the colonel if his regiment might contain a suitable successor to Samuel Baker. The candidate must organize a vast, chaotic wilderness, expunge the great barbarism of slavery, and open a lost tract of Africa to civilization. Suddenly, as if struck by the colonel's reserved manner and intense gaze, Nubar wondered if the task might interest the colonel himself?

Colonel Charles George Gordon had clear blue eyes, and their sapphire glow gave him a visionary aspect. "What eyes they were!" marveled his underling Arthur Stannard. "Keen and clear, filled with the beauty of holiness, bright with an unnatural brightness, their expression one of settled feverishness, the color blue-grey, as is the sky on a bitter March morning." Yet they were not what they seemed. Color-blind, Gordon lived in a monochrome world, discriminating the value of postage stamps by peering at their numerals.[2]

Born at Woolwich, a garrison suburb on the Thames, Gordon had the migrant childhood of an army child. His father, Henry, was an officer in the Royal Artillery, and the family followed him from posting to posting—Woolwich, Dublin, Leith, and Corfu—their transits marked by promotions and deliveries; Henry reaching the rank of major general, his wife, Elizabeth, a tally of five boys and six girls. Somewhere in the middle of the sequence, "Charley" was the youngest boy in a brood raised on the values of the army and the church: faith, duty, and hard work. At ten, he left Corfu for the ritual brutalities of an English boarding school, and at thirteen he passed into another adolescent underworld, the Royal Military Academy at Woolwich.

The stocky cadet raised in the shadow of the barracks seemed ideal officer material. Physically fearless, Gordon had a quick, practical mind unburdened by intellect, and an artist's hand for mapmaking. Yet he would not conform to authority, exceeding the cadet culture of pranks, brawls, and petty rebellion that inspired him to butt a fellow cadet in the stomach, tumbling him down a flight of stairs, or to release a plague of mice into the house of the academy's commandant. Berated for a minor infraction, Officer-Cadet Gordon tore off his epaulettes and threw them on the floor. Later, he beat a younger boy around the head with a bone hairbrush. For bullying, Cadet Gordon lost six months' seniority, and with it the chance to follow his brothers and father into the Royal Artillery. Instead he was disinherited into a lieutenant's commission in the Royal Engineers.

Although Gordon never forgot the slight, he had found his home. The Royal Engineers was meritocratic and unconventional. The officers of the regular army bought their commissions, but an Engineer earned his through mastering the science of modern warfare. The mechanic of empire, he built bridges, barracks, and forts, laid explosives, and commanded native irregulars. Skirting the snobs and social climbers, Gordon now stood a greater chance of swift promotion.

Unfortunately, the empire first needed Gordon at the naval fortifications at Pembroke, on the damp coast of Wales. Lonely and lost, he found pantheist solace in country rambles. A local couple, Captain and Mrs. Drew, identified the turbulent, troubled young officer as a soul in need of salvation. Guided by their gentle evangelizing, Gordon began a lifelong habit, an autodidactic dig through the occult fringe of Victorian religion. Shunning church services as conformist and inauthentic, he read the Bible every day using the calendar devised by Robert M'Cheyne, the "Prophet of Dundee," taking for his study guide the *Commentaries* of Thomas Scott, which revealed the hidden sense of every verse. God, he learned, was everywhere, an invisible hand in history: "No such thing as *chance*, every emotion is felt for the great object, His glory."[3]

Short and stocky with curly hair and fashionable sideburns, Gordon spoke quickly with a slight stammer. His letters flowed with an untutored facility, the stammer replaced by a compulsive "D.V."—*Deo Volente*, God willing—attached to any mention of the future. In 1854 he secured a posting to the front. In the Crimea, the British and French, having neglected to seize the port of Sebastopol when it was available, now besieged its Russian defenders, among them the young Leo Tolstoy.

Yet the War Office had neglected to plan for the Russian winter. The soldiers slept on the frozen ground without overcoats or tents, and subsisted on raw salt pork. Without fodder, cavalry horses chewed off each other's tails and ran crazed through the camp. By January 1855, the British had eleven thousand fit soldiers, and twenty-three thousand invalided out by dysentery, cholera, starvation, frostbite, gangrene, and self-inflicted wounds. At the hospital in Scutari, the ward floors seethed with rats, and dysenteric patients lay in their own filth. While the Russian public read of the heroic, brutal defense in Tolstoy's *Sebastopol Sketches*, the British public had the *Times'* correspondent William Russell. His telegraphed reports raised an outcry, forcing the dispatch of winter kit and nurses, among them Florence Nightingale.

Tolstoy's characters progressed from nervous idealism to shellshocked fatalism, but Gordon found war thrilling. The Royal Engineers blasted trenches and gun emplacements from the rocky ground, fortified captured positions, dug mines for explosives, and prepared detailed sketches of the enemy lines. Gordon lay on the frozen mud in front of the British trenches, deliberately drawing Russian fire so he could plot the firing positions in his sketchbook. "I do not think I was ever in better health, and I enjoy the work amazingly," he wrote to his mother. Dismissing Russell's reports as "an atrocious fib," Gordon's letters home dwelled more on the beauty of the

Crimean spring. "Our wounded have everything they want, and all comforts," he reported. "I have got a splendid outfit, and two chamois leather vests and drawers." Unwilling to leave after the Russian withdrawal and the end of the war, and awarded the *Legion d'Honneur* by Britain's French allies for his bravery, Gordon stayed on for three years as a member of the commission charged with mapping the new Russo-Turkish border. He returned to Britain at the end of 1858 but, bristling at the peacetime diet of dress uniforms, parades, and dinners, he escaped as soon as he could to China.[4]

Britain wanted to trade Indian opium for Chinese silver, but the Manchu emperors did not want an epidemic of addiction. Prime Minister Lord Palmerston had already applied "gunboat diplomacy" to force the Manchus to grant Europeans the right of residence, trade, and garrison at seventeen "treaty ports," and to cede Hong Kong as a British naval base. In 1860, when the Manchus refused to open China to Free Trade, a British force under Lord Elgin went up the river to Beijing. Gordon was among the soldiers who looted and burned the Summer Palace, and sent souvenirs back to his family and the regimental Mess.

The advent of European trade and Christian missionaries tipped feudal China into the Taiping Rebellion, a civil war setting newly evangelized Christian peasants against the corrupt cities. Its leader, Hung-Sen Tuen, called himself the Heavenly King and believed he was Jesus' brother. He announced a Dynasty of Perpetual Peace that slid into mass starvation, beheadings, crucifixions, and the ingathering of wealth among the revolution's leaders. By August 1860, the Taiping were at the gates of Shanghai, the largest Western entrepôt. The Shanghai merchants raised a militia of Taiping deserters officered by hard-drinking American mercenaries and dubbed them the Ever Victorious Army. When the British and French governments took over the defense to protect their trade interests, Gordon became the Ever Victorious Army's new leader.

Gordon inherited a rabble of varying strength, where uniforms were optional and supplies irregular. With strict discipline, uncompromising courage, and calculated modesty, he turned it into a crack brigade. Spurning any salary over his British army pay, he lived mainly on raw eggs sucked from the shell and tea from a pot carried under his arm. He went into battle in his Royal Engineers' undress uniform, armed with nothing more than a lit cigar and a short cane, his Wand of Victory. He wept over his wounded, but shot mutineers and captured enemy officers. With a natural gift for irregular, small-scale warfare, he outmaneuvered the Taiping by launching ferries and gunboats on the canal system around Shanghai. Fighting sixteen battles in as many months, in June 1864 he took Nanking. The Heavenly King committed suicide, and the Taiping Rebellion collapsed. The Manchu emperor appointed him to the ranks of mandarin and field marshal, the empress gave him a solid gold medal, and Queen Victoria made him a Companion of the Bath. At home, he became a hero.

As uncomfortable with attention as he was compelled to seek it, Gordon told his mother to keep his return secret. He bought a bowler hat and a secondhand suit, which he squashed and soiled, and slipped away from the Mess without saying good-bye. The subterfuge failed. His troops had festooned his launch with the banners of the Ever Victorious Army, and as it carried him to a waiting steamer, they fired off rockets, cannons, and horns for the "Great General Ko."

It was worse at Southampton. He stepped off the boat as "Chinese" Gordon, the iconic product of patriotic journalism. Loathing his celebrity, he refused invitations to dinner, edited out references to his bravery from accounts of his battles, and scratched his name from the empress of China's medal before donating it anonymously to a charity for starving cotton workers. With fifteen months' leave still remaining, Gordon asked to return to duty. The War Office distrusted celebrities and eccentrics. Pettily, it sent one of the army's most brilliant soldiers to supervise a mixed force of masons and drain-diggers at the fortifications of Gravesend on the Thames Estuary.

After a decade of violent adventure and purposeful proximity to death, Gordon fell into depression by the gray Thames. The death of his father deepened his gloom. "Is this all we have come to?" he wondered at the deathbed. In mourning and with little else to do, Gordon fought "the doles" with icy baths, more brandy in his water than usual, and a return to his religious speculations. Struggling toward a mystical personal theology, he began an intense correspondence with his sister Augusta, an Evangelical spinster twelve years his senior who shared his desire "to be too closely acquainted with G-d." He spent his evenings reading at his kitchen table with a saucer of tea and a hunk of stale bread, or with August and Octavia Freese, local Evangelicals who shared his taste in heavy theology and clean jokes. It was months before Octavia Freese realized that the sad, sunburned colonel in her parlor was "Chinese" Gordon.[5]

Relief and revelation came one evening as he dressed for dinner. The Gospel of St. John lay on the dressing table before him: "Whosoever confesseth that Jesus is the Son of God, God dwelleth in him, and he in God."[6]

"Something broke in my heart," he recalled, "a palpable feeling, and I knew God lived in me." Gordon had found "the great secret of the new life," "the key to happiness and holiness": "the indwelling of God." Born again, Gordon bounced from misery to ecstasy. He devoted himself to sharing the revelation. Shy of buttonholing strangers, he printed up a pamphlet, pressing copies into people's hands, flinging handfuls from train windows, strewing them across the fields on his country walks. He imparted the great secret to the poor, elderly, and sick of the Workhouse infirmary, gave his afternoons to teaching the urchins of the Ragged School, and attended deathbeds to pray the departed into Heaven. But he reserved his greatest efforts for young and poor boys, his "scuttlers" and "kings."[7]

Turning his house into a school, Gordon gathered boys from the cottages and slums of Gravesend and the barges and fishing boats of the river. He scrubbed new recruits in the horse trough, then stood them before a mirror. "You see a new boy, don't you?" he asked. "Well, just as you are new outside, so I want you to be new inside." Priming his scuttlers with Christ, cricket, and cheese sandwiches, he found them jobs in the army, plotting their progress on a giant map of the world, its trail of pinpricks marking the travels of Jack, Willie, Alex, and dozens more. Only shyness held him back. "There were boys running about worth millions, and I could not have the courage to speak to them," he confided to Octavia Freese after one expedition into the backstreets. When he dared approach a prepubescent sinner, the rewards were thrilling. "Great blessings in Perry Street. Got three rough lads into a room and found they were kings! A country lad of Our Lord's, a Hebrew 14 years' old, has fallen to me, and I hope to get him a job in the Survey."[8]

"The creature is in bondage, waiting for the redemption of the body." Ears tuned to celestial harps, Gordon missed the clanging erotic overtones of his mission. When Gordon soaped his rough lads, Sigmund Freud was still a Viennese schoolboy. Victorians prized the innocence of children, and found the notion of childhood sexuality repugnant. Pederasty was an unmentionable Turkish vice or, as a contemporary study explained, *A Problem in Greek Ethics*. Progressive science held "male love"—the term "homosexuality" did not yet exist in English—to be an "inversion" caused by brain malformation at the foetal stage. To Christians, the body was God's temple: "Do not disgrace the throne of Thy glory."[9]

Apart from matronly spiritual companions like his sister Augusta or Octavia Freese, Gordon avoided women. He withdrew when he sensed a friendship developing and fled from physical desire; using the fashionable Spiritualist terminology, he called the body the treacherous "sheath" of the spirit. "I wished I was a eunuch at 14," he admitted in a letter to his evangelist friend, Reverend R. H. Barnes. In another letter, Gordon traced this wish to an unspecified "breach" that had occurred at boarding school. "I never had a sorrow like it in all my life." The physical world itself seemed irredeemably corrupt. "The world contains the people of two kingdoms, acknowledging two separate kings and two separate systems of government. The one is an everlasting, undefiled and incorruptible kingdom; the other is mortal, defiled and corruptible. Christ is the King of the Kingdom of God, and the Devil, Anti-Christ, is the King of the Kingdom of Earth." His sexuality, crushed in the struggle with satanic physicality, remained as arrested in development as it was furtive in expression. "We are so hampered by our carnal nature that it is not easy to speak as one should."[10]

After a biblical exile of seven years by the rivers of Gravesend, Gordon secured a posting to another backwater, Galatz in Turkey. He said good-bye to his mother and her irritating requests that he marry and joined the international commission regulating free navigation on the Danube. The work was dull, Galatz was muddy, and his career stalled. Letters arrived reporting the death of Gordon's mother, and the demise of favorite scuttlers in imperial adventure; "the doles" descended again. When Gordon met Nubar Pasha at the British Embassy in Constantinople in September 1873, he was ripe for a born-again career that promised virtuous struggle, brutal conditions, and eternal glory. So enthusiastic and naïve was he that he did not wonder if Nubar had deliberately tracked him down in order to make his apparently spontaneous offer.

Returning to Gravesend to pack, Gordon left England on January 28, 1874, as the morning papers carried the death of David Livingstone in Central Africa. The last words of the abolitionist missionary beseeched and challenged the enlightened conscience, "May Heaven's high blessing come down on every one, American, English or Turk, who will help this open sore of the world." The great Evangelical cause, the redemption of Africa, needed a new figurehead. Before Gordon left, he sketched the Freeses a last postcard. Shaded by a single palm, a stick figure walked an empty road toward a low sun. The message read, "Isaiah 35. Goodbye."[11]

"The wilderness and the solitary place shall be glad for them; and the desert shall rejoice, and blossom as the rose," Isaiah had prophesied, "and a highway shall be there, and a way, and it shall be called the way of holiness; the unclean shall not pass over it . . . the wayfaring men, though fools, shall not err therein . . . and the ransomed of the Lord shall return."

It was unclear whether the stick figure was walking toward a sunset or a sunrise.

GORDON COULD NOT resist Ismail. A prince of the world of desire and power that Gordon renounced yet pursued, the khedive wallowed in earthly pleasures like a hippo, but appealed from the depths for the redemption of his Sudanese kingdom from the slavers.

"The lesson must be made clear," said Ismail, "even in those remote parts, that a mere difference of color does not turn men into wares, and that life and liberty are sacred things."[12]

Ismail knew that good intentions bought him British support for his empire. At the same time, he profited cynically from the slave trade. No judge of character, Gordon believed him, and cast himself as Ismail's redeemer. Blaming Nubar Pasha and the "Greek or Hebrew" speculators for the "rottenness of Egypt," he cast Ismail as the victim, "quite innocent (or nearly so)," of unscrupulous Levantines. "You have no idea of the intrigues here," he wrote to Augusta, "it is a regular hot-bed, and things cannot last long like this."[13]

To inspire Ismail's redemption, Gordon turned down Baker's large salary, accepting only two thousand pounds to cover his expenses. "My object is to show the khedive and his people that gold and silver idols are not worshipped by all the world. They are very powerful Gods, but not so powerful as our God."[14]

Ismail, used to artful diplomats and swivel-eyed bankers, happily ceded the worthless commodity of moral comfort. He flattered his awkward, ascetic employee, saying that Gordon was his ideal. "When that man comes into the room, I feel I am with my superior."[15]

"The Khedive is an honest fellow, and I like him very much," Gordon decided as he accepted the title of governor of Equatoria. In a two-week whirl at Cairo, the new governor alienated most of Ismail's ministers, collected a staff of European and American adventurers, told them not to call him "His Excellency," visited the dentist, and took ship for Suakin. "I wear Engineer undress, with fez. It is very fine in its effect!" Then he vanished in the direction of the equator.[16]

ISMAIL RETURNED TO more important business. Equatoria was not his only imperial project, and the entertaining naïf Gordon not his only ally. While Ismail pandered to Britain's slavery obsession with boilerplate about sacred life and liberty, the greatest slaver in the Sudan wore an Egyptian fez and took a governor's salary.

A crown would have been more appropriate. Zubair Rahmat was the informal king of the Gazelle River district, the province to Equatoria's northwest. Born in an Arab village near Khartoum, he had followed the expanding slave trade into the Gazelle River, using his connections among the Arab tribes to set up an export network reaching as far as Tripoli and Jeddah. The massive wealth he accrued bought him a private army, and notoriety among the British abolitionist lobby. In 1869, Ismail had sent twelve hundred Egyptian soldiers from Khartoum to the Gazelle River with orders to crush Zubair's militia and incorporate the district—and its lucrative slaving—into his Sudanese provinces. Zubair's men massacred the Egyptian troops. So Ismail tried a more emollient approach. Instead of killing Zubair, Ismail made him governor of the Gazelle River district, accepting in return an annual tribute of fifteen thousand pounds. In effect, Zubair's bribe paid Baker's salary: the slave trade in one province funded its repression next door.

Untouchable, Zubair took over the Gazelle River slave trade. He ruled from a pastiche of an African chief's palace, where visitors waited on carpeted divans among chained lions. His network of thirty *zaribas* became the infrastructure of a government-licensed slave factory. He grew so rich that, on hearing that a rival slaver had bought an amulet rendering him immune to lead, he melted down twenty-five thousand silver dollars and armed his men with silver bullets.[17]

In 1873, Ismail's collaboration with Zubair deepened with the invasion of Darfur. Constant British pressure on Egypt to adhere to the Ottoman antislavery edict of 1857, and the consolidation of Egyptian control in the Nile Valley north of Khartoum, had gradually closed the lower reaches of the Sudanese Nile to slave shipping. This forced the slavers away from the river and onto the Forty Days' Road, the ancient overland route that ran north through the desert from El Fasher in Darfur. The transit revenues of this trade further enriched Zubair's biggest rival in the slave trade, the sultan of Darfur, who also happened to be the only African power west of the Nile capable of resisting Egypt's imperial expansion. So Ismail and Zubair carved up Darfur. Zubair invaded from the south, and Ismail Ayoub Pasha, the governor of Khartoum, invaded from the east. In November 1874, Zubair's troops killed the sultan of Darfur and captured El Fasher. Ismail gained a new province, and Zubair got control of the caravan routes.

Ismail launched another war against his rival to the east of the Nile, the independent Christian kingdom of Abyssinia. Apart from holding the source of the Blue Nile, the Abyssinian highlands overlooked the other export route of Sudanese slavery, the road from Berber, on the Nile south of Khartoum, to Suakin on the Red Sea. Ismail engaged French and Danish mercenaries to lead his troops. He fomented civil war in Abyssinia by shipping hundreds of Remington rifles to its rebellious border tribes. He launched a series of border campaigns to secure the Abyssinian foothills that, strategic value aside, also happened to be a source of valuable female slaves. Yet the feeble performance of Ismail's conscripts, and the fierce response of King John of Abyssinia, led to a deadlock, with Abyssinian troops hovering in the hills overlooking Massowa. So in 1875, at a cost of £1 million, Ismail sent an army of thirty thousand into Abyssinia, to "re-establish Egyptian prestige" and "secure the future tranquillity of the border districts" so that Egypt might "retain her African empire." While Ismail indulged Gordon's evangelizing abolitionism in Equatoria, his generals and governors enslaved Christians in Abyssinia.[18]

BY THE EARLY 1870s, Ismail was broke. Egyptian loan stock soaked up so much capital in the European stock exchanges that in 1869 Ismail's rival for credit, Sultan Abdul Aziz, had banned him from taking out foreign loans for five years. It had taken over £1 million in bribes and the raising of Egypt's annual tribute to £700,000 to restore his right to borrow abroad. In the meantime, Ismail's European cronies had set up banks in Egypt, so that the khedive might borrow domestically, with the loans secured against Ismail's private estates. In 1870, he borrowed £7 million from the Franco-Egyptian Bank. In 1872, he borrowed £4 million from the Oppenheim bank at Alexandria, £3 million at Constantinople, and then another £2 million at Alexandria. In 1873, when revenue was £7.3 million, of which £6.3 million went on the interest on his existing loans, Ismail took another huge loan from Henry Oppenheim, converting the national debt of £27 million into a long-term loan of £32 million. This device freed up cash, but created a spiral of compound interest and coupon payments that swiftly throttled the economy. Even the loans did not add up. Commissions, bribes, theft, and devaluation shredded their value on the way from the bank to the treasury. Of the Oppenheim loan, a paper credit of £32 million had shrunk to £17.8 million by the time it reached Egypt. The difference could only be made up by further loans, on increasingly reckless terms. By 1874, Ismail had received over £37 million in Egypt's name, and personal loans of just under £10 million. The amount to be repaid, over periods of between ten and thirty years, was £139,767,000 on the national debt, and £27,760,000 on his private debt. Revenue for 1874 was £10 million.[19]

Ismail did find the money for a private palace complex in the shadow of the Pyramids at Giza. He diverted irrigation channels to create a horticultural fantasia in the desert, where artificial streams plashed under fairy-tale bridges and the air tinkled with the chirping of caged African birds. Like a genteel debtor, the khedive devoted his income to keeping up appearances. When Nubar Pasha tried to slow the rush to the precipice, Ismail sacked him. When Nubar's replacement, Ismail Sadyk Pasha, concocted a plan that mortgaged what remained of Egypt's future, Ismail was delighted.

Ismail owned a fifth of Egypt's arable land, but he paid no tax. The European traders in Egypt earned a lot of money, but they paid no tax. The next-highest earners were the Turkish landlords, who reduced their income tax by bribing the inspectors, but were still liable for annual assessment on their landholdings. Ismail Sadyk Pasha made the landowners an offer: If they paid six years' tax on their landholdings in one year, the land would be taxed at a 50 percent discount forever. He called this deal the *Muqabala*, the Compensation. It was not clear who compensated whom: The landowners produced £8 million in cash, tiding Ismail over for a few months, but Ismail lost millions in future revenues. After that, only one source of tax revenue remained: the *fellahin*.[20]

The slowdown of the cotton boom had deprived the *fellahin* of the small pleasures of owning slaves and dodging the *Corvée*. "The *kourbash* has been going on my neighbors backs and feet all the morning," recorded the émigré Scottish aristocrat Lucie Duff Gordon. "The system of wholesale extortion and spoliation has reached a point beyond which it would be difficult to go." She had written in 1865, a golden year for the Egyptian economy. "The poor *fellahin* are forced to take the bread from the mouths of their starving families and eat it while toiling for the profit of one man. Egypt is one vast plantation, where the master works his slaves without even feeding them." By the 1870s, the situation was out of control. Egypt was ripe for revolution.[21]

KHARTOUM WAS THE permanent boomtown of the wild south. After decades of Egyptian influence, life was almost bearable. The telegraph had arrived, and there was talk of a railway. Apart from guns and tent pegs, the local Greek merchants now offered French wines and perfume, tinned fruit and the elixir of the Briton abroad, Bass's Pale Ale. On the river, Egyptian police boats hunted slave smugglers with sluggish enthusiasm.

The town's governor Ismail Ayoub Pasha greeted Gordon with a banquet, followed by dances from gyrating Nubian girls wearing only bangles and leather thongs. Aroused and drunk, Austrian consul Martin Hansal jumped up and jiggled along. Sober and disgusted, Gordon slipped away unnoticed. Obliged to return the governor's hospitality at the British Consulate, Gordon's party deployed from the storeroom the remainders of Samuel Baker's supplies: Sèvres plates, crystal goblets from Bohemia, vintage burgundy and champagne. Gordon bought forty pudding bowls and whipped up a giant vat of tapioca as a Spartan finale. Then he sailed south for Equatoria, the wood-burning boiler of his little steamer *Khedive* puffing industriously.

Ismail Ayoub Pasha wanted to dispose of Gordon before he could detect the intimate connection between the Khartoum government and the slave trade, and he had already cut Gordon a path through the rotten gates of the Sudd. South of the reeds, Gordon disappeared into a primeval interior of naked animists and mapless swamps, where the connected world of Cairo and the coast lost all meaning. His new subjects had words for east and west, because they moved from bank to bank of the Nile, but not for north and south. Conversely, Equatoria had a northern border six hundred miles south of Khartoum, where the Sobat and Gazelle rivers met the White Nile, and a southern border somewhere near Lake Victoria; but its eastern or western borders could stretch as far as the Indian or Atlantic oceans. Its capital, Gondokoro—Baker's name of Ismailia had not stuck—was a collection of huts a thousand miles from Khartoum. In 1874, a telegraph message from Bombay reached London within five hours, and a steamer took thirty days. By contrast, Gordon took twenty-six days to sail the thousand miles from Khartoum to Gondokoro, and without Ismail Ayoub Pasha's help, the journey could have taken up to a year.

As an engineer, Gordon saw his commission as a question of logistics. He could not rule without communications, so he would begin by setting up a logistical spine for Equatoria: a chain of forts running south toward the Great lakes "at intervals of a day's journey," connecting Gondokoro to Foweira and Fatiko, the surviving outposts of Baker's tenure. Then he would map the last vague section of the Nile between Fatiko and Lake Victoria, completing the labors of Speke, Grant, and Baker, while his soldiers brought up Baker's metal steamers in sections. Launching the steamers on Lakes

Victoria and Albert, he would open the lakes to "legitimate trade," and the Christianity and Commerce that made for Civilization.[22]

He repeated all of Baker's mistakes. His Turkish fez and Egyptian soldiers marked him as a collaborator in the corruption of the Turkiyya. Announcing that the motto of Equatoria would be *Hurriyet*—Turkish for "Liberty"—Gordon declared martial law and restored the government's monopoly on ivory trading, an economic blow that drove the native tribes and the slavers into an alliance. Like Baker before him, he caused outrage at the Anti-Slavery Society by hiring Abu Suud—a prime agent of the Gazelle River slave trade and a director of Rataz Agat, Khartoum's leading slave and ivory company. He hoped to set one thief to catch many more, but his crude strategy foundered in repeated betrayals. Through it all, he depended on a minimal budget and untrustworthy soldiers.

Gordon had come to save an irredeemable regime. None of its members wanted to be there. The Cairo government used Equatoria as a dumping ground for rebels, criminals, and slave conscripts. "I never in the course of my life saw such wretched creatures dignified by the name of soldiers." His officers colluded with the slave dealers behind his back and sold their own men. Their idea of order was to license *ghazwas* in their territories. To collect taxes, they strung men and women upside down and beat the soles of their feet to a pulp with a *kourbash*. Little of the money they extracted reached Khartoum. Their men ran amok, their principal activities theft, murder, rape, and slavery, facilitated by Remingtons from the British dealer at Cairo. At permanent war with the tribes, they became prisoners of their own forts, venturing out only to hunt slaves and cattle, delivering mail and supplies by armed convoy. "The fact is that the people who annex the province need quite as much civilisation as those they attempt to civilise."[23]

Gordon sailed south to set up his forts, his boat making four knots against a current of two knots. He crept through a "pestiferous" flat country of muddy greens and browns, a sea of "rank jungle-grass" that parted for the odd acacia tree or the conical brush roof of a native hut. Traumatized by the slave trade, the native Shilluks stared silently at Gordon as he passed, running away if he tried to approach them. He could not speak to them directly; he spoke no Arabic, and his French interpreter had died from fever after only ten days. There remained only nine Europeans in Equatoria. Gordon soon fell out with the other eight. His Bible was the only book for miles around, his letters to Augusta his only escape.[24]

"No steamer as yet: very trying for the flesh." Weeks passed in a hut waiting for supplies, the "horrid" climate alternating between burning heat and torrential rain that turned his mess kit moldy and rusted his instruments. Cockroaches nested in his rice and sugar, scorpions lurked in the folds of his mosquito net, hippos lunged out of the Nile at his boats, elephants smashed up his vegetable garden, and the mosquitoes ate him alive, queuing up under his wicker chair to drink from the veins of his buttocks. The diet was tedious and barely nutritious: dry biscuits with boiled macaroni—"*most* ordinary, I can assure you"—supplemented with incessant bananas and mangy bits of broiled meat. Within three months, seven of his ten staff had died or been invalided back to Khartoum, and one of his captains had broken down and shot himself. Communication broke down between his posts; his Egyptian couriers could not deliver a letter without pillaging any villages en route. When his men ventured too far from the camp, the natives murdered them with spears and stuck their heads on poles.[25]

Gordon boiled his water and laced it with brandy to fortify his liver. He concocted his own supplement, "a splendid daily pill" of ginger, rhubarb, and ipecacuanha, washing it down with swigs of Warburg's Tincture, an anti-malarial brew of quinine, alcohol, cloves, and ginger whose recommended dose was a single teaspoon at times of fever. He took to his sleeping bag at dusk to evade the mosquitoes, rose at dawn for the "fearful mysteries" of Bible study in the prehistoric forest, and drove his party down the river, more fearful of "the doles" than of disease or death. By the end of 1875, he had managed to build a chain of posts between Gondokoro and Foweira. He had hauled up the fifty-ton steamer *Nyanza* in three sections, and assembled them at the village of Dufilé, midway along the line of posts. He was ready for the final push to the lakes. Then, a few miles south of Dufilé at a place called Fola, came the crushing honor of discovering the last secret of the White Nile.[26]

"IT IS ALL OVER! I started from Dufilé this morning and, keeping on the higher level to avoid the wet edges of the river, came on it about five miles from here. I fancied for some time I had heard a voice like thunder, which increased as we approached the river. At last we stood above it, on a rocky bank covered with vegetation which descended abruptly to the stream, and there it was, appalling to look at, far less to think of getting anything up and down, except in splinters."[27]

Gordon looked down on a two-mile stretch of boiling rapids, the only totally impassable stretch between Lake Albert and the Mediterranean. There could be no steamer service between Khartoum and the lakes. The great civilizing project of "opening up" Central Africa via the White Nile had been revealed as a delusion. Seeking to salvage a smaller victory over the wilderness, Gordon pushed on southward through "mosquitoes, marsh, forest and misery," to finish his geographical work. Typically, he gave his Italian aide Romolo Gessi the glory of sailing onto Lake Albert. A few months later, their tiny force came up against King Mutesa of Uganda, a tyrant who honored his European guests by decapitating batches of insignificant subjects in their presence, and threatened the same fate for any Egyptian soldiers who entered his territory. Gordon's force was too small and too tired to risk a battle with Mutesa. The Egyptian frontier stopped sixty miles short of Lake Victoria.[28]

As Gordon's mission reached its end, "the doles" closed in. Like Samuel Baker, he had found that the easy prescriptions of the humanitarians, and the easy promises of the khedive, meant nothing in the face of African reality. Policing the White Nile north of Khartoum made little difference to a slave trade whose hunting grounds had shifted to the Gazelle River, and whose export routes now ran overland. Those routes lay outside Gordon's authority, and were controlled by the slavers and senior Egyptian administrators. So long as a corrupt Egyptian governor-general steered this conspiracy from Khartoum, the trade would continue. "What right have I to coax the natives to be quiet, for them to fall into the hands of a rapacious Pasha after my departure?"[29]

To Gordon, the collapse of his grand project was a moral failure, proof of his secret vanity and his lust for worldly status. Malarial and morally exhausted, his assumptions melted in the heat. The Egyptians, he concluded, would never be agents of progress. "Oh! I am sick of these people. It is they, not the black, who need civilisation. There is little difference between white men and black men, I feel more and more assured." He fell prey to "effeminate" fantasies of first-class railway carriages, the taste of fresh oysters, lying in a real bed all morning, and the luxury of turning down invitations to dinner. "Poor sheath, it is much worn!" Consumed by futility and ready to resign, he began the long journey back down to Cairo.[30]

"You are a barnacle to the world and its judgments," he berated himself. If Gordon needed proof of his smallness, it lay in events in Egypt in his absence. While he had hauled stores past the rapids, Ismail's Egypt had shot over the cataracts of credit.[31]

THE CRASH BEGAN on October 5, 1875, when Sultan Abdul Aziz announced that he could not afford the interest on Turkey's £100 million of debt. The value of Turkish securities tumbled, and Egyptian securities followed. The umbilicus connecting Egypt to Turkey, to whose severance Ismail had devoted so much diplomacy and cash, tightened around his neck. If Ismail did not find a new source of revenue, Egypt would default on its next coupon, defrauding investors in London, Paris, Amsterdam, Brussels, Antwerp, Geneva, and Constantinople. He and his ministers had already taxed men, butter, animals, and salt. They had sold tax exemptions, devised stock frauds, hocked the titles to Egypt's best farmland, and turned debt to short-term loans and long-term consolidations. There remained only one asset: his private shares in the Suez Canal Company.

A whisper went out from Cairo that Ismail's 44 percent stake in the Canal was for sale. Ismail's friend Henry Oppenheim mentioned it over dinner with Frederick Greenwood, the editor of the *Pall Mall Gazette*, who told his proprietor George Smith, who mentioned it to Lord Derby, the foreign secretary. Derby followed the traditional Conservative line: "All we want is trade, and land is not necessary for trade; we can carry on commerce very well on ground belonging to other people." So long as Egypt provided mutton chops and post horses, Britain had no need to intervene directly in its economy or politics. But Derby's prime minister disagreed. Although he did not follow the mathematics, Benjamin Disraeli understood that two decades of rapid globalization had changed the international balance of power.[32]

In 1815, a coalition of European monarchies—Britain, Austria, Prussia, and Russia—had defeated Napoleon at Waterloo. To prevent further revolutionary outbreaks, the victors devised the Concert of Europe, a security system that defused international tension at regular summits. The result was four decades of economically productive but socially conservative peace. The Concert was a multilateral system resting on the unipolar authority of Britain, which possessed enormous industrial, economic, and military advantages. This peace eroded through the decline of the Sick Man of Europe and the rise of the Eastern Question. The Russian and British members of the Concert fell out over control of the Eastern Mediterranean. Fueled by a French partner seeking to regain global importance, this rivalry sparked the short but significant Crimean War of 1853–56, a shock from which neither the Sick Man nor the Concert ever recovered.

The breakdown of the Concert coincided with the ripening of other eighteenth-century legacies: the Enlightenment notion of national identity, the French Revolution's demand for mass enfranchisement, and the Industrial Revolution's steam-powered machines. Europe, once imperial, feudal, and agricultural, became a continent of rising nationalism, sharp political division, and rapid industrialization. The new nations of Germany and Italy arose. In 1870, Gallic vanity and Prussian ambition led to the Franco-Prussian war, collapsing the Third Empire of Napoleon III and creating a unified German Empire. Although European statesmen still invoked the Concert of Europe, their relations turned into a multipolar struggle between "Great Powers."

The newly powerful European states turned abroad for materials and markets. Playing out their local rivalries on a global scale, governments used private businesses as assets in strategic competition. Free Trade gave way to protectionism, and private traders to government-run colonies. Rather than a utopia of economic liberalism and international harmony, the opening of the Suez Canal inaugurated an era of trade tariffs and chauvinism. The informal influence that governments gained through private investors and gunboat diplomats hardened into formal empires and global strategies. National honor and prosperity now depended on what became known as "Imperialism." Within five years of the fireworks at Port Said, some Europeans feared that Imperialism might ignite a general European war.

THE BRITISH HAD the most to lose. Their advantage over their fellow Europeans eroded as they lost the patents on their industrial technology. Their campaign for global Free Trade foundered on protectionism. Their ally the Turkish sultan played them off against Bismarck's shiny Germany. Benjamin Disraeli, the British prime minister, understood that Britain must compete or decline. He also had a Romantic's fondness for the Orient, and a showman's feel for the public. He offered voters a choice between "a comfortable England" or "a great country, an imperial country, a country where your sons, when they rise, rise to paramount positions, and obtain not merely the esteem of their countrymen, but command the respect of the world." The million working class voters that Disraeli created through the 1867 Reform Bill responded to his spicy vision of Eastern power. The prime minister who, as a baptized Jew, had joked, "I am the blank page between the Old Testament and the New," became the pivot of Britain's imperial development.[33]

When the Egyptian crash came, the British government had no policy other than its traditional laissez-faire distaste for entanglement in its subjects' foreign speculations. But while British politicians, Disraeli included, had held aloof from Ismail's wild dance of debt, French politicians had supported their businessmen and bankers in Egypt as a means of recovering their Napoleonic influence. By the time Disraeli heard that Ismail's Suez Canal shares were available, two French banks had already tabled offers, one organized by Ferdinand de Lesseps, and both backed by their government. Meanwhile, Britain held the largest share of Egypt's debt, took 80 percent of its exports, and supplied 44 percent of its imports. Egyptian cotton had become as integral to Britain's economy as the Canal had become to its strategy.

Business had become too important to be left to businessmen. Overriding Lord Derby, Disraeli secured Queen Victoria's permission to enter secret negotiations with Ismail and Nubar Pasha, raised £4 million from the banker Edmund de Rothschild, and bought all of Ismail's 177,646 shares. Although the Canal Company remained a French company run by French engineers, the controlling stake now sat in the vaults of the Bank of England. Disraeli's assertive "forward" policies, and the omnipotence of the Royal Navy, had combined to establish Britain as the Canal's effective proprietor. Believing that he had secured the India Route, Disraeli set a symbolic capstone on Britain's formal empire by dubbing Queen Victoria the empress of India.

ISMAIL PREFERRED THAT his government collapsed into British arms. Selling his shares to Disraeli created a pleasing balance of foreign interest. Now Britain and France both had deep political interests to go with their crucial private investments in Egypt. By manipulating the tension between the two states, Ismail could play them off against each other. First, however, he had to restore his credit after the embarrassment of Sultan Abdul Aziz's default on the Turkish debt, in order to tempt foreign creditors back to the pink suite at the Abdin Palace. In January 1876, Ismail invited his new British friends to send "some competent Government official" to assist Ismail Sadyk Pasha in "remedying the confusion" of Egypt's finance ministry, so that he might reconstitute it along British lines.[34]

The Disraeli government was aggressive, but it was not foolish. Responding cautiously, it sent its paymaster-general, Stephen Cave, M.P., to prepare a confidential report on the Egyptian finances. Cave had trouble deciphering Ismail's accounts; the finance ministry was the sinecure of several Coptic families, who had kept out interlopers by writing the accounts in Arabic code. Despite their refusal to help him, Cave produced a detailed Parliamentary Report. He concluded that Egypt was £76.5 million in debt, but the country might yet stay afloat, if only Ismail would stop spending. "Egypt is well able to bear the charge of the whole of her present indebtedness at a reasonable rate of interest, but she cannot go on renewing floating debts at 25%, and raising fresh loans at 12 or 13%."[35]

Ismail responded by establishing a Commission of the Public Debt, to implement Cave's recommendations for recovery. To secure British and French support, he suggested that it be furnished with an advisory panel of Europeans. The commission was a smokescreen. Ismail was confident that competition between its British and French members would prevent it from offering any real advice. And as the commission had taken over Ismail's debts, he considered himself free from the need to pay his creditors. On April 8, 1876, he followed Sultan Abdul Aziz into bankruptcy and suspended payments on all bonds and debts.

Ismail's strategy produced the desired division. The French government sent a candidate to the commission's panel, but the British government refused to name a representative. When Disraeli refused to publish the Cave Report because he did not wish to frighten the markets, the French and British bondholders united in concern for their money and launched their own inquiry. The French government weighed in behind its bondholders and nominated a Paris banker named Joubert as its investigator, but Lord Derby refused to support the British bondholders: A business gone bad was not the responsibility of Her Majesty's Government. The British bondholders sent the British banker George Goschen anyway.

In October 1876, Goschen and Joubert began to excavate the debris of Ismail's finance ministry. Determining that the Cave Report had overstated the scale of Egypt's debt, they arrived at a figure of £59 million, and drew up a new austerity plan for the Egyptian economy. Goschen did not expect Ismail to implement it. He warned the Foreign Office that the khedive "would repudiate if he got the chance," and that "there was reason to believe he was holding back funds which he had in hand."[36]

Gordon's return from Equatoria coincided with the last act of the Goschen-Joubert inquiry. In their labors, they had uncovered evidence of systematic fraud: false invoices, fake receipts, and duplicate bonds. When they asked Ismail, he suggested that they had only found evidence of innocent clerical blunders. And when they pressed him, he reminded them that in a modern state like Egypt, all financial complexities were the province of the finance minister, Ismail Sadyk Pasha.

As Gordon sailed down from Khartoum, Ismail Sadyk Pasha went in the opposite direction. In chains and under armed guard, the windows of his steamer boarded shut, Sadyk Pasha was taken to the military camp at Dongola in the Sudan. "Sadyk Pasha has sought to organise a plot against His Highness the khedive, by exciting the religious sentiments of the native population against the scheme proposed by Messrs. Goschen and Joubert," announced the government-owned *Egyptian Monitor.* "He has also accused the khedive of selling Egypt to the Christians."[37]

"What an affair!" Gordon wrote to Augusta. "Everyone speaks of it in bated breath."[38]

In early December 1876, the foreign consuls received a circular reporting Sadyk Pasha's natural death at Dongola from "fatigue, grief and excess." It omitted to mention that in his fatigue and grief he had bitten off one of his murderers' thumbs.[39]

3

God's Diplomacy
1879–81

Sheikh Said Jamal ed-Din al-Afghani, the "Sage of the East."

Religion is the Mainstay of Nations and the Source of their Welfare. In it is their Happiness, and around it is their Pivot. Materialism is the Root of Corruption and the Source of Foulness. From it comes the ruin of the Land and the Perdition of Man.

—Jamal ed-Din al-Afghani, *The Truth about the Materialists*, 1881[1]

AT THE SOUTHEAST CORNER of the Ezbekiyyeh Gardens, on the plot between the Opera House and Ismail's estate offices whose previous occupant had been the Cairo circus, a team of imported Syrian stonemasons finished their work. Facing Ataba Square and the kiosks and promenades of the Gardens, and backing onto the alleys of the old city, the Mattatias Building was one of the last gasps of Ismail's golden age. Neoclassical arches sheltered an arcade of shops, overlooked by two upper stories whose arched windows owed more to Italian Gothic than the Ottoman vernacular. The developer and namesake of this polyglot design was Mattatias Nahman, a Greek Jewish businessman who had engaged the French architect Ambroise Baudry and, after pausing to avoid bankruptcy in the Debt Crisis of 1875, spent six hundred thousand francs building it.

A café sheltered in the arcade. It was open all night and served meals in a small alcove. The regulars were a hybrid bunch: journalists, playwrights, Freemasons, and, the café being near al-Azhar University, unconventional clerics. Lately having turned down a post at al-Azhar for tenure at Mattatias's café and a small rented house in the Jewish Quarter, fueled by tea, coffee, tobacco, and the odd brandy, the Sage of the East held forth at his usual table.[2]

Bearded, voluble, and a little bug-eyed, Sheikh Said Jamal ed-Din al-Afghani was a prophet without honor in many lands, usually under an assumed identity. In Afghanistan and India, he pretended to be a Turk called Said al-Istanbuli: "Said of Istanbul." In the Ottoman Empire, he called himself al-Afghani: "The Afghan." In both guises, he claimed to be a defender of mainstream Sunni Islam. None of this was true. He was a Shia, not a Sunni; from northwest Persia, not Afghanistan; and rather than being an orthodox scholar, he was a highly unorthodox revolutionary. Afghani believed that Islamic civilization was under deliberate military and cultural assault from the Christian world. The only solution was to beat the infidels at their own game. Western technology and ideas would be the weapons of a modern, reformed Islamic society.[3]

Afghani grew up in Persia, its shah the chief defender of the Shiite minority that had splintered off from Islam in the decades after Mohammed's death. While messianism was incidental to Sunni Islam, it was integral to Shia faith. As a child in Tehran, Afghani learned that the twelfth in the series of infallible *imams* that had led the Shia had disappeared over a thousand years earlier, but would return as the *Mahdi*, the Expected Redeemer who would inaugurate a new millennium. In a further deviation from Sunni custom, Afghani's education in the Shia seminaries of Najaf included both the rationalist, Greek-derived philosophy of medieval Islam—banned as heresy in the Turkish and Arab worlds—and also Sufi mysticism. In Afghani's youth, the blending of these streams of thought produced the Shaikhi sect, a stew of rationalist philosophy, mysticism, and a cult of strong, hidden leadership. While the Sunni clerics of the Ottoman lands endorsed the sultan and stability, Afghani was a philosopher, a heretic, and a mystic who expected a messianic redemption.

Afghani dwelt on Islam's intellectual frontier in an era when European exports and armies broke the borders between the Islamic and Christian worlds. By economics or war, the outcomes were the same: the eclipse of Muslim power. The shah of Persia intrigued weakly between the British and Russians as the borders of their empires converged on Central Asia. The Mughal emperors of India were crushed by first the French and then the British. The Ottoman sultan betrayed his caliphate, entering military alliances with the Christian nations against whom previous sultans had waged jihads of conquest and conversion.

The rise of the Christian West mocked the Muslim conviction that in the unfolding of the divine plan that was history, theirs was the final and true religion. More than modern Judaism or Christianity, Islam was a total system. Accepting no separation between religion and state, its ambit included all life, including politics. The past power of Islamic empires attested that Islam was the true religion. Yet if Muslims possessed the final revelation and the duty to spread it, how had Christians, their infidel inferiors, taken over the world?

The only reason could be that Muslim rulers and their subjects had drifted from true Islam. Some preached a return to an idealized past of authoritarian purity and desert tribalism. In Arabia, the Wahhabi sect rejected the corrupt sultan's claim to the caliphate and attacked the Ottoman occupiers of Mecca. In Libya, the Wahhabi-influenced Senussi sect retreated from the cosmopolitan coast to the desert, reconstructing an idealized Koranic society. Others, especially in the borderlands of Islam, incorporated Western elements. In Turkey, a rumbling movement for political reform dressed its ambition in concern for the independence of the sultan-caliph. In Persia, the years of Afghani's boyhood saw the rise of the modernizing, messianic Babi sect, whose leader called himself the *Bab*, the gate that would lead to the arrival of the Twelfth Imam. All believed that the best future resembled the distant past, whether that was located in the militant austerity of the Prophet's wars or the messianic restoration of the Twelfth Imam.

Afghani's early life took him across the Islamic world, east to west, each stop overlaying unorthodoxy with political radicalization. Symptoms of crisis stretched from the Himalayas to the Mediterranean. In Persia, a failed Babi attempt to kill the shah caused the expulsion of the sect. In India, Afghani saw a jihad against Christian control, known to the British as the Indian Mutiny, which ended in defeat and the consolidation of Christian power. In Afghanistan, he saw how imperial competition created a civil war.

Believing in the unity of Islamic civilization, and the imperative of its global mission, he assumed a unity of Christian purpose. He decided that the Christian empires, rather than growing through trade, had an expansionist program to destroy Islam. The British, subverters of the Mughal, Persian, and Turkish empires, were the prime agents of the war on Islam.

At the same time, British India also demonstrated to Afghani the value of modern weapons and ideas. He did not repeat the error of the Ottoman sultans, who had identified machines with their inventors, and banned imports of technology from Christian countries: To Afghani, economic and scientific progress were weapons of defense. No less useful were European ideas of revolutionary politics and religious skepticism. These confirmed his suspicion that in the new world political power counted for more than spiritual depth. The result was a dilemma of attraction and repulsion: attraction to the power of the industrial, skeptical West, and repulsion at its heretic, atheistic intent. Like those European liberals who, disillusioned by the failure of the 1848 revolutions, succumbed to nihilism and anarchism, what Afghani really believed in was the utility of power. The further he developed his ideas in its pursuit, the further he drifted from the faith he wished to restore.

Although his blend of religious and political heresies marked him as a radical, new type of Muslim, the only viable path to power obliged him to dress his rebellion in orthodoxy. His travels had shown that religion was the great unifier of the Islamic world, and that simple appeals to tradition could raise revolutions against the Christian empires. His enemies also invoked transnational ideas to justify their expanding influence. The Russians used pan-Slavism to push the Turks from the Balkans, and the British saw the colonies of their emigrants as elements of a global Anglo-Saxon civilization. Like his European contemporary Karl Marx, Afghani blended philosophy, mysticism, and vestigial messianism into an ideology designed to resist the imperial, commercial onslaught. While Marx looked to the shared miseries of the Western industrial city as the fuel of revolution, Afghani turned to the foundation of his world.

He realized that philosophy would never bring revolution to conformist Sunni Islam. He had to appeal to the international patriotism of Islam, to the simple orthodoxies of popular tradition. So the father of modern Islamic politics disguised himself as a Turkic Sunni to overcome the double handicap of being a minority Shia, and a Persian in Indian, Arab, and Turkish societies.

Afghani inverted the Islamic belief that politics was an aspect of religion:

to him, religion was an implement of politics. He went to great lengths to mask this heresy at the heart of his thought. Unlike Marx, he never formulated his thoughts in a manifesto; articulating his program would have revealed his profound modernity. Instead he campaigned relentlessly, his ambitions masked in local issues, his agitations less an answer than the parameters of a new question. He claimed to speak for all Islam, although only a small coterie of intellectuals, many of them not Muslim, knew who he was. He mobilized the technology of propaganda to create an impression of influence, introducing the tools of European activism—the journal, the leaflet, and the secret society—to the Islamic world. He began the carving of a modern political ideology from traditional Islam, adapting the weapons of the West to create a weapon for confronting the West: pan-Islamism, an attitude as much as an agenda.

Wherever Afghani went he tried to adapt local opportunities to his jihad. In Afghanistan, he spied for the Russians. In Turkey, he signed up with the liberal reformers. In Egypt, where hostile clerics threw stones through his windows, the Shia sheikh from Persia added to his repertoire a pose from eighteenth-century Paris: the coffee-drinking, café-haunting, freethinking *philosophe.* He slept all day, stayed up all night at the café, got himself elected the head of a Masonic lodge, the Star of the East, and even made saucy comments to the waitresses in the outdoor café in the Ezbekiyyeh Gardens. Not that Afghani indulged in sex. Like Charles Gordon, Afghani deferred consummation to the end of the world. "Owing to his preoccupation with great things, he had lost the need and capacity for marriage," explained Rashid Rida, an early adherent who would become the intellectual link between Afghani and Hassan al-Bana's Muslim Brotherhood. When the sultan of Turkey offered Afghani a spare woman from his harem, Afghani refused, citing his impotence, and threatened that if the sultan insisted on bestowing his gift, he would "cut the organ of procreation."[4]

The disciples at the table of this bloodthirsty bachelor made unlikely harbingers of Islamic revolution. Most were educated dropouts from government service, stepping off the ladder of promotion in protest at the slowness of their climb. Yacub Sanna was an Italian Jew who had switched from teaching in a government college to become Ismail's court playwright; when the khedive stopped laughing, he had become a salon agitator, satirical journalist, and Masonic organizer. Adib Ishaq, an atheist Syrian Catholic, had also left the theater and Ismail's patronage for journalism. Abdullah Nadim had left a post in a provincial telegraph office for the life of an itinerant poet and handkerchief salesman.

Only one of Afghani's recruits might become more than a useful ideologue. Sheikh Mohammed Abdu was a fellow renegade from Islamic orthodoxy. A brilliant scholar from al-Azhar and a "complete votary" of the café circle, Abdu rejected traditional Islamic interpretation, called for the study of "the sciences of the Franks," and grew his hair long like a Whirling Dervish. Afghani groomed him as the bearer of the revolution, and Abdu responded with moist-eyed idolatry. "You have made us with your hands," he gushed, "invested our matter with its perfect form, and created us in the ideal shape. Through you we have known the entire universe."[5]

A Jewish comedian, a Christian playwright, a footloose haberdasher, and an infatuated sheikh: Afghani's collection of misfits and dreamers made an unlikely cadre to lead the renewal of the Islamic world. But to the true revolutionary, as to the servant of God, the end justified all means.

KHEDIVE ISMAIL did his best to prevent the growth of civil society, but it grew anyway. Having invited the flood of private capital, international communications, mass literacy, and immigration, he proved powerless to channel it. The props and scenery of the modern state, littered artfully for the benefit of European investors and politicians, assumed malevolent animation. Railways, the telegraph, and a postal system imported foreign information and ideas. French and English, the languages of technical manuals for engineers and soldiers, were also languages of ideas, of fiction and philosophy. The army that intimidated the sultan and enslaved the Sudanese developed a native core of Egyptian officers who expected equal rewards. The Masonic lodges established by networking businessmen became incubators of radical politics. The mass education that created a civil service also created a reading public, and cheap printing allowed the production of independent newspapers. The days when an autocrat could arrange Egyptian society around his throne had gone forever.

When Ismail had come to power, Egypt had no Arabic newspaper. As part of his program of furnishing Egypt with the amenities of the modern West, he had reconstituted the government *Gazette* as a useful tool of control and publicity. In the late 1860s and early 1870s, however, a sheaf of privately owned newspapers grew up to serve Egypt's expanding readership. First, Ismail and his ministers tried to contain the press by bribery. Secret "donations" guided the newspapers' editorial stance, and the government rewarded their assistance by buying advertising space for its announcements. Originally, this worked; *Nile Valley*, the first Arabic weekly, subsisted entirely on the khedive's money and consequently praised the policies that drove Egypt into bankruptcy. By 1873, the government allocated nine thousand pounds to its "Newspaper Intelligence Offices," a figure equivalent to a fifth of the education budget, and far more than it gave to the antiquities museum. But the Debt Crisis of 1876 diverted funds to more urgent ends. At the same time the reading public expanded and more newspapers opened. As printing costs fell, and editors began to sell advertising space to private buyers, low-budget independence became feasible. By 1877, the Afghani protégé Adib Ishaq could afford to print the first issue of *Egypt* on a budget of one pound, the contents of his pocket.[6]

For the first time, Ismail's Egypt, and the khedive's character, came under independent examination. Like all of Ismail's innovations, the press was a double-edged sword. While *Mahroussah* allowed investors to follow the daily prices of Sudanese commodities, and *Nile Valley* loyally distributed government propaganda, brave reporters from *The Pyramids* exposed mass starvation, child labor, beatings, and corruption in the villages of the Nile Delta. Most popular of all were satirical journals that mocked the corruption, incompetence, and inertia of Ismail's officials. Entire print runs of *To Laugh Or To Cry* sold out within minutes of delivery, while *Mr. Blue Spectacles* ridiculed the government so skillfully that Ismail exiled its editor, Afghani's accomplice Yacub Sanna.

"I used to see them in the streets of Cairo and the old city," recalled the historian Mikhail Sharubim. "Crowds of them, gathered about a man, or a boy from among the Koran-schooled pupils, while he read to them the translation of a piece by the publisher of the London *Times* or another foreign newspaper. All the time, they clamoured and shouted, *There is no power save through Allah!*"[7]

Egypt now had an independent press to formulate political ideas, a communications infrastructure to distribute them, and enough readers to ensure that their message reached all levels of society. The titles showed how local interests were creating a national identity, at least in the minds of intellectuals: *Nile Valley, The Pyramids, The Nation, Egypt*. Their editors requested that Ismail grant what he already claimed to have offered: a constitution, equal legal rights for all, an independent judiciary, and representative government. Like Ismail, the political journalists framed their program in "Ottomanism," the idea that Egypt could reform without compromising its subordinate relationship to Turkey. But while Ismail used Ottomanism as a gesture to cover his drive for independence, the political journalists used it as a means to import a revolution.

In Turkey, Sultan Abdul Aziz had initiated a program of mild reforms as the key to escaping his debts but had halted in the face of religious and aristocratic opposition. In May 1876, students inspired by Mazzini's revolutionary Young Italy movement rioted in Istanbul with the cry "Turkey for the Turks!" Allying with progressive nobles, disaffected clergy, and a populace punished by Turkey's foreign debt, the Young Ottomans managed to tip Sultan Abdul Aziz from his throne. The caliphate passed into the shaking hands of Aziz's alcoholic son Murad V, whom the rebels forced to rubber-stamp a constitution and proposals for total political liberalization. This bracing dose of secular constitutionalism drove ex–sultan Abdul Aziz to suicide, and reactionary aristocrats to overthrow Murad V in favor of his brother Abdul Hamid II.

Thoroughly hostile to reform and foreigners, Abdul Hamid II led Turkey into a disastrous confrontation with Russia. He waged war on the Christian secessionists of Serbia and Montenegro and massacred Christians in Bulgaria. When Russia weighed in on behalf of Orthodox Christians everywhere, Turkey's *Sheikh el-Islam* declared jihad against the Christians. A bungled political reform had mushroomed into a war between Christianity and Islam. God, it appeared, backed the Russians, who were soon at the gates of Constantinople. Rallying to prevent the collapse of the Ottoman Empire, the Concert of Europe called the parties to a peace conference in Berlin. Neither Russia nor Turkey gained any great advantage from the resulting treaty. In a remarkable feat of conjuring by Disraeli and his foreign secretary Lord Salisbury, Britain became the main beneficiary of a war it had not fought. In return for a renewed promise of British protection, Turkey surrendered Cyprus to Britain. The island became the fortress from which the Royal Navy supervised the Mediterranean approaches to both the Black Sea and the Suez Canal, further cementing its maritime supremacy. With Cyprus overlooking the Eastern Mediterranean, Aden at the tip of the Red Sea, and Ismail's shares in a vault in the Bank of England, only the collapse of Ismail's Egypt could imperil the India Route.

Ismail was caught between the same forces as the sultans: the reformers agitating from below, and the Europeans imposing from above. Although Ismail favored everything modern in principle, if he imported Young Ottoman ideas into Egypt, he risked deposition and the fate of "Abdul the Damned," as the erstwhile Defender of the Faithful was now known. Meanwhile the Anglo-French Commission of the Debt gave birth to the inevitable commission of inquiry into Egypt's accounts. Not unreasonably, the inquiry concluded that Ismail could not be trusted with Egypt's finances and advised further austerities. Less wisely, they refused to reschedule Egypt's debts and insisted that the bondholders should receive their dividends on time. More concerned with their banks than Ismail's peasants, the British and French forced Ismail to send "iron-fisted" tax collectors into the Delta so that he could pay the biannual dividend paid to European bondholders. Scraping the last piastre from the peasants, the tax collectors extracted a "great diversity of currency," much of it in antique or small coinage, still strung together as jewelry. Where beatings failed, moneylenders loaned the *fellahin* cash to pay their taxes, the security being the next harvest. The dividend due on May 1, 1878, was paid with hours to spare.[8]

That summer the Nile flood broke its banks, sweeping away over thirty villages, hundreds of villagers, and crops to the value of five hundred thousand pounds. Already broke, the *fellahin* now had nothing to eat. Ismail had no further source of income. The commissioners made him an offer he could not refuse: They would organize a loan so that Egypt could meet the next coupon, but Ismail must abandon his autocratic methods. There must be a Council of Ministers and an independent Finance Ministry supervised by Europeans. Ismail must subsist on a fixed salary, and he must surrender to the state the million acres of prime land he had accumulated. It was a design to turn Ismail into a bearded cherub adorning a European bank.

Hopeless, Ismail consented to the hostile takeover. The British and French brought Nubar Pasha back from Parisian retirement and installed him as head of the council. An official from the British treasury, Sir Rivers Wilson, took over the Finance Ministry. Rivers Wilson knew nothing of Egypt, but he spoke excellent French. He needed it to converse with his French counterpart M. de Blignières, newly resident at the Ministry of Public Works. Between them, they sacked dozens of Egyptian employees, replacing them with Europeans. Rivers Wilson went to Paris and borrowed £8.5 million from the Rothschilds' bank, so that Ismail could pay the coupon due on November 1.

"I have a strong impression that the proceedings of the Commission are wholly wanting in commonsense," observed Lord Salisbury, Disraeli's foreign secretary. "If they want to dethrone the khedive, their policy might lead to the desired result. But they do not want to dethrone him. What then is the use of driving him to desperation?"[9]

Squeezed between the rebels, the Royal Navy, and the commissioners, Ismail had no room for maneuver. If he chipped at the brittle plaster of the Egyptian state, the entire edifice would collapse and crush him. He had cultivated a bourgeoisie as the human decoration of his European boulevards, but it had mutated beyond recognition. The educated children of the middle class demanded more than seats at the opera and concerts in the Ezbekiyyeh Gardens. They formed secret societies with names like Young Egypt, impersonating the revolutionaries of Italy and Turkey. At the Star of the East lodge, budding Freemasons imbibed Afghani's preaching that all religions were the same, and that this banal heresy somehow commanded the overthrow of the European empires. At study circles led by Afghani's crony Yacub Sanna, they mined rebellious ideas from eighteenth-century novels and ancient philosophy, hiding their sedition behind innocent names like the Circle of Progress or the Society of Lovers of Knowledge. And if, like many respectable young Muslim men, they were repelled by the theological cavorting of the Freemasons, or the prominence of Christians and Jews in Young Egypt and the reading circles, then the handkerchief-vending poet Abdullah Nadim was on hand to induct them into the ostensibly traditional Islamic Philanthropical Society or the Young Men's Association. Even the progressive Turkish nobility joined in, devising its own mildly impertinent suggestions about how Ismail might improve his ways.

Ismail knew what these groups were plotting, because his spies had infiltrated them all. Their existence posed a serious problem. If he repressed the most productive element among his subjects, he lost their contribution to the economic recovery that was his only way out of debt. Yet if he indulged the fashion for free speech and constitutionalism, he undercut his own power. It was Ismail's good fortune that Egypt's rebels were as remote from the people as the Turkish aristocrats they sought to topple.

Ismail's enemies slid into the traditional Ottoman politics that they hoped to disrupt. Organizing into rival elites, they sided with one aristocratic patron against another. As Mohammed Abdu explained, the *fellahin* and the urban poor were too mired in "political ignorance" to take part in a republican government. Facing the same problem, Marx had admitted that the leaders of the revolution were more likely to emerge not from the proletariat, but from among the overeducated children of its bosses. Similarly, Afghani and Abdu wanted to create an alliance of enlightened minds to lead the struggle. So the rebels retreated to their private salons to play parlor games of factional rivalry and theoretical delusion. Afghani had a lifelong weakness for powerful patrons and ready cash. Instead of leading his followers to liberty, he led them into the bogs of Ottoman conspiracy. He and his followers became partisans of Ismail's exiled uncle Halim, who plotted his nephew's overthrow from Istanbul and drew support from the reactionary sultan Abdul Hamid II. Afghani served a greater tyrant to overthrow a lesser, more progressive one. It made no political sense, but it paid well.[10]

The intellectuals ignored or dismissed the most discontented Egyptians of all: the poor. While the beverages and conversation flowed at Mattatias café, the least literate, least educated Egyptians stirred without theoretical guidance. In his field in the Nile Delta, the ordinary *fellah* had borne the brunt of Ismail's ineptitude. He paid the most tax, he ate the least food, he sweated in the *Corvée*, and he suffered random floggings and extortion at the hands of corrupt officials. His only recourses were to the khedive's mercy, an increasingly limited commodity, and to the Islam that had been the backbone of Egyptian society before Ismail had wrecked it. Abstract ideas of nationalism bore no relation to *fellahin* life, but the continuity and consolation of traditional religion did. Many Egyptian Muslims saw their country's crisis not as a result of Ismail's folly or the caprice of the European markets, but as a divine punishment. Like the Crusaders of the past, the *Faranji*—"the Franks"—had taken over the economy and set up an illegitimate Christian government. Instead of rhetoric about parliaments and constitutions, popular rebellion took the simpler forms of native xenophobia and religious revivalism. To the *fellahin*, God's diplomacy was not Free Trade, but what it had always been: religion.

Ismail cared little for Islam and less for religious dissent. The Islamic clergy endorsed his line, and when they did not, he replaced them. But as the economy crashed and society unraveled, he lost control of his subjects. The Capitulations and the police no longer sufficed to protect Egypt's privileged Europeans from the wrath of a starving public. Foreign consuls sensed a rumbling of popular resentment, and sporadic, spontaneous expressions of rising religious anger.

During Ramadan of 1876, irate Muslims beat up an Italian who smoked in the streets of Cairo in daylight. The British consul reported rumors that arms were being stockpiled in the city's mosques, and that unseen agitators were making "clever attempts" to direct popular discontent at Europeans. A Sufi from Mecca and his father, a Turkish war veteran, paraded through the center of Alexandria under the Prophet's green flag, calling for an uprising and the slaughter of Egypt's infidels. The police shipped them swiftly back to Arabia. One morning, residents in the Arab quarter of Cairo awoke to find their neighborhood plastered in decrees from one Sheikh Ahmed, who called himself the "servant of the Prophet's tomb in Medina." The sheikh had used the infidel telegraph system to exhort Egypt's Muslims to abandon drink and sex for prayer. He warned that the Last Day, when the sun would rise from the west, was imminent.[11]

"I WISH, I WISH the King would come again and put things right on earth," Charles Gordon confided to his sister Augusta. Gordon could not resist Sudan. The grandeur and despair of his Equatorial adventure, the drama of corruption and redemption offered by the war on slavery, the power of his office, and the scale of his task all provided the cosmic drama he craved. Three months after resigning in disgust, Gordon returned to the khedivial suite at the Abdin Palace, charmed by a telegram from his "affectionate Ismail," begging that he "complete the work which we began together."[12]

This time, Gordon would not settle for a provincial governorship and the thwarting of his work by his corrupt superior at Khartoum. "Either give me the Sudan, or I will not go," he demanded.[13]

Ismail gave it to him: absolute authority over seventeen provinces and a million square miles of territory, the rank of marshal, a uniform trimmed in £150 worth of gold lace, and orders for "the suppression of slavery and the improvement of the means of communication."[14]

Gordon was surprised by Ismail's apparent surrender, but Gordon never bothered with politics. Ismail had British officials combing through his accounts, and British merchant shipping in the Suez Canal. He needed to demonstrate his suitability as a British client. The cheapest way to do this was to indulge Britain's humanitarian lobby. Six months later, a similar blend of weakness and cynicism prompted his agreement to the Anglo-Egyptian Convention, the fruit of twenty years of humanitarian pressure. The convention emphasized Ismail's obligation to suppress immediately all hunting and trading in slaves. It gave Egypt seven years to phase out the ownership of slaves, and its Sudanese empire twelve years. It also granted the Royal Navy the right of stop and search in the Red Sea.

Even Gordon saw the contradiction it created in British policy. "It is rather amusing to think that the people of Cairo are quite oblivious that in 1884 their revenue will fall to one-half, and that the country will need many more troops to keep it quiet. Seven-eighths of the population of the Sudan are slaves, and the loss of revenue in 1889 will be more than two-thirds." Order would never come to Sudan if the convention dismantled Egypt's imperial economy. "Here slavery touches everyone. How can you deal with it so as to avoid a servile war or a rising of the people?" If Britain imposed legislation without offering the alternative of legitimate trade, and the Egyptians still insisted on their taxes, there could only be one outcome: "If the liberation of slaves takes place in 1884, and the present system of Government goes on, there cannot fail to be a revolt of the whole country."[15]

Uncertain if the physical world merited redemption or destruction, Gordon forced a crisis. He saw the likely consequences of British policy and did his best to make them inevitable. Returning to the Sudan, he found it on the verge of breakdown. Starved of funds and soldiers from Egypt, Gordon's kingdom ran at a loss of ninety-seven thousand pounds per annum. Most of its territory was beyond government control. To the east, Ismail's war with Abyssinia had turned the borderlands into militia fiefdoms. To the south and west, the slavers had only to dodge the patrol boats on the Nile to rampage more freely than ever. Even in the north, government authority was so weak that a Greek impostor who had awarded himself "a grand uniform and plenty of decorations" was able to con bribes from the locals by passing himself off as a pasha. The Khartoum government maintained its authority over a delinquent population through random public floggings, and it exercised its judgment according to the size of its petitioners' bribes. When Gordon took over the governor's palace, he found that the sister of his predecessor Ismail Ayoub Pasha had smashed all of its 130 windows and "cut the divans in pieces." Ismail's Sudanese empire was falling apart.[16]

"With the help of God, I will hold the balance level," he promised Augusta. As he and Baker had done in Equatoria, Gordon divided his plan into two stages. First he would establish order in the government, then he would use it as a springboard for a war on the slavers. He canceled the floggings, fixed the windows, pinned up a box to gather his subjects' petitions, and passed the bribes to the empty treasury. Then he left for an extended camelback tour of his kingdom, accompanied by a small bodyguard. "The people want justice," he wrote hopefully.[17]

Riding thirty miles a day through "torrid wastes," sunburn, saddle sores, and chest pains, he felt the camel's gait rattle his liver and lungs loose and tied a sash around his waist and under his armpits to keep them in place. Gordon believed that the sudden appearance at a country barracks of "a single dirty, red-faced man on a camel, ornamented with flies" had an inspirational effect on Arab rebels, Egyptian soldiers, and African tribesmen alike. Yet after correcting the local abuses that caught his eye on the day of each visit—a sleeping sentry, a slaving officer, a mosque stocked with militia rifles—Gordon vanished into the bush with a whiff of Warburg's Tincture. The garrisons drifted back into their corrupt slumber.[18]

Gordon barely possessed the means to impose occasional order. He had the Convention of 1877, which called slave-hunting "robbery with murder."

He had a decree from Ismail that slaving carried a five-year prison sentence. He had permission to execute any slave catchers and dealers who offended him. But he also had a letter from Nubar Pasha, reminding him that while the Convention banned the taking of slaves, their sale and ownership in Egypt would remain legal until 1884. Gordon had only half the law on his side, less of the economic balance, and none of his Egyptian subordinates. They subverted him at every turn, and he responded with wholesale sackings. In May 1878 alone, he fired one provincial governor, three generals, a brigadier, and four lieutenant colonels. Soon he had sacked fourteen of his seventeen provincial governors. He replaced them with inexperienced Sudanese or Egyptian officers, and passing European mercenaries.[19]

Alienated from his own administration, Gordon fell back on personal magnetism, arbitrary assertions of strength, and sordid pragmatism. Among the "furtive, polecat race" of Abyssinian brigands and the heavily armed Darfur slavers, Gordon's drive for "justice" crumbled into Ismail's tactic of legitimizing local tyrants with a government stamp. In Darfur, he licensed the slavers of the Baggara tribe to intercept their rivals in the trade, the itinerant Jallaba merchants. Returning to Khartoum, he shot without trial a suspected murderer, and a slaver for "mutilating a little boy." Claiming to strike "daily deadly blows against the slave trade," he called his wild methods his "Government of Terror." The description was more accurate than he realized.[20]

In Sudanese eyes, Gordon's Turkish fez and Egyptian soldiers marked him as merely the latest dictatorial import from Cairo. While Gordon dreamed of justice, the Egyptian soldiers slogging along behind his camel grabbed children from the roadside as if stealing chickens. In districts where he stopped the slave trade, the tax collector's *kourbash* still flogged the Sudanese tribes. His British uniform and Christian faith advertised the intrusive reach of an infidel empire, and its pact with Ismail's tyranny. Always skeptical of the Evangelical trinity of "Christianity, Commerce, and Civilization" as a universal cure, he could not help but empathize with his subjects and enemies. "Consider the effect of harsh measures among an essentially Mussulman population, carried out brusquely by a Nazarene," he explained to Augusta, "measures which touch the pocket of everyone."[21]

The Muslims clung to slaving as their religious and historical right, and the animists seemed impervious to evangelism. Faced with the murderous paradox of the Sudan, Gordon retreated to the conventional explanation of his day: "I look upon the Negro races as I would on children of three or four years of age, incapable of understanding these truths." Contrary to the

Evangelical vision, Sudan was no running battle between humanitarians and slavers, Christian universalism and Islamic obscurantism. These incompatible ideologies did not make direct contact. They were mediated through Ismail's Egypt, which aspired to the former while profiting from the latter. "His Highness never punishes the men I send down. They appear at his balls with the greatest coolness." Much as Gordon hoped his Sudanese ordeal was a divine calling, he could not ignore the evidence that he was the voluntary instrument of a corrupt regime. Worse, the "hermaphrodite administration" that the European bankers had imposed on Ismail showed no interest in Sudan, slavery, and salvation. In the choice between "God or Baal," they chose Baal and the next debt payment.[22]

"The only thing I can do to these slave dealers is to flog them and strip them, and send them like Adams into the desert." Within eighteen months, most of the south and west of Sudan erupted in slaver revolts. Gordon responded in kind, taking over two thousand troops into the Gazelle River region. On the road across southern Darfur, the enormity of the trade became clear. A torrent of small caravans streamed north for El Obeid and the Forty Days' Road. Every petty trader had his handful of exhausted, dying merchandise. "Nothing could exceed the misery of these poor wretches. Some were children of not more than three years' old. They had come across that torrid zone from Shaka, a journey from which I on my camel shrink." He flogged the slavers and set their cargo free. One morning Gordon woke to find a female slave had crawled into his tent at night to escape a caravan. When he encountered emissaries from the slavers offering a truce, he executed them. The campaign ended with the execution of their leaders by firing squad.[23]

"I wish the great mystery of evil was revealed to you," he complained to Augusta in faraway Southampton. His campaign barely dented the slave trade. By his own count, in 1878 he intercepted just over two thousand slaves from the estimated thirty thousand exported that year. All the elements that made Sudan a slaver's paradise remained in place: massive demand from the Islamic world, an absence of local alternatives, and an exploitative, corrupt Egyptian government. Gordon's forceful tactics exacerbated Muslim hostility to the Turkiyya and tipped Egypt's tense accommodation with the slavers into open warfare. Alert to the volatility of the situation, yet personally and logistically unequipped to solve it, Gordon turned a mess into a crisis. Rather than establishing justice, Gordon had accelerated Sudan's slide into anarchy.[24]

Within two years, he had repeated his equatorial tangent. "The long crucifixion that a residence in these horrid countries entails appals me. I do not think I can face the cross of staying here on physical grounds." His legs were scabbed with sores from over eight thousand camelback miles. He ate little more than dates munched in the saddle. His liver ached from the brandy. He suffered fevers, prickly heat, boils, and recurrent attacks of malaria, one of which sent him staggering through the corridors of his empty palace at night, pursued by hallucinatory petitioners. He smoked so heavily that he developed heart problems: pains across his chest, numbness in his arms, and dizzying panic attacks. "A rush of blood takes place to the head, and you think all is over. I may say I have died suddenly over a hundred times." He concluded he had finished his task, or that his task would finish him.[25]

Once again Gordon had driven himself to collapse, defeat, and a ghastly epiphany. "I have brought it on myself," he confessed, "for I have prayed to God to humble me to the dust, and to visit all the sins of Egypt and the Sudan on my head." The clouds of altruistic glory parted. "It would be little to say, take my life for theirs, for I do earnestly desire a speedy death. I am weary of the continued conflict with my atrocious self."[26]

"THERE IS NO DELIVERANCE except in killing," Afghani raged, "there is no safety except in killing." Afghani and Abdu planned to kill the khedive, the wicked pharaoh whose death would spark revolution. Every day, Ismail took his afternoon constitutional. An assassin would be waiting for him with a bomb when his carriage slowed to turn onto the Kasr el-Nil bridge. This cast-iron symbol of Ismail's claim to the Nile would be the site of a political murder. It was a scene from the Russian playbook, an emulation of the nihilists and anarchists who had tried repeatedly to kill Czar Alexander II, and would succeed in 1881.[27]

"I strongly approved," Abdu recalled, "but it was only talk between ourselves, and we lacked a person capable of taking a lead in the affair."[28]

Afghani and Abdu were scholars, not soldiers, and for all their revolutionary interest in the masses, elitists in concept and deed. While the mosques fizzed with resentment and the *fellahin* grew lawless in starvation, they operated on the tattered fringe. Lacking a popular power base or military strength, their Masonic rites, reading circles, and high-placed patrons were more likely to assist a palace putsch than inspire a popular revolt. Afghani's transit from religion to politics had swapped one passive daydream for another. He felt diminished by the loss of consolation. "If a philosopher puts on rough clothing, lengthens his prayer beads, and spends his time in the mosque, then he is a mystic," he admitted, "But if he sits in Mattatias' coffee house and smokes the hubble-bubble, then he remains only a philosopher."[29]

ALTHOUGH AFGHANI AND ABDU did not realize it, the missing muscle of their revolution already existed: the army. Its ranks divided like Egyptian society: The senior officers were Turkish, the rank and file were *fellahin* and Sudanese slaves, and the middling officers were the Egyptian graduates of the new systems of education and military schooling. The Turkish generals discriminated against these *fellahin* officers. Though they were more likely to be sent to a Sudanese outpost or an Abyssinian battlefield, none of them ever rose beyond the rank of colonel. In 1876, a handful of frustrated *fellahin* officers had formed a secret society under the robust title Strong Egypt. Its members drifted through the Masonic groups and salon reading circles of Afghani's ideologues, their radicalization accelerated by the government's inability to pay their salaries. When the foreign commissioners sacked twenty-five hundred officers and placed the rest on half pay, the disaffected *fellahin* officers grew mutinous. A group of colonels emerged as their leaders, with Ahmed Urabi at their head.

"The first book that ever gave me ideas about political matters," recalled Urabi, "was an Arabic translation of the *Life of Bonaparte*.' A lanky, ponderous *fellahin* from the Delta, Urabi was deliberate in gesture and heavy in limb. Although he looked more like a farmer than a soldier, his life read like a précis of the reforms and failings of Ismail's Egypt. The son of a country sheikh superannuated by the new bureaucracy, Urabi passed through Ismail's village schools and, via two years' religious education at al-Azhar in Cairo, into the army at fourteen. Rising rapidly to the glass ceiling as a colonel in the transport corps, the ambitious Urabi came home from the "disastrous" Abyssinian campaign to find the starving Delta "in a fearful state of oppression." Returning to al-Azhar, he fell in with Afghani's circle, taking instruction from Afghani's deputy Mohammed Abdu and joining Yacub Sanna's Society of the Lovers of Knowledge. "After this, I thought much about politics."[30]

Ismail's despotic interpretation of his French inheritance had recreated the circumstances that had produced the French Revolution. A repressive Ancien Régime of aristocrats allied with tame clerics and corrupt landowners to tyrannize a starving peasantry. Urban intellectuals inspired by the ideals of the Enlightenment agitated for accountable, representative government. The only element missing was a military strongman. In Urabi, the café rebels thought they had found their plaster Napoleon. But when the officers entered politics, they did not ally with the radical opposition. They aligned with Ismail. With discontent simmering at every level of Egypt's fractured society, and no other option available, the khedive had turned to the refuge of the scoundrel, and now posed as a patriot.

"I admire the khedive exceedingly," Gordon had written. "He is the perfect type of his people, thoroughly consistent to all their principles—a splendid leopard! Look at the numberless cages out of which he has broken his way, when it seemed quite impossible for him to do so."[31]

By excluding Ismail from meetings of his own ministers, the commissioners had turned him into a guest of his own government. To shake off the Europeans in his ministries and regain control over Egypt, Ismail tried to turn Egyptian nationalism to his advantage. As Afghani, Abdu, and the most radical journalists had chosen to back Ismail's uncle Halim, the khedive was spared the indignity of having to indulge their demands. Instead he maneuvered his traditional allies and instruments—the Turkish aristocracy and the army—back into his camp. He dusted off the Chamber of Notables. He promised a ministry to Sharif Pasha, head of the moderate aristocrats, and privately promised Urabi and his colonels the cancellation of cutbacks in their ranks and the payment of full salaries. Then he organized a riot.

Over three days in February 1879, hundreds of sacked, hungry officers converged on Cairo to demand their overdue salaries. The Nubar Pasha government had no money: The Rothschilds' £8.5 million had already been paid out to the Europeans. On February 18, four hundred officers staged an apparently spontaneous demonstration before the Finance Ministry, waving sabers and revolvers and demanding their salaries. Into this brew converged the carriages of Nubar Pasha and Rivers Wilson, on their way to a meeting at the ministry. When Wilson saw armed officers grabbing the reins of Nubar's carriage, he jumped down from his own carriage and ran to help, hitting out at the rioters with his cane. The officers kicked and punched him back, pulling his beard. They knocked Nubar to the ground, cravat torn and fez awry. Then they dragged the rulers of Egypt upstairs into Wilson's office, crying, "Death to the dogs of Christians!"[32]

While the officers forced Nubar and Wilson to hear that their children were starving, the British consul raced to the Abdin Palace to warn Ismail that the revolution had begun. The khedive seemed unperturbed, and although Abdin was only five minutes' drive from the Finance Ministry, two hours passed before Ismail went to his ministers' assistance. Confident of the officers' allegiance, Ismail rode alone to the ministry. When he stepped down from his carriage and strode into the ministry, the officers cheered him. He then appeared on a second-floor balcony and told them in Turkish, "If you are my officers, you are bound by your oaths to obey me. If you refuse, I will have you swept away."[33]

The officers duly dispersed. Nubar Pasha resigned. Rivers Wilson and de Blignières fell out over whose policies had caused the riot. The British consul, taken in by Ismail's political theater, reported to London, "The Khedive alone is able to maintain order."[34]

Then Ismail sacked the commissioners.

REPLAYING THE SCENE with which he had opened his reign, Ismail summoned the foreign consuls to his palace. Announcing the total reformation of the state, he produced three letters. One was from the Chamber of Notables; they expressed their gratitude at being invited to convene for the first time in three years by denouncing Anglo-French control of their finances. The second letter offered an alternative: Signed by many of the notables and several radical clerics, it demanded constitutional government. The third letter proposed a financial plan. It overestimated Egypt's income, reduced its debt obligations, and omitted any mention of a limit on Ismail's personal spending.

Ismail addressed the consuls with a straight face. "My family has given up a large part of its landed estates in order to help the State. We are prepared to make still greater sacrifices. The jewels of the ladies of the Khedivial family are at the disposal of the creditors of Egypt. Every acre that we own and every diamond that we possess is at the beck and call of the bondholders. We refuse to admit that we are bankrupt."[35]

Ismail had launched a coup against himself. The portly leopard sprang so lightly from his cage that the Europeans were thrown. Of all the costumes in Ismail's wardrobe, that of constitutionalist seemed the least fitting. But he had acted within his constitutional rights, if not within financial possibility. And precedent demonstrated that so long as he honored Egypt's debts, he could manipulate the rivalries of the Great Powers and avoid serious common action.

What Ismail underestimated was the possibility of unilateral action by a single creditor. To the Disraeli government, the internal economy and politics of Egypt could no longer be the sole interest of cotton traders and loan sharks. They were integral to the global security concept that, based on British India, defined the stability of the Ottoman Empire and the Suez Canal as key British interests. Now Britain held Ismail to account. A brief look at Egypt's balance sheet showed that without further loans or a return to imposed austerity, Ismail would soon default again. It was obvious that his sacking of the foreign ministers and his conversion to constitutionalism were a smokescreen for an escape from foreign debt. Britain would not permit it.

"This is a grave and apparently intentional breach of international courtesy to friendly powers," Lord Salisbury warned Ismail from the Foreign Office. If Ismail ignored his debts and excluded Britain and France from direct control of the Egyptian economy, the two powers would use "an entire liberty of appreciation and action" to force Egypt into line.[36]

At the same time, Rivers Wilson cut off Ismail's last line of credit. Hurrying to Berlin, he denounced Ismail to the Rothschilds. When the Rothschilds passed on their alarm to the German financier Bleichroeder, Otto von Bismarck weighed in on behalf of Germany's investors. Wilson had accidentally internationalized the crisis. Backed by Bismarck, Sultan Abdul Hamid II offered Ismail's uncle Halim as an alternative khedive. The British and French refused to invite Turkey and Germany into Egypt, and they rejected Halim. Instead, they settled on Ismail's shallow, timid son Tawfik. Lord Salisbury advised Ismail "officially to abdicate and leave Egypt."[37]

One by one the consuls trooped through the pink reception room. The representatives of Britain, France, Germany, Austria-Hungary, Italy, and the United States all begged Ismail to avert a public humiliation that might permanently compromise Egypt's independence. The British and French consuls offered Ismail a large payoff and assured him that his debts would pass to Tawfik along with the khediviate.

Ismail thought this was just another financial crisis. As usual, he dispatched a bribe to Constantinople and waited for it to take effect. In the meantime, he kept his new supporters happy by announcing the expansion of the army to 150,000 men and the launch of a megalomaniacal farming project that would flood the countryside around Alexandria. He believed that his debts, £93 million and rising, made him indispensable to his creditors. But he had misunderstood the corporate nature of the modern state. Ismail had signed for the loans, but they had been issued on the security of Egypt. Like shareholders overthrowing their chairman for the good of the share price, the British and French simply wanted to fire him. To preserve legal decorum, they forced his sleeping partner to do the job. On June 26,

1879, Ismail, the great modernizer and *Grand Dilapidateur,* received a telegram from Constantinople. Its contents were obvious from the address: "Ismail Pasha, ex-Khedive of Egypt."

"It has been proved that your maintenance at your post can result only in multiplying and in aggravating present difficulties. His Imperial Majesty the Sultan has therefore decided, in conformity with a decision of his Council of Ministers, to appoint Mehmet Tawfik Pasha [the] Khedive of Egypt."[38]

At the same time, Tawfik opened an envelope to find he had been promoted. Ismail took the news with customary elegance. Containing his distress, he summoned his treacherous son and recognized him as the new khedive. At six-thirty that evening, a thunderclap of cannon fire from the Cairo Citadel called the local diplomatic corps to Tawfik's investiture.

Ismail did not attend. In his private quarters at Abdin Palace, he packed for exile. Having lately offered "the jewels of the ladies of the Khedivial family" to the cause of liberty, he now took back all the jewels he had bestowed on his harem, stripping the stones from their mountings to make them more portable. He rolled up the Aubusson carpets, boxed twenty-two dinner services of cutlery, lifted the silver sconces off the walls, selected his favorite mistresses. As the rejected members of his harem smashed the mirrors and furniture of their gilded cage, the khedive's retainers lugged all his spoils to Cairo station. It took four days to load up the train. There was so much loot and luggage that a second train had to be found for Ismail and his retinue.

Ismail left the station that he had commissioned on tracks that he had laid, crossing the Delta irrigation channels that he had dug on bridges that he had built. On the waterfront at Alexandria, he shook hands and exchanged pleasantries as if he was only off for another European jaunt, fundraising in London, shopping in Paris, gaming at Cannes. Two million pounds in cash from the British and French may have helped. Ten years earlier, the *Mahroussah* had followed the *Eagle*'s ample stern into the Suez Canal. Now Ismail's yacht edged past the sea wall and into the Mediterranean to another, more muted round of salutes. He sailed for Naples, never to return.

4

The Redeemer
1881–82

Mohammed Ahmed, the Mahdi.

Permission has been given to us to revive religion among Muslims. Innovations have spread through the land and are being followed by both Muslim clerics and people. Nothing is left of Islam but its name; nothing of the Koran but its Arabic script.

—Mohammed Ahmed, October 1880

THERE HAD ALWAYS BEEN something different about Mohammed Ahmed. He had trained with his three brothers in their father's boatbuilding business, but his heart was in the other family tradition. They were among the *Ashraf,* those who claimed descent from the House of the Prophet. From the boatyard on an island in the Nile just beyond Dongola, the boy traced back his ancestry through thirty generations to Imam Ali, the Prophet Mohammed's cousin and son-in-law. Little

Mohammed's family tombs marched into the desert beyond Dongola, a lineage of sheikhs and scholars, adepts of the Sufi cults that had carried Islam up the Nile Valley. Legend blots out his childhood. Baby Mohammed spoke at two weeks of age. A virgin who carried him home lactated spontaneously. Once, when he trod on a thorn, a bird swept down and plucked it out.[1]

Signs of corruption surrounded him. Egyptian tax collectors depopulated the countryside. Irrigation channels dried up and wells collapsed. Even the palm trees sagged. The sugarloaf dome of Dongola's mosque glittered whitely over a waste of sand, but the regional center of northern Sudan had become an Egyptian military station. The governor, Hafiz Ibrahim Effendi, was a hunchbacked Greek-speaking Turk. Waited on by slaves bearing sherbet, coffee, and pipes, Ibrahim Effendi ruled from his divan. He enriched himself with fraud, torture, and grain speculation. As a modernizer, he replaced traditional methods of punishment—chopping off the hands and ears of criminals—with the bastinado. His subjects lived in a ramshackle smear of mud-brick hovels. Dongola was the penultimate stop on the Forty Days' Road, the last halt before Wadi Halfa and the Egyptian border. Berber Arabs like Mohammed Ahmed scraped a living from the dry earth and passing slave caravans. North of the Egyptian camp, the crumbling ruin of a medieval Christian city mocked the broken present.[2]

While the people suffered, Mohammed Ahmed's father profited from the occupation. As the Turkiyya pushed south for slaves and ivory, demand rose for boats and boatbuilders. When Mohammed was five, his father secured a contract from the Khartoum government. Although Mohammed's mother was heavily pregnant, the family packed its possessions and tools. They sailed for Kariri, just north of Khartoum, a riverside village surrounded by acacia hardwood. Mohammed's father died on the way. His brothers took over the business. His mother named her new baby for her dead husband.

Mohammed Ahmed withdrew into grief. He prayed constantly. It consoled him, like the single cloud said to have hovered over his head, protecting him from the pitiless sun. His brothers noticed his sharp mind and spiritual habits. Scholarship was a greater honor than carpentry. They used some of the Turkiyya's money to pay for his lessons and board at a Khartoum madrassa. Mohammed rose before dawn, recited from memory the previous day's koranic portion, then memorized the next portion. His lessons ran all day. The children paused only to pray, kneeling five times daily by their slates. If they made an error, they were beaten. At night they begged food in the alleys of Khartoum or scavenged firewood from the fields and citrus groves. At eleven, Mohammed was a *hafiz,* one who could recite the entire

Koran from memory. By seventeen he was fluent in Islam: theology, koranic exegesis, sharia law, and the *hadith*, the reported sayings of the Prophet.[3]

The young scholar left the madrassa for a Khartoum that was a fount of religious corruption, public drunkenness, and sexual license. The only two buildings in the Sudan with glass windows were the governor's palace and his harem. The slave and ivory trades attracted criminals, Christian missionaries, and a scuffling underclass of hungry Berbers. Official Islam collaborated with the Turks, endorsing the governor's every whim. Even the Sufi brotherhoods were on the Turks' payroll. Just as the Turks had taken over the slave trade, they had overrun Sudanese Islam. They profaned it and turned it into a commodity.

Mohammed Ahmed turned from this sleaze. He left his brothers to their collaborators' contracts with the government. He looked back to the local tradition displaced by the Turkiyya: the mystical Sufi sects. Developed in the thirteenth century by minority Shia as a refuge from the legalism and politicking of the Sunni majority, the cults had been integral to the spread of popular Islam in Africa and India. Sudanese Islam, though Sunni, bore a Sufi influence: a belief steered by saintly holy men, ascetic miracle workers, and a mystical belief in direct intervention from Allah. Much of this cultish mysticism derived from contacts with other religions. If the preachers who had carried their faith up the Nile in the fifteenth century resembled the mendicant friars of medieval Christianity, their emphasis on mysticism, poverty, and seclusion bore a further monkish trace. The Sufi brotherhoods were organized like monastic orders. The novice apprenticed himself to a sheikh; the sheikh derived his authority from his own teacher, and so on back to the founder of the sect. Blending conventional Islam with the precepts of its saintly founder, each sect collected its prayers and quotations in a *ratib*, a unique anthology.

Sailing into the political vacuum beyond Khartoum, Mohammed Ahmed went south. One hundred miles down the Nile lay the base of the Sammaniya order, a sect ascetic by even the bare standards of Sudanese life. Swearing loyalty to its sheikh, Mohammed Nur al-Daim, he donned the jibba, the Sufi's rough garment of patched wool, and renounced the world. For seven years he starved himself, proving his humility through grinding grain and gathering firewood. In imitation of the Prophet, he stood alone through the night reciting the Koran. He learned the Sammaniya *dikr*, the rhythmic combination of koranic quotation and the ninety-nine names of Allah. Like the Whirling Dervishes who made Sufism famous throughout the world, he worked himself into an ecstatic trance through breath control, physical movement, and repetition of the *dikr*. Sheikh al-Daim was impressed. "How he fasted! How he prayed! How he recited the word of Allah, tears running down his face! How he prayed long into the night, through to mid-morning!"[4]

Throughout the Islamic world, Muslims reacted to the intrusion of Western ideas and technology with a revivalist call for purification and restoration. In the Sudan, three ancient trade routes crossed, and each carried a revivalist message that appealed to a society destabilized by modernity. Wahhabi puritanism floated across from Jeddah to the Red Sea ports. The Senussi ideal of retreat into the desert crossed the northern Sahara from Libya. Sokoto militancy, inspired by a sharia state in West Africa, crossed the arid belt below the Sahara. In the Sudan, the mixing of these currents gave rise to a revolutionary maelstrom. Aided by Egypt's imperial infrastructure, its ripples spread across huge distances, and across tribal lines. Soon, Mohammed Ahmed refused to eat the communal Sammaniya meal if it had been paid for by the khedive's subsidy.

At twenty-eight he graduated from Sheikh al-Daim's order, with a license to teach his own adepts. He could do little else. With no experience of work or women, he was so zealous that he could not earn a living. He failed as a wheat trader, because he did not want to profit from others' hunger. He failed as a charcoal vendor, after discovering that his customers used it to brew sorghum beer. He rejected the government salaries that tempted other brilliant but less scrupulous Sufis. He rejected study at al-Azhar University, where Sudanese scholars had their own quarters, because al-Azhar compromised with the Egyptian government. He felt driven to the radical fringe. In 1869, the year of Ismail's parades and parties at the Suez Canal, Mohammed Ahmed again moved against the current. Like the Prophet, who had taken to a cave near Mecca, Mohammed Ahmed took to a cave in the riverbank of an island south of Khartoum, fasting, praying, and waiting for revelation.

"This is the hour of need for which you have been created." The spot he had chosen for his reflections was both the Sammaniya heartland and the epicenter of the chaos caused by Egypt's repression of the slave trade. Aba Island lay one hundred miles south of Khartoum, on the border between Kordofan and Sennar, two provinces whose main business was slaving. The Turkiyya's troops imposed two equally unpopular policies, stealing the profits of the trade, or repressing it violently. By the late 1870s, the Anglo-Egyptian Convention and Gordon's war on the slavers pointed to a likely future. The government broke Islamic law, intercepting slaver boats on the

Nile, executing leading slavers, and freeing legally held slaves. Traditional society was breaking down before Mohammed Ahmed's eyes.[5]

Aba Island was heavily wooded, and well sited for the slave trade. His brothers moved their boatyard down to join him, and other exiles from Dongola followed. A settlement grew up on the island, funded by the boatyard but built around the charismatic holy man in his cave. Mohammed Ahmed became famous for his amulets, his piety, and his spiritual presence. The local people called him The Renouncer. He offered his visitors sweet milk, beatific smiles, and tears for the fallen world. In 1878, he moved into politics. His experience of Sufi factionalism had trained him for the fragmented tribal politics of the Sudan. Mohammed Ahmed was a natural politician: artful in his choice of alliances, and always preferring to negotiate with his rivals rather than fall into feuds. He married strategically. At Aba Island, he took two wives, one from the local Dinka tribes, another from the Dongolawi exiles in his camp. Secure at Aba, he turned to his power base, the Sammaniya brotherhoods, and attempted to overthrow his mentor, Sheikh Nur al-Daim.

Attending a party to celebrate the circumcision of the sheikh's son, Mohammed Ahmed denounced the music, the dancing, the gorging on food and drink. His tactic misfired. The sheikh excommunicated him, cutting him off from his potential power base in the sect. Mohammed Ahmed donned a slave's yoke, sprinkled his head with ashes and wrote apologetic poems. But Nur al-Daim, threatened by his protégé's rising fame, withheld forgiveness.

"Get away, you wretched Dongolawi, who fears not Allah and opposes his master and teacher," the sheikh shouted at his kneeling pupil. "You show the truth of the saying, *The Dongolawi is the devil in the skin of a man.* By your words you try to spread dissension among the people."[6]

Mohammed Ahmed removed his yoke and stopped writing poems. He transferred his allegiance to Nur al-Daim's greatest rival, Sheikh Qureishi, leader of the Sammaniyas of the Blue Nile. He married the daughter of the eighty-six-year-old sheikh, and when the old man died in the summer of 1878, he inherited his authority. His eminence among the Sammaniya became the foundation of a tribal coalition.

Mohammed Ahmed emerged from his cave and began to campaign for adherents. Again he eschewed tradition. Instead of making the *haj* to Mecca, he conducted a *haj* among his own people, a pilgrimage to resentful tribes and neglected principles. He used his brothers' boats to jump the vast distances of the Sudan, south to Sennar, north as far as Dongola, west to

Kordofan and the Gazelle River, often sailing in the company of smuggled slaves. Like an ordinary traveler, he slept in the homes and mosques of Sammaniya members. He preached piety, resistance, and redemption. He reached out to the disenfranchised, the desperate, and the mystical. He crafted alliances with tribal leaders, Sufi cults, and slavers.

Kordofan seemed the most susceptible area for evangelism. Gordon's campaign against the slavers of the southwest threatened the future of two rival Muslim groups: the itinerant Jaalayin traders and the nomadic Baggara Arabs. In early 1880, while the Sudan swung leaderless after Gordon's resignation, Mohammed Ahmed headed for its capital, El Obeid, the key station between the source of slaves on the Gazelle River and the start of the Forty Days' Road at El Fasher.

"After midnight we heard recitation of a new *dikr* from the outskirts of town," recorded his convert Yusuf Mikhail. "In the middle of the night, he would start with his disciples and circle around the town until dawn, when it would be time for morning prayers." Mohammed Ahmed was intensely charismatic. When he prayed, he would go into a trance, collapse unconscious, or burst into a fierce sermon of redemption that stopped the faithful in the midst of their devotions. The people flocked to him, swearing allegiance to Allah, the Prophet, and Mohammed Ahmed, the renunciation of sin and material pleasure, the pursuit of eternal life through faith and jihad. "He was, so to speak, watering parched soil," Yusuf Mikhail remembered of these early, glorious days. By 1880, Mohammed Ahmed commanded twenty thousand followers, more numerous and more committed than the entire Egyptian army in the Sudan.[7]

Aba Island became the center of a new cult. The third and smallest Sammaniya faction joined him; taking his fourth wife, Mohammed Ahmed again married the daughter of its leader. Delegations of Baggara Arabs came from Kordofan to swear loyalty and place their weapons at his disposal. Aided by the Egyptian postal service, a torrent of letters flooded out from Aba Island, spreading the word and steering his coalition. When government steamers stopped at Aba Island to reload with wood, the captain, crew, and passengers all knelt on the deck and prayed toward his cave. The fortunate disembarked for a cup of sweet milk and a blessing from the famous cave-dwelling sheikh. By late 1880, he was ready. The fasts, prayer vigils, meditations, and mortifications coalesced to mobilize a massive popular discontent. Sufi-style, the initiates were ready for induction into the great secret.

"Lights, good omens, prophetic secrets and instructions, divine revelations, all have appeared to me repeatedly," he told his disciples. "I wrote to you earlier, before I received the supreme command, which has now happened. Happy are those who responded quickly and joined us with their families, sons and possessions. Those who ignore this command are outcasts, whom Allah and his Prophet will judge."

"This affair is secret, a secret which is not meant to be revealed. It must be kept secret, for your eyes only, until Allah himself reveals it."[8]

KHEDIVE ISMAIL had never liked his eldest son. Tawfik was a pampered, puppy-faced boy with a wispy mustache. An accident of Ismail's scramble through the harem, he spoke no European languages and received little formal education. When they met at one of Ismail's formal parties, they stood next to each other embarrassed and silent. It appeared that Ismail intended to rule forever.

Tawfik was a devout Muslim, a frugal administrator, and a uxurious husband. Inheriting the catastrophe that was modern Egypt, he did nothing to improve the country. Like his attributes, his failings derived from his fear of change. Isolated, inexperienced, and unsure that when he fell asleep, he would still be khedive when he awoke, he foundered. On the way up, Tawfik had promised everything to everybody. The native army colonels expected promotion. Sharif Pasha and the reformist nobility expected a constitution. Afghani and the rebels of Young Egypt expected even more. Tawfik delivered nothing. The "Dual Control" of Britain and France had installed him against the wishes of Sultan Abdul Hamid II, and he stayed in the shadow of his European patrons.

The "Dual Control" wanted stability and debt repayment. To satisfy them, Tawfik ignored the Chamber of Notables, rejected the writing of a constitution, and fell back on the narrow but powerful support of the old Turkish aristocracy. To deal with the people, he clung to the paternal despotism of Ismail's old adviser Mustapha Riaz Pasha, who clamped down on any opposition, and any criticism of the Europeans. Combing back issues of newspapers and journals for incriminating statements, Riaz Pasha closed down Young Egypt and imprisoned editors who objected. Most of Afghani's circle went into exile. A foreign passport was no protection: when the French journalist Jules Barbier attacked the closure of Young Egypt in *Reform*, Riaz closed him down, too. The Freemasons avoided the purge by assuring Tawfik that their speculations did not include politics. To demonstrate their loyalty, they ejected Afghani from the Star of the East lodge.

Afghani had overplayed his hand. One night in Cairo's Hassan mosque, he had harangued a huge crowd of four thousand, explaining that Tawfik was a pawn of foreign interests, that British annexation of Egypt was only a matter of time, and that the only solution was "revolution to save the independence of Egypt." In *Egypt,* he had announced his conversion to republican democracy. He and his sidekick Mohammed Abdu moved to the top of Riaz Pasha's list. In late August 1879, the secret police raided Afghani's house. The director of publications—the government's chief censor—announced the discovery of documents proving that Afghani had set up a secret society of "young thugs" with the aim of causing "the ruin of religion and rule." At the same time, Afghani's erstwhile allies in the Masonic lodges alleged that he had publicly denied the existence of a higher being. The police hustled the Sage of the East to Suez, and put him on a boat to Jeddah.[9]

Separating mentor and protégé, Riaz Pasha sentenced Mohammed Abdu to internal exile at the village of his birth. Abdu attempted to escape to Alexandria, but was detected. For a year, the promising scholar scuttled around the Delta as a vagabond, dodging the secret police. When Riaz Pasha permitted Abdu to return to Cairo, he completed the neutralization of Afghani's dangerous legacy. Riaz appointed Abdu the editor of the government *Gazette,* and Abdu employed the remnant of his journalist friends. All had been chastened by Riaz's crackdown. The revolution, it seemed, had been canceled.

With the repression of the intellectuals, opposition devolved to two groups: mildly reformist Turkish aristocrats led by Sharif Pasha, and the native army colonels. The aristocrats had served in Ismail's nationalist government, but now Riaz Pasha sidelined them in favor of tight collaboration with the British and French. In November 1879, they responded with a reform program: the exclusion of Europeans from the government, the nationalization of Ismail's private lands—at the time mortgaged to the European banks—and the reduction of Egypt's debt repayment schedule. To avoid Riaz Pasha's wrath, they retreated to Helwan, a rundown spa village near Cairo. Though they claimed to speak in the name of *al-Hizb al-Watani,* the National Party, their manifesto was in French, not Arabic; one elite group spoke to another. Their hideout gave them a name more appropriate to their narrow interests, the "Helwan Society." Riaz Pasha barely bothered with them. He had already silenced the journalists, expelled Afghani, and emasculated Abdu. His police state would not be ruffled by a few bored aristocrats. He miscalculated. Through the deputy minister for war, Mahmoud Sami al-Barudi, the Helwan Society made contact with the native army officers.

Ahmed Urabi and his friends did not have the luxury of biding their time at a spa. The army, their only hope of preferment in a society run on ethnic discrimination, was disappearing before their eyes. In 1875, at the height of Ismail's Abyssinian ambition, the army had numbered 90,000. By Tawfik's accession, it had halved to 45,000. Now Riaz Pasha's economy drives shredded it to 18,000. To sack almost an entire army was to create a militia in waiting. Worse, Tawfik's new war minister, Osman Rifki Pasha, persecuted the remaining native soldiers. Regarding the *fellahin* as cannon fodder, he passed a law limiting military service to four years, effectively denying them the possibility of promotion. He fired most of the Egyptian officers and restored the officer corps to the Turkish elite. He hired out *fellahin* soldiers as forced laborers on Tawfik's estates. Even his installation at the War Ministry reeked of corruption and favoritism. Rifki Pasha had commanded Ismail's Abyssinian fiasco. William Dye, an American mercenary who had served under him, thought that Rifki Pasha's incompetence merited not promotion, but a firing squad.[10]

Urabi had not been promoted in nineteen years. He and the other native colonels had petitioned Tawfik, protesting against discrimination and the use of their men as forced laborers. Their complaints went unanswered. Salaries and pensions went unpaid, and families unfed. At a barracks banquet in early 1881, he heard that Osman Rifki Pasha intended to purge the Egyptian colonels. With Ali Fehmi, colonel of the palace guard, and Abd el-Al, colonel of the Sudanese regiment, Urabi drew up a second petition. They took it to Riaz Pasha.

"Your petition is a hanging matter," said Riaz. "What is it you want, to change the ministry? And what would you put in its place?"[11]

Tawfik and his ministers took the petition as a direct challenge to Turkish authority. On February 1, 1881, Osman Rifki Pasha summoned the colonels to the War Ministry. Rifki Pasha claimed that he wanted their assistance in planning the parades for the upcoming wedding of Tawfik's daughter.

"We were on our guard," wrote Urabi, "and made the preparations necessary for our rescue."[12]

Instead of planning Princess Jamila's wedding party, Osman Rifki had prepared a court-martial. As the three colonels entered the ministry, Circassian officers disarmed them, abused them, and marched them into a temporary courtroom. Rifki's generals sacked all three for sedition. Just as these commands were issued, the court's deliberations were interrupted by the sound of marching. Junior Egyptian officers loyal to Urabi and the colonels had led their troops into the streets. From his balcony, Tawfik watched in disbelief as a battalion appeared on the parade ground outside Abdin Palace. Two more battalions surrounded the War Ministry. The soldiers stormed the ministry and freed the colonels. Osman Rifki Pasha climbed out of a window and ran away. Drums beating, the troops carried their colonels back to their barracks in triumph.

Modern Egypt had been built on the army. Tawfik's British and French handlers advised that if he could not fight the native colonels, he must compromise. Promising to reform the army, he reinstated the colonels and sacked Osman Rifki Pasha. The Helwan Society's Mahmoud Sami al-Barudi became the new war minister. Without firing a shot, the reformers had taken over the army and the War Ministry.

The riot at the court-martial turned Urabi from obscure officer to nationalist icon. While Sharif Pasha and the Turkish aristocrats of Helwan saw him as a blunt instrument with which to menace Tawfik, the villagers of the Delta looked to him as their savior. Alone among the oppressed Egyptians, Urabi had resisted the tax-hungry Turks and won. They called him *El Wahid:* The Only One.

FOR A WEEK Mohammed Ahmed had refused all food and drink. His disciples waited as he emerged from his cave in the riverbank.

"I am empty," he told his disciples. "I am powerless. But I have received an order from Allah through his Prophet. I am *al-Mahdi al-Muntazar.*"[13]

Al-Mahdi al-Muntazar: The Expected Guide. The Prophet had not mentioned a messiah in the Koran: His was the final revelation. But the messianic idea was central to Judaism and Christianity, and it soon appeared in Islam, too. In religious societies where religion doubled as politics, messianism was the politics of despair. The Abrahamic faiths all agreed that God acted through history. Religious authority gave divine sanction to the social divisions and customs of a society. When that society collapsed, the disintegration of the familiar world became a harbinger of the end of history itself: A local catastrophe indicated a total apocalypse. Judaism, Christianity, and Islam had all produced would-be messiahs. They rose at times of crisis, when established custom and authority collapsed, unable to respond creatively to rival values and armies. Their careers tended to be brief and fiery, ending not in redemption, but in miniature apocalypse.

Islamic messiahs fared no better than their Christian and Jewish counterparts. One after the other, they sprang to failure whenever a dynasty wavered, a society crumbled, or a hostile horde invaded. An elaborate Mahdist literature grew up in the *hadith,* the collected sayings attributed to the Prophet. The Mahdi would be a descendant of the Prophet. He would have the same name as the Prophet, and his father would be called Abdullah, like the Prophet's. He would be tall, balding, and have a brown, Arab complexion, an aquiline nose, and a gap between his front teeth. He would appear at the end of a century when Islam had fallen into corruption and weakness. He would restore Islam just as the Prophet had spread it, by military conquest of the enemies of Allah. He would fill the earth with justice and equity where it had been overrun with oppression and tyranny, and would reduce the rate of taxation to the 2.5 percent recommended by the Prophet. He did not have much time in which to conquer the world, as he would rule for only seven years.[14]

The Christian year 1881 was the Islamic year 1298. The thirteenth Islamic century was drawing to a close, and with disaster on every front. From Africa to India, Muslim societies failed to adapt to modern technology and communications, and seemed paralyzed before modern banking and science. Intellectuals like Afghani investigated the sources of the infidels' strength, but alliances of religious and monarchic conservatives ensured that their conclusions remained marginal. More powerful was the call to revival, its urge for strong leadership so amenable to the millenarians' dream of a redeemer and a war of redemption. The Wahhabis of Arabia eschewed the Mahdist idea as an impure deviation. But other revivalists, often primed by Sufi influence, were ripe for it. In Libya, the followers of Mohammed al-Senussi speculated that he was the Mahdi, and though al-Senussi denied that he was, he did not punish them for their heresy. In west Africa, the jihadi Usman dan Fodio claimed that personal visions of the Prophet had commanded him to set up a sharia state.

In Egypt and the Sudan, the influence of traders from Libya and pilgrims from West Africa fueled popular hopes. Mohammed Ahmed was not the first of the khedive's subjects to declare himself the Mahdi. In 1865, one Ahmed the Good had challenged Khedive Ismail's hold on the Upper Nile. Ahmed called for the overthrow of the Turks and their allies from al-Azhar, and the redistribution of property. When his followers drove off Ismail's tax collectors with stones, the troops went in. They destroyed whole villages, shooting every man, woman, child, and animal, burning every building. Like the Romans in Judea, they sowed the land with salt to render it barren.

Mohammed Ahmed had asked both his mentor Sheikh Nur al-Daim and the state-funded Khartoum sheikhs if one of them might be the Mahdi.

None of them had taken up his leading question. Gradually, he realized that it must be *his* destiny to lead the redemption of the Islamic world. The first hint was visible to all: a series of comets in the night sky, heralds of the new Islamic century. The second had come when he was up a ladder, building the dome of Sheikh Qureishi's tomb, burying his father-in-law as he praised him.

A tall, thin Arab had appeared beneath the workers. Abdullahi al-Taishi was a Baggara from Darfur. His family lost their home to Zubair Pasha and Ismail's troops. Although his father had taught religion, Abdullahi could barely recite a few Koranic phrases. His dying father had exhorted him to find a teacher, and to escape the impure Sudan by emigrating to Mecca. Abdullahi never acquired much religious expertise, but he had the tactical skills of a Baggara. The disintegration of Egyptian control had left the Sudan open to the strongest party. So he searched for the most powerful Sudanese he could find: Zubair Pasha, the only man capable of driving out the Turks. Abdullahi sought out the archslaver and told Zubair that he had dreamed that Zubair was the Mahdi. Zubair told him that he was not. So Abdullahi scoured the Sudan in search of a mentor. As he traveled east with his donkey, his waterskin, and his bag of corn, he heard about the Renouncer of Aba Island and tracked him to Sheikh Qureishi's tomb. For several hours he waited at the foot of the scaffold, too timid to speak.

"At length I plucked up courage, and in a few words told him my story. I begged him, for the sake of Allah and his Prophet, to allow me to become one of his disciples." Mohammed Ahmed put out his hand for Abdullahi to kiss. "I swore entire submission to him as long as I lived."[15]

Abdullahi did more than carry bricks up a ladder. The Baggara were the fiercest and most independent of Sudan's tribes. They were paramount in Kordofan, the site of Mohammed Ahmed's political campaign. Any revolt against the Turks must either strike a deal with the Baggara or contend with them. Abdullahi would become Mohammed Ahmed's general, the Baggara the key troops in his tribal coalition.

In March 1881, not long after Abdullahi's appearance at the foot of his ladder, Mohammed Ahmed initiated his inner circle into his great secret. The Prophet had revealed himself to Mohammed Ahmed. This occurred within a month of the riot at Urabi's court-martial. Simultaneously, Riaz Pasha informed the Khartoum government that to save money, it would be incorporated into the Cairo government. There could not have been a better moment for divine intervention. "I was awake and in good health. I was not asleep or in a trance, nor under the influence of intoxication or madness," Mohammed Ahmed testified. "No, I was in possession of all my faculties of reason—prepared to command what He commands and prohibit what He prohibits."[16]

Mohammed Ahmed returned to Kordofan and activated his network. On June 29, 1881, he dropped the "Ahmed" that did not conform to prophecy. Calling himself Mohammed al-Mahdi, he declared publicly that he was Allah's messenger, come to redeem the Sudan and the world for Islam. Then he retreated to Aba Island, gathering his followers and waiting for the Turkish response.

Gordon's heir in the white palace at Khartoum was Mohammed Rauf Pasha. The son of a Nubian father and Abyssinian mother, Rauf had risen from Egypt's menial underclass to become Sudan's first Egyptian, Arabic-speaking governor; as in the British Empire, the less pleasant corners of the Egyptian empire abounded with opportunity. While Urabi and his friends protested discrimination in Egypt, Rauf spent his entire career in a region viewed by most officers as a punishment posting. As a young officer, he had been Samuel Baker's chief of staff in Equatoria. He had served Gordon twice, and been sacked twice for corruption. As governor, his job was to mollify subjects driven to the edge of revolt by Gordon, and to implement Riaz Pasha's cutbacks by reducing the Sudanese garrisons. He performed both duties with his usual mediocrity. Beyond following orders, he had little power. Riaz Pasha had centralized the imperial government and now ran the Sudan by remote control from Cairo. Mohammed Rauf Pasha did what he was told.

When Rauf Pasha heard that the Expected Redeemer had manifested in his jurisdiction, he sent him a friendly letter, assuming that this holy fool could be paid off with a government stipend. The Mahdi went to the local telegraph station and fired back a message.

"I must reveal to you that my call to re-establish the way of the Prophet, and to reclaim our religion from its present evil ways, is mandated directly by the Prophet Mohammed. I declare that I am the Expected Mahdi, and that my arrival was heralded by heavenly signs. He who follows me will be victorious. He who refuses will be punished by Allah in this world and the next. The sermons preached to the faithful have been absolutely clear: He who does not believe in me will be purified by the sword."[17]

This was heresy and treason. Worse, it was beyond bribery. Rauf Pasha decided to summon the fakir to Khartoum for examination by the government's theologians. He sent an old friend from his schooldays to fetch him: Abu Suud, the one-eyed slaver who had subverted both Baker and Gordon in Equatoria and now combined slave-trading with a post in the Khartoum government. If the troublesome sheikh had a worldly agenda, Abu Suud could strike a bargain with him.

Sitting on a rush mat, the Mahdi and his inner circle received Abu Suud in the hut that was their madrassa. Abu Suud explained that the Mahdi must go to Khartoum and acknowledge that the chain of temporal authority led from Mohammed Rauf Pasha to Khedive Tawfik, Sultan Abdul Hamid II, and Allah.

"You misunderstand," the Mahdi replied. "Who can be set above the Mahdi, personally selected by the Prophet? It is Rauf who is duty bound to obey me."

Abu Suud grew angry. "How can you hope to fight the government?"

The Mahdi waved his hand. "If need be, I will fight the government only with those present here." The disciples stirred, offering their lives for Allah, his Prophet, and the Mahdi. It was time for Abu Suud to leave.

Three days later, Abu Suud returned by steamer with two hundred Egyptian soldiers, a cannon, and theological heavy artillery in the shape of Sheikh Ahmad al-Azhari, a government jurist. Arriving at dusk, they tied up a quarter of a mile from the Mahdi's village and stepped into the shallows. As night fell, they divided into two companies. The officers had been promised promotion if they caught the false prophet. As they hurried forward in the dark, they lost contact with each other. The Mahdi's men waited, hidden behind rocks and bushes. A heavy rain began to fall.

The Egyptian troops heard a war cry from the darkness. Both columns fired a ragged volley toward the village. As they fumbled to reload, the Mahdists surged out of the night, ghostlike in their white jibbas. They fell on the soldiers, clubbing and hacking at them with spears, sticks, and knives. Panicking, the soldiers fled, scrambling through the mud and bushes toward their steamer. Its frightened captain cast off, leaving the soldiers splashing in the shallows as the Mahdists hunted them down. By dawn, the abandoned wounded had been killed where they lay. After the slaughter, the Mahdi led the dawn prayer. He had been shot in the shoulder by the first Egyptian volley, and Abdullahi had hidden the wound so that his men would not lose their faith in his immortality. The next day, they buried their dozen dead in the cave where the Mahdi had communed with the Prophet.

The Mahdi knew that Mohammed Rauf Pasha would send a larger force. Just as the Prophet had hidden from the hostile tribes of Mecca and made his Hejira to Medina, so his heir would escape the Turkiyya's soldiers. Using his brothers' boats to ford the White Nile, the Mahdi led his followers southwest into the Nuba Mountains of Kordofan, a trek of seventy-nine days. He rallied his party by comparing them to the Prophet's first adherents: They were the *Muhajiroun,* the exiles who blazed the trail for the *Ansar,* the followers who rallied to the Prophet at Medina.

When the Mahdi's secret shoulder wound had healed, he halted at a hill called Jebel Gadir. To conform to another precedent, the Mahdi renamed it Jebel Massa, after the hill in northwest Africa where a tenth-century Mahdi, Mohammed Ubaidallah, had declared himself.

The fugitives built a mosque and a settlement. Their leader sent letters and messages across the Sudan. The Successor of Allah's Messenger announced the end of the Egyptian tyranny. He called all Muslim allies, partisans, and enemies to his jihad. A new caliphate had arisen. The reign of the Mahdi had begun.

WILFRID SCAWEN BLUNT spent that summer at Crabbet Park, his country estate in Sussex. Surrounded by the blooms of the English summer, he worked quickly on a series of essays. He called them *The Future of Islam.*

"I began life rather early," Blunt admitted. A tall, stooping rake with a thick ginger beard, Blunt had served briefly as a diplomat, before an inheritance had allowed him to pursue his real passions: poetry, thoroughbred horses, radical politics, and Lady Anne King-Noel, the granddaughter of his hero Lord Byron. For five years Blunt and Lady Anne had traveled throughout the Ottoman East, from Turkey to Arabia and Egypt, structuring their exotic tours as business trips. The most successful bloodlines in English and American racing stemmed from a trio of eighteenth-century Arab horses— the Byerly Turk, the Darley Arabian, and the Godolphin Arabian—and the Blunts were determined to create a stud at Crabbet Park. An obsession with origins was the common thread between their disparate interests. Both traced their bloodlines back to the Norman Conquest. Both derived their "sympathies of the cause of freedom in the East" from Anne's grandfather Lord Byron, the poet who had sacrificed himself in the Greek war of independence from Turkey. Both viewed the politics of Islam through this aristocratic prism.[18]

The Blunts found their horses, but their travels in the Ottoman Empire so radicalized Wilfrid that he left the stud farm to Lady Anne. The Ottoman government seemed "a moral plague" on the Arabs, "infecting its subjects with its own corruption." Blunt empathized with the Arabs, especially the Bedouin, who, like the English gentry, valued tribalism, honor codes, and the company of horses over women. Blunt decided that as the Sick Man declined, the Arabs, like Byron's Greeks before them, should be encouraged toward independent modern nationhood—"to champion the cause of Arabian liberty would be as worthy an endeavour as had been that for which Byron had died."[19]

Blunt's infatuation with Arab society deepened in tandem with his disaffection from his own society. In Britain, money and merit were displacing birth and privilege. Commerce and industry had created a liberal middle class. Blunt considered it vulgar in origin and conformist in politics, and that the displacement of the gentry meant the death of "the patriotic idea." Once, he had believed in Britain's "providential mission in the East," but now he saw Britain as complicit in tyranny, supporting the Ottomans in order to preserve British India and the balance of trade. He traced the moral decay of British foreign policy to the rise of "Semitic influence" at home: the "cosmopolitan finance" of Disraeli and his friends the Rothschilds, the "too powerful Hebrew house." Blunt was not alone in his conspiracist reading of the global economy. In 1879, while the Blunts shopped for pure-blooded horses in Syria, the unemployed German journalist Wilhelm Marr published a pamphlet, *The Victory of Judaism over Germanism*. He called his platform "Anti-Semitism."[20]

Although Blunt's visions of Arab nationalism put him on the cranky fringe of Britain's politics, his background gave him access to the private houses and clubs of its elite. When Disraeli's government lost the 1880 election to the Liberals, Blunt's close friend Eddy Hamilton became secretary to the new prime minister, William Gladstone; Blunt's cousin Philip Currie performed the same duties for the foreign secretary, Lord Granville. Blunt refined his ideas in similarly refined circumstances, usually at parties hosted by fellow "Philo-Asiatics."

In the drawing room of "a fine lady's house in Belgravia," the Persian ambassador Malkum Khan described the Babi movement to Blunt. "I knew that it was useless to attempt a remodeling of Persia in European forms," Khan explained, "And I was determined to clothe my material reformation in a garb which my people would understand, the garb of religion."[21]

Spellbound, Blunt realized he had started "at the wrong end." If he was to help the Arabs, he must first understand their thinking. He hired as his teacher Jean Louis Sabunji. A Syrian priest who had converted to Islam and journalism, Sabunji edited *The Bee*, a minor Arabic newspaper that propagandized against the Ottoman Turks. Sabunji taught Blunt about "the

Caliphal question and its modern aspects": The caliphate must be returned to its rightful owners, and if the Arabs were to recover their spiritual independence from Turkey, they must create their political spiritual independence. Blunt decided to trace the caliphate to the source of Islam. "I am full of the notion of going to Arabia and heading a movement for the restoration of the Arab Caliphate. People have been called great who sacrificed themselves for smaller objects."[22]

En route to Arabia, Blunt stopped in Cairo to learn Arabic. One afternoon in January 1881, his tutor took him to "a little house in the Azhar quarter" to meet Mohammed Abdu, lately returned by Riaz Pasha from internal exile.

Blunt's host wore the white turban and dark kaftan of an al-Azhar scholar. He was about thirty-five, of middling height, with a "quick intelligence revealed in singularly penetrating eyes" and a "manner frank and cordial and inspiring." He told Blunt about Afghani, the "wild man of genius," and the reformist vision. The Islamic polity, said Abdu, must resist hostile empires not by reform, but "total reformation." For two hundred years, the Turkish sultans had cared "almost nothing for religion." Holding the caliphate "only by right of the sword," they had lost their spiritual authority. The caliphate must be reconstituted on a "more legitimate and "more spiritual" basis: returned to the Arabs. Most radically of all, it must be separated from secular law; to Abdu, revivalism was only a means, and the end was an Islamic version of the separation of church and state.[23]

These ideas were the basis for Blunt's *Future of Islam*, serialized in the *Fortnightly Review* while Urabi and his friends seethed at Cairo and the Mahdi fled into Kordofan. The Islamic world, said Blunt, was like Catholic Europe before the Reformation. The "bondage of a too-strict tradition" impeded its evolution. It needed "the freeing of its thought" by "a religious reformation." Britain, heir to the Mughal Empire and protector of the Ottoman Empire, had a special responsibility. Rather than profit from Islam's decline, Britain should encourage "the better elements of Eastern thought," as embodied in Egypt by Mohammed Abdu. "In God's name, let her take Islam by the hand and encourage her boldly in the path of virtue." In the summer of 1881, while the Mahdi declared the advent of a new caliphate, Blunt gave Sabunji money for a new periodical, its platform evident in its title: *The Caliphate*.[24]

Blunt, Abdu, and the Mahdi could not have been less similar. Blunt was a European radical, ignorant of the Islamic world. Abdu was an orthodox

Sunni scholar in the pay of the Egyptian government, secretly dabbling in forbidden ideas from the West. The Mahdi was a Sufi cultist inspiring local rebellion through religious reaction. But they had all arrived at the same conclusions. Only a renewed caliphate could save Islam from the West. Ottoman Turkey was the enemy, and its rule over the Arabs must be overthrown.

AS IN THE SUDAN, in Egypt religion gave legitimacy to revolt. After the riot of February 1881, the rebellious Egyptian army colonels and the junior members of Sharif Pasha's aristocratic reform faction formed a grand alliance with Mohammed Abdu's religious rebels. In secret meetings at private houses, they worked out a common interest in forcing Tawfik toward reform.

The aristocrats wanted to regain the fruits of office and obtain a constitution that would free Egypt from both Turkey and Europe. The colonels wanted an end to the long misery of the *fellahin* at the hands of the Turks: no more ethnic discrimination, and more *Corvée*. The religious politicians wanted a constitution that would protect their cultural revolution from the inevitable clerical backlash. Each group accepted the others not from principle, but from pragmatism: They all agreed that the most important policy of all was to get rid of Britain and France. So the Turkish aristocrats promised the colonels that they would end discrimination against Egyptians, and the colonels put the weight of the army and the peasantry behind the aristocrats' call for a constitution. The religious reformers decided that both positions were compatible with a liberal Islamic republic. Privately, Abdu and Sharif Pasha both believed that Urabi was an ignorant peasant, that the Egyptians were not yet ready for liberty, and that they were most likely to reach it via their preferred strain of paternalism. Publicly, each faction in this awkward alliance spoke as the voice of the National Party.

Although Khedive Tawfik had promised to reform the army, he and Riaz Pasha worked to break the colonels. Over the summer of 1881, Riaz Pasha's spies shadowed the colonels, infiltrating their meetings and trying to provoke street brawls. The colonels dodged the provocations. So in early September 1881, Tawfik and Riaz sacked Mahmoud Sami al-Barudi, the colonels' ally in the War Ministry, and ordered the colonels' regiments to the provinces.

The colonels called an emergency meeting. One of Urabi's supporters suggested that if the colonels boarded a train for the provinces, they would end up in the Nile at Karf ez-Zayat like Khedive Ismail's unfortunate brothers. Sensing that they had been followed to the meeting, several officers admitted that they feared assassination by the police. Others mentioned a rumor that the sheikh of al-Azhar had given Tawfik a *fatwa* branding the colonels as traitors marked for death. Urabi was for marching on the Abdin Palace, but Mohammed Abdu spoke against military confrontation, and the Turkish aristocrats agreed with him.

"A foreign occupation will come," Abdu warned. "A malediction will rest forever on him who provokes it."[25]

But the Colonels overruled the aristocrats and the clerics. The next morning, Urabi sent Tawfik a letter containing the National Party's demands. He ended with an ultimatum that if Tawfik had not answered by lunchtime, then the colonels would march on Abdin Palace.[26]

Tawfik panicked. Most of the ministers and foreign consuls had left Cairo to avoid the stifling late summer heat. Only one controller was on hand. Sir Auckland Colvin knew little of Egypt, but had long experience of native effrontery in India. He and Riaz Pasha advised Tawfik to meet Urabi's insolent demands with an ambush. When the rebels marched onto the parade ground in front of Abdin Palace, troops loyal to the government should open fire from the palace windows. The khedive and his advisers spent the morning racing around Cairo, trying to rally regiments loyal to the government. Their last stop was Urabi's barracks. When they got there, they found that they were too late. Urabi had already left for Abdin Palace.

Khedive Tawfik sneaked back by side roads and slipped into his palace by a back door. When he looked out of a front window, he saw that the parade ground contained twenty-five hundred soldiers and eighteen field guns, all pointed at the palace. Every regiment in Cairo had broken its oath. Not a single soldier had sided with him.

On the parade ground, the troops stacked their rifles and stood at ease, cracking pistachios and rolling cigarettes. The colonels waited on their horses for the khedive. It was the height of the tourist season. Curious visitors wandered over from the Ezbekiyyeh Gardens to watch.

Tawfik emerged from a doorway, followed by Sir Auckland Colvin and a few brave attendants. As they walked toward the troops, Colvin kept muttering advice. Tawfik should order Urabi to surrender his pistol, and then shoot him with it. Tawfik should order Urabi to give up his sword, and then walk with the colonel from regiment to regiment, ordering them back to barracks.

Tawfik had no intention of following Colvin's advice. He was terrified.

Colonel Urabi rode up to them, backed by infantrymen with bayonets fixed. Tawfik ordered him to dismount. Lowering his heavy frame to the ground, Urabi marched forward and saluted. His sword stood between his face and the khedive's.

"Now is your moment," hissed Sir Auckland Colvin. "Give the word!"

Tawfik froze. "We are between four fires," he whispered. "We shall be killed."

"Have courage!"

"We are between four fires," Tawfik repeated, turning to Colvin and his attendants as if in apology.

He ordered Urabi to put his sword away. Urabi seemed relieved. His hand shook so much that he had trouble finding the scabbard. Tawfik walked up to him and demanded an explanation.

"I am the khedive of the country, and shall do as I please," the khedive warned.

"We are not slaves, and never shall be from this day forth," replied Urabi.[27]

Sir Auckland Colvin could not believe his ears. The khedive was haggling in public with a rebellious colonel. He suggested they withdraw to the palace.

While Tawfik recovered in an anteroom, the British consul menaced Urabi with the threat of military intervention. But Urabi insisted that his troops demonstrated not against Turkey or Britain, but for the liberty of the Egyptian people. When Urabi repeated his demands to Tawfik, the khedive caved in. The Riaz Pasha cabinet would be dissolved. Mahmoud Sami al-Barudi would return to the War Ministry, and Urabi would be his undersecretary. The army would be expanded to eighteen thousand men, and there would be no more discrimination. The Chamber of Notables would hold elections and prepare a constitution. Tawfik and Urabi appeared on a balcony. The troops cheered and the marching bands struck up. Urabi kissed Tawfik's hand.

The soldiers returned to their barracks. The revolt had achieved its object, and in time for the military band to give its customary afternoon concert in front of the New Continental Hotel. Once again, the colonels had intimidated Tawfik and bluffed the British and French. They had won the war, but their supposed ally Sharif Pasha had his own plans for the peace.

The next morning, a special train brought Sharif Pasha back to Cairo. He had watched from his estate while Urabi cleared a path to the palace. True to Turkish habit, he had no intention of sharing power. When he met Urabi, he insisted that Urabi place the army under his orders. Urabi refused. This gave Sharif an excuse to exclude the colonels from influence over his government. He pacified Urabi with a promise to expand the army and bought off Mohammed Abdu by loosening control over the press. Calling an election, he rigged its results, packing the Chamber of Notables with pliant Turkish landowners.

"The Egyptians are children, and must be treated like children," Sharif said. "It was I who created the National Party."[28]

AFTER FINISHING *The Future of Islam*, Wilfrid Blunt returned to Egypt as the new Chamber of Notables convened. Previously, Blunt had discounted Colonel Urabi as a force for progress. Mohammed Abdu had convinced him that reform would come from Islam, not the army. The British press had depicted Urabi as a budding dictator, and the National Party as a screen for a military takeover. But Philip Currie, Blunt's cousin at the Foreign Office, demurred, hinting, "Perhaps you might find in Urabi just the man you have been looking for."[29]

Blunt found Urabi at a barracks outside Cairo. Petitioners waiting to see The Only One spilled from the waiting room into the doorway. Urabi now styled himself Ahmed Urabi al-Misri: "Ahmed Urabi the Egyptian," his people's Everyman. Urabi admitted that he had not read Lord Byron's poetry, but esteemed his work for Greek liberty. He promised Blunt that the army's involvement in politics would end as soon as possible. "We have won for the people their right to speak, in an Assembly of Notables, and we keep the ground of it to prevent their being cajoled or frightened out of it."[30]

Sharif Pasha having betrayed his allies in the National Party, both Urabi and Abdu were trying to work out how to recover the initiative. Blunt suggested to Abdu that they appeal directly to Britain over Sharif Pasha's head, by drawing up a National Party program and dispatching it to London. Britain's new Liberal premier, William Gladstone, loathed Turkey for the savagery of its repression of Christian minorities in the Balkans. He had campaigned on an ethical foreign policy. Blunt felt "certain" that he would recognize the legitimate aspiration of the Egyptians for freedom.[31]

Abdu agreed. Blunt's plan would bypass Sharif and the notables, and return the National Party to its true founders. Blunt and Abdu composed a program, and showed it to Urabi and Mahmoud Sami al-Barudi, the minister of war. They approved, and Blunt sent it to 10 Downing Street and the *Times*.

Moderately, the National Party accepted the sultan as its caliph. Radically, it promised to fight for its "national rights and privileges." Moderately, the party expressed "loyal allegiance" to Tawfik. Radically, it conditioned this allegiance on Tawfik's "exact execution" of the promised "parliamentary government," and warned him against continuing his "despotic power." Moderately, the party recognized the Dual Control as "a necessity of their financial position," and the debt as "a matter of *national honour.*" Radically, it rejected the Control's method: direct control of Egypt's finances. Moderately, the Nationalists disavowed violence, but radically they hailed the army as "the armed guardians of the unarmed people," and "the only power in the country" capable of establishing constitutional government.

The National Party insisted it was a pluralist movement, "a political, not a religious party." Its government would make no distinction between Muslims, Christians, and Jews, "holding all men to be brothers and to have equal rights." This clause, a revolutionary break with the sharia law and the *dhimmi* status by which the Ottomans had governed religious minorities, had the approval of the sheikhs of al-Azhar, "holding the true law of Islam to forbid religious hatred and religious disabilities." To demonstrate its tolerance, the National Party also had "no quarrel" with European residents, providing they would "live conformably with the laws and bear their share of the burdens of the State"; in other words, if they forsook the Capitulations and the Mixed Courts, and their tax exemptions.

Having vaulted over Islamic tradition and the Capitulations, the program soared into Utopia. "The general end of the National Party is the intellectual and moral regeneration of the country by a better observance of the law, by increased education, and by political liberty, which they hold to be the life of the people. They trust in the sympathy of those of the nations of Europe which enjoy the blessing of self-government to aid Egypt in gaining for itself that blessing." Again Blunt could not resist confrontation. "But they are aware no nation ever yet achieved liberty except by its own endeavours; and they are resolved to stand firm in the position they have won."[32]

There was no more talk of gradual reforms and cautious constitutionalism. Excited by Urabi's image of the army as the irresistible guarantor of Arab liberty, and unable to resist his poet's fluency, Blunt had composed a direct challenge to British influence in Egypt. He had even twisted Urabi's surname in translation, calling him "Arabi," the embodiment of Arabs everywhere.

Lord "Pussy" Granville, Britain's foreign secretary, wrote a note to Prime Minister Gladstone. "It will be desirable for us to have a little talk about Egypt."[33]

5

Egypt for the Egyptians!
1882

William Ewart Gladstone, M.P.

Remember that He, who has united you together as human beings in the same flesh and blood, has bound you by the law of mutual love; that the mutual love is not limited by the shores of this island; is not limited by the boundaries of the Christian civilisation; that it passes over the whole surface of the Earth, and embraces the meanest along with the greatest in its unmeasured scope.

—William Gladstone, M.P., 1879

M R. GLADSTONE LIVED by his conscience. It commanded a life of Christian service. At first it called him to the Church, but then it led him into the Commons. He followed its summons into the Tory Party, and then across the floor and into the Liberal Party. It guided him through an ideological struggle with Benjamin Disraeli, and it advised him not to attend Disraeli's funeral. It compelled him to broaden the electoral system, to bring aid to suffering Lancashire mill workers, to advocate Home Rule for the Irish, and to support the Confederacy in the American Civil War. It sent him at night into the streets of London to pick up prostitutes and exhort them to turn to God, and when a less spiritual urge raised its head, it obliged him to flagellate himself afterward.

In 1881, the "Grand Old Man" was seventy years old, a straight-backed, fierce-eyed prophet whose iron chin jutted over the high wing collar of a passing generation. Liberals compared his craggy face to an eagle's, and Tories to a hawk's. The greatest orator of the age, Gladstone relaxed by reading theology, chopping down trees, and walking miles across rough country. Even his hair defied time, springing up in wild clumps despite lashings of Macassar oil. After four decades in Parliament, Gladstone's conscience had shaped liberal England as surely as his political talent had shaped the Liberal Party. He never stopped inspecting both for impurities of egotism and greed.

Family money from Caribbean sugar plantations had dispatched young William to Eton and Christ Church, Oxford, and then to a "rotten borough" Tory seat in the Commons. The young High Tory had opposed the emancipation of British slaves and condemned electoral reform. In his second decade in Parliament, Gladstone had served Palmerston as the chancellor who found the funds for the Crimean War. But then conscience demanded a breach. Converted to social and electoral reform, he left the Tories. When the Liberals won the 1868 election, Gladstone became their prime minister.

"It has been experience which has altered my politics," he explained. Gladstone struggled constantly to reconcile Christianity with modern thought and modern society. In the 1870s, that meant a personalized battle with Disraeli. They had been antithetical. While Disraeli planted an arboretum on his estate, as if lending permanence to his ennoblement as the earl of Beaconsfield, Gladstone turned down an earldom and delighted in taking an axe to an unworthy tree. While Disraeli wrote novels, idealistically glossing the relations between Church and State in *Coningsby* or the religious implications of empire in *Tancred,* Gladstone reflected on his favorite subjects—religion, politics, and classical literature—at joyless length with titles like *The Impregnable Rock of Holy Scripture, The State and its Relations with the Church,* and *Homeric Synchronism.* Gladstone thought Disraeli "hopelessly false." Disraeli called Gladstone "a sophisticated rhetorician, intoxicated with the exuberance of his own verbosity."[1]

Queen Victoria preferred "Dizzy," with his charming patter and sensitivity to her widowhood, to Gladstone, with his starchy clergyman's manner and his presumption to know the conscience of an empress. It was the question of empire that caused the bitterest split of all. Disraeli had modernized Palmerston's view that Britain must keep the *Pax Britannica* in a malevolent world: In the face of spreading competition, Britain's global interests now required protection through formal empire. Gladstone was an idealist. He believed that the "operations of Commerce" created "the amity of nations": Free Trade created a rational interest in peace. If needed, the Concert of Europe could correct bellicose "lusts and appetites" through collective action based on Christian principle. The "great moral purpose of the repression of human passion" was secured not by tyranny, but by spreading commerce, consensus, and "public law." His critics called him a "Little Englander," ignorant of "over-sea" matters.[2]

Turned out of office by Disraeli in 1874, Gladstone attempted to retire. Yet he could not resist politics, with its high principles and profane intrigues. The Eastern Question fascinated Gladstone like the prostitutes he intercepted on the road to Hell: alluring, guilt-inducing, and redeemable. It was Gladstone's "noble" duty to sustain Britain as a Christian, nonexpansionist member of the international community. "The curtain rising in the East seems to open events that bear cardinally on our race."[3]

Two years after retiring, Gladstone returned to the stage. He struck at the weak point of Disraeli's Eastern strategy: its ethics. In March 1876, Turkish troops repressing the Christian nationalists of Bulgaria massacred fifteen thousand men, women, and children. In *Bulgarian Horrors and the Question of the East,* Gladstone savaged Ottoman rule as "like a deluge of blood rained from the windows of heaven," and Disraeli for having allied Britain with heathen tyranny. Disraeli held to his policy. He installed the Dual Control in the Egyptian government and further entwined Britain and Turkey in the Treaty of Berlin. Gladstone, his politics and principles converging, chose the unfamiliar ground of foreign policy as the battlefield of the 1880 election. As a less couth candidate put it, the liberal public must unite against "Jingoes, Jugglers, and Jews."[4]

In the winter of 1879, the great orator launched the first modern election campaign, using public set pieces, print media, and rapid transport. Trailed by a horde of journalists, Gladstone toured his Scottish constituency of Midlothian, addressing thousands of voters at every stop. He had always excelled on the soapbox, but his real audience was the newly educated and enfranchised public who would read his speeches over breakfast the next morning. In the spring of 1880, he mounted a second tour, using the railway to target key constituencies from London to Edinburgh.

From "the highest grounds of principle" Gladstone assailed the "pernicious fanaticism" of Disraeli's foreign adventures: war in Afghanistan, annexations in Fiji, Cyprus, and Africa, and the shaming alliance with the "cruel and grinding oppression" of Ottoman Turkey. The public must resist Disraeli's "hoodwinking," his "theatrical" costuming of Queen Victoria as an empress, his "gratuitous, dangerous, ambiguous, impracticable and impossible" engagements. The Suez Canal shares were "a mere delusion." Cyprus was "a valueless encumbrance." Turkey repressed minorities with a cruelty "perhaps entirely unequalled in the history of mankind." Disraeli's imperial strategy was a "monstrous" recipe for permanent preemptive war: "A little island at one end of the world, having possessed itself of an enormous territory at the other end of the world, is entitled to say with respect to every land and every sea lying between its own shores and any part of that enormous possession, that it has a preferential right to the possession or control of that intermediate territory, in order, as it is called, to safeguard the road to India."[5]

"Do not suffer appeals to national pride to blind you to the dictates of justice," he declaimed. "Remember the rights of the savage, as we call him."[6]

Disraeli had invoked ancient Rome as an ideal of "Empire and Liberty," but the days of the Caesars would not be returning under a Gladstone government. "Modern times have brought a different state of things. Modern times have established a sisterhood of nations, equal, independent; each of them built up under that legitimate defence which public law affords to every nation, living within its own borders, and seeking to perform its own affairs." Britain must stand for "the equal rights of all nations" and must "always be inspired by a love of freedom."[7]

The public returned the Liberals to power, and Gladstone to Downing Street, but the Liberals were a coalition in all but name. On one side were the Whig aristocrats who had founded the party. On the other were the middle-class Radicals who knew how to speak to the new voters. At the pivot was Gladstone, eloquent incarnation of the liberal, Free Trading inheritance. He would need all his eloquence. On the big issues, Ireland and empire, the cabinet divided not along the Whig-Radical split, but rather along personal beliefs. Alliances formed and broke on single issues. At times, Gladstone had more in common with a rogue Tory like Lord Randolph Churchill, anti-imperial and pro–Home Rule, than with his own ministers. After the election, Gladstone hoped to drop his opportunistic focus on "over-sea" and concentrate on granting Home Rule to Ireland. But Britain's accumulated interest in the Eastern Question soon drew Gladstone's ethical foreign policy into the Egyptian quagmire.

Gladstone had always condemned interference in Egyptian affairs. "Our first sight of Egypt," he had warned in 1877, "be it by larceny or be it by emption, will be the almost certain egg of a North African Empire that will grow and grow . . . till we finally join hands across the Equator with Natal and Cape Town."[8]

Although the "Bulgarian Horrors" had convinced Gladstone that Islam was "radically incapable of establishing a good or tolerable government over civilized and Christian races," he was wary of intruding into the Islamic world. "The susceptibilities which we might offend in Egypt are rational and just. For very many centuries she has been inhabited by a Mohammedan community. That community has always been governed by Mohammedan influences and powers." It also seemed immoral. Conscience demanded that, like any other people, the Egyptians be encouraged to reach "the ends of political society, as they understand them," and without foreign interference.[9]

At the same time, Gladstone invested heavily in the Egyptian economy. In 1875, he bought Egyptian loan stocks worth £25,000, in 1878 £5,000, and in 1879 he speculated a further £15,000. By December 1881, Gladstone owned Egyptian stock with a paper value of £51,000. Apart from affecting Britain's global position, his Egyptian policy would directly affect his holdings, then underperforming with a market value of only £40,567. The Gladstonian conscience remained mute on this conflict of interest. It remained a hidden imperfection, like the middle finger of his left hand, mutilated in a shooting accident, and always covered in public by gloves, hats, and tailored leather fingerstalls.[10]

"We shall be in a scrape, if we are not prepared with any policy," his foreign secretary Lord Granville warned. "Ought we to have a Cabinet?"

Chubby and deaf, with a halo of white curls that made him resemble a debauched cherub, "Pussy" Granville was a Whig traditionalist with a Mayfair mansion and an aristocratic style. Experience had proven that success came from "dawdling matters out" rather than jumping in. Egypt perplexed him. "I am not prepared to propose anything," he admitted to Gladstone.[11]

Nor did Gladstone want to suggest a policy. He felt that he lacked "information on the merits of the quarrel," and rightly. The British press gave a very partial view of Egyptian affairs. Through its Cairo correspondent Moberley Bell, the *Times* reported Egyptian politics as a series of share issues, while the Cairo stringer for the *Pall Mall Gazette* was Sir Auckland Colvin of the Dual Control. At the Foreign Office, Lord Granville received a similarly narrow view. Sir Edward Malet, the British consul at Cairo, believed the reformers were no threat to British interest. Malet's information about Urabi came from his regular tennis game with Wilfrid Blunt on the court in the consulate garden, and Blunt painted Urabi in the colors of European liberalism. In the absence of a dissenting impression, Gladstone and Granville agreed that the most important principle was to maintain amiable relations with France, the other Dual Controller, and its new premier, Leon Gambetta.[12]

The lack of a British response to the crisis in Egypt allowed France to dictate Dual Control policy. In November 1881, Gambetta had taken office facing revolts in Tunisia and Algeria. He attributed them not to burgeoning nationalism, but to pan-Islamic agitation fomented by Sultan Abdul Hamid II. French prestige, still deflated after defeat at the hands of Prussia in 1871, forbade concessions to Muslim nationalists in North Africa. French and British gunboats should be sent to Alexandria at once, and preparations made for a joint Military Control that would introduce "order and discipline" to the Egyptian army.[13]

"They will propose joint occupation, which is very awkward," Granville warned Gladstone. Granville managed to talk Gambetta down to issuing a "Joint Note" to the Egyptian nationalists: a warning that any move concerning the status of the khedive, the Dual Control, and the budget would be met with force. He felt sure that this would call the Egyptians' bluff. If the Egyptians stayed in line, it did not matter that Gambetta believed the Joint Note was a preamble to annexation.[14]

Gambetta's draft of the Joint Note reached London on New Year's Day, 1882. The same morning, the *Times* published Urabi's manifesto. The sudden appearance of modern nationalism in Muslim Egypt surprised Gladstone. The "very ideas" of a national sentiment and a national party seemed "quite incompatible" with the Egyptian people. "How it has come up, I do not know. Most of all is the case strange if the standing army has reared it. There, however, it seems to be." Gladstone believed that everyone had the right to be like him, and the defender of oppressed minorities could not fail this first test of his foreign policy. "*Egypt for the Egyptians* is the sentiment to which I should wish to give scope; and could it prevail it would, I think, be the best, the only good solution of the Egyptian Question."[15]

Yet in the same note to Granville, Gladstone endorsed Gambetta's draft for the Joint Note. Conscience also commanded respect for the "public law" of the "Anglo-French concert," not forgetting "the bond-holders' interests." So long as the National Party recognized these limits, there would be no need for gunboats, let alone annexation. Gladstone believed that the Joint Note would remain what Granville had intended it to be, a rhetorical ploy.[16]

Five days later, the Joint Note reached the Cairo consulate. Sir Edward Malet realized that the Egyptian rebels would not interpret the Note's threat of an Anglo-French invasion as mere rhetoric.

"They will take it as a declaration of war," Malet warned Wilfrid Blunt. He asked Blunt to go to his friend Colonel Urabi and convince him of Britain's goodwill. Blunt found Urabi at his desk in the War Ministry, his face "like a thunder cloud" and "a peculiar gleam" in his eye.[17]

"It is the language of menace," Urabi raged, "a menace to our liberties." He began to shout. "Let them come! Every man, woman and child in Egypt will fight them!"[18]

"WHAT A BLUNDER!" said Sharif Pasha as he read the Note.[19]

Sharif Pasha had done his utmost to placate the French and British. He had excluded the colonels and the clerics from his government. He had stacked the Chamber of Notables with mild Turks. His draft of a Basic Law for the constitution had prioritized debt repayment over liberty. Now, caught between Blunt, Urabi, and Abdu's radical appeal to the British, and the threat of the Joint Note, Sharif lost the center ground. The Joint Note had convinced even Sharif's tame notables that, just as France had annexed Tunisia, so Britain was about to annex Egypt. Led by Urabi's patron Mahmoud Sami al-Barudi, a majority of the notables demanded that the proposed Basic Law recover full control of Egypt's finances. Sharif Pasha did not want to head a government that breached Egypt's international obligations. He resigned.

"I have offered them a constitution which is good enough for them, and if they are not content with it, they must do without one," he explained to Blunt.[20]

"For many days after this, I hardly heard anything from my friends but the language of pan-Islamism," Blunt noted, not without satisfaction.[21]

For their new leader, the notables chose Mahmoud Sami al-Barudi, whose surname meant "the powder works." A Turkish aristocrat with ambitions as a poet, al-Barudi was a sensualist who adored women, wine, and his own family tree. While Urabi drew on koranic schooling and an Arabic biography of Napoleon, al-Barudi read in French, mixing the *Collected Works* of Montesquieu and *The Dictionary of Politics* with smut like *Mysteries of the Harem* and *The Thousand and One Nights of Paris.* By adopting Urabi and the colonels, he hoped to gain the further pleasure of power. He made Urabi a major general, and appointed him minister for war. He hired and promoted hundreds more Egyptian officers and filled his new government with Egyptians. But he took care not to invite European gunboats to Alexandria. Promising to honor Egypt's debt schedules, al-Barudi envisioned a constitution little different from Sharif Pasha's.[22]

The subtleties of al-Barudi's policy did not reach London and Paris. Urabi spoke no languages other than Arabic and Turkish, and both he and al-Barudi negotiated with Britain and France only through local intermediaries. The Dual Controllers, the consuls, and the freelance intriguer Wilfrid Blunt all skewed their reports to suit their prejudices. Meanwhile, the French government saw the rise of al-Barudi and Urabi as a military coup, and the British government saw the issue in terms of their French alliance. These confusions pushed al-Barudi and Urabi toward Ottoman Turkey as their only possible protector. Hoping to manipulate Egypt back into the Ottoman orbit, Sultan Abdul Hamid II encouraged them. He promoted Urabi to brigadier general and pasha.

To complete the chaos, Gambetta, who had instigated the Joint Note, fell from office within weeks of its dispatch. His successor was Charles de Freycinet, nicknamed "The White Mouse" for his caution. De Freycinet could not afford to back down on Gambetta's threat to Egypt, but nor did he want to antagonize the French chamber by calling a vote on a military expedition. So he insisted that Britain and France stand by the Joint Note, knowing that the preponderance of British interest in Egypt would force Britain to take the lead.

In London, Gladstone and Granville fumbled for a response. While they had pondered the terms of an Egyptian constitution, the international order had crumbled.

"Smouldering fires in Egypt," warned the *Pall Mall Gazette.*[23]

"It would be childish to discuss the pattern of a carpet when the house in which it was laid down was in flames," warned de Freycinet.

Sir Auckland Colvin extended the metaphor. "The house is tumbling about our ears," he warned from Cairo, "and the moment is not propitious for debating whether we would like to add another storey to it." Egypt, he said, was under "military despotism." The Dual Control had ceased to exist.[24]

The Anglo-French duo having failed, Gladstone attempted to internationalize the problem by constructing various trios and quartets from the Concert. Overcoming his revulsion for Turkey, the author of *Bulgarian Horrors* proposed that Turkish troops be sent to Egypt. The sultan bristled that before he could address this request, Britain and France must apologize for issuing the Joint Note without consulting him. Granville humbly apologized, but Abdul Hamid II refused to send troops anyway: He had no desire to stop the Egyptian drift toward Turkey. Nor would he permit an internationalized solution, refusing a French request that he invite the Concert to an emergency conference at Constantinople. He did, however, agree to send a Turkish general to reason with the rebels, and that was because it seemed an invitation to turn events in his favor.

"The Sultan is intensely false and fraudulent," Gladstone complained, "and tries to work everything against us."[25]

While the sultan would not let Gladstone off the hook by sending troops, the French would not allow him to negotiate with the rebels. In early May, the option of retreat closed, too. In a demonstration of the link between domestic and foreign policies, and the power of terrorism, Gladstone's Egyptian policy became hostage to his Irish policy.

Gladstone had sent two emissaries to Ireland to negotiate with the Fenian nationalists. In Dublin on May 6, 1882, members of a paramilitary splinter group called the Invincibles murdered them with surgical knives in broad daylight at the gates of Phoenix Park, the seat of British authority. One of the dead was Thomas Burke, the undersecretary for Ireland. The other was Lord Frederick Cavendish, brother of the secretary for war, Lord Hartington, and Gladstone's nephew by marriage. The "Phoenix Park Murders" hardened attitudes in the cabinet. Hartington insisted that there be no negotiation with terrorists. Gladstone had to choose between abandoning his Irish policy or breaking up his cabinet. He chose to keep his cabinet. Egyptian policy followed suit: consensus in the cabinet, and a tough policy.

The only option was to overthrow the Nationalist government, replace it with a reliable puppet government, and then withdraw. The French insisted on sending a joint fleet. Gladstone tried to internationalize that, too, but the French foreign minister Tissot blocked him. On May 13, Gladstone caved in. From the Royal Navy base at Suda Bay in Crete, the fat, fierce admiral Sir Beauchamp Seymour, known as "The Swell of the Ocean," set forth.[26]

"DO NOT FEAR THE SHIPS," Blunt blithely cabled Urabi. "No interven-tion."[27]

Blunt interpreted Gladstone's vagueness as an endorsement of the Egyptian revolution. Misinformed and inexperienced, Urabi misplayed his hand. While Gladstone drifted into war and Seymour steamed south, Urabi clumsily provided a pretext for intervention. He made a play for total power.

As soon as Urabi took control of the War Ministry, he turned the old policies of discrimination on the Turkish elite. He rehired unemployed na-tive officers, sacked over seven hundred Turks, and sent dozens more to the Sudanese outposts. In protest, some of the remaining Turkish officers left the country and defected to the sultan. Not long after this purge, the Ura-bists discovered a plot to poison Abd el-Al, head of the Sudanese regiment. Urabi detected a Turkish conspiracy against his takeover of the army, appar-ently funded by ex-khedive Ismail. He arrested forty Turkish officers, among them his old enemy, Osman Rifki Pasha. By the end of April, when the mass courts-martial began, Urabi was sleeping in the Abdin barracks to avoid assassination, and Abd el-Al's mother was keeping his drinking water under lock and key. The courts convicted all forty officers of treason, stripped them of their ranks, and sentenced them to exile in the Sudan.

The sentences reached Khedive Tawfik for approval. Tawfik realized that the purging of the Turkish officers turned him into the mascot of a native revolution. Although the state still functioned, it had undergone a military coup. Foreign intervention was his only hope. Guided by Sir Edward Malet, he refused to endorse the sentences and put them to the vote in the Cham-ber of Notables. The Turkish majority among the notables also sensed that al-Barudi and Urabi were turning Egypt into a dictatorship, and they voted down the sentences. The khedive, in genuine fear of his life, was now in a standoff with his own army.

Next, a cable arrived from London, warning that British and French war-ships were on their way to Alexandria, and that any disorder in Egypt would bring intervention. Al-Barudi and Urabi tendered their resignations, but Tawfik refused to accept them. Neither side wanted to be responsible for what happened when the gunboats arrived. The rebel ministers decided to stay in office. If war was inevitable, it made more sense to fight it from a po-sition of strength.

ON THE MORNING of May 19, 1882, Urabi's sentries on the walls of Alexandria reported that a British ironclad had anchored outside the harbor.

The next morning, a French warship appeared. One stream of Alexandrians fled the city, and another converged on Urabi's house. All order collapsed.

The British and French consuls issued a "Dual Note": The al-Barudi government must resign, all troops must withdraw to the countryside, and Urabi must go into exile. The entire government resigned. Tawfik sent for Sharif Pasha, but Sharif refused: It did not seem possible to assemble a new government without the army's involvement. Then the army officers weighed in with a telegram refusing to accept Urabi's resignation. More worried by rifles at Cairo than battleships at Alexandria, Tawfik turned around and requested Urabi to return.

Urabi accepted. He assured the consuls that he was in charge, that there would be no shooting, that Egypt still honored its sultan and its debts. At the same time, he fortified the walls of Alexandria. Meanwhile, Tawfik prepared for civil war. Thousands of his Bedouin supporters flooded into Alexandria. Omar Lutfi Pasha, Alexandria's pro-Tawfik police chief, bought up all available stocks of *naboots*—the wooden clubs used by the city's night watchmen—and distributed them among the Bedouin and the poor Arabs of the city. Stocking up with guns and supplies, Alexandria's Europeans barricaded their homes.

On June 8, the sultan dropped two sparks into the Egyptian tinderbox. Abdul Hamid II sent two emissaries, one to persuade and the other to coerce the rebels into the Ottoman camp. The first was Sheikh Ahmed Assad, one of the pan-Islamists Abdul Hamid collected at Constantinople as a bulwark against Arab secessionism. Sheikh Assad promised Urabi and the al-Azhar scholars that the sultan would protect the Islamic aspect of their nationalism. In return, Urabi assured the sultan of his loyalty, his willingness to accept Tawfik's great-uncle Halim as the new khedive, and that he was "fighting for Islamic unity, and was prepared to sacrifice his life."[28]

The second was the notorious general Dervish Pasha. In Albania, Dervish had tied pairs of rebel prisoners back to back, executing one and leaving the other roped to a corpse. "Dervish is a man of iron," chortled the *Pall Mall Gazette.* "And Arabi may well quail before his eye. One saucy word and his head will roll upon the carpet."[29]

Tawfik greeted Dervish Pasha with fifty thousand pounds in *baksheesh* and jewels worth twenty-five thousand pounds. The Nationalists greeted him with an ovation, "Allah give victory to the Sultan! The note? Reject it, reject it!"[30]

Neither swayed Dervish. He had come to raise the tension in the sultan's favor. Again, Urabi provided the pretext. He boasted to Dervish Pasha that for the previous four years, he had been "preparing an Islamic league, from the depths of Africa to the extremities of India." In Libya, Algeria, Tunisia, the Sudan, and "other distant countries," members of this secret "Islamic union" were poised to rebel in harmony with the Egyptians. This claim, soaked in the flammable visions of Jamal ed-Din al-Afghani, was as much a threat to the sultan's caliphate as to European influence. The flexible virtues of Pan-Islamism attacked the Ottoman Empire as easily as they validated it.[31]

Dervish ordered Urabi to Constantinople, but Urabi refused to go. To counteract Mohammed Abdu and his followers, Dervish toured the mosques of Cairo, denouncing the radical sheikhs for threatening the interests of the sultan-caliph. His campaign backfired. Whipped up by Afghani's protégé Abdullah Nadim, thousands of al-Azhar students rioted in the streets. The Urabists rallied around their leader. Mohammed Abdu devised a Masonic-style oath of loyalty: If they abandoned Urabi to exile, their throats would be cut, their tongues and hearts removed. More conventional but more radical, Sheikh el-Ullaish, the head of al-Azhar, issued a *fatwa* against Tawfik. The khedive had sinned against Islam by inviting a Christian fleet into an Islamic land. [32]

"He shall be cast out," el-Ullaish decreed, "and in his place shall be named one who will watch over the law and defend it, and respect the rights of the Commander of the Faithful." He cited the Koran, *"O ye who believe! Take not the Jews and the Christians for your friends and protectors; they are but friends and protectors to each other. He among you that turns to them is one of them."*[33]

As the Urabists rolled more cannon onto the ramparts, Dervish Pasha retreated to one of Tawfik's palaces. Egypt appeared to be breaking loose from Constantinople on a nationalist wave that frothed with Islamic ire. From the harbor at Alexandria, Sir Beauchamp Seymour telegraphed to London, "Admiral wants more ships in consequence of earthwork erected opposite *Invincible.*"

On June 1, Gladstone told the Commons that Urabi had "thrown off the mask." The Egyptian national movement had revealed itself as a front for a military takeover. Conscience and the national interest demanded the restoration of "public law." More British battleships steamed for Alexandria.[34]

"Everything seems to be going on beautifully," Blunt wrote in his diary. "Arabi acknowledged master of the situation in Egypt."[35]

"Intelligence from the Sudan reports an affray between the population and the military, caused by the preaching of a 'false prophet,' the *Times* reported. "The rise of the Nile is satisfactory."[36]

While Egyptian eyes focused on the Nile Delta, the flight of a religious fanatic and his followers to the most distant corner of Kordofan barely registered in Cairo. Riaz Pasha's economy drive had divided Sudanese affairs between the relevant ministries of the Cairo government and shrunk the army in both Egypt and the Sudan. Urabi's agitations had secured the reversal of the army cutbacks, but the new regiments remained in the Delta, where Tawfik, Sharif Pasha, and Urabi all wanted them as leverage in the political struggle. Although the War Ministry was responsible for repressing the Mahdi's revolt, Mahmoud Sami al-Barudi and Urabi ignored the Sudan in favor of their campaign against the khedive. As the ministries rose and fell at Cairo, policy disintegrated and funds dried up.

As an Urabi sympathizer, Governor-General Mohammed Rauf Pasha's first concern was to keep his position. Complacently, he had dismissed warnings from the Sammaniya leader Sheikh Nur al-Daim that the Mahdi was massing support for a revolt. Nor had Rauf Pasha sounded the alarm when the Mahdi had taken up arms against the government. His report to Cairo had downplayed the night battle at Aba Island as an "affray." To Rauf Pasha, the Mahdi was a *Mutamahdi,* a false prophet. To crush him, Rauf Pasha had sent the governor of Kordofan and a thousand soldiers to Aba Island.[37]

While the soldiers had marched northeast, the Mahdi and his followers had fled in the opposite direction. Finding Aba Island deserted, the soldiers had paused to burn down the entire settlement—mosque, village, and orchards—and then followed the Mahdi's trail southwest. Spies had watched the column's every noisy move. Traveling light, the Mahdi had easily evaded his pursuers. When the September rains had flooded the roads and riverbeds, the column had given up the chase and returned to El Obeid, leaving the Mahdi free to set up a new base in the Nuba Mountains.

Simultaneously, Colonel Urabi had marched his troops up to Abdin Palace and pulled down Riaz Pasha's government. For the next nine months, Rauf Pasha had ruled in a vacuum, deprived of money and orders, as the Sudanese conscripts that he had fired on Riaz Pasha's orders flocked to the Mahdi's camp. Most of Rauf Pasha's officers were Egyptians sidelined in Sudan by discriminatory policies. Mutinously, they looked to the turnover of governments as an invitation to a cozier posting in the Delta. A visitor to Rauf's office just after Urabi's mutiny found him "despondent," tinkering with plans as the army shattered into ethnic camps, and unable to decide which of his unreliable regiments to deploy.[38]

The government's next move misfired so badly that Rauf Pasha disclaimed any knowledge of it. The closest garrison to the Mahdi's camp at Jebel Gadir lay at Fashoda, 150 miles to the southwest. Governor Rashid Ayman did not want to spend the rest of his career in malarial obscurity. Hoping that victory might get him out of Fashoda and into Rauf Pasha's seat at Khartoum, Rashid Ayman set out for Jebel Gadir with four hundred troops and a mass of friendly Shilluk tribesmen. A woman from the unfriendly Kinana tribe hurried to the Mahdi's camp and warned him of the approaching force.

At sunrise on December 8, 1881, the Egyptians rose for their dawn prayers. The Mahdists had already finished their devotions, and waited, arrayed in a crescent, with the Mahdi's boatmaking brother Mohammed poised at the center. Over their white jibbas they wore oddments of medieval armor, loose-ringed chain mail shirts, helmets from Abyssinia, and padded armor from Darfur. In their hands they held sticks, spears, knives, broadswords, and throwing stars. Rashid Ayman, confident in his troops' white uniforms and Remington rifles, ordered his bleary men forward. They fired a volley at short range. The *Muhajiroun* held their ground, then charged into the Egyptian troops, slashing with spears and knives. They killed Rashid Ayman and cut off his head to show the Mahdi. A few soldiers ran away fast enough to escape. The rest were enslaved into the Mahdi's army.

The Mahdi appeared later in the day. Although nobody had seen him at the battle, he wore a bloodstained jibba. He also had a growing arsenal of government rifles. He banned his followers from using the infidels' Remingtons. "The Prophet has repeatedly informed us that our victory is through the spear and the sword, and that we have no need for the rifle." Yet he did not destroy his stash of modern weaponry. He centralized it in the hands of Abdullahi, his Baggara general. "After the collection, we shall see what Allah wills."[39]

THE ROUT OF Rashid Ayman fueled the legend of the Mahdi. Letters went out from Jebel Gadir, spreading the word. Sticks and spears had overcome government rifles. The *Muhajiroun*'s chanted prayers had turned Egyptian bullets to water. The wrath of the Mahdi caused corpses to catch fire where they lay. Like the Prophet at the Battle of Badr, the Mahdi had smashed a superior force with only 313 men. Fighters arriving too late to die in the jihad had wept in grief. The Mahdi's name appeared on stones, eggs, and watermelon seeds. His camp overflowed with limitless food and water.

Kordofan and Darfur hummed with expectancy, not all of it theological. Many tribes had resisted the Mahdi's religious call, but now almost all responded to his political call. Overthrowing the Turks meant relief from taxation and control of the slave trade. The Mahdi's core supporters had come from the tribes settled along the Nile, but now his camp swelled with Baggara nomads. Although the Nile tribes derided the Baggara as recent, ignorant converts to Islam who still worshipped rocks and trees, the Mahdi adopted the Baggara as the backbone of his army. Just as he had prophesied, the *Ansar* had arrived.

The Mahdi inducted recruits divided by lifestyle and language into a martial regime designed to obliterate all difference. Sufi cultists, Egyptian deserters, riverain farmers, and desert nomads all received the patched white jibba. All received a copy of the Mahdi's *ratib*, cobbled together from Sammaniya ritual and the Mahdi's favorite quotations from the Koran. "I seek refuge in Allah. I commit myself to Allah. How good Allah is. There is no power but with Allah." All hung their *ratibs* around their necks as an amulet and prayed from them five times daily, chanting and breathing themselves into hypnotic fury. All chanted "He gives life and death and is almighty" one hundred times, and "There is neither might nor power but with Allah" 101 times.[40]

The Mahdi invoked the tribes' common bonds, Islam and resentment, to forge the sword of the Prophet. He directed it toward the Turks. The "ultimate aim" was jihad, "the attainment of martyrdom" in battle. The ultimate owner of all property was the Mahdi. As the Prophet had laid down, "Those who love me love to follow the two virtues of poverty and jihad." All dissent was banned: The Mahdi was in "a permanent state of beholding the Prophet without screens," and his word was the word of Allah.

Tradition was an error that had to be purged. The Mahdi had studied the four legal schools that medieval Islam had built upon the Prophet's revelation. Centralizing all authority in his person, he destroyed their texts and annulled their judgments, dissolving the traditions that made the Prophet's vision workable. He canceled all prior legal judgments, except those concerning four financial categories: fraud, debt, the property rights of orphans, and the manumission of slaves. Laying waste to a thousand years of Islamic culture, he attempted to reconstruct the society of the Prophet, building a fanatical simulacrum of seventh-century Arabia on a Nubian hillside. He regressed to a fantasy of Prophetic inspiration, when the ideal society existed for war in the name of Allah.[41]

The only law was sharia in its crudest form. A man who called his fellow Muslim "a dog, a pig, a Jew, a pimp, a dissolute, a thief, an adulterer, a fraudster, cursed, an infidel, a Christian or a homosexual" received eighty lashes and a week in prison, as did a man caught in possession of alcohol. Tobacco, the Turkish habit, was expunged from the face of the earth: A man caught smoking, chewing, or even taking snuff received eighty lashes. A man who donned the jibba but refused to pray would suffer eighty lashes, a week in prison, the confiscation of all assets, and if he was still alive after that, death. A revolt whose followers rebelled against the Turkish *kourbash* imposed its law through whippings, stonings, judicial mutilation, and public executions.[42]

The Mahdi rewarded men with the holy task of jihad and its guarantee of heaven. He punished women for their existence. At five years of age, a girl had to be fully veiled. She could not go outside "unless strictly necessary." She could not speak in public. She could not speak to a man unless she wore a veil. When she did speak, she must whisper. She was banned from "wailing and lamenting" at a funeral. If she uncovered her hair, "even for the blink of an eye," she received twenty-seven lashes. If she spoke "with a loud voice" or "immodestly," she received another twenty-seven lashes. If she used "obscenity," she received another eighty. Her duty was to put her womb at the service of jihad. If she refused to have sex with her husband, she forfeited her property. If she disobeyed him, she was "confined in a dark house or hut," and if she did not repent, she was left to die. The Mahdi's order to a woman who had passed child-bearing age was "let her wage jihad with her hands and feet."[43]

Men and women had equality before the sharia in two rulings only: Adulterers were stoned to death, and everyone was expected to inform on his or her neighbor. Claiming to defend traditional society, the Mahdi subverted the family by turning its members into informants. Then he reconstituted the broken pieces on military lines. He promoted his carpenter brother Mohammed to commander of the armies. Imitating the Prophet, he named four khalifas, caliph-generals, each named for his koranic forerunner, each commanding a wing of the Mahdist league. The western Baggara followed the black flag of Abdullahi, rewarded for his long loyalty. The eastern Baggara followed the green flag of Ali wad Helu, a small, hirsute al-Azhar graduate. The riverain tribes and the Mahdi's *Ashraf* relatives followed his Dongolawi son-in-law Mohammed al-Sharif.

The fourth khalifa refused the honor. Hoping to export the revolution, the Mahdi had sent an offer across the Sahara to his Senussi namesake in Libya, Mohammed al-Mahdi. Receiving no reply, the Sudanese Mahdi wrote again, and heard nothing. The Libyan Mahdi spurned him totally. After receiving the first letter, Senussi envoys had ventured into the Sudan to examine the Sudanese Mahdi's claims. Instead of a koranic paradise on earth, they found a bloodbath inspired by "idle yarns, fables and falsifications" and "a burning country, dying and reeking of death."[44]

BREAKING THE BAD NEWS of Rashid Ayman's death, Rauf Pasha requested that Khedive Tawfik send reinforcements. But in December 1881, Tawfik needed all the loyal troops he could muster. Three days after Rauf asked for help, Urabi, Abdu, and Blunt launched their National Party manifesto. Tawfik was more worried by radical Islam on his doorstep than in the Sudan. When the French editor of *L'Egypte* called the Prophet Mohammed "a false prophet," death threats forced him to flee the country. At al-Azhar, Mohammed Abdu's increasingly restive allies had overthrown their prokhedive rector. Rauf did not get his reinforcements.[45]

When the Sharif Pasha ministry fell in February 1882, hapless Rauf Pasha fell with it. Distrusting his new war minister, Ahmed Urabi, Tawfik turned the Sudan back into a separate government ministry. If Urabi incited a revolt of the Sudanese garrisons, the khedive would lose his empire as well as his throne. Tawfik entrusted the garrisons to Abd al-Qadir Pasha, a loyal Turk. Rauf Pasha left Khartoum in early March, but Abd al-Qadir Pasha took eleven weeks to arrive in his new post. The governorship passed to one of Gordon's protégés, Carl Giegler, a lanky red-bearded telegraph engineer from Germany.

Egypt was in turmoil. The throne in Khartoum was empty. The Mahdi sensed his moment. By the time Abd al-Qadir Pasha arrived in Khartoum, a thousand *Ansar* had moved north and surrounded El Obeid, the capital of Kordofan and the key to western Sudan.

Giegler the amateur succeeded where Mohammed Rauf had failed. In the Jazira, the district south of Khartoum, Giegler crushed the tribes loyal to the Mahdi and stuck their leader's head on a spike in Khartoum's marketplace. But when Abd al-Qadir Pasha arrived, he displaced Giegler in favor of a political appointee: Brigadier Yusuf al-Shallali, a Sudanese who had fought for Gordon on the Gazelle River. In early May 1881, al-Shallali gathered 3,000 infantry, 500 cavalry, four field guns, two rocket launchers, a train of 600 camels, and a mass of porters. As they set out into the wooded foothills of the Nuba Mountains, Mahdist spies shadowed their advance, even infiltrating their ranks and stealing their horses. To rally his apprehensive troops, al-Shallali chopped off the arms and legs of four captured spies.

On the night of May 29, 1882, ten days after Admiral Seymour steamed into Alexandria harbor, Brigadier al-Shallali camped in a wood near Jebel Gadir. His men cut down spiky acacia branches and stacked them into a rough *zariba,* but he was so confident that he did not bother to post sentries. As the army slept, the *Ansar* crept up.

At dawn, thousands of "almost naked" warriors descended on the *zariba* before the Egyptians awoke. The thorn walls became a trap for their defenders, who were slashed and stabbed as they fumbled for their rifles. Still in his underclothes, Brigadier al-Shallali was hacked to death at the door of his tent. Some of the troops formed up and fought their way out of the *zariba,* only to disappear under a human tide. The entire expedition was slaughtered, their weapons, slaves, animals, and food looted.

The Mahdi took a fifth of the loot and established a *Beit al-Mal,* a treasury for his sharia state. He now controlled all of southern Kordofan. The garrison at El Obeid subsisted on rats. Egypt was in revolution. Nothing could stop him. "My progress to Mecca is guided by the Prophet at the time ordained by Allah."[46]

That summer, a succession of comets fired the night skies. Fifty miles south of Asyut, a British expedition led by Professor Arthur Schuster took the first photograph of an Eclipse Comet. They named it "Tawfik" for the khedive. Schuster identified it and the previous summer's comet as part of a sequence of Kreutz Sungrazers, giant fragments of a greater comet that had broken up centuries earlier, their orbits plunging into the sun.[47]

AT ALEXANDRIA, the morning of June 10, 1882, dawned hot and bright. On the harbor wall, Urabi's men returned to their fortifications. On HMS *Superb,* Admiral Seymour returned to his telescope and gave his batman Strackett a day's shore leave among the seamy delights of the Orient. In the city, the British missionary H. P. Ribton decided to take his five-year-old daughter on a boat trip.

In the Carcacol Laban—the "White Quarter" by the harbor—a Maltese trader decided to spend the day crawling the bars. To save valuable drinking time, he hired an Egyptian boy with a donkey cart to ferry him around. As the noonday sun reached its apogee, he fell into a slurred dispute with the boy outside the Café et Gazaz. A crowd gathered, the Maltese grabbed a cheese knife and stabbed the donkey boy in the stomach, and the boy fell dying to the café floor. A brawl erupted between natives and foreigners, and a mob of angry Egyptians forced the Europeans back into their houses. Breaking out the guns they had hoarded in expectation of disorder, the Europeans fired indiscriminately into the crowd. The Alexandria Riot had begun.[48]

The *Mustafezzin,* or city police, were ready. Their leader, Omar Lutfi Pasha, was a Tawfik loyalist. When the *Mustafezzin* heard shooting, they broke out their stocks of wooden *naboots,* passing them from the windows of their police stations to mobs of irate Bedouin. When the *Mustafezzin* reached the riot, they joined in, attacking passing Europeans with knives and bayonets. Lured by a request from Omar Lutfi Pasha, the British consul Charles Cookson appeared at the scene. Rioters clubbed him to the ground, but he escaped to sanctuary in a police station. Then Lutfi Pasha appeared, having swapped his pasha's uniform for plain clothes. He left without giving any orders. The rioters needed no guidance. A cry went up, "Kill the Christians!"

The rioters clubbed to death a five-year-old boy outside the Austrian Post Office and a well-dressed man they found staggering along the Rue des Soeurs covered in blood. Further down the street, they shot one European in the head, stabbed another in the chest, and fractured the skull of a third, stripping him of his shoes and socks as he lay dying. Looting shops and cafés, the mob spilled along the Rue des Soeurs toward the Place Mehmet Ali, surging around the equestrian statue of the founder of modern Egypt as the air rang with gunfire and smashing glass. Beneath the metal gaze of Mehmet Ali, one policeman walked down the street holding a chandelier; another a toy horse; and a third a stack of trousers.

The rioters moved on to Frank Street and the marina. Clubbing and stabbing to death any Europeans they found, they robbed, stripped, and mutilated the corpses, then tipped them into the sea and fought the *Mustafezzin* for their valuables. Returning from the marina, H. P. Ribton, his two friends, and his five-year-old daughter were pushed back toward the mob by police bayonets. The three men were beaten to death trying to prevent the child's abduction. A policeman carried her away on his shoulder, but a friendly sheikh who heard her screams saved her and hid her in his house. As Europeans commandeered carriages and raced for the harbor, the mob pulled them down and attacked them, stabbing a Greek sea captain and shooting a Frenchman. They beat up five tars from HMS *Superb* with *naboots*, stabbing one to death, and attacked merchant sailors from the SS *Tanjore*. When a soldier helped one of them to a police station, the policeman at the gate took out his sword, split the sailor's skull with his first stroke, and decapitated him with his second.

Three hours passed before Osman Lutfi Pasha requested military assistance. When he did, the commanders of the seven thousand soldiers in the Alexandria barracks refused to move without orders from Minister Urabi, and he wanted to demonstrate that only the army could prevent the collapse of Egypt. Three more hours passed. At six in the evening, the troops finally marched out and took up position outside the European consulates. The mob melted away, leaving empty streets littered with bodies and wreckage. Most of the forty-nine corpses in the hospital morgue carried wounds from *Mustafezzin* bayonets.

Forty years a sailor, Admiral Seymour fumed impotently as the smoke rose in the eye of his telescope and the boats ferried survivors back to his warships. The rioters had killed Strackett, too.[49]

"BUTCHERED UNDER THE very guns of the fleet, which had never budged an inch to save them!" Lord Salisbury, now leader of the Opposition, blamed Gladstone for the riot. The British press unanimously denounced the massacre as an insult to national dignity: An Arab mob had slaughtered innocent Europeans and beaten a consular agent in the street. But the most alarming response came from within Gladstone's cabinet. Led by Lord Hartington at the War Office, the Whigs rebelled. "Harty-Tarty" threatened to resign and bring down the government.[50]

"I am afraid that we are going to give in and submit to a total defeat in Egypt," Hartington warned. "I do not think that I can stomach this."[51]

The Radicals split. John Bright, a Quaker pacifist and Free Trade purist, opposed force on principle. But the younger Radicals joined their Whig rivals in the revolt. Joseph Chamberlain, president of the Board of Trade, warned that "a military adventurer" like Urabi meant "bankruptcy and anarchy" for Egypt. Sir Charles Dilke, the undersecretary for war, raised the strategic fear of a Suez Canal blocked by Islamic nationalists.[52]

Gladstone faced a decision that revolved around the essence of Britain's Egyptian policy, and the incarnation of everything he loathed about imperialism: the Suez Canal. Although he had derided it to the voters of Mid-lothian, Gladstone knew that the Canal was vital to Britain. British steamers carried 70 percent of the Canal's traffic. Their cargoes weighed over a hundred million metric tons and were worth over £65 million to the British economy. Gladstone had three options: to surrender the Canal to the Egyptians; to protect its neutrality through annexation by the Concert; or to protect it unilaterally by British arms. Having overcome his initial conviction that the Egyptian rebellion was a genuine national movement, Gladstone discarded the first option with a clean conscience.[53]

For three weeks, he tried the second option. The sultan refused to help. While Abdul Hamid II agreed to host a Concert summit at Constantinople, he blocked any fruitful outcome. Instead of condemning Urabi as a rebel, the sultan honored him with Turkey's highest honor, the Grand Cordon of Medjidieh and, via Dervish Pasha, offered him a monthly pension of £250. The French turned on Gladstone, too. De Freycinet did not want to spark a reaction in France's Arab colonies. He refused to take part in any punitive action at Alexandria, or to commit troops to the inevitable land expedition. Instead, he secretly tried to draw Urabi to France, by doubling the sultan's offer to £500 a month.[54]

Urabi had no way back: Tawfik and Omar Lutfi Pasha had steered the riot and made him look like a crude xenophobe. He had no way to turn: On one side, Dervish Pasha squeezed him in a treacherous Turkish embrace, and on the other, European gunboats took aim at Alexandria. Only the forward path remained: the narrowing tracks of nationalism and Islam. Urabi broke out stores of rifles stocked up by Khedive Ismail for the day of his independence from Turkey. He accelerated the fortification of Alexandria and laid plans to sabotage the Suez Canal. Writing to Gladstone, he threatened that if British ships fired on Alexandria, he would confiscate all European property, cancel the Dual Control, disown the debt, destroy the Canal, and cut the telegraph connecting Britain to India. Then he would ignite the Islamic world against the British and Ottoman empires.

"Use will be made of the religious zeal of Mohammedans, to preach a holy war in Syria, in Arabia, and in India," Urabi wrote to Gladstone. "Egypt is held by Mohammedans as the key to Mecca and Medina, and all are bound by their religious law to defend these holy places and the ways leading to them.

"I repeat again and again, that the first blow struck at Egypt by England or her allies will cause blood to flow throughout the breadth of Asia and of Africa.

"England may rest assured that we are determined to fight, to die martyrs for our country, as has been enjoined on us by our Prophet; or else to conquer, and so live independently."[55]

Gladstone had no choice but his third option. Admiral Seymour reported up to ten thousand Egyptian soldiers on the fortifications of Alexandria, strengthening the defenses and dragging up heavy cannon. As the Channel squadron steamed south to join Seymour, Egypt's Europeans crammed onto boats and trains, desperate to escape. British consular staff evacuated Egypt on a P&O steamer, led by the stricken Cairo consul Sir Edward Malet, who suspected that the Urabists had poisoned him. As the Egyptian post offices closed and the Eastern Telegraph Company withdrew its staff and instruments to British ships, communication with India became interrupted. In London, the Stock Exchange fell.

Gladstone insisted he would be "no party" to unilateral annexation, "an act full of menace to the future peace of the world." But the War Ministry and the Admiralty kept up the pressure: Either Urabi would annex the Canal, or the French would buy him out, and Egypt with him.

"My brain is *very* weary," Gladstone admitted in his diary. At dawn on July 10, Admiral Seymour gave Urabi twenty-four hours to surrender, or face bombardment. Gladstone hoped that a little gunboat diplomacy would persuade Urabi to back down. He felt certain that the rebels would not dare to breach the Canal's neutrality. To do so would make "the whole world their enemies." It was "improbable that they meditate or desire such a course, unless under the most desperate extremities." Which was where he had placed Urabi.[56]

THE MORNING OF JULY 11 was bright and clear, the sea still and glassy. At dawn a gentle northwest wind rustled the leaves of the acacia trees in what remained of Place Mehmet Ali. Sudanese house slaves squatted at their owners' gates, city employees watered the streets, and Bedouin women from the country sold fresh milk to the soldiers who had passed the night on benches and doorsteps. The clock of St. Catherine's church struck seven.

As the chimes faded, a single blast issued from the harbor, followed by a wild shriek and a second blast that shook the city. Smoke issued from the burning barracks of the Ras el-Tin palace. Admiral Seymour had run out of patience.

His order was simple. "Attack the enemy's batteries."

A mile from the shore, the fleet steamed back and forth, firing constantly at the batteries in perfect shooting weather. The Egyptian gunners, many exposed on open ramparts, blasted back an irregular response. The harbor filled with gunsmoke and the air sang with shellfire. With each hit on the defenses, gouts of debris as tall as the Pharos lighthouse spouted into the air. The forts were made of soft limestone, with sand parapets coated in cement. Their French architects had built them to resist cannonballs, not the eighty pounds of high explosive in each shell fired by the *Inflexible's* four guns.

Yet each time the dust cleared, the Egyptian gunners crawled back to their places and reloaded. Their firing was not all wild. They blew a hole ten feet by four just above the *Superb's* waterline. They holed the mainmast and funnel of the *Sultan*. When the *Alexandra* sailed too close, they landed twenty-four direct hits, leaving five-inch-deep dents in her armor plating. One shell exploded by the ship's sheep pen, another blew up the captain's cabin, and a third landed fizzing at the feet of Gunner Israel Harding, then standing at the entrance to the magazine and its twenty-five tons of gunpowder. Harding picked up the shell—"It was heavy, hot and grimy"—and dropped it in a bucket of water. He won the Victoria Cross.[57]

The fleet's bombardment was unrelenting. Stray British shells burst all over the city, hitting the Ras el-Tin harem, the German Consulate, the police headquarters, several schools, a convent, a synagogue, and many private houses. At 1400, with the gunners on the walls either killed by direct hits or fleeing their stations, Seymour dispatched a landing party to spike the guns of the westernmost fort. But by then, the populace had realized that the British only intended to bombard the harbor forts, and not the city behind them.

"Death to the Christians!" went up again. Children beating petroleum tins paraded down the Rue Sharif Pasha beneath a green flag, calling on Allah and his Prophet. Looters, arsonists, and angry soldiers descended on the European quarter. With stray shells exploding around them, they attacked shop shutters and doors with hammers. They threw petroleum-soaked cloths into the houses, or stacked mattresses in the doorways, burning alive the inhabitants or killing them if they tried to flee. By 1600, the British Consulate was on fire. By 1715, when Admiral Seymour called "Cease fire," the European quarters and Ismail's avenues had gone up in smoke.[58]

Omar Lutfi Pasha ordered the inhabitants to quit the city. A tide of people struggled through the Rosetta and Moharrem Bey gates, some in stolen carriages, others lugging mirrors, sofas, and gilt chairs. Bedouin gathered outside the gates to rob the fugitives. The open space before the city walls turned into a mass of looters, brawling over the spoils. When the women and children of the royal harem arrived, all turned on them, hacking off hands and ears to get at the khedive's jewelry. Behind them, Alexandria went up in smoke.

The fire took two days to burn out. When Admiral Seymour's marines ventured a landing, they found devastation. Decomposing bodies bobbed in the harbor and swelled in the streets. The damage ran into millions. The entire European Quarter had been destroyed, and five consulates lay in ruins. In Place Mehmet Ali, where only the equestrian statue had survived the flames, looters scavenged in smoldering rubble. Seymour appointed Lord Charles Beresford, captain of the *Condor,* as Alexandria's temporary chief of police. Bluejackets armed with Gatling guns took over the city. When they caught a Sudanese slave looting in Place Mehmet Ali, they tied him to a tree and shot him. Order had returned.[59]

"The fire is a sad misfortune," admitted Gladstone. He tried to persuade the sultan that the bombardment had "made a clear way" for Turkish troops, but no troops were offered. The French did not help, either. At least the cabinet had held together. Only John Bright followed his Quaker conscience and resigned. Yet though the bombardment had eased tensions in Downing Street, it had worsened the situation in Egypt. The rebels refused to surrender, and Gladstone's imperial adventure moved to its second phase. Britain had gone in alone, and had to finish the job alone. It was time to send in the troops.[60]

"Instructions to Wolseley: Put down Arabi and establish Khedive's power."[61]

6

The Wind and the Whirlwind
1883

Adjutant General Sir Garnet Wolseley.

I have always been ambitious, and thought that the higher I mounted the military ladder, the better I should serve the idol I have worshipped since I was capable of understanding what love of country meant. To see England great is my highest aspiration, and to lead in contributing to that greatness is my only real ambition.

—Adjutant General Sir Garnet Wolseley, 1882[1]

O N T H E *Calabria* with a cargo of Guardsmen and a heavy cold, Sir Garnet Wolseley rested in his cabin. He had picked up a chill while paying a farewell visit to the queen at Osborne Castle on the Isle of Wight. On the way back to London, it had turned into a fever. For several days Britain's favorite warrior lay bedridden, worrying that his rivals at the Admiralty might take over the Egyptian expedition. Escaping his sickbed as the fever broke, he had planned to take the speedier route, across Europe by train to catch a steamer at Marseilles. But the doctors had forced him to take the restful but tedious sea route all the way to Egypt.

Their representative on the *Calabria* was a rotund, red-faced pipesmoker in a too-tight uniform. He inspected the Wolseley bowel movement and sentenced the patient to a light diet and complete rest. For lunch, Sir Garnet ate the grapes Lady Louisa had given him as he had left London. He tried not to think of his "Dearest Loo"—"My eyes fill unpleasantly when I do"—but as the doctor had restricted brainwork to "light literature," he had little else to contemplate as the *Calabria* chugged south. Although the Wolseley brain possessed advanced faculties for romance, sentiment, and the Savoy operas, it relished most the heavy mechanics of military strategy, and the glory of their skillful execution.[2]

Slight and sprightly, with a blind eye from the Crimea and a temper like grapeshot, Garnet Wolseley was a self-made legend. As a boy, he had studied "every work on the theory and practice of war" he could "beg, borrow or afford to buy." As a young officer, he had been wounded in Burma and blown up at Sebastopol. He had fought the Mutiny in India and the Taiping rebels in China. In Canada, he had organized an expedition up the Red River against French rebels, conquering the "Mississippi of the North" with Canadian *voyageurs* and the rebels by logistical diligence. In the Ashanti campaign of 1874 and the Zulu War of 1879, Wolseley had found glory in Africa, clearing up the accidents of "forward" policy and leaving a trail of dead Africans.[3]

The public adored the peppery Jingoist whom Disraeli called "our only General." He was "The Man Who Wouldn't Stop," the fireman of empire, dousing border conflagrations with irregular warfare. His *Soldier's Hand Book in War* became the *vade mecum* of the ambitious officer out to chastise the natives on a tight budget. Everything was "All Sir Garnet," said his soldiers: in strict order. Gilbert and Sullivan lampooned the Wolseley method in *The Pirates of Penzance*.[4]

> *I am the very model of a modern Major-General,*
> *I've information vegetable, animal and mineral,*
> *I know the kings of England, and I quote the fights historical,*
> *From Marathon to Waterloo, in order categorical.*[5]

Wolseley's life was a pincer assault on the heights of glory, edging along the narrow paths of patriotism and promotion while treachery massed at his back. In his mind, the enemies of Britain lurked everywhere: Boers and blacks in Africa, mullahs and Russians in Afghanistan, Fenians in Ireland, Jews in the banks, Radicals in the streets, and not forgetting the French. The army had to prepare for the defense of the empire, but a coalition of high-ranking snobs and penny-pinching Radicals cut its ranks and funds. To save it, Wolseley was prepared even to pander to the man he loathed as the chief Radical, William Gladstone.

Gladstone's first ministry of 1868 had used the Crimean fiasco as a pretext for army reform. To create an efficient, professional army, Lord Cardwell, the secretary for war, had cut back the bureaucratic weeds and rooted out the sale of commissions. But Cardwell had left the upper branches unpruned. Queen Victoria insisted that her obese cousin the Duke of Cambridge remain commander-in-chief, and she rejected Cardwell's request to create a meritocratic General Staff.

Though Wolseley despised Gladstone, he valued army reform as a means of strengthening the empire. He campaigned ceaselessly to oust the duke of Cambridge, the "Great German Sausage." He intrigued at the War Office and whispered to the press. Cannily identifying the new staff college of Sandhurst as the "Grand Key" to promotion, he built up a circle of ambitious young officers: the "Wolseley Ring," a party within the army.[6]

The strategy of subversion backfired. Queen Victoria objected to the upstart general's vendetta against her cousin. Liberal politicians recoiled from his loud trumpeting of military answers to political questions. The Duke of Cambridge deprived Wolseley and his friends of the greatest prizes, high ranks in the India command. By 1882, Wolseley's star had ceased to rise. In a rare moment of harmony, Queen Victoria and Gladstone both distrusted him. Defeat at the hands of Afghans, Boers, and Zulus embarrassed the reformed army and tarnished the brilliance of the Wolseley Ring. The Egyptian expedition represented Wolseley's best and final chance of salvaging the twin destinies of the British Empire and the Wolseley career.

While Gladstone had fought his rearguard action against his cabinet, Wolseley had planned every detail of his campaign. He took no chances, insisting on the latest artillery, twenty-four thousand soldiers from Britain, and a further seven thousand from India. The shortest route to Cairo—from Alexandria—was heavily defended, so he would take the longer but safer route. From Ismailia on the Suez Canal, Cairo lay one hundred miles across the crunchy sand of the Eastern Desert. He would use Ismail's railway to resupply his troops, and the Sweetwater Canal to sustain his horses. En route he would smash the Egyptian army and silence his domestic foes. To Lady

Louisa, he confided, "I long for a real success to make the world feel that England has a lot left in her, and that her soldiers' strength and courage is unaffected by the influence of Radicalism."[7]

On the *Calabria*, the general ate an invalid's supper of fried sole and a bowl of jelly. He thought of his little daughter Frances, and the gifts he had promised her when he returned in triumph: a little pony, and the tip of Urabi's nose, cut off with the Wolseley pocket knife.

WHILE THE FIRES of Alexandria still burned, Urabi sent four hundred soldiers to surround Khedive Tawfik at his al-Raml palace by the city gates. Tawfik bribed his way out and defected to a British warship, taking Dervish Pasha with him. Almost all the notables backed the khedive, some congregating in Alexandria under Admiral Seymour's guns, others fleeing to Istanbul. The government collapsed. In the Delta, mobs of homeless Alexandrians attacked Jews and Christians, and *fellahin* tore up their contracts with the government's Greek moneylenders.

Urabi declared martial law. He told all ministers and officers to ignore their superiors and the khedive, and to report to him only. He formed a General Council of fourteen soldiers and administrators, and ran the country from a nightly meeting in the War Ministry. To ensure the people's loyalty, Urabi canceled all debts owed by *fellahin* to the government. Then he sent orders to the countryside, requisitioning all mules and horses and enlisting twenty-five thousand new recruits. The government *Gazette* announced a jihad against the British, quoting the Prophet: *Truly Allah has purchased a Believer's life and possessions so that he may attain Paradise fighting for Allah's religion.* Abdullah Nadim, Afghani's protégé turned Urabi's secretary, launched a propaganda campaign. In *al-Taif,* he accused the British of plotting to seize Mecca. In the countryside, he sent Urabist preachers to rouse the *fellahin:* Islam was in danger, and Urabi's party was the *Hizb Allah,* the Party of God. The mosques took up the call at Friday prayers. The momentous, millennarian events promised by the comet that heralded the turn of the Islamic century appeared to be coming true.[8]

Next, Urabi dispensed with the Chamber of Notables. He summoned seventy of Egypt's most influential nobles, merchants, religious leaders, and civil servants to an emergency meeting at the Interior Ministry. With hours to go before Ramadan began, only a handful of notables attended. Debate was furious and brief. The rebels quickly outflanked the rump of Tawfik supporters by claiming the supreme sanction of religion. Before the meeting even opened, Sheikh el-Ullaish of al-Azhar had called for jihad against the infidel trespassers, and his ally Sheikh al-Idwi had made the case for Tawfik's deposition.

"What say you of a Sovereign who, being named by the Commander of the Faithful to govern his subjects with justice, and to act according to the rules of Allah, has violated the compact and sown dissension among the Muslims, and has broken their staff of unity?"[9]

Once chairman Mohammed Abdu called the meeting to order, two Turkish notables tried to speak for the khedive and caution, but army officers shouted them down. Sheikh el-Ullaish spoke again for jihad, and this time Mohammed Abdu stood up and demanded the overthrow of Tawfik in the name of Islam and Egypt. Then he called for a vote.

Although the soldiers and clerics wanted war, the nobles, civil servants, and merchants were in no hurry to fight Britain, the sultan, and his appointed deputy the khedive. They voted for compromise: Military preparations should continue, but as the khedive's position was still unclear, no decision should be made on his future until he had been consulted. The meeting deputed a commission to go to Alexandria.[10]

With Admiral Seymour on his side Khedive Tawfik felt no need to negotiate his own demise. Rejecting the commission as illegitimate, he responded to Urabi's impertinence by sacking him as minister for war. The sultan backed him: Urabi must cease from challenging the Ottoman order, and must repair the damage he had caused by rebelling against it. The sultan and the khedive had both profited by Urabi's revolt, but now he was on his own.[11]

Urabi hid the sultan's letter from all but the General Council. Abdullah Nadim wanted to publish it in *al-Taif*, to show that the sultan had betrayed Islam as cravenly as Tawfik had. But Urabi would not let him. Although Urabi posed as a nationalist, he knew that Egyptian nationalism was strongest among the new elite: intellectuals, army officers, and wealthy Turks. The *fellahin* came out in support of Islam, not Egypt. If they discovered that their revolt no longer acted in the name of Islam and its caliph, they might abandon Urabi. So while Urabi continued to claim to have the sultan's support, and continued to endorse "Ottomanism," he worked toward another end: the establishment of a revolutionary government.

Calling provincial governors and officers to Cairo, he held a second, larger meeting at the Interior Ministry. Ali al-Rubi, founder of the secret Strong Egypt group that had seeded of the officers' revolt, raged passionately against the British and the khedive. To support Urabi was to support resistance and patriotism, and to defend Islam and Egypt. Who could oppose the cause of Allah?

The meeting did not dare to. It voted to ignore the khedive's orders, and to pass all authority to Urabi and his General Council. Soldiers posted at the doors made sure that everyone signed its declaration, sent to Constantinople in the name of "the Egyptian people" and "Islamic-Ottoman Egypt."[12]

Now a military dictator, Urabi dug in for war. Like Wolseley, he saw there were two likely routes to Cairo: from Alexandria, and from the Suez Canal. Urabi pulled his troops back from Alexandria, blocked the Mahmoudiya Canal, the city's only supply of drinking water, and cut its telegraphic and postal links with Cairo. While his headquarters at Kafr Dawar blocked the Alexandria-Cairo road, the capital's eastern flank lay exposed. Urabi suspected that the British would breach the Canal's neutrality; their warships had already been sighted off Suez, where they were poised to plug the Canal's southern exit. He and his generals had identified four points at which to block the Canal to all traffic, commercial and military. On August 16, Urabi's generals informed him that Wolseley had arrived at Alexandria, and they advised that he block the Canal preemptively. Urabi ignored them. He had the word of Ferdinand de Lesseps that the British would observe the Canal's neutrality.

When de Lesseps had heard that his greatest creation was in danger, he had hurried to Egypt and mounted a one-man diplomatic campaign. He assured Urabi that France would prevent Britain from using the Canal for military purposes. Urabi, whose vanity had grown in tandem with his authority, believed him.

Unlike Wolseley, Urabi had little battle experience and no training in modern warfare. Instead of blocking the Canal—and forcing the British to advance along the difficult, easily defended road from Alexandria—he cabled de Lesseps that he would not be the first to breach the Canal's neutrality.

Instead, he fortified the chokepoint of the Ismailia-Cairo road at Tel el-Kebir, where a military camp sat on a mile-wide wedge of elevated land, with the Sweetwater Canal to its south and soft sand dunes to its north. He expanded its defenses, digging trenches and artillery emplacements. His plan was to hold up the British, and force the Concert to intervene by sending Turkish troops who would be more likely to sympathize with their fellow Muslims than with the British. While Urabi waited, he spent more time consulting with Islamic ideologues from as far afield as Algeria and Tunisia than he did with his generals. Among his reading was a Mahdist handbook expounding the necessity of jihad against non-Muslims who had invaded *Dar al-Islam*. Even Blunt, his avid publicist, admitted, "Much of the time which he should have given to the secular duty of organizing the defense was wasted with them in chants and recitations." Urabi did find time, however, to treble his private landholdings.[13]

Wolseley did not take the bait at Alexandria. He had planned to bypass the city entirely, but Admiral Seymour's "criminal" bombardment obliged him to land and split his forces, in case Urabi made a move on the city from Kafr Dawar. On August 18, Wolseley took ship with the rest of his troops. Under cover of darkness, he raced for the Canal.[14]

When de Lesseps heard that the British were coming, he cabled Urabi grandly, "Take no action towards blocking my Canal. I am there." With no grounds for the claim, de Lesseps added, "Not a single British soldier will embark without the company of a French soldier. I take full responsibility."[15]

Urabi wanted to believe him. But in a war council at Kafr Dawar, his generals overruled him.

"Sincere thanks," they replied. "Assurances consolatory, but not sufficient under existing circumstances. The defence of Egypt requires the temporary destruction of the Canal."[16]

That night, Urabi sent an order to Ismailia for the dynamiting of ships in the Canal. With the telegraph interrupted by the revolution, his message took fifteen hours to travel from Kafr Dawar to Cairo to Ismailia. By then, British warships had moved up from Suez and into the Canal's southern reaches. At the northern mouth of the Canal, residents of Port Said woke in the small hours to musket fire and the rumble of artillery in the streets. By dawn, the people of Ismailia found their town seized by Wolseley's soldiers.

AT KHARTOUM the new governor-general, Abd al-Qadir Hilmi Pasha, received an order from Khedive Tawfik: He must ignore all communications from War Minister Urabi. Shortly afterward, Urabi told Hilmi Pasha to ignore the khedive's orders. Neither offered Hilmi Pasha the reinforcements he had requested.[17]

Tawfik and Urabi used the Mahdi's revolt against each other. Tawfik wanted to grant Hilmi Pasha his reinforcements; he wanted to draw Urabi's troops away from the Delta. Urabi refused to send them. He would do nothing that might help Tawfik, and he needed all his troops in Egypt, to fight the British, and to "maintain internal security." Urabi underestimated the Mahdist threat. Unlike Tawfik, he should have known better. Mohammed Rauf Pasha, the previous governor-general of Sudan, had resurfaced as a member of Urabi's revolutionary cabinet, the General Council.[18]

To win over Hilmi Pasha, Urabi sent telegrams describing imaginary victories over the British. Hilmi Pasha could not tell if he served an Ottoman monarchy or a nationalist republic, but when he read Urabi's claim that the Alexandria batteries had sunk the entire British fleet, he burst out laughing. Declaring for Tawfik and the Turks, the governor-general proceeded with the only possible strategy. He tried to take the war to the Mahdi without risking a military expedition.

Hilmi Pasha abandoned the Kordofan countryside to the rebels and fortified its garrison towns. He strengthened the walls of Khartoum, digging a ditch around its southern flank, and patrolled its streets with soldiers. He gave a year's tax relief to tribes that stayed loyal to the government, and offered them blood money: two pounds for a member of the *Ansar*, eighteen pounds for a sheikh. He hired assassins to attempt to kill the Mahdi with bullets and poisoned dates, and asked Tawfik to organize a letter bomb that might blow up in the Mahdi's hands.[19]

Although he could not take the war to Kordofan, Hilmi Pasha did take it to the Mahdi's theological territory. Handwritten Mahdist propaganda seeped constantly from southern Kordofan. To counter it, Hilmi Pasha mobilized the Khartoum clergy. The government's sheikhs obliged with the *Message on the Mahdi and the False Mahdi*, and some *General Advice to the People of the Sudan on Disagreement with Rulers and Disobedience of the Commander of the Faithful*. The sheikhs emphasized the rights of the sultan to the caliphate, and Tawfik to the khediviate. They warned that the Mahdi was an impostor, and that the wrath of Hilmi Pasha was fearful. They did not reject the idea of a Mahdi, only that he might be the Renouncer of Aba Island.[20]

"Our refuge," they said, "the refuge of all, does exist: it is His Highness the khedive and His Excellency the Governor-General."[21]

Their argument made no impact in the face of the Mahdi's swelling revolt. All through the summer of 1882, the garrison towns of Kordofan fell, as wave upon wave of wild tribesmen descended on isolated contingents of demoralized Egyptian soldiers. The revolt spread to Darfur and the Gazelle River district. Refugees poured into El Obeid with terrifying tales of suicidal savages armed with sticks and spears, climbing over their dead to fling themselves onto rifles and rocket launchers, massacring women and children.

The Mahdi's camp grew into the largest settlement in the Sudan. By August, over one hundred thousand warriors and their families had gathered around him. From sympathizers in Egypt, the Mahdi heard that the khedive had been deposed, and that the British had landed at Ismailia. He knew that the Egyptians could not afford a major campaign in the Sudan, and the British had no reason to launch one. This was the moment to carve out his Islamic empire. The Mahdi moved on El Obeid.

The garrison of El Obeid knew what to expect. Directed by their commander, General Mohammed Said, they had dug two concentric trenches, one around the town perimeter, the other around its core: the barracks, wells, food store, and arsenal. They built thick *zaribas* in front of them, raising earthworks behind them with loopholes for firing.

At dawn on September 8, as Garnet Wolseley edged toward Tel el-Kebir, the garrison at El Obeid squinted into the rising sun and saw the glitter of thousands of spearheads pouring toward their eastern flank. General Said waited until the *Ansar*'s front runners had almost reached the *zariba* before giving the order. A massive fire of rifles, cannon, and rocket launchers stopped the *Ansar*'s first wave. "We killed hundreds and thousands of them, though they continued to fall on us, fearless and dauntless." As the bodies piled up by the *zariba*, further waves descended on the trench. The defenders' rifle barrels became so hot that they had to wrap them in wet handkerchiefs. At one point, a wave led by the Mahdi's brother Mohammed burst through the outer trench and into the town. They were stopped at point-blank range by fire from the rooftops. When the human tide ebbed, there was "nothing but dead people heaped everywhere."[22]

The Mahdi had planned to mark the new Islamic century with a triumph. Instead he had lost over ten thousand followers, and many members of his family. The revolution faltered. The Mahdi was meant to be invincible, but infidel weapons and faithless Turks had stopped the *Ansar* in its tracks. Khalifa Abdullahi counseled retreat to the hills, but the Mahdi had no choice. His was a divine claim, and to moderate it was to abandon it. Instead, he revised his tactics; the Prophet had conducted sieges, too. The Mahdi sent parties to fill in the wells on the road between El Obeid and Khartoum. In addition, the voice of the Prophet spoke to him, advising that he reconsider his earlier aversion to modern rifles.

One night, a comet lit the sky just before dawn, a brilliant, narrow band of reddish light, terminating in a flaming nucleus as large and bright as Venus. The *Ansar* knew nothing of Professor Schuster and his Kreutz Sun-grazers. They could not know that for the previous two weeks astronomers in Auckland, Panama, and Cape Town had tracked its progress across the sky. To the *Ansar*, it was not the Great Comet of 1882. It was a sign from the heavens. Their leader was the true Mahdi.

"I HAVE RESOLVED upon fighting Urabi next Tuesday or Wednesday," Wolseley informed his "Dearest Loo."[23]

From Ismailia, Wolseley had edged forward forty miles, skirmishing with Urabi's cavalry until he came to the defenses at Tel el-Kebir. Cairo lay sixty miles away, but first Wolseley had to break Urabi's web of trenches. He had no way around them. If he tried to outflank them in a long, looping march around the sand dunes, Urabi could withdraw his army intact into a countryside crisscrossed with irrigation canals. But if Wolseley attacked the lines, the Sweetwater Canal and the sand dunes would force him to advance frontally across gentle pebble slopes. His troops would be in the Egyptians' view five miles before they reached the trenches, and the Egyptian artillery would blow them to pieces. The only option was "a new thing" that he had not tried before: to advance at night and attack at dawn.[24]

In the small hours Wolseley and his generals rode out into the desert. At first light, they saw Egyptian scouts riding out from the lines. It was 0545.

"Note the time," said Wolseley. "Our attack must be delivered before this hour."[25]

He picked 0500 the next morning for the attack. That night, his officers ordered their men to strike camp, but leave their fires burning. The men filled their pockets with one hundred rounds of ammunition and their water bottles with cold tea, and they stacked their tents and blankets by the railway line. Navigating by the stars, at 2300 they paused behind a low hill, the last cover before the Egyptian lines. The order of battle listed the risks: no fires, no bugles, no smoking, no talking, each man to paint a diagonal white stripe on the back of his uniform.

The plan was audacious and dangerous. They would advance frontally, the First Division on the right, the Second on the left, the Artillery Brigade in the center. The reserves of the Indian and Naval brigades would move up the wadi containing the Canal and railway line, keeping well behind the main advance in case they disturbed the dogs and insomniacs of the villages

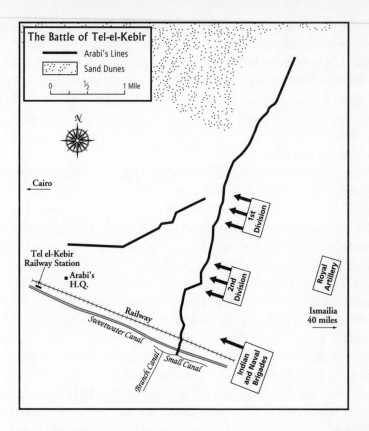

The Battle of Tel-el-Kebir

in the wadi. The Muslim dragoons of the Bengal cavalry waited on the far right. If Wolseley's plan worked, they could dash to Cairo in the long day ahead. If it did not, his men would be caught on open ground.

At 0130 Wolseley's whispered order to advance rippled down the ranks in hushed waves. A single soldier, drunk on rum rations and fear, started shouting in the darkness. Before the Egyptians noticed, his companions seized him, tied him up, and chloroformed him.

On the left, the Highland Brigade led the Second Division forward. In the center of the brigade, Major General Sir Archibald Alison halted periodically to check his position. As each order passed to the edges of the brigade, its flanks drifted out of position. Its line turned into a crescent, the battalions on its tips marching toward each other in the darkness. Alison halted them in time. Wolseley sent Colonel William Butler to locate the lost battalions. It took him half an hour to straighten the line. One mile more, and at 0300 they halted to wait for dawn and the reserves in the wadi. For over an hour they waited in the dark in total silence. Major General Graham and the leading troops of the First Division crouched only half a mile from the Egyptian trenches.

Suddenly, a streak of brilliant light appeared on the eastern horizon behind the trenches, as though dawn had come early. It was the Great Comet. A single shot rang out from an Egyptian sentry, and then the entire Egyptian line exploded into fire. The troops in the trenches had been waiting for them. Egyptian scouts had seen the British troops packing up their tents. There was no way back.

Major General Graham ordered the First Division forward. They fired a volley at 300 yards, rushed up and fired a second at 150 yards, then jumped and scrambled past a defensive ditch and onto the parapet of the Egyptian trench, bayonets fixed. The Egyptian troops turned and fled, their white uniforms blurring into the gray desert. Behind them, the Royal Artillery opened up, firing canister rounds of grapeshot into the Egyptian ramparts.

To Graham's right, Major General Alison marched the Highland Brigade forward, the drums beating a tattoo, the bagpipes' shriek mingling with the fall of Egyptian shells. At 150 yards, they fixed bayonets. A bugle sounded, Colonel Leith galloped to the front, shouting, "Come on the Seventy-ninth!" and the Cameron Highlanders ran cheering up to the trenches. Alone among the Egyptian troops, the Sudanese conscripts in the trenches did not run away. The first private onto the parapet fell back shot in the head, but the Camerons climbed into the rifle fire over each other's shoulders to fight hand to hand in the narrow trenches. They took the trench with bayonets as the pipers struck up "The March of the Cameron Men."

At dawn, the sun rose to reveal thousands of Egyptian soldiers, horses, and camels in flight. The Royal Artillery rained shells down on the flat desert. Then the cavalry swept in with their sabers, slashing at men raising their hands in surrender. Successive waves of infantry killed pack animals and wounded men. The plain filled with dead. "Anything seemed good enough to let off a rifle at," Colonel Butler admitted. At 0620, Wolseley ordered the Bengal cavalry to race for Cairo.[26]

Urabi had been asleep in his tent when the shooting started. Fleeing Tel el-Kebir on horseback without his boots, he reached Cairo just half an hour before Wolseley's cavalry. The revolutionary council had prepared a decree to be read at morning prayers, ordering that the city be set on fire, but Urabi knew he was beaten, and he countermanded the order. At sunset, the Bengal cavalry reached the walls of Cairo and saw a white flag. In the Citadel, four thousand of Urabi's troops surrendered to two squadrons of dragoons. The next day, Egyptian garrisons all over the Delta surrendered. In Alexandria, Europeans stopped trading and marched in the streets, crying "Viva Inghilterra!" as the bands struck up the Khedivial Hymn and "God Save the Queen." Just as Wolseley had planned, he had smashed the revolution in a single battle.

Steaming into Cairo station on a commandeered train, the victor took a suite at the Abdin Palace as the Highlanders pitched tents on Ismail's parade ground. "What a change in forty-eight hours!! From the squalor and misery of the desert, with all its filth and flies, to the cool luxury of this spacious palace. Yesterday living on filth, today having iced Champagne."[27]

Wolseley had failed to cut off Urabi's nose for little Frances—the nose and its owner were locked up in the Citadel—so he posted her one of Urabi's visiting cards instead. Lady Louisa received a "charming little book, done by hand": the Mahdist legal book that Urabi had read in his tent before the battle.

Ten days later, British troops escorted the khedive to Cairo. The city came out to celebrate with bands, bunting, and obsequious cheers. Tawfik trundled along in his carriage with his new friends and "tears in his eyes." Sharif Pasha and Riaz Pasha settled their differences to form a government. Only the mass graves at Tel el-Kebir and the wreckage of Alexandria attested that anything had happened.[28]

Protocol obliged Wolseley to surrender the seat of honor next to the khedive to the Duke of Connaught, who, though only a colonel, was also Queen Victoria's son. The architect of victory rode backward, next to the consul, Sir Edward Malet. Wolseley had been "very nervous" before Tel el-Kebir, but soon reverted to sour habit as the politicians took over. He griped that the Turkish reward—the Order of the Osmaniyeh, First Class—had recently been granted to the sultan's favorite bootmaker. Nor did Gladstone's gift of a baronetcy satisfy him. He felt it should have been a viscountcy. Gladstone had further cheapened the honor by giving it to the Swell of the Ocean for his part in the war.

"Seymour destroyed Alexandria," Wolseley grumbled, "I saved Cairo."[29]

"ANOTHER FLOOD OF good news," Gladstone reacted with delight. "Wolseley in Cairo: Arabi a prisoner: God be praised."

Wolseley's swift victory silenced complaints from bondholders and criticism from the back benches, and it gave Gladstone a chance to show that Liberals could be patriots, too. The prophet who had warned of "the egg of

a North African empire" now ordered the church bells to be rung and can-
nonades to be fired in the London parks in celebration of its delivery. The
next day, the *Economist* reported a "fresh great rise" in Egyptian and Turkish
Loan stocks. Parliament voted Seymour and Wolseley a baronetcy and
twenty thousand pounds apiece. The only sour note came from Blunt's
friend Sir Wilfred Lawson, who moved that "a vote of thanks should be
given to the Egyptian army for running away."[30]

When Wolseley returned to a tumultuous welcome at Charing Cross
Station, Gladstone and Granville met him on the platform. A "whirlpool of
people descended" on Wolseley, sweeping away the Grand Old Man and his
ministers. "If Garnet's campaign is supposed to have set Mr. Gladstone on
his legs politically, the return of the hero very nearly carried him off them
practically, for the poor gentleman was sadly pushed and pummelled in the
crowd," joked Lady Louisa Wolseley. Garnet went on to an audience with
the queen at Balmoral, her Scottish castle. This time, they got on much better. It turned out that they both loathed Mr. Gladstone and his Radical accomplices.[31]

Having successfully managed a war, Gladstone now faced the problem of
the peace. He wanted to restore the khedive to his broken throne, uphold
the bondholders' rights, and pull out the troops, but the invasion had destroyed Egypt's political infrastructure. Egypt had a broken army, an unpopular monarch, a wrecked civil society, and a rebellion in the Sudan. As a
Liberal and an internationalist, Gladstone could not bring himself to annex
Egypt into the British Empire: That would wreck relations with the sultan,
the Concert, and the cabinet. Yet nor could he pull out and leave a vacuum
that might endanger the Suez Canal.

"The difficulty, I feel at this moment," Lord Granville ruminated, "is not
that of persuading the Egyptians to do as we wish, but that of arriving at the
plan which we desire."[32]

Informal empire had indulged a khedivial tyranny that had crashed in
debt and revolution. The Dual Control had collapsed: "The parties did not
act jointly in upholding it." The only local alternative, the constitutionalist
movement, had been crushed along with Urabi's military government.
Britain's bilateral partners Turkey and France had both betrayed her in the
moment of crisis. As Wolseley put it with soldierly bluntness, Tawfik's authority rested only on British bayonets. Having broken the Egyptian state in
the name of security, somehow Gladstone had to rebuild it.

The only answer was an interim authority, with which Britain might "plant solidly western and beneficient institutions in the soil of a Mohammedan community." British soldiers and administrators must train up Egypt's failed institutions, and then withdraw, handing back a working state. The British taxpayer would cover the £2.3 million bill for Wolseley's expedition, but Egypt must pay the wages of the twelve thousand British soldiers who stayed on. Turkey would be forgiven: The sultan would keep his tribute, but lose everything else. France would be punished. The Gladstone who had warned that a British occupation would "bid a long farewell to all cordiality of political relations between France and England" now excluded France from any role in Egypt.[33]

With the confidence of a man settling between two stools, Gladstone imposed his model of liberal imperialism: discreet enough to calm the Concert and his conscience, but strong enough to give Britain complete control over Egypt. Lord Dufferin, the ambassador to Constantinople, arrived to prepare a constitution. The Wolseley Ring stalwart Major General Sir Evelyn Wood stayed on as *sirdar,* commander of the Egyptian army. Sir Samuel Baker's younger brother Valentine, disgraced after molesting a female passenger in a First-class railway carriage en route to Waterloo, arrived to retrain the Egyptian police. The ex–Dual Controller Major Evelyn Baring returned to inherit Sir Edward Malet's villa and tennis court. Although Baring had the rank of consul, Gladstone's arrangement for Egypt turned him into a virtual viceroy, the supreme link between the London government, the Abdin Palace, and the *sirdar.* Meanwhile, the Turkish aristocrats crept back into their ministries: Sharif Pasha, Riaz Pasha, and Omar Lutfi Pasha, who received Urabi's seat at the War Ministry as a reward for fanning the Alexandria riot.

To calm the Concert, Lord Granville sent a circular to the chancelleries of Europe, the first of sixty-six such protestations.[34]

"Although for the present a British force remains in Egypt for the preservation of public tranquility, Her Majesty's Government are desirous of withdrawing it as soon as the state of the country and the organization of proper means for the maintenance of the khedive's authority will permit it."[35]

Surveying the wreckage, Lord Dufferin had no illusions about the immensity of the task facing Britain: "For some time to come, European assistance in the various departments of Egyptian administration will be absolutely necessary."[36]

Turning to the "proper means," Lord Dufferin's constitution was a masterpiece of enlightened despotism. Justice would be fairer—the police would be retrained, the courts reorganized, the army kept out of politics—but power would not be shared. He reduced the Chamber of Notables to forty-six members, with advisory powers only, just as Khedive Ismail had planned. The Chamber communicated the national will to a Legislative Council, which passed it onto a Council of Ministers, who told the khedive, who asked Evelyn Baring, who checked if Egypt could afford it. Opinion flowed upward, but all power remained at the top.

Lord Dufferin advised Tawfik to declare an amnesty for all junior officers and other ranks that had taken part in the revolution, and to establish a commission of inquiry. Tawfik had no choice but to accept this puppetry, but he and Riaz Pasha wanted revenge. They intended to execute Urabi and destroy the constitutionalists forever.

"The Egyptians are serpents," said Riaz, "and the way to prevent serpents from propagating is to crush them underfoot."[37]

Within weeks, his officers had bagged twelve hundred suspects, many of them innocents denounced by their neighbors. The charges included "stirring up the public," "assisting the rebels," and "dressing up dogs to imitate Sir Garnet Wolseley and then shooting at them." The guards extracted evidence against Urabi with thumbscrews and the *kourbash*. The prisons overflowed, and dysentery broke out. Touring the cells, Tawfik's eunuchs spat in the faces of Mohammed Abdu and other ringleaders. The local Europeans called for executions.[38]

Gladstone wanted the Egyptians to dispose of Urabi quickly, but Wilfrid Blunt had ensured that his hero could not be executed quietly. With A. M. Broadley, a lawyer in the consular courts at Tunis and occasional stringer for the *Times,* Blunt had formed an Urabi Defense Fund and hired a sympathetic London lawyer, Mark Napier. The Urabi Defense Fund paid Napier's costs, and not all the donors were Radicals. They included Lord Randolph Churchill, "Chinese" Gordon, and many others incensed by the imminent show trial. Tawfik and Sultan Abdul Hamid had both used Urabi against the British for their own ends. Now they were collaborating on a judicial murder. It seemed unlikely that the trial would be fair. When Broadley and Napier arrived at Cairo, the Egyptian government refused to allow them access to Urabi and returned their letters unopened. The European liberal press started comparing Urabi to an "African Garibaldi."[39]

The trial began on the last day of October 1882, in the court next to the Mattatias Building. It swiftly turned into a farce. For the government, the French lawyer Borelli Bey charged Urabi with setting fire to Alexandria following the British bombardment; inciting the people to civil war; and treason against the sultan and the khedive. For Urabi, Mark Napier swiftly demonstrated that his client had played no role in the burning of Alexandria. He also produced Urabi's private papers, hidden from Riaz's policemen by Urabi's wife, and demonstrated the sultan's covert encouragement of Urabi's revolution. Napier then announced his intention to summon four hundred witnesses in Urabi's defense.

Tawfik did not want his role in the Alexandria riot to come to light. Gladstone did not want a drawn-out circus. The Defense Fund could not afford one. Defense and prosecution agreed to a deal out of court. Only Mahmoud Sami al-Barudi, Urabi, and their army inner circle would be tried. The charges would be reduced from treason to rebellion, and though a death sentence would be passed, Tawfik would commute it to exile. Lord Dufferin convinced Tawfik to accept this compromise. Gladstone wondered if Hong Kong was far enough from Egypt, but accepted Ceylon as the site of exile.

At 0900 on December 4, 1882, armed guards took Urabi from the Citadel to the courtroom. Thin and pale, in a dark greatcoat and a graying beard, Urabi had aged in his cell. The charges were heard, his lawyers pleaded "Guilty," the sentence was read and commuted. Mrs. Napier rushed over with a bouquet of white roses, to loud hisses from the Europeans and Turks in the gallery. The court had been in session for six minutes. The artist from the *Graphic* barely had time for his sketch.

Late at night on December 26, a sealed train took Urabi, Barudi, and four colonels to Suez. Accompanied by sixty women, children, and servants, and thirty men from the Sixtieth Rifles, they boarded the steamer *Mareotis*. As they sailed for Ceylon, further decrees exiled most of their minor accomplices to Massowa, Suakin, and other distant, inclement Sudanese garrisons.

The revolution had been erased. Tawfik and the British were more in control than ever. Three days later, Gladstone sat down to compile his annual accounts. His "Egyptians," the underperforming loan stocks that comprised nearly 40 percent of his portfolio, had risen to a record high.[40]

At El Obeid, the defensive trench around the town turned into an open grave filled with decaying bodies. For three months, the defenders had worked their way down the food chain: camels, cattle, donkeys, mice, locusts, and cockroaches. By the end of the year, they grubbed in the earth for ant nests, boiled the leather of their shoes, and picked through animal feces for undigested scraps. Scurvy and dysentery broke out. Refugees lay dying in the streets. At their loopholes, soldiers died from exhaustion and sickness. The air stank with putrefaction, and the sky blackened with hundreds of birds. Carrion-kites grew so bloated from gorging on the dead that they could no longer fly. Soldiers killed and ate them, stomachs and all.[41]

From beyond the trench, the Dervishes mocked the defenders for eating dog's meat, and experimented with their new rifles. When the Mahdi caught smugglers bringing food to El Obeid, he cut off their right hands, tied the stumps to their necks, and paraded them around his camp. The *Ansar* had plenty of food, and had slaughtered a feeble relief expedition from Khartoum. El Obeid could not resist for long.[42]

General Mohammed Said wanted to blow up the arsenal and most of the town and its defenders with it, but his officers preferred to take their chances in a jibba. On January 19, 1883, he surrendered. Barely half of his garrison staggered out of the lines with him. They stood in the heat as the *Ansar* stripped them of their valuables, then watched as the Dervishes climbed over the bodies in the trench to rob the town. The capital of Kordofan, El Obeid was stocked with the profits of the slave and ivory trades. The Mahdi looted it systematically. He posted guards outside every large house to prevent its inhabitants from escaping. To find out where valuables had been hidden, his men flogged children, servants, and slaves. For two weeks they tortured the inhabitants, emerging loaded with gold, silver, and jewelry.

The booty included thousands of slaves, six thousand Remington rifles, and five artillery pieces. In General Said's house alone, they found gold worth six thousand pounds. The Mahdi's generals embellished their filthy jibbas with silk and their sword hilts with silver, exchanging the life of poverty for harems and divans. When everything had been stolen, they hacked Mohammed Said Pasha to death with axes. They killed his deputy Ali Sharif Bey in front of his wife and children. An executioner tried to decapitate him with a sword, but failed, so a mob threw him down a well, crowding around its mouth to watch him drown. After these killings, most Egyptian conscripts promptly switched sides, swapping their uniforms for the jibba.[43]

Having revised his aversion to infidel technology, the Mahdi issued the six thousand Remingtons to Khalifa Abdullahi and his Baggara. A compliant Egyptian artillery officer drilled the Mahdi's gunners. Like the Turks, the Mahdi forced black slaves into his ranks. They formed a new wing of the army, the *Jihadiya,* his holy warriors. He would need them and his new arsenal in the next stage of the jihad. Immediately after the surrender of El Obeid, the Prophet had appeared to the Mahdi and ordered him to sacrifice three cows to celebrate the conquest of Kordofan. He returned a few nights later with a strategy for conquering the entire Ottoman Empire.

"As you have prayed in the mosque of Obeid, so you will also pray at Khartoum, then you will pray in the mosque at Berber" (the junction of the White Nile and the overland route to the Red Sea ports), "then in the Kaba of Mecca, then in Medina, then in the mosque at Cairo, then in the mosque at Jerusalem, then in the mosque of Iraq" (at the Shia center of Samarra), "and finally in the mosque of al-Kufa," the Shia shrine at Najaf.[44]

The Prophet's strategy bore remarkable resemblance to the plans of previous enemies of the Ottoman Empire. Mehmet Ali, Napoleon, and the czars had all planned to sever its provinces one by one, leaving a limbless Turkish torso at Constantinople. The Mahdi would begin at the weakest points: remote Sudan and puritan Arabia, where the Wahhabis would help with arms and legitimacy. Then down the Nile to Cairo, pushing the Turks and Europeans from North Africa, and on to the eastern Ottoman provinces. At Samarra and Najaf, he would heal the Sunni-Shia split, imposing his caliphate on the entire Islamic world.

The Mahdi had never been out of the Sudan, had never made the *haj* to Mecca, and knew nothing of the blurry world beyond the borders of Islam. But his theological mandate obliged this rhetoric of world domination. Even as he consolidated his local success, concentrating on Kordofan and leaving Khartoum for later, he planned in global terms. He now received visitors from as far afield as Tripoli, Mecca, and India. He corresponded with sympathizers in the Red Sea hills, in Damascus and Cairo, and sent his call to jihad beyond Darfur to Sokoto on the West African coast. As he had always believed, his visions had the power to create reality.

"I have been enabled to capture Kordofan and all the surrounding country, and Allah will also open your country to me, accepting me as the true Mahdi. Woe, therefore, to those who do not believe in me, for they shall all be destroyed. Why did you not set forth to help the jihad as soon as you heard of me? Are you afraid of the Turks and their strength? Are you not aware that all their armies must fall into my hands? Do you not know that all the infidels will be destroyed by us? Do you not believe that I am the Expected Mahdi?"[45]

"IT IS NO PART of the duty incumbent on us to restore order in the Sudan," Gladstone insisted. "It is politically connected with Egypt in consequence of its very recent conquest, but it has not been included within the sphere of our operations, and we are by no means disposed to admit without qualification that it is within the sphere of our responsibility."[46]

To Gladstone, the only specter worse than permanently occupying Egypt was to be dragged upriver into the Sudan. He wanted to withdraw from Egypt, not defend its empire. Faithful to the necessary fiction of Egyptian independence, he insisted that British advisers were in Egypt at Tawfik's request. He could not admit that Britain, having taken over the government of Egypt, now bore responsibility for the Sudan. Like Granville, he preferred to concentrate on the more appetizing aspects of the Egyptian problem: rebuilding the international consensus and totting up the indemnity that Egypt should pay for the property lost at Alexandria.

Within weeks of the British takeover, reports arrived in London of a hidden catastrophe in the Sudan. All of Lord Granville's correspondents advised urgent action. Sir Charles Wilson, military attaché at the Cairo embassy, recommended abandoning Darfur and Kordofan to the Mahdi. Sharif Pasha and Omar Lutfi Pasha backed him, and both requested that British officers supervise whatever survived of the Egyptian Sudan. On the other extreme, Lord Dufferin suggested Egypt be forced to draw a line in the sand at Wadi Halfa, abandoning totally a failed empire that had proved "a constant drain upon the Egyptian resources." Diplomatically straddling the middle ground, the outgoing Cairo consul Sir Edward Malet restated the Foreign Office's position back to the foreign secretary: The Egyptians should be encouraged to take all possible measures to repress the revolt, but "without aid or advice from Her Majesty's Government." This sounded more sensible than it was. Egypt had no army with which to fight the Mahdi.[47]

Nevertheless, Lord Granville endorsed it. He had little choice. Khedive Tawfik refused to abandon the Sudan. He had already lost his dignity to Urabi and his kingdom to the British. He would not surrender his empire to the Mahdi. He spurned his ministers' advice that he save the core of the Sudan by surrendering Kordofan and Darfur to the Mahdi. Instead, he ordered Omar Lutfi Pasha to recruit a new army and asked for British officers to command an Egyptian expedition to Kordofan.

Sir Edward Malet found the compromise that gave Tawfik his British officers without breaching the British policy of nonintervention. Several retired officers had contacted Malet, offering their services to the new Egyptian army and police force. Why not pick a handful of these retirees and adventurers and recommend them to the Egyptians? Once again,

Scenes from Ismail's Egypt: (*top*) The Cairo citadel and the graves of the Mamelukes; (*middle*) lunchtime traffic outside Cairo's new railway station; (*bottom*) Place Mehmet Ali at Alexandria, with its cab rank, equestrian statue, and stock exchange.

4

Scenes from Ismail's Sudan: (*above*) Native sheikhs at Khartoum; (*below*) the subjects who stocked the slave trade.

(*Left*) Sultan Abdul Aziz, Ismail's rival for foreign credit; (*below*) Nubar Pasha, architect of the khedivial finances.

(*Left*) Sir Samuel Baker, pioneer of Ismail's rule in Equatoria; (*below*) Khedive Tawfik, inheritor of Ismail's empire and debts.

8

9

11

The Eastern Question: (*above left*) Sultan Abdul Halim II, caught between European strategists and domestic reformers; (*above right*) Queen Victoria, proprietor and enthusiast of empire; (*right*) Benjamin Disraeli, the prime minister who bought Ismail's shares in the Suez Canal and dubbed Victoria the Empress of India.

12

13

"Egypt for the Egyptians!": (*above left*) Colonel Ahmed Urabi; (*above right*) his patron Mahmoud Sami al-Barudi; (*left*) their supporters Wilfrid and Lady Anne Blunt.

15

"Attack the enemy's batteries": (*left*) Admiral Sir Beauchamp Seymour, "The Swell of the Ocean"; (*below*) Rue Rosetta, Alexandria, after the bombardment and riots.

16

17

Jihad in the Sudan: (*left*) Mahdist warriors in their decorated jibbas; (*below*) the officers of the Hicks Expedition. Hicks sits second from right, Colonel John Colborne of the *Daily News* sits at the far left, and Colonel Farquahar stands second from left.

18

1

20

21

22

(*Above left*) The archslaver Zubair Rahmat in his pasha's uniform; (*above right*) Osman Digna, the Mahdi's opportunist ally in the Red Sea hills; (*left*) a Hadendowa warrior, or "Fuzzy-Wuzzy."

23

The ministers who sent Gordon to the Sudan for the last time: (*above*) Lord Granville and (*right*) Lord Hartington.

24

The making of a legend:
General Gordon's Last Stand
by William Joy.

"Too Late!": Britannia bereft on
the cover of *Punch* magazine.

Scramblers for Africa: (*left*) Leopold II, King of the Belgians; (*below*) the sporting Lord Rosebery, lampooned in *Punch* as "A Doubtful Stayer."

27

'A DOUBTFUL "STAYER."

L-by. "YOU AIN'T GOT MUCH OF A MOUNT, GUV'NOR!"
R-s-b-ry. "PE'APS NOT,—BUT I'LL RIDE HIM FOR ALL HE'S, WORTH!"

28

29

"From the Atlantic to the Red Sea":
(*above*) French foreign minister Théophile
Delcassé; (*right*) Captain Jean-Baptiste
Marchand, dreaming of Fashoda.

30

31

The modern traveler: British officers, Egyptian soldiers, and Sudanese laborers take a break from laying the Sudan Military Railway, 1897.

32

"A very *Good* Friday": Kitchener's intelligence officer Colonel Reginald Wingate smokes a cheroot as he interrogates the wounded Mahdist emir Mahmoud Ahmed after the Battle of the Atbara, April 8, 1897.

"Of course, there would be a charge":
Second Lieutenant Winston Spencer
Churchill in the uniform of the Fourth
Hussars, 1895.

33

"Old Mac": Major General Hector
MacDonald, whose Egyptian and
Sudanese troops broke the khalifa's
charge at Omdurman and saved
Kitchener's reputation.

34

35

Shell damage to the dome of the Mahdi's tomb, September 3, 1898, shortly before "Monkey" Gordon blew it up.

36

"Whatever happens, We have got / The Maxim gun, and they have not": The bodies of Khalifa Abdullahi (*center left*) and his commanders at Umm Debeikerat in Kordofan, November 24, 1899.

Britain sought to achieve its policy goals by renting mercenaries to the Egyptian government. At a meeting on the verandah of Shepheard's Hotel at Cairo, Valentine Baker Pasha pulled a name from a hat: Colonel William Hicks of the Royal Engineers.[48]

Tall, handsome, and polite, with fierce eyes and a long gray goatee, Hicks had been decorated in the Indian Mutiny. With no Sudanese experience, he felt "anxious" about his abilities and "overwhelmed" by responsibility. But he could not resist the hope of "some wonderful decoration" or "£10,000 *backsheesh* from the Khedive." Collecting eight officers from the bars of Cairo, a batch of khaki jackets hurriedly trimmed with gold lace, and a geriatric Egyptian general named Suleiman Nyazi Pasha, Hicks drank "the inevitable coffee" with Tawfik, and sailed for Suakin.[49]

An army sailed with him. Omar Lutfi Pasha had scraped together four thousand conscripts from the defeated soldiers of Tel el-Kebir. None of them wanted to go to certain death in the Sudan, most of them had lately rebelled against the khedive they now served, and many of them sympathized with the Mahdi. Their officers trusted them so little that they sent them to Khartoum separately from their arms and ammunition. When Hicks drilled them, he discovered that many did not know how to load their rifles.

"I have never seen such a disgraceful thing in my life," Hicks thundered. He sentenced them to daily training, but expected no improvement. "Here I have 4,000 of Wolseley's enemies under my command. He got great *kudos* for breaking them—my great anxiety is lest they should run away when I take them before the rebels."[50]

In one session, an exasperated Hicks ordered several conscripts to point their empty rifles at his head and pull the trigger, so that he might check if they kept the barrels steady as they fired. He was appalled that none of them even tried to shoot him. "Who would have thought a short time ago, when they were behind the trenches at Tel el-Kebir, that an English officer would be asking them to pull a trigger at his eye at two feet distance—and they wouldn't slip a cartridge in?"[51]

His officers turned out little better. "It is simply heartbreaking to try to do anything with them." The Egyptians were "dolts and fools," the British "helpless as babies." Several were alcoholics. "Walker is very seedy—he vomits after he eats." One, Colonel John Colborne, was a notorious Cairo soak who scraped a living as a stringer for the *Daily News*. The *Daily News* had also sent its regular war correspondent, Edmund O'Donovan. He spent his first four days in Khartoum getting violently drunk, "using inflammatory language to the natives in the bazaar" before he passed out in the street. When he woke up two days later, he resumed his binge with Frank Vizetelley, a roaming artist for the *Illustrated London News*. To Hicks's horror, the two staggered around the streets threatening the natives with revolvers.[52]

Suleiman Nyazi Pasha turned out to be a further burden, scheming against Hicks with the governor-general, Ala al-Din Siddiq Pasha. "I cannot tell you how disgusted I am with everything in this place. I am surrounded by intrigue, deception, and liars. The situation is too disgusting."[53]

Watching the long-awaited reinforcements, Carl Giegler Pasha reflected, "It would be difficult even if one tried to gather together again such a bunch of incompetents."[54]

After six months of futile drill, Hicks marched seven thousand men out of Khartoum. He planned to take the shortest route: south 100 miles along the west bank of the Nile to Dueim, then southwest 130 miles to El Obeid. The army marched across a waterless, treeless plain, the temperatures exceeding 120 degrees Fahrenheit. Colonel Colborne was soon invalided back to Khartoum. Even the camels began to collapse. Governor Siddiq Pasha turned up, leading the delegation of Khartoum merchants that he intended to impose on Kordofan once Hicks had killed the Mahdi. Siddiq Pasha and Suleiman Nyazi Pasha forced Hicks to change his plan. They were to divert south towards rumored supplies of fresh water, and then loop round to attack El Obeid from the south. Hicks agreed. The guides led the expedition south, into a terrain of thick mimosa forest, spiky acacia, and impenetrable tall grass. Suspecting that he was being led into an ambush, Hicks kept his guides under armed guard by day and tied them together by the neck at night.[55]

The Mahdi watched the infidels stumble into a trap. As scouts blocked up the wells in Hicks's path, a small force of three thousand *Ansar* moved up behind him, cutting his supply line and peppering the stragglers with fire from their new rifles. The Mahdi intended to defeat Hicks through geography. The cumbrous Turkiyya army would destroy itself searching for water. When it collapsed like an exhausted elephant, the main body of the *Ansar* would attack.

Helpless, Hicks watched his army disintegrate. A tight square turned into a long column. When thirsty soldiers broke away from the march in groups of four or five, Hicks's officers ignored his orders to bring their men back into line. His guides led him into thick thorn forests where the trees were festooned with Mahdist tracts. In the day, constant rifle fire from both flanks picked off his men, and at night, the Mahdi's men probed the *zariba*. After a stray bullet entered Hicks's tent and pierced the stool on which he sat, Colonel Farquhar wondered to O'Donovan of the *Daily News* where they would all be in a week's time.

"In Kingdom Come," replied O'Donovan.[56]

The net was closing. On November 1, men sent out to collect water vanished in the woods. At night, the Remington fire was so heavy that the soldiers could not sleep and lay hugging the ground while the bullets stripped the bark from the trees. The next morning, Hicks ordered them into a giant square: one battalion on each side, cavalry on the flanks, guns and stores in the middle. As they crawled forward, suddenly the *Ansar* appeared.

"All around, we saw Arabs innumerable. The whole world surrounded us, and flags were waving and spears gleaming in the sunshine."[57]

Hicks opened fire. Although the *Ansar* had Remingtons, Hicks had new American-made Gardner machine guns that, though susceptible to malfunction in desert conditions, could fire over three hundred rounds a minute. Unusually, they worked perfectly, blasting into the bushes through the day and night. When Hicks resumed his trek the next morning, he passed *Ansar* bodies piled six deep. Some of the Egyptian soldiers, realizing that the drifts of dead were only a fraction of the Mahdi's army, lay down and hid in the grass. When Hicks sent his staff officers to tell them to keep marching, the soldiers killed some of the officers.

"These are bad times," noted one of Hicks's officers. "We are in a forest, and everyone very depressed."[58]

No one had any water left. Hicks ordered the bands to strike up, but the fire from the hidden *Ansar* was so heavy they could not hold a tune. Men, mules, and camels collapsed from thirst. As they convulsed on the ground, groups of twenty or more *Ansar* fell on them, stabbing them to death. Hicks's guides now led him into a forest of three-inch thorns. Again the march stalled, and the battle raged through the night. At dawn they pressed on toward a rumor of fresh water, the *Ansar* firing at them through the trees from all sides. The woods were so thick that Hicks's artillery and machine guns were useless. As he ordered his force into a triangular shape and tried to wheel onto open ground, he found his path blocked by the main body of the Mahdi's army.

"Allahu Akbar!" the Mahdi called three times. "God is great!"[59]

The noonday sun was at its apogee, and fresh water within sight, when Hicks's soldiers heard a rushing sound, "terrible and sudden, sweeping like a torrent from the mountain." They heard the oceanic roar of the *Ansar* before they saw its spears. Thousands of screaming tribesmen poured out of the trees. The ground beneath the Egyptians' feet opened up: *Ansar* fighters had hidden in pits covered with brushwood as the lead units of Hicks's army marched over their heads, and jumped up at their backs with spears.[60]

Hicks's lead battalion disappeared like chaff in the wind. As the *Ansar* poured into the center of Hicks's troops, the battalions on either side turned inward as if seeking protection, frantically firing in all directions, killing Egyptians and *Ansar* alike. Hicks and his staff spurred their horses out of the slaughter, and the survivors of the onslaught formed up a short distance away. They emptied their revolvers at the *Ansar*. When the bullets ran out, Hicks ordered the officers to draw swords and the men to fix bayonets. As a final defiance, Hicks charged his horse straight into the midst of the *Ansar*. He swung at a sheikh in armor, his saber skidding across a chain mail shirt and slashing the sheikh's face and arm. A club struck him on the back of the head, a spear cut his sword arm at the wrist, and a lance pierced his body. He fell from his horse into a pile of bodies, blood pouring onto his homemade uniform.

The *Ansar* cut off his head and showed it to the Mahdi. His sheikhs queued to mutilate Hicks's headless body, each stabbing it with a spear so that he might claim to have assisted in the killing.

The Mahdi had not taken part in the battle. That afternoon he came to inspect the battleground. The destruction was total. The woods were strewn with the bodies of men and animals, arranged in three rough piles in the shape of a triangle. Further trails of bodies streaked in all directions, marking the paths of flight. Only a few camp followers survived. The Mahdi mounted the heads of Hicks and his officers on the walls of El Obeid. Now only Khartoum stood between him and Egypt.

Four days later, Britain's political and financial elite gathered at the Guildhall in the City of London for the annual Lord Mayor's Banquet. In his speech, Prime Minister Gladstone restated his Egyptian policy. Contrary to recent impression, Britain had no empire in Egypt, and it never would have one.

"We are about to withdraw. The order has been given. That withdrawal will include the evacuation of Cairo."[61]

7

The Unrolling of the Scroll
1884

Sir Evelyn Baring.

The dawdling policy, or to put it another way, the policy of not having a policy at all, is often very good diplomacy, particularly when it is carried out by a man of Lord Granville's singular tact, quickness and diplomatic experience. This line of action, which involves delaying any important decision until the last moment and not looking far ahead, is rather in conformity with English customs and habits of thought. It was generally practised by many of the statesmen and diplomatists of Lord Granville's generation.

—Sir Evelyn Baring[1]

GOOD FORTUNE ATTENDED Evelyn Baring like a loyal retainer. Born into the Barings Bank family, he ascended to office with such ease and grandeur that people called him "Evelyn Over-Baring." After his father bought him a commission in the Royal Artillery, his connections secured him the post of private secretary to the viceroy of India. When the Egyptian Debt Crisis began, Britain needed a representative with diplomatic skill and financial connections. Major Baring became Britain's commissioner of the debt. He left Egypt for India in June 1880, just as Tawfik's regime began to unravel, and returned with equal good timing in September 1883, just after Urabi's defeat. When the Foreign Office blamed Consul Malet for not having foreseen the obvious, Baring took over.

Tall and heavy-set, with a mustache that strove for gravitas and the plump face of one used to good food, Baring was the pivot of the new Egypt, linking the Foreign Office, Tawfik, and the British army of occupation. He kept his modest rank and villa, but his powers were akin to those of a viceroy. He interpreted Lord Granville's vague cables with mandarin clairvoyance. At his daily meetings with Tawfik's ministers, he steered them toward compromise. He explained Egypt's interests to Khedive Tawfik, never needing to raise the military threat. Cool and competent, he built a regime within a regime. Liberal in politics, imperialist in vision, and pragmatic in policy, Baring saw in Egypt the seed of a second India.

He saw no such potential in the Sudan. "The origin of the Egyptian Question was financial," he insisted, not strategic. Although Baring never forgot the Suez Canal and the India Route, he rejected an imperialism of "military or Jingo feeling, which simply desires to annex." Empire served a considered purpose, the stability of Britain's economy. The Sudan was economically irrelevant to Britain. It could not be turned to a profit, and the financial verdict was final. Neither the "superficial philanthropy" of the humanitarians, nor the "decided roguery" of "promoters and financiers," nor even "a magic wave of the diplomatic wand" could turn Sudan into an "Equatorial Arcadia."[2]

Nor was Baring's position at Cairo secure. Egypt's treasury was empty, its economy disrupted by the revolution. Tawfik's enemies plotted against him from abroad: Abdu at Beirut, Afghani at Paris, Halim at Constantinople, and Khedive Ismail from a hotel suite on the French Riviera. Nationalist rage still bubbled beneath the restored khediviate. In the summer of 1883, a clandestine group calling itself the Egyptian Patriotic League threatened Tawfik with terrorist attacks if the British did not withdraw immediately. The letters were signed "The Avenger." The police traced them to a Urabist cell. When they broke it up, "The Avenger" turned out to be Dr. Mohammed Said al-Hakim, the French-born son of an Algerian immigrant.

More urgently, within days of the destruction of Hicks's column, the Mahdist spark had leaped from the far west of Sudan to its east. Led by an erstwhile gin distiller and slave dealer named Osman Digna, the Hadendowa tribesmen in the hills overlooking the Red Sea ports rose for the Mahdi and the slave trade. They besieged Egyptian garrisons at Sinkat and Tokar, threatened the port of Suakin, and cut the Suakin-Berber road. The ports guarded the southern exit of the Suez Canal, and they linked the Sudan with Jeddah and Mecca. The Mahdi's shadow now fell upon the India Route and the Arabian provinces of the Ottoman Empire.[3]

Baring swiftly reversed his opinion, and recognized what Gladstone and Granville refused to admit. Although the Sudan had no economic value, Britain could not "separate the Egyptian question from the Sudan question": By taking over Egypt, Britain had inherited Egypt's empire. Through the autumn of 1883, while Hicks Pasha blundered around Kordofan, Baring discovered the alarming implications. Egypt faced "a serious religious movement" in the Sudan, and no means of defending itself. If the Mahdi took Khartoum, the Nile Valley was open all the way to the Mediterranean. If he took the Red Sea ports, his army could reach Arabia. The provinces of the Ottoman Empire would tumble like dominoes, and their fall would block the India Route.[4]

In the absence of an indigenous army, Baring saw no choice but a strategy of containment. To keep the Mahdi out, Egypt must withdraw from part or all of the Sudan and fortify the Red Sea ports. This required British officers to organize a defensible border and train new troops. So Britain must delay its withdrawal from Egypt until the Sudan had stabilized, and must provide officers and administrators. All Baring's partners in Egypt agreed with him: Khedive Tawfik, Sharif Pasha, *Sirdar* Sir Evelyn Wood, and commander of the British garrison General Sir Frederick Stevenson.

Gladstone had justified his unilateral invasion of Egypt by promising a swift withdrawal. If he reversed this policy, he opened himself to domestic assault by his own Liberal supporters, and ridicule from the Opposition. Privately, he admitted that British troops must remain in Egypt "till the danger has overblown." But publicly he refused to alter his policy, only the time required to implement it. "Our engaging in warfare to recover the Sudan is quite another matter, especially now that it seems so clear that Egypt has not the strength enough to hold it."[5]

Yet the Egyptians insisted on holding the Sudan, or at least its core territories. Egypt's governing class of Turkish landowners, officers, and merchants identified national dignity with Ismail's empire. Their authority had been shaken by the Urabi revolt, the British invasion, poor harvests, and outbreaks of cholera. Abandoning the empire would encourage the disaffected from Wadi Halfa to Alexandria and fan the flame of Islamic expectancy that Urabi had lit among the *fellahin*. To salvage what he could, Sharif Pasha prepared to abandon the western and southern provinces of the Sudan, in order to preserve the curved spine of the Egyptian empire: the long meander of the Nile Valley from Khartoum to Aswan. He asked for British, Indian, or even Turkish soldiers.[6]

"Very ticklish," Lord Granville advised.[7]

"The Egyptian government will find it impossible, with the forces at its disposal, to hold the Sudan," warned the British generals at Cairo.[8]

"Khartoum is the center of an important commerce, and belongs to Egypt geographically and commercially as truly as Cairo itself," claimed Garnet Wolseley from the War Office.[9]

"We are resting on the edge of a knife," Granville reflected, and took no action whatsoever.[10]

ON THE STEPS of Shepheard's Hotel in Cairo, a telegraph messenger slipped a piece of paper into the shaky hand of Colonel Colborne.

"Hicks' army annihilated."[11]

After Hicks had vanished into the hills of Kordofan, rumor filled the silence: Hicks had won a great victory and besieged El Obeid; Hicks and his officers had been massacred by their Egyptian conscripts; the Mahdi had captured Hicks and cut off his hands; only Mr. Vizetelley of the *Illustrated London News* had survived because he had sketched the massacre from an elevated rock. Unable to clarify matters, the Khartoum government sent out scouts. The Mahdists caught one and fed him alive to termites by jamming him upside down into an anthill.

In mid-December 1883 a survivor finally reached Khartoum and reported the annihilation of Hicks's army. The city panicked. A garrison of two thousand defended sixty thousand inhabitants, many of whom looked to the Mahdi to restore the slave trade. The whole Sudan, from Wadi Halfa to Equatoria, was held by only twenty-four thousand Egyptian soldiers, marooned in their fortified islands against a rising tide of rebellion. In the east, Osman Digna besieged the Red Sea ports that were Khartoum's lifeline. To the west and south, garrisons in Darfur, the Gazelle River, and Equatoria surrendered. In the north, the riverain tribes of Berber and Dongola stirred to join the revolt. The Mahdi had at least one hundred thousand warriors, with the same rifles as the Egyptians, and much more motivation. Europeans began to flee Khartoum while the road north was still open.[12]

After two months without a clear answer from London, Khedive Tawfik and Sharif Pasha grew desperate. If they did nothing in the Sudan, they lost everything. Sharif Pasha moved to save Khartoum and the Nile Valley. He ordered all southern garrisons to retreat toward Khartoum and dispatched Valentine Baker Pasha's new police force to secure the Suakin-Berber road. Then he begged Baring for British troops.

In increasingly urgent tones, Baring repeatedly asked London for "more definite instructions." The Egyptian government lay "absolutely in the hands of Her Majesty's Government," and it drifted "without any very definite or practical plan of action." Correspondents at Khartoum warned Baring that the city could not be held. Its granaries contained only two months' supplies, its populace could not be trusted, the tribes to its north might rise and block the overland route, and the Nile would soon fall and become impassable to steamers. The consequences would rebound on Britain and Egypt, and on Baring as Britain's man in Egypt.[13]

"If the whole valley of the Nile is to be abandoned down to Wadi Halfa," Baring warned, "the political and military situation here will become one of very great difficulty."[14]

Yet that was the course on which Gladstone and Granville finally settled. Forty-five days after Baring's first request for guidance, Granville ordered Egypt to abandon its empire in the Sudan. He deployed Britain's veto over Egypt's finances: Britain could not accept "increasing the burden on the Egyptian revenues" through military operations "of doubtful advantage to Egypt." Britain would maintain order in Egypt, and would secure the Red Sea ports. But Egypt must withdraw all Sudanese garrisons and "abandon all territory south of Aswan, or at least of Wadi Halfa." Gladstone, having disclaimed any responsibility for the Sudan, now took full charge of Egypt's Sudanese policy.[15]

Baring warned Granville that "only the very strongest language, and possibly a change of ministry" would force the Egyptians to accept this humiliation. Imposing a withdrawal meant surrendering Sudan to the slave trade, and "an increase, rather than a diminution, in the amount of interference" in Egypt. But Gladstone insisted. To preserve its untenable policy of nonintervention in Egypt, Britain intervened in the Sudan.[16]

Sharif Pasha refused the order. The Sudan belonged to the Ottoman Empire, and neither Egypt nor Britain could abandon it. "We have thousands of men in the Sudan, and nothing shall ever induce me to allow them to be abandoned to the miseries of Mahdi rule. I am sure I am right. Time and posterity will judge between me and Mr. Gladstone in this matter."[17]

Mr. Gladstone insisted. Sharif Pasha resigned in disgust. For the second time in little more than a year, Britain's anti-imperialist prime minister had overthrown an Egyptian government. This time, Khedive Tawfik made no trouble. "He is in very good humor, and has behaved exceedingly well," Baring reported. "He will do anything he is told."[18]

When Sharif's old rival Riaz Pasha refused the poisoned chalice, Baring summoned Nubar Pasha from retirement. On January 18, 1884, Nubar Pasha ordered all nonmilitary residents at Khartoum to make their own way north, carrying their own food. War Minister Omar Lutfi Pasha drew up a plan to evacuate the Sudanese garrisons, but when Governor-General Abd al-Qadir Hilmi Pasha read it, he refused to implement it. While the politicians in London and Cairo had debated the necessity or desirability of evacuating Sudan, none of them had considered its feasibility. The Sudan had no railway, and the roads were closed. The Mahdi was rumored to be marching on Khartoum. It would take months to move fifteen thousand civil servants, soldiers, and dependents by boat. As soon as Hilmi Pasha announced the evacuation, the whole Sudan would turn to the Mahdi to avoid massacre, and the escape routes would be severed.[19]

Nubar Pasha turned to his minister of war, but Omar Lutfi Pasha refused certain death at Khartoum. Baring had a policy, but no one to enforce it.

"The Egyptian government," he told Granville, "would feel obliged if Her Majesty's Government would send at once a qualified British officer to go to Khartoum with full power, civil and military, to conduct the retreat."[20]

With Sir Samuel Baker in gouty retirement, only one "qualified" candidate remained. To Baring's distaste, his name had floated around the "Sudanese question" for weeks. In spontaneous appeals to Lord Granville, soldiers, parliamentarians, abolitionists, and imperialists had all recommended "Chinese" Gordon.

"He has always exercised a very remarkable influence over wild, uncontrollable, uncivilised peoples," declared Sir Harry Verney, M.P.[21]

"His name alone would do wonders," advised Colonel Bevan Edwards.

"If the Mahdi is a prophet, Gordon in the Sudan is a greater," agreed Sir Andrew Clarke of the Royal Engineers. [22]

After Queen Victoria had joined the chorus of Gordon admirers, Lord Granville admitted that Gordon might be the quick fix he needed in the absence of a policy.

"Do you see any objection to using Gordon in some way?" Granville mused to Gladstone. "He has an immense name in Egypt—He is popular at home—He is a strong but very sensible opponent of slavery—He has a small bee in his bonnet."[23]

"I can quite understand there might be some advantage," Gladstone replied. "But for what? And by whom?"[24]

"IT IS ODD THAT, longing with a great desire for death, I am now quite well," Charles Gordon confessed to his sister Augusta.[25]

For four years the man whom *Vanity Fair* called "the grandest English-man now alive" had drifted around the British Empire. He had delighted in his liberation from English manners—"I nearly burst with the trammels which are put on one"—but nothing satisfied him. From India to Hong Kong, Ireland, Mauritius, and South Africa, his obsessions trailed him like an albatross. Life without the dramatic proximity of death had little meaning. "I strike against garden parties, archery and lawn tennis!"[26]

All that mattered was the moment of revelation, the Unrolling of the Scroll. He continued to find it in unexpected locations. In the Seychelles, the resemblance of the *coco de mer*, a local palm fruit, to the female pudenda, convinced him that the island of Praslin had been the Garden of Eden. He struck up a botanical correspondence with Mr. Scott of the Royal Botanical Gardens at Mauritius, sending photographs and drawings. Perhaps Mr. Scott would clarify whether the breadfruit was male, female, or hermaphrodite? And on that note, would Mr. Scott put him in touch with the doctor in Liverpool who had examined a pregnant man?[27]

With little else to do, Gordon went to the Holy Land. Restricting his imitation of Christ to geography, he walked around Jerusalem with his Bible in his hand, identifying eccentric locations for the sites of Jesus' life. "All events in this life tend to the willing or unwilling death of the flesh," he concluded, "Life is one continual crucifixion, whether we look on it as such or not."[28]

The collapse of the Egyptian empire gave grim satisfaction. "I foresaw the Egyptian and Sudan affair, and was not listened to. I am glad I was humiliated, for the things of this world will pass away." Gordon sympathized with the Sudanese and the Egyptians, not the corrupt pashas or the squalid policies of the Foreign Office. He detected a divine hand in the Mahdi's revolt. "I feel for the rebels, and am proud of their prowess, and Our Lord will work good for them out of it." Against all evidence, he prophesied that the Mahdi's revolt would end "in the suppression of the slave trade and slave-holding." In London, he snubbed an invitation to dinner from the Prince of Wales—"Tell him that I always go to bed at half-past nine"—but took breakfast with Wilfrid Blunt and donated to the Urabi Defense Fund. [29]

Revolted by Gladstone's adoption of Disraeli's imperial style, in late 1883 Gordon accepted an offer from King Leopold II of Belgium to develop the swelling Belgian empire in the Congo. Leopold II's territory now reached to within 250 miles of the Gazelle River. With Sudan closed by the Mahdi's revolt, Gordon believed that the Belgian Congo offered an alternative path to cutting off the slave trade "at its head." He appeared set to repeat his Sudanese vanishing trick, and this time for good. Agreeing to terms with Leopold II, Gordon took ship for Southampton, arriving on the day that Sharif Pasha resigned. Lying low at Augusta's house, where he could only smoke in the kitchen, he cut his last bond with England. On January 8, 1884, he wrote to the War Office and resigned his commission in the Royal Engineers.[30]

The next morning, the War Office came to him. A personal deputation appeared on his doorstep, comprising his War Office friend Captain Henry Brocklehurst and W. T. Stead, editor of the *Pall Mall Gazette* and pious imperialist. Gordon had returned only two days after the government's Sudanese problem had spilled onto the front pages. The *Gazette* had run the story even before the evacuation policy had been announced. The likeliest source of the leak was the War Office: Lord Hartington's private secretary Reggie Brett, M.P., was an erstwhile *Gazette* staffer with a financial interest in the paper. He was also an admirer of Gordon's.

The War Office had a different Sudanese policy in mind. Lord Hartington and Garnet Wolseley wanted a "forward" policy. The besieged Red Sea ports could not hold out for long. At Sinkat, the defenders were eating cats and dogs. The Egyptian government could only offer Valentine Baker Pasha's half-trained police force, but Gladstone and Granville resisted sending British troops. With the Mahdi's revolt spreading to the borders of Egypt and the India Route, the War Office could not afford to lose the army's Sudanese expert.

"I hate the idea of your going to the Congo," Wolseley wrote to Gordon. "You have had enough of liver-grilling climates, and the world does not seem bounded with the clear horizon that would warrant our very best man burying himself among niggers on the Equator."[31]

Gordon relished Stead's invitation to savage the government's inept policy. Gleefully, he demonstrated to Stead the absurdity of Gladstone's plan, and the immorality of abandoning the Egyptian garrisons.

You have 6,000 men in Khartoum. What are you going to do with them? You have garrisons in Darfur, in Gazelle River, and Gondokoro. Are they to be sacrificed? Their only offence is their loyalty to their Sovereign. For their fidelity you are going to abandon them to their fate.

You say they are to retire to Wadi Halfa. How will you move your 6,000 men from Khartoum—to say nothing of other places—and all the Europeans in that city, through the desert to Wadi Halfa? Where are you going to get the camels to take them away? Will the Mahdi supply them? If they are to escape with their lives, the garrison will not be allowed to leave with a coat on their backs. They will be plundered to the skin, and even their lives will not be spared.

Whatever you decide about evacuation, you cannot evacuate, because your army cannot be moved. You must either surrender absolutely to the Mahdi or defend Khartoum at all hazards.[32]

Gordon then demonstrated his profound ignorance of what had happened in the Sudan since 1880. The Mahdi's movement, said Gordon, was "not really religious, but an outbreak of despair." An amnesty and a fair government would placate the rebels. "If this were done and the government entrusted to a man whose word was truth, all might yet be re-established." As Stead left, Gordon gave him a copy of *The Imitation of Christ*.

"Chinese Gordon for the Sudan," ran the *Gazette*'s headline.

"We cannot send a regiment to Khartoum," Stead admitted, "but we can send a man who on more than one occasion has proved himself more valuable in similar circumstances than an entire army. Why not send Chinese Gordon with full powers to Khartoum, to assume control of the territory, to treat with the Mahdi, to relieve the garrisons, and to do what he can to save what can be saved from the wreck of the Sudan?"[33]

The next day, the *Times* reprinted the interview. Sir Samuel Baker, the big beast of Nile politics, stirred in his lair and endorsed Gordon's analysis. Queen Victoria sent a note to Granville, agreeing with Gordon, and Lord Hartington sent one, too. Even the Liberal *Morning Advertiser* agreed: "No effort that H.M. Government could make would be too great for securing the safety of the defenders of Khartoum and the remnant of the European population under its protection. If disaster, and possibly massacres, should overtake the column of fugitives from Khartoum, there would be an outburst of indignation from the civilised world."[34]

The following day, the *Advertiser* added, "It is not too much to say that all

England has been looking for the employment of General Gordon in the present crisis in Egypt."

"There is a storm brewing over the question of Khartoum," warned the *Pall Mall Gazette*, "which ministers will do well to take heed."

Now GLADSTONE FACED the failure of his Egyptian policy. He had invaded Egypt, then sacked its government when it refused to cooperate. He had redrawn the map of the Egyptian empire to suit British interests, devising a policy that the governor-general of Sudan considered unenforceable, and the Egyptian war minister considered suicidal. He could not rely on Turkey: "The Sultan's whole political nature seems to be so absorbed in vice that he is incapable of entertaining any subject in a straightforward manner." He could not orchestrate the Concert of Europe and contrive a multilateral shield for the occupation of Egypt. Although he privately conceded that Britain must occupy Egypt for "a few years" to give "confidence to the commercial class," he did not want to formalize British control. Apart from being "a grave mischief," that would be an embarrassment to liberalism, as "bastinadoed *fellahin* would be reported to Parliament at the rate of a hundred cases a week." As Britain slid into "the wreck of the Sudan," Gladstone forgot his humanitarian sympathies: "I care *more* that we keep out of the Sudan than who goes in." But he could not forget the press and the cabinet.[35]

On January 14, Gordon and Baker launched a coordinated attack in the Letters page of the *Times*. The next day, Gordon met Wolseley at the War Office, where he agreed to go to Suakin and "inquire into the condition of affairs in the Sudan." Hemmed in by Liberal opinion and the War Office, Granville reminded Gladstone that while the Sudan might be of minimal use to Britain, its loss would harm the government. "The destruction of these poor people will be a great disaster, and will of course create a great sensation here and abroad."

The government's prevarications on Ireland had already sapped its support among both Radicals and Liberals. It could not afford to be called unpatriotic by ignoring Baker, losing Gordon to the Belgians, and abandoning the Sudanese garrisons. Once again, Granville fell back on Gordon as a talisman. "If Gordon says he believes he could by his personal influence excite the tribes to escort the Khartoum garrison and inhabitants to Suakin, a little pressure on Baring might be advisable."[36]

Granville cabled Cairo, suggesting Gordon for the third time. Only the previous day, Baring had pleaded again for the dispatch of a British officer with full powers. Regardless of his reservations about Gordon, Baring judged that the government would give him no alternative, so he conceded.

"Gordon would be the best man," Baring replied, "if he will pledge himself to carry out a policy of withdrawal from Sudan as soon as possible, consistently with saving life." Baring still did not trust Gordon. "He must also fully understand that he must take his instructions from the British Representative in Egypt, and report to him."

Gladstone agreed, and added a further condition: "While his opinion on the Sudan may be of great value, must we not be very careful in any instruction we give, that he does not shift the center of gravity as to political and military responsibility for that country? In brief, if he reports what should be done, he should not be the judge *who* should do it, nor ought he to commit us on that point by advice officially given."[37]

The government had taken seven weeks to make up its mind. Meanwhile Gordon was at Brussels, and the *Times* had announced that he was about to become a Belgian mercenary.

"Come to London," Wolseley cabled.

At dawn the next morning, Gordon stepped off a Channel ferry. After taking a nap at the Knightsbridge barracks, he reported to the War Office. Wolseley asked him to return that afternoon to meet with cabinet ministers. It being Friday, Gladstone and most of his ministers had already left London for the weekend. Apart from Granville and Hartington, the only other available ministers were Lord Northbrook, who was Baring's cousin, and the Radical M.P. Sir Charles Dilke, president of the Local Government Board and erstwhile undersecretary for foreign affairs. No secretaries could be found to assist them in clarifying a policy. As no cabinet secretary was available, and as ministers were forbidden to make their own notes, there would be no minutes of the meeting. When Hartington suggested they wait until the next cabinet, scheduled for the following Tuesday, Granville overruled him. Apart from securing Gordon's services before the Belgians did, Granville wanted to avoid splitting the cabinet.

Waiting in an anteroom, Gordon watched a solitary clerk at his desk, and asked him, "Do you ever tell a lie?" Before Gordon could explain whether he was referring to his own experience as an aide or his strategy for the imminent meeting, Wolseley appeared. The ministers had sent him out to secure Gordon's consent for a principle on which, they said, the whole cabinet agreed.[38]

"Her Majesty's Government want you to understand this Government are determined to evacuate the Sudan, for they will not guarantee future government," said Wolseley, "Will you go and do it?"

"Yes."

"Go in."

By Gordon's account, the meeting was brief. One of the ministers, presumably Lord Hartington, began, "Did Wolseley tell you our ideas?"

"Yes. He said you will not guarantee future government of Sudan, and you wish me to go and evacuate it?"

"Yes."[39]

The ministers' accounts suggest a longer encounter, and that the cabinet dispatched Gordon without abandoning its constructive ambiguity over the aims of his mission.

The next day, Lord Northbrook would cable Gordon's assessment to Baring: "Does not believe in the great power of the Mahdi. Does not think the tribes will go much beyond their own confines, and does not see why the garrisons should not get off. He did not seem at all anxious to retain the Sudan; and agreed heartily to accept the policy of withdrawal."

"The upshot of the meeting," Northbrook told Baring, "was that he leaves by tonight's mail for Suakin to report on the best way of withdrawing the garrisons, settling the country, and to perform such other duties as may be entrusted to him by the khedive's government through you." Northbrook did not clarify what those "other duties" might be.[40]

Lord Granville's telegraph to Baring began with the same impression, and ended with similar ambiguity: Gordon had been engaged in an advisory role, but might carry out unspecified executive actions. As an adviser, Gordon was to "report on the military situation"; "consider the best mode of evacuating the interior of the Sudan, and of securing the safety and good administration by the Egyptian Government of the ports of the Red Sea"; and make recommendations for counteracting "the possible stimulus to the slave trade which may be given by the revolution which has taken place." Like Northbrook, Granville went on to imply the executive role for Gordon that Baring and the War Office had requested. "Gordon will be under the orders of H.M.'s Minister at Cairo, and will report through him to H.M.'s Government, and perform such other duties as may be entrusted to him by the Egyptian Government through Sir Evelyn Baring."

To Granville, Gordon's mission for the British government would be simultaneously a mission for the Egyptian government, with Sir Evelyn Baring as the link. This partitioning of Gordon's duties observed Gladstone's policy of nonintervention in the Sudan, while placating the interventionists at the War Office, and the mixed corps of imperialists and humanitarians in the press. Granville saw no potential for conflict in Gordon's simultaneous engagement as a British adviser and an Egyptian executive. After all, Evelyn Baring had shown how well such an arrangement could work.[41]

As war minister, Lord Hartington reported the decision to Gladstone. He did not mention the key elements of Gordon's orders, calming the revolt and extracting the garrisons. Nor did he mention that Gordon would be under the command of both Britain and Egypt, via the person of Evelyn Baring. He told Gladstone only that Gordon had been sent to report and make recommendations. Either Hartington had failed to follow the conversation, or he had chosen not to report it. Granville supported him in this omission, telling Gladstone, "Northbrook, Hartington, Dilke and I took a good deal of responsibility on ourselves, but I think we have acted within the limits of your views." Gordon, he added, had been "very pleasing and childlike."[42]

The ministers had engaged a zealot, but they hid their work in ambiguity and denial. Hartington assured Gladstone that they had followed his policy. Unaware that his ministers had misled him, the prime minister passed a pleasant weekend at Hawarden Castle. Attending church twice on Sunday, he read Wright's *Confessions of an Almsgiver* in the library that he called his "Temple of Peace."

Wilfrid Blunt would claim to detect a conspiracy in this: The War Office had manipulated the press, and a cabal of ministers had subverted official policy, forcing a deep intervention in the Islamic world. Certainly, Wolseley and the generals in Egypt agreed that the garrisons could not be withdrawn without military cover. Further, the four ministers who dispatched Gordon had all pressed Gladstone to launch the bombardment of Alexandria. But Hartington had attempted to delay the decision until a formal cabinet, hardly the act of a conspirator subverting his government. There was no conspiracy, only individual ministers sensitive to "sensation" and rivalry. Gordon's confused orders expressed the divisions and discomforts of a cabinet whose members, like Gladstone, recognized the need for action but did not want to take responsibility for ordering it.[43]

By the time Gladstone read his ministers' reports, they had hustled Gordon out of the country. As if to confirm that they did not expect Gordon to merely report and recommend, they appended to him the stabilizing influence of Lieutenant Colonel John Donald Stewart, an intelligence officer with Sudanese experience. From the War Office, Gordon went to the Chelsea house of Reginald Tilney, a friend from the Royal Engineers.

When a cab arrived to take Gordon to Charing Cross Station, Tilney found him in the nursery, in his muffler and overcoat, cradling Tilney's infant son.

The ministers were waiting for him at Charing Cross. Lord Granville bought his ticket, Sir Garnet Wolseley carried his bag, and the duke of Cambridge opened the carriage door for him. When the grandest Englishman now alive realized he had forgotten his wallet, Wolseley turned out his pockets and, finding only small change, gave Gordon his gold watch and chain. At eight on a winter night, the train pulled out for Dover.

"IT IS NOT my finding out, it is G-d's revelation." Gordon had tried to escape his destiny, but the Lord had summoned him to the Sudan. That night, as his express train hurtled across Europe to Marseilles, his mind spun with schemes. The next morning, when Lord Granville rose for breakfast in his Mayfair mansion, he found eight telegrams from Gordon waiting for him. Two called on the tribes of eastern Sudan to meet him at Berber to negotiate a withdrawal. Two announced him as governor-general, with powers to evacuate the Sudan. One restored the Sultanate of Darfur as a buffer between British Egypt and the abandoned Sudan, and another ordered the recruitment of Sudanese troops into the Egyptian army. Even before he had reached Cairo, Gordon was making policy in the field. And if the ministers did not grasp the implications of their orders to Gordon, W. T. Stead of the *Pall Mall Gazette* did.[44]

"At Last!" cried the *Gazette.* "The whole Egyptian question has been revolutionized in one hour. At yesterday's informal meeting of the Ministers at the War office there was taken one of those decisive steps that make or mar the destinies of Empires. Henceforth, we have full and undivided responsibility for affairs in the Sudan." And that meant Egypt, too. "Whether the public realises it or not, the dispatch of General Gordon to the Sudan, exercising practically unlimited powers not as Governor-General of the khedive, but as the accredited representative of the British Government, must entail, as a natural and inevitable corollary, the assumption sooner or later of a similar responsibility, as direct and as unlimited, for the affairs of Egypt."[45]

Alarmed, Granville asked Hartington, "We were very proud of ourselves yesterday. Are you sure we did not commit a gigantic folly?" If the garrisons really were a British responsibility, the only way to save them would be to send troops to Berber, not Gordon to Khartoum. If the garrisons were not a British responsibility, and the aim was to negotiate with the Mahdi, then the best emissary would have been a Turkish or Egyptian Muslim, not a

Christian from Britain, whose actions carried an inevitable whiff of annex-ation. And if a reconnaissance was required, then the reliable Stewart, who had recently toured northern Sudan, would have been a better choice.

Gordon was a cult figure, his name a panacea for the government's prob-lems. At the next cabinet, Gladstone and his ministers unanimously en-dorsed his dispatch. "Gordon's mission—a mission to report," Gladstone noted in his diary.[46]

Now on the Mediterranean aboard the SS *Tanjore,* Gordon shot off an-other memo. He would "restore" Sudanese independence by dividing the country among local "sultans," letting them decide for themselves whether to ally with the Mahdi or remain independent. To make this rule by divi-sion workable, the cunning slaver Zubair Rahmat must be kept out of the Sudan, preferably at Cyprus, or he "would in no time eat up all the petty Sul-tans and consolidate a vast state." Gordon was reheating old ideas: Both Colonel Stewart and Abd el-Qadir Pasha had suggested reviving the Sul-tanate of Darfur as a counterweight to the Mahdi, while both Urabi and Sharif Pasha had considered throwing western Sudan to the Mahdi as the price of keeping the Nile Valley. But though times had changed, Gordon had not. He still could not imagine that the Mahdi was more than "a mere figurehead," that his prophetic stance was more than an opportunist pos-ture, or that the impetus and passion of his revolution would allow him to form a coalition and advance "beyond the frontiers of the tribes who were immediately under him" to Khartoum.[47]

While Gordon risked his life, Evelyn Baring risked his career. He had asked for a steady hand, and had received Gordon instead. But Baring, cov-eting Egypt as his destiny, did not argue with Lord Granville. He accepted Gordon, and tried to contain his willfulness. When Gordon attempted to bypass sinful Cairo and head straight for Khartoum via the Suez Canal and Suakin, Baring ordered him back. He forced Gordon to observe the ele-mentary politeness of meeting his nominal commander Khedive Tawfik. He told Gordon bluntly that he was not to attempt to hold Khartoum, as he had advised in the *Gazette* interview. To Baring, Gordon had been sent to Khar-toum in order to abandon it. His job was to help create a defensible Egypt-ian border, and not to make "trouble."[48]

Gordon complied meekly. Reporting to Cairo, he apologized to Tawfik for his past rudeness. Immediately afterward, he and Stewart conferred with Baring, Wood, and Nubar Pasha at Baring's villa. Gordon received a budget of £1 million and two *firmans.* One, to be announced immediately, made him governor-general of the Sudan. The other, to be kept secret and revealed at a suitably stable moment, announced the evacuation of Khartoum.

"What a curious creature he is!" Baring wondered to Granville. "He is certainly half-cracked, but it is impossible not to be charmed by the honesty and simplicity of his character."

Gordon agreed with everything Baring said, and emphasized his assent to the withdrawal policy. But Baring still worried that Gordon was "terribly flighty," and capable of alarming reversals of opinion. So he drafted a set of orders, expanding upon the final clause of Gordon's orders from London and clarifying his duties for the Egyptian government. In these, Baring accepted Gordon's opinion that withdrawal might take "a few months"; that the territory should be handed over to a "confederation" of "the different petty Sultans who existed at the time of Mehmet Ali's conquest"; and that the Egyptian government should assent to surrendering its empire. To accomplish this, the Egyptian government gave Gordon "full discretionary powers" to retain the Egyptian garrisons, but only to accomplish the withdrawal "with the least possible risk to life and property," and not to underpin the power of the confederacy of sultans. The implicit gap between Gordon's advisory and executive powers now became clear: He advised for London, but governed for Cairo.[49]

Gordon's first executive action widened the gap. "I wish Zubair to come to the Sudan with me," he announced.

Only a day earlier, Gordon had identified Zubair as the greatest threat to his mission. Now Gordon had a "mystic feeling" that Zubair was his ideal partner. In the absence of British troops, Zubair was Gordon's best hope. Zubair was a skillful, violent politician. He was a direct descendant of the Prophet. He was a leader of the Jaalayin tribes who had turned to the Mahdi. "The Mahdi's chiefs are ex-chiefs of Zubeir," reasoned Gordon. "All the followers of the Mahdi would, I believe, leave the Mahdi on Zubair's approach."[50]

He was also under a death sentence for slaving and treason, and had sworn to kill Gordon for executing his slaver son Suleiman on the Gazelle River. Baring excluded "mystic feelings" from his calculations, but Zubair had pragmatic appeal, and with Osman Digna threatening the Red Sea ports, Baring had to do something. So he arranged a melodramatic reconciliation at which Zubair, reverting to professional habit, declared himself Gordon's "slave for life." Gordon prepared to leave for Khartoum, with Zubair to follow when Baring had secured permission from London.[51]

"Zubair's appointment was received here with astonishment," reported

Frank Power, the *Times'* man at Khartoum. "It will nullify Gordon and Baker's work."[52]

The hero of the abolitionists was about to pass Sudan to the king of the slavers. Though Gordon misunderstood the Mahdi, he grasped fully the implications of his orders from London. Abandoning the garrisons meant surrendering to slavery. The Anti-Slavery Society had already warned Lord Granville that Britain was about to shame its record as humanitarian enforcer. Hiding behind the pretense that Egypt still ruled the Sudan, Granville had replied that the government did not consider it "desirable to interfere with the measures which the Egyptian Government may be disposed to adopt." The Gladstone government needed stability in Egypt more than liberty in the Sudan. As Baring's friend Moberley Bell of the *Times* put it, at least Zubair would be a British client; when the crisis had passed, he would be "more amenable to humanitarian influence." This did not mollify the Anti-Slavery Society and its supporters on the Liberal benches. While Gordon packed his dress uniform at Cairo, confident that Baring would arrange for Zubair to join him, a humanitarian revolt against the Liberal government stirred in London.[53]

On the evening of January 28, 1884, Gordon and Baring rode through the Cairo streets to Ismail's magnificent railway station. On the platform behind him, Abdel Shakur, the new sultan of Darfur, levered onto the train twenty-three of his wives, sixty servants, and a mass of baggage. Gordon and Baring shook hands, both believing that Zubair Pasha would soon follow. Then Gordon bravely endured the embrace of Nubar Pasha, and boarded the train with General Graham and Colonel Stewart.

"I leave for Sudan tonight," he wrote to Augusta. "I feel quite happy, for I say, if God is with me, who can or will be hurtful to me? May he be glorified, the world and people of the Sudan be blessed, and may I be the dust under His feet."[54]

He had a year to live.

AT ASYUT they boarded a Thomas Cook steamer for the south. Thrilled by power and the proximity of the telegraph key, Gordon bombarded Baring with messages. Gordon's ideas rested on three contradictory assumptions. The first was that the Mahdi would not dare to leave Kordofan and attack Khartoum. The second was that if he did, then Britain would be compelled to fight back. As Gordon confided to the archaeologist A. H. Sayce when his steamer stopped for coal at Luxor, whatever happened, he expected to be "supported by troops." An Egyptian withdrawal from Sudan was bound to endanger British control of Egypt, so reinforcements seemed inevitable. This was the soldier's perception, shared by Gordon with Wolseley, Wood, and Graham. It was also the perspective of "forward" politicians like Baring, Northbrook, Hartington, and Dilke. Unspoken in the attempts to create a Darfur buffer state, or carve off Khartoum and the Nile Valley from western Sudan, was the expectation that Britain would maintain indirect control over the Sudan via Egyptian agency. "I have always contemplated making some arrangements for the future government of the Sudan," admitted Baring, as he implemented a policy intended for the opposite effect.[55]

Gordon miscalculated hugely. His fellow passengers Colonel Stewart and General Graham did their best to dissuade him. The Mahdi did not need to attack Khartoum. Its populace had only three months' supplies, and would soon be starving. Nor was it obvious that a British government, faced with a revolt on two fronts, would send troops to Khartoum instead of the Red Sea ports. A man of faith, Gordon ignored their advice.

His third assumption was that the Mahdi was a mere bandit. Gordon decided that he would go to the Mahdi, and treat him to a dose of charisma and a bribe of ten thousand pounds. Then Gordon and the Mahdi would divide Sudan between them as Egyptian governors, with Gordon governing the Nile Valley from Khartoum, and the Mahdi as governor of Kordofan. After that, Gordon could build up an army of Sudanese troops, sack their corrupt Egyptian officers, read out the *firman* announcing the withdrawal, and hand over control to Zubair Pasha.

Hardly believing his ears, General Graham repeated Gordon's own words from the *Gazette* interview. Even without Zubair's help, such a strategy would create "deluge, anarchy and slavery." Ignoring Graham, Gordon announced that when he had completed his Sudanese mission, he would proceed to the Congo, to force Britain and Belgium into an antislavery alliance.[56]

"Rather wild," Baring admitted to Granville.[57]

"As you aware, General Gordon is rather hasty," wrote Stewart, exasperated. "I shall be glad we are actually in Khartoum and face to face with the situation."[58]

On the last day of January, Gordon and Stewart left the river for the desert. From the village of Korosko, they would bypass the Second, Third, Fourth Cataracts and the great loop of the Nile, taking a 260-mile desert track to Abu Hamed. General Graham walked them out of Korosko, then said good-bye. Climbing a black volcanic hill, he watched Gordon, Stewart, and their Arab guides in his telescope until they shrank into dust specks. Then they disappeared.

As Gordon crossed the desert, his advice diverged from the policies of both British and Egyptian governments. On February 8, he informed Baring that Egypt should keep all the Sudan and rule it with Egyptian officers. He reasoned that as the khedive's authority derived from the caliph at Constantinople, his religious "prestige" might buttress Egypt against the "violent and protracted commotion" that would follow the evacuation of Khartoum. The revised British policy should be "evacuation, but not abandonment," and Zubair Pasha was "the only man who is fit for Governor-General of the Sudan if we wish it to be quiet." The next day, Gordon requested that Baring publish all his cables to Cairo. This decision would inflame public opinion in Britain more than it would help the British government. It turned Gordon's mission into a public drama. Not for the first time, he sought to use his admirers in the press to pressure the government.[59]

While these instructions were on their way to Cairo, Gordon attempted to make his recommendations a *fait accompli*. He offered the sultanate of Kordofan to the Mahdi. Gordon had been forbidden to meet the Mahdi; Baring feared he would be abducted. Regardless, Gordon wrote to the Mahdi at El Obeid and requested a meeting.

"Know, respected sir, that I would like to be in your presence on terms of the utmost affection and cordiality," Gordon wrote. "My intentions are nothing but good."[60]

No less respectfully, he wrapped the letter in silk, and sent it off with a parcel containing a scarlet cloak and a fez, the adornments of a Turkish governor. Giving the Mahdi the detested costume of the Turkiyya showed how little Gordon understood his rival. Sudan was vast, but to Gordon it was big enough only for one prophet. The Mahdi had to be a fraud. Gordon's offer of Kordofan derived from the same miscalculation. Egyptian rule was collapsing all over the Sudan. Why should the Mahdi settle for Kordofan?

Next, Gordon reversed his strategy entirely. At Berber, an insomniac Gordon woke Stewart at 0530. Having "pondered all night," Gordon announced that it was time to open "the Pandora Box," and proclaim "the divorce of the Sudan from Egypt." Before Stewart could stop him, Gordon revealed his secret, second *firman* to the local Egyptian authority, Hussein Pasha Khalifa, whom Stewart suspected as a Mahdist agent. The following day, Gordon declared Berber's independence from Egypt and appointed himself its first governor-general. Naturally the first question on the lips of his new subjects was whether the Egyptian government's antislavery ordinances still applied.

"No," he replied, proclaiming, "whoever has slaves shall have the full right to their services, and full control over them."[61]

Already beyond effective communication with Cairo, Gordon had exceeded every aspect of his orders. Making policy as he went along, he dragged the British Empire up the Nile in his wake.

At 0930 on Sunday, February 18, 1884, the steamer *Tawfikieh,* having survived Mahdist ambush at the Sixth Cataract, docked at the landing stage of the governor-general's palace at Khartoum. As the Egyptian officials waited in their dress uniforms, a crowd of frightened, grateful citizens gathered. When Gordon disembarked in his gold-fringed uniform, hundreds pressed forward to kiss his hands and feet. The *firman* restoring him as governor-general was read out, and he gave a short speech.

"I have come here alone, without troops," he told them. "And we must ask Allah to look after the Sudan, if no one else can."[62]

Then he ordered the building of a huge bonfire in the market square, piled with Turkish whips, stocks, and tax records. Stewart rustled up a celebratory banquet of turkey and Bass's Pale Ale from the stores, but Gordon spent that night at his desk planning his campaign. While cultivating a "mission of peace" among the local tribes, he would begin evacuating from Khartoum its fifteen thousand Europeans and Egyptians, described by Stewart as "the white element and the whitey-brown." Barring interference from the *Ansar,* he calculated that he could evacuate them all before the level of the Nile dropped in October. In the meantime, he identified at least a third of the population as Mahdist sympathizers.[63]

"I am watching these things closely, and you should not think I am ignorant of what is going on," Gordon informed the townspeople. "The troops of the British government are now on their way, and in a few days will be at Khartoum."[64]

This was a lie, and it bound Gordon to the people of Khartoum. "Pray do not consider me in any way to advocate the retention of the Sudan," he told Baring. "I am quite averse to it, but you must see that you could not recall me, nor could I possibly obey, until the Cairo employees get out from all the places. How could I look the world in the face if I abandoned them and fled?"[65]

Yet even if evacuation succeeded, it could not help Egypt. Gordon's recognition of the strategically obvious compelled him to recommend action unpalatable to the British government. "When evacuation is carried out, Mahdi will come down here, and by agents will not let Egypt be quiet. Of course, my duty is evacuation and the best I can for establishing a quiet government," he telegraphed Baring. "If Egypt is to be quiet, Mahdi must be smashed up. Mahdi is most unpopular, and with care and time could be smashed. Remember that, once Khartoum belongs to the Mahdi, the task will be far more difficult; yet you will, for the safety of Egypt, execute it."[66]

"MORE LIKE THE Arabian Nights than real life," Lord Granville wondered. Gordon was not the least of it. The bizarre events at Khartoum seemed less urgent than another Egyptian fiasco, one overlooking the southern approaches to the Suez Canal. At dawn on February 4, as Gordon had crossed the desert, Valentine Baker's thirty-five hundred policemen had sighted Osman Digna's tribesmen at the wells of El-Teb, on the outskirts of Suakin.

In mist and heavy rain, Baker ordered his gendarmes to form a square. Their fire was so heavy that the whole area had disappeared beneath a fog of gun smoke, and no orders could be heard above the cacophony. Digna waited until smoke occluded the field, and then launched his horde from all sides. They killed more than two thousand of Baker's men, many of them as they ran back to Suakin. On hearing the news, the seven hundred surviving members of the Sinkat garrison spiked their guns and attempted to reach Suakin on foot. The Hadendowa caught them a mile from its gates, massacring all the men and most of the women and children.[67]

Now only a small party of marines held Suakin, Britain's last foothold on the Red Sea coast. To compound the government's problems, a platoon of journalists reported on the siege from a Royal Navy ship anchored in Suakin harbor. With the India Route under threat, Gladstone's "forward" ministers rebelled. From the India Office, Lord Kimberley demanded that British influence in Egypt should develop "a more formal character." From the War Office, Hartington and Wolseley pushed for sending British troops to Suakin under General Graham. Queen Victoria joined in.

"A blow *must* be struck," she urged Gladstone, "or we shall never be able to convince the Mohammedans that they have not beaten us." She backed the patriots at the War Office. "These are wild Arabs and they would not stand against *regular* good troops at all. The Queen *trusts* Lord Wolseley's plan will be considered and our *whole position remembered.* We must not let this fine and fruitful country, with its peaceful inhabitants, be left a prey to murder and rapine and utter confusion. It must be a *disgrace* to the British name, and the country will *not* stand it."[68]

"Another element of trouble in the cauldron," sighed Gladstone. Over-ruled in cabinet, Gladstone suffered further humiliation when the Conservatives launched a vote of censure in the Commons. Why, asked Lord Randolph Churchill, was Osman Digna to be punished for one rebellion, and the Mahdi rewarded for another? And why, if Gordon had been dispatched to negotiate peace in western Sudan, should British troops make war in its east?[69]

For five days the debate raged. The government dived for cover, and its positions lost all consistency. Gladstone had previously insisted that Gordon had no executive powers, but now he announced that Gordon had been dispatched for the "double purpose" of overseeing an evacuation and creating a system of "petty Sultans." Lord Hartington, who had been instrumental in creating Gordon's executive role, now denied that Britain bore any responsibility for the Sudan. He claimed that the Red Sea ports, though technically part of the Sudan, were really a distinct geographical entity; therefore, intervening at Suakin could not be a Sudanese issue. Rather, as Gladstone explained, it was "a simple service for humanity."

The government survived the vote, and the troops went off to Suakin. After a brutal second round at El-Teb, General Graham quickly forced Osman Digna's tribesmen back into the hills. His unsporting use of the latest Martini-Henry carbines, and the publication of battlefield sketches showing British soldiers bayoneting wounded "Fuzzy-Wuzzies," further discomfited Gladstone's party.[70]

Next, Gordon's plan to engage Zubair Rahmat detonated in the press. A government allergic to "sensation" came under attack from moralists of all stripes. The Anti-Slavery Society called Gordon's scheme "a degradation for England, and a scandal for Europe." The Liberal M.P. William Forster, the Quaker conscience of the pacifists, denounced Gladstone for undermining Britain's historic campaign against African slavery. "For generations we have been the champion of the slave in every part of the world, and one of our boasted historical traditions has been that we have never ceased for many years to do what we could to stop this terrible evil." Lord Granville thought that Gordon had gone "Oriental crackers." Only Baring supported Gordon.[71]

"Public opinion here would not tolerate Zubair," replied Granville.[72]

The Liberal *Newcastle Chronicle* laid out the dilemma. On one side, strategic and economic necessity; on the other, conscience. "Englishmen will stand a great deal for party interest, but they will be false to all their traditions and principles if they openly recognise the appointment of an unscrupulous and tyrannical slave-driver over the Sudanese."[73]

As he had done before in moments of crisis, Gladstone fell ill. He took to his bed with "strong perspiration," a chest infection, and a copy of Disraeli's *Sybil*. When the cabinet met to debate the engagement of Zubair, he communicated with it by passing notes to Granville. In one, Gladstone suggested that the government might be able to dodge domestic criticism if it claimed that Gordon had hired Zubair in his capacity as an employee of the Egyptian government; that way, the moral aspect of the crisis was Cairo's problem. The cabinet rejected this fever dream.

Four days passed. Gladstone and Granville played for time. Lord Hartington, afraid to face the Commons without Gladstone's support, played along. On March 16, the waverers in the cabinet finally sided with Gladstone. The cabinet cabled its verdict to Baring: Zubair must not be engaged.

By then, Baring could only contact Gordon through smuggled notes.

On March 12, as Gladstone finished *Sybil* in bed, four thousand *Ansar* had routed the Khartoum garrison's northern outpost of Halfaya. They cut the steamer route to Berber and severed the telegraph cable connecting Gordon to the outside world. As soon as Gordon heard, he wrote to Augusta.

"This may well be the last letter I send you, for the tribes have risen between this and Berber and will try to cut our route. They will not fight us directly, but will starve us out. What I have to do is to submit my will to His, *even* however bitter may be the events which happen to me."[74]

The siege of Khartoum had begun. If the Mahdi held Gordon hostage, so Gordon held Gladstone.

Armies of God
1885

Sheikh Mohammed Abdu.

Oh, East is East, and West is West, and never the twain shall meet,
Till Earth and Sky stand presently at God's great Judgment Seat;
But there is neither East nor West, Border, nor Breed, nor Birth,
When two strong men stand face to face, tho' they come from the ends
of the earth!

—Rudyard Kipling, "The Ballad of East and West," 1895[1]

O N THE DAY KHARTOUM was cut off, in a Paris attic eight feet square Jamal ed-Din al-Afghani and Mohammed Abdu read the first issue of their new journal. Taking its name from the Koran, *The Indissoluble Bond* called every Muslim in the world to unite against "the Root of Corruption and the Source of Foulness": Western materialism, which subverted Islam through variegated perversions like the Anglo-Ottoman alliance, socialism, communism, nihilism, Free Trade, Darwinian evolution, international banking, and sex. Afghani wrote the editorials, Abdu wrote most of the articles, and the French government was the likeliest source of its funds. Curiously, the name of their journal doubled as the title of their latest, and supposedly secret, society.[2]

Afghani planned to use Western communications technology against Western power. In the attic, bales of "journals and clippings" awaited export to "the remotest corners of the Islamic world." Cheap steam and rail travel would spread "the spirit of insurrection." In 1884, while the teenager Mahatma Gandhi was learning English at high school so he could follow his father into government service, Afghani prophesied, "England believes it has made a great political stroke by imposing the English language on the Hindus, Muslims, and idolaters. She has made a great mistake. Today they understand the newspapers published by their conquerors, and make themselves perfectly aware of the state of subjection to which they have been reduced."[3]

While planning the revolution, Afghani and Abdu enjoyed themselves among the materialists. When Wilfrid Blunt came to visit, he found Abdu "somewhat Europeanized." Abdu no longer shaved his head, wore a fez instead of a turban, and spent much of his time in cafés. His mentor Afghani had publicly debated with the philosopher Ernest Renan. Responding to Renan's scathing assessment of the gulf between Islamic tradition and modern science, and addressing skeptical Christians in French, Afghani had effectively endorsed Renan's analysis. "In truth, the Muslim religion has tried to stifle science and stop its progress. It has thus succeeded in halting the philosophical or intellectual movement, and in turning minds from the search for scientific truth."

Like an Enlightenment *philosophe,* Afghani cited the Church's persecution of Galileo, concluding, "Religions, by whatever names they are called, resemble each other. Religion imposes on man its faith and belief, whereas philosophy frees him of it totally or in part." Afghani's idea of freedom was not the secular paradise of the Enlightenment, but the freedom to domesticate Western methods in order to empower the Islamic world. A thoroughly modern jihadi, his true passion lay in killing the thing he loved: the modern, secular West.[4]

In Paris, he had no shortage of visitors: Urabist exiles, Catholic nationalists, Irish revolutionaries, religious cranks, and Wilfrid Blunt. When Blunt visited in March 1884, he found the Sage of the East lecturing "a very curious party of strangers." They were led by Madame Helena Blavatsky, the Russian Jewish inventor of Theosophy, a fashionable medley of Spiritualism, personality cult, and quasiscientific search for the common origin of all religion. Blavatsky saw Afghani as an authentic Persian mystic, one of those "Aryans" who seemed somehow related to the Theosophical quest. He was also the ex-master of the Star of the East lodge at Alexandria, many of whose founders had been inspired by Blavatsky when she had visited Egypt to study Sufism.

Both shaping new ideologies to bridge East and West, and both convinced of their imminent global triumph, Blavatsky and Afghani met to discuss a third mystic. What, asked Blavatsky, did Afghani think of the Mahdi? She thought he must be "a humanitarian," because he fought against the Ottoman and British empires, but she was troubled by his "attachment to the slave trade."

Hiding his amusement, Afghani replied by explaining "how much slaves gained among Mohammedans in exchange for their freedom." The Theosophists left shortly afterward, convinced that the Mahdi's revolt was part of their global upsurge of religious consciousness.[5]

Privately, Afghani and Abdu saw a different kind of opportunity in the Mahdi. "He is the forerunner of the Caliph who will be," Abdu explained to Blunt. Afghani had already initiated contact with the Mahdi via sympathizers at Cairo. In early 1884, a French freelance named Olivier Pain secured a commission from *Le Figaro* to report on the Sudanese revolt. When Pain approached Afghani for help, Afghani gave him letters of introduction, and ordered his contacts at Cairo to prepare "a caravan of fake merchants" to escort Pain to the Sudanese border. He also gave Pain "secret letters" for the Mahdi, proposing an alliance.

The Mahdi's enemies were Afghani's enemies: the Ottoman caliph, the Egyptian khedive, and the British Empire. They were also Ahmed Urabi's enemies. So Afghani appointed himself as interlocutor between the Sudanese holy warrior and the Egyptian general. Afghani hoped that the Mahdist revolt would spread downriver to Egypt, forcing Britain to return Urabi from exile. Through smuggled letters and visitors, Afghani and Blunt maintained regular contact with Urabi at Ceylon. Inflating his credentials, Afghani described the Mahdi, who had never left the Sudan in his life, as "my old pupil at al-Azhar." With Blunt, he devised an exit strategy that Blunt would offer to the Gladstone government. Meanwhile, the British consul at Constantinople reported pro-Mahdi demonstrations and poster campaigns in Beirut and Damascus.[6]

Blunt had been banned from Egypt as an agitator and denounced in the Commons for having advised Urabi of Wolseley's intended line of attack, but he still possessed the social key to the political class. Three days after his Paris intrigue, he visited another attic room. This one was in London's Connaught Place, and its bed contained the flu-stricken form of Lord Randolph Churchill. Blunt tried to mobilize the maverick Tory as "the champion of the Mohammedans." On April 23, Blunt offered himself to Gladstone as "mediator for the relief of Gordon." Offering "opportunely received information" from unnamed sources, Blunt promised to secure both Gordon's freedom and "the pacification of the Upper Nile," and all without diverging from Gladstone's "general principles of policy." In fact, as Blunt admitted that day in his diary, he intended to use his "mediation" to force the British government to accept a more radical agenda: the withdrawal of all non-Muslims from Sudan, a "treaty of peace" between Britain and the Mahdi, and the return of Urabi to Egypt.[7]

Gladstone brushed away the offer. In the *Pall Mall Gazette*, W. T. Stead lambasted Blunt acidly. "If all are to be handed over to the Mahdi and the garrisons are to trust their lives to his tender mercies, our proper agent in the Sudan is not General Gordon, but Mr. Wilfrid Blunt. General Gordon was prepared to go a great length to conciliate the Mahdi. Mr. Blunt is prepared to go to all lengths . . . Mr. Blunt, then, is obviously the man to whom the Government should turn in this, their hour of need. He represents their policy to a nicety . . . Mr. Blunt is not less brave than General Gordon, and he could be sacrificed at least as safely."[8]

Blunt's was not the only proposal. All the strands of British interest had knotted around Khartoum. A chorus of Gordon advocates joined Sir Evelyn Baring's lonely solo, demanding Gordon's rescue for reasons foreign, domestic, and ethical. Abolitionists were appalled by the abandonment of the Sudan and its patron saint. Liberal universalists revered Gordon as a Christian martyr in the making. Conservative cynics took him up as a martyr to Gladstone's prevarication. Jingoists warned of defeat by savages. Strategists warned of the implications for Egypt and the India Route. The great mass of Evangelicals, businessmen, soldiers, bigots, and ordinary Britons were enthralled by Gordon's bravery and faith.

Mass meetings gathered in London and Manchester. Gordon's admirer Mrs. Surtees-Allnatt started a subscription fund to raise eighty thousand pounds as a ransom. In the absence of a governmental address, a torrent of unsolicited donations for funding a relief force poured onto the editor of the *Times*. He sent them back, but passed the task to the Almighty, calling for public prayers for Gordon. Armchair warriors wondered if the veteran big-game hunter "Curly" Knox, whom Blunt called "a somewhat decayed blood, a rabid damned-nigger Guardsman," would go alone to Khartoum in disguise and spirit Gordon to safety. Urabi's lawyer Mark Napier toured clubland, trying to recruit "a thousand sportsmen" willing to blast a passage from Suakin to Berber with elephant guns.[9]

The government resisted every public pressure and private entreaty. The policy was withdrawal, not invasion by troops or "Curly" Knox. And judging from his letters, Gordon did not want to be rescued.

"THE ENEMY HAS established himself about nine miles from here, and we hear his drums from the palace," Gordon wrote to his brother Henry in mid-March. "We are well off for food, and the people are in good spirits. We shall, D.V., go on for months. The steamers are a great advantage to us, and we only await the rising of the Nile in two months' time to be still more powerful."[10]

At first, Khartoum did not seem like a city besieged. The local Mahdists set up three camps, to the north, southeast, and southwest of Khartoum, but they did not attempt to encircle it. The Mahdi suspected that Gordon was only the advance party of a major force, and he remained with his *Ansar* at El Obeid. The gates of Khartoum remained open. Scouting parties went out to gather firewood and skirmish with the rebels, and local farmers came in to sell grain. The government steamers chugged up and down the White Nile and the Blue Nile, buying supplies and exchanging potshots with the rebels on the banks. Food was rationed, but it included fresh meat, and milk for the sick.

Gordon remained ebullient. The situation suited him: a mortal drama devoid of grubby politicians. Faith, charisma, and a Royal Engineer's talent for siege warfare would be pitted against a false Messiah and a feeble Foreign Office. If destiny had called him to Khartoum, reason and honor demanded that he stay there. Having evacuated 2,140 Egyptian personnel and their families, on March 11 Gordon suspended all further evacuations, reasoning that he would soon need all available men under arms. Although the escape route north lay open, and the rebels did not yet control fully the White Nile or the desert routes, he made no effort to leave or to lead the remaining inhabitants south to the equator or north toward Berber. Gordon trusted that Baring would secure him Zubair or British troops. He felt sure that flight would be more dangerous than a short siege.

On March 22, Gordon received the first inkling that he had miscalculated. Three armed Dervish messengers arrived, bearing a letter and a parcel. The Mahdi had refused the Sultanate of Kordofan. Refusing to disarm, they waited while Gordon opened the letter.

"I am not a trickster, nor do I aspire to thrones, money or prestige. I am a servant of Allah," the Mahdi announced. "I value humility and hate pride, the boasting of sultans and their deviation from the truth. . . . For God says, *Oh ye who believe, take not the Jews and Christians to be your friends and protectors. They are only friends and protectors to each other.* . . . So renounce your infidel faith and turn to Allah and his Messenger, looking forward to the life hereafter, and then I will take you as my friend and brother.

"You should know that the *Hizb Allah,* the party of God, can reach and remove the false authority with which you claim sovereignty over Allah's worshippers and land. . . . Know that I am the Expected Mahdi and the successor of God's Prophet. I have no need of the sultanate, nor of the kingdom of Kordofan, nor of the wealth of this world and its vanity. . . . If you surrender and follow the true religion, you will gain honor in this world and the next, and will save yourself and all those under you. . . . Then, if I see improvement and piety in you, I shall grant you a rank."[11]

As Gordon read the letter, the messengers repeatedly prompted him to open the parcel. Angered, he threw it across the room. After they had left, his clerk opened it, and found a jibba, "a filthy patched Dervish's coat." The Mahdi had returned Gordon's compliment. In response, Gordon severed all contact—"I cannot have any more communication with you"—and went to war, sending out raiding parties on land and water. Cut off from Cairo, he had now cut himself off from the Mahdi.[12]

"The town is all right and has become accustomed to firing," he wrote on March 31. "Be assured for the present and the next two months, we are as safe here as in Cairo."[13]

The communication breakdown between Khartoum and Cairo allowed Gordon to continue in his error, and London to underestimate its dangers. Contact with Cairo, previously instantaneous, now took four weeks or more. Instead of regular, verbose telegrams, Gordon now communicated with Baring via couriers, who tied tiny notes into their hair. But his communication difficulties only complicated a position of his own choosing. Gordon did not leave Khartoum because he did not want to. As a soldier, he saw no reason to retreat before a "trumpery" revolt. As a gentleman, he felt bound to the people of Khartoum by his promise of British troops. He could accept an orderly evacuation, but he would never abandon the people of Khartoum:

They had responded to his call to resist the Mahdi, and the fall of the town would be a massacre. A mystic, Gordon felt entitled to follow the urge of conscience and the whisper of glory, regardless of the politicians.[14]

On April 9, Gordon received Baring's letter informing him that London had refused him Zubair. Khartoum was now under daily sniper fire from "some 500 determined men and some 2,000 rag-tag Arabs." One of Gordon's palace clerks had been killed at his desk. Most of the White Nile from Halfaya to Berber was still open to his steamers, the Shaygia tribes on its banks remained hostile to the Mahdi, and the seasonal rise in water level made river travel easier. Gordon could still have organized an evacuation. Instead, he replied with open disobedience, turning on Baring, the temporary ally he had always despised.[15]

"I consider myself free to act according to circumstances. I shall hold on here as long as I can and, if I can suppress the rebellion, I shall do so. If I cannot, I shall retire to the Equator and leave you the indelible disgrace of abandoning the garrisons of Sennar, Kassala, Berber and Dongola, with the certainty that you will eventually be forced to smash up the Mahdi under great difficulties, if you would retain peace in Egypt."

Gordon had sought this drama, and detected a divine hand behind his return to Khartoum. On the frontier between Christianity and Islam, empire and wilderness, he prepared for the last act of his cosmic drama. It would be a fight to the death. "I do not see the force of being caught here, to walk about the streets for years as a Dervish with sandaled feet; not that, D.V., I will ever be taken alive. It would be the climax of meanness, after I had borrowed money from the people here, had called up them to sell their grain at a low price, etc., to go and abandon them." Gordon was a prisoner not of the Mahdi, but of honor. "I feel sure," he told Baring, "whatever you may feel diplomatically, I have your support—and that of any man professing himself a gentleman—in private."[16]

Then he sent word that he appointed Zubair as deputy governor-general of the Sudan. Baring intervened, sending Zubair to Cyprus for safekeeping instead. Gordon now knew he could expect no assistance, and he prepared for a long siege. With supplies in good order but money running short, he ordered the printing of a temporary currency. He spent much of April signing the notes, and the rest of it organizing his defenses, occasionally dueling with Mahdist snipers from the roof of the palace, and nearly losing an eye when a cartridge blew back.

Khartoum sat on a triangular peninsula. Its two vertices were the Blue and White Niles. Its base, the eight-foot-deep ditch and rampart dug by

Hilmi Pasha, ran for four miles between the two rivers. Outside the perimeter were two fortified outworks, Omdurman on the west bank of the White Nile, and North Fort on the east bank of the Blue Nile, both connected with Gordon's headquarters in the palace by field telegraph. With a fifteen-mile perimeter and only nine thousand regular and irregular soldiers, Gordon identified Hilmi Pasha's earthwork as his weakest point. He studded the ditch and rampart with spearheads, the first hundred yards of open ground with triple-spiked iron "crow's feet," the next five hundred yards with broken glass—"You know the Mahdi's men are all in bare feet"—and then laid homemade mines composed of "tin biscuit boxes full of powder, nails and bullets" among the obstacles. When Gordon ran out of electrical triggers, he devised triggers built around matchheads. "*Messieurs* the rebels will have a *mauvais quart d'heure* before they get to the ditch," promised Frank Power of the *Times*.[17]

While Gordon prepared his defense, the level of the Nile dropped. The Mahdi realized that Gordon really had come alone. Gordon's escape routes closed. In late April, the Shaygia tribes of the Nile Valley surrendered to the Mahdi. On May 18, they took Berber, the key town of northern Sudan, capturing two steamers, sixty thousand pounds in cash, and Gordon's medals, sent north for safekeeping. Since mid-March, Gordon had claimed to be cut off and unable to escape. Now his prophecy had been fulfilled.

"GENERAL GORDON IS under no constraint, and under no orders to remain in the Sudan," Gladstone told the Commons to cheers from his own benches. Nor, Gladstone added, was he aware that Gordon was under "any inability to leave the Sudan at this moment if he chooses."[18]

As far as Gladstone knew, this was true, but with no word from Khartoum since mid-March, he could not know if Gordon's position had changed. After the cutting of the telegraph on March 12, no word from Gordon reached Cairo for three months. In that time, Gladstone faced a rising tide of public pressure, and an Opposition that used the Gordon affair to stalk Gladstone's Irish policy and his plans for domestic reform. Capitalizing on the silence from Khartoum, Gladstone cited Gordon's insouciant final messages to insist that the government needed no new Sudanese policy. This served his immediate needs: The *Times* and the Tories seemed more dangerous than Gordon and Khartoum. It also accorded with his antiimperial principles.

"I have from the first regarded the rising of the Sudanese against Egypt

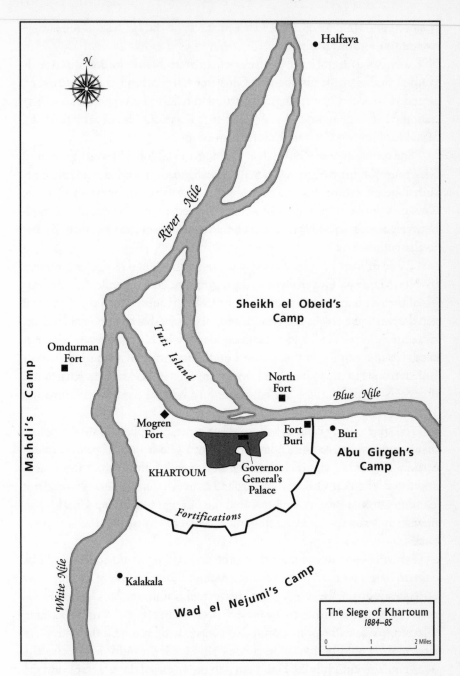

Halfaya

River Nile

Sheikh el Obeid's
Camp

Omdurman
Fort

Tuti Island

North
Fort

Blue Nile

Mahdi's Camp

Mogren
Fort

Fort
Buri

Buri

Abu Girgeh's
Camp

KHARTOUM

Governor
General's
Palace

Fortifications

White Nile

Kalakala

Wad el Nejumi's Camp

The Siege of Khartoum
1884–85

0   1   2 Miles

as a justifiable and honorable revolt," Gladstone admitted privately to his
secretary Eddy Hamilton in early April. The Liberal universalist could not
understand how "one who bore in his hands a charter of liberation should be

besieged and threatened." His ideals at stake, he did his best to remain ignorant of Gordon's position.[19]

Baring, Hartington, and Wolseley all advised that if Gordon was not already stranded, he would soon be. Giuseppe Cuzzi, Baring's man at Berber, issued a series of dire warnings: "Situation in Khartoum very critical.... Situation critical, do not delay. . . . Apparently Khartoum is cut off. . . . All are afraid for Gordon, Stewart and the Europeans."

"The question now is how to get Gordon and Colonel Stewart away from Khartoum," Baring warned Granville. Baring recommended immediate action. The government should ignore the humanitarian lobby and engage Zubair Rahmat; it should build a two-hundred-mile railway and telegraph between Suakin and Berber; and it should send armed steamers from Berber to Khartoum.[20]

"These officers have been sent on a most difficult and dangerous mission by Her Majesty's Government," Baring reminded Granville. "Their proposal that Zubair Pasha should be sent to Khartoum, which if it had been acted upon some weeks ago would, without doubt, have entirely altered the situation, was rejected; and the consequences which they foresaw have ensued. No one can regret more than I do the necessity of sending British or Indian troops to the Sudan, but having sent General Gordon to Khartoum, it appears to me that it is our bounden duty, both as a matter of humanity and policy, not to abandon him."[21]

"You shot a heavy cannon ball, your last protest," replied Granville, before dismissing every recommendation. He and Gladstone suspected that a Suakin-Berber railway might become a bridgehead, from which the annexationists at the War Office would expand their African empire. And had not Gordon's brother Henry lately assured the Foreign Office that Charley had previously "extricated himself from more dangerous positions than the present"?

Granville contrived a marvel of procrastination. As no action could be contemplated without accurate information, the government should draw up a questionnaire for Gordon as to his "actual conditions," his "plans of proceeding," and his "wishes in the present position of affairs." Two weeks later, Gladstone was still working on it. No courier willing to risk the journey to Khartoum would be found until May 18. Gordon would not receive the questionnaire until July 29. Habituated to the world of the telegraph and the steam train, Gladstone and Granville forgot the extent of Gordon's disconnection. This error fortified their unwillingness to send troops to Berber, build railways into Africa, or cede rhetorical ground to the Opposition.[22]

"Gordon is our officer," Lord Hartington reflected. "Can we sit still and do nothing?" As secretary for war and leader of the Liberal party's Whig aristocrats, he could have forced Gladstone's hand. To Hartington, Gordon's silence indicated imminent crisis. Lord Wolseley warned him that it would take at least three months to prepare an expedition and reach Khartoum. Hartington urged that Gordon be saved.

"I think it is now clear enough that, whether he has a right to do so or not, he expects help in some shape or another," Hartington told Granville. "The first thing we have to do is to decide whether to leave Gordon to his fate, because if we do not, the sooner we begin to make preparations, the better."

Hartington passed on a plan devised by Wolseley and his intelligence adviser, Sir Charles Wilson, to send troops to Khartoum via Suakin and Berber. He also advised that after rescuing Gordon, Britain should retain influence in the Sudan through "some sort of independent government under our protection."[23]

To Gladstone, this sounded less like a program for rescue than a conspiracy for annexation. Replying that an expedition should only be sent "in the last and sad necessity," he then devoted himself to demonstrating that this necessity had not been reached. To avoid splitting the cabinet, Hartington did not insist. This permitted Gladstone to continue playing for time. On April 21, he explained to the House that Gordon's description of Khartoum as "hemmed in" did not mean that the town was "surrounded." Rather, the "bodies of hostile troops" in its vicinity formed "more or less a chain around it." Two days later, he claimed, "If Berber was to fall into the hands of the tribes around it, the position of General Gordon would not then become one of peril."[24]

It was not Hartington who forced Gladstone to defend his position, but the Opposition. On May 1, the government published Gordon's correspondence, with its warning of "indelible disgrace" and its criticism of Gladstone's inertia. Supported by prointervention Liberals and Radicals, the Conservatives called a vote of censure against the government, forcing the debate that Gladstone and Granville wanted to avoid.

From the gallery above the seething Commons, Wilfrid Blunt watched Gladstone wriggle from the charge of incompetence "more as a man might in a debating club, than as a statesman arraigned on a dishonourable charge."[25]

Gladstone began by rolling out a Liberal broadside. What did the sending of an army to the Sudan mean? "It meant a war of conquest against a people rightly struggling to be free."[26]

"No! No!" the Opposition benches exploded.

"Yes, these are people struggling to be free, and rightly struggling to be free!"[27]

"You will incur indelible disgrace!" the old Tory Sir Michael Hicks shouted, jabbing an accusing finger at Gladstone.

"What does he mean by pointing to me?" Gladstone screamed back. "What does he mean by pointing to me, to dishonor me in the eyes of my country?" Gordon had criticized the abandonment of four garrisons, but what of the other six in more remote corners of the Sudan? Did the Conservatives intend to send expeditions to relieve all of them? Had they an alternative policy?

"What is the answer of the Right Honourable gentleman?" cried Gladstone, pointing to the Opposition benches. "I think he has no answer to give—probably does not want to give me an answer . . . the Right Honourable gentleman is dumb!"[28]

Scaling the moral high ground, Gladstone conceded that he had entered into "a solemn covenant with General Gordon."

"It may," he allowed, "be our duty to plant a British force in that terrible country." If he received "reasonable assurance" that Gordon was in danger, he would "use the resources of this country" to protect him. But Parliament must consider "the treasure of the nation, the blood of the nation, the honour of the nation" before it sent "British and Christian arms among the Mohammedan people struggling for their liberty in the Sudan."[29]

This was bravura stuff, but when the disaffected Liberal W. E. Forster insisted that Gordon was in danger, it looked as if Gladstone would not get away with it.

"I believe everyone but the Prime Minister is convinced of that danger. I do not say that he is aware of the danger himself; I think he would act very differently if he was. And I attribute his not being convinced to his wonderful powers of persuasion. He can persuade most people of most things and, above all, he can persuade himself of anything."[30]

It was Hartington who saved Gladstone. By promising that the government would, with sufficient evidence, "grudge no sacrifice to save the life and honour of General Gordon," Hartington mollified the dissident Liberals, and persuaded them to abstain from the censure vote.[31]

The government won by twenty-eight votes. Sending their questionnaire to Cairo, Granville and Gladstone ordered Gordon to withdraw: He must avoid "aggressive operations" and prepare "measures for his own removal." To lay the ground for Gordon's escape or his rescuers' advance, they ordered that a British intelligence officer be sent to negotiate with the tribes on the Suakin-Berber road.[32]

The next day, Berber fell to the Mahdi, and Giuseppe Cuzzi, his warnings ignored, chose conversion to Islam over death.

Gladstone's questionnaire would take three months to reach Khartoum.

"WE ARE ALL WELL and can hold out for four months," Gordon wrote to Baring on July 13.[33]

Every Friday and Saturday night through the hot summer of 1884, the garrison band played jaunty tunes outside the palace. When not supervising the daily duel with the Mahdist snipers, Gordon drilled platoons of citizen irregulars, tracked down hidden supplies of grain, inspected his sentries day and night, sent backgammon and chess boards to the wounded in the hospital, and smoked incessantly. He did all he could to convince the populace of Khartoum not to abandon him. When Ramadan began at the end of June, he persuaded the Khartoum clergy to announce that as the town was at war, its people were freed from the obligation to fast. He ordered the town foundry, already producing forty thousand rounds of Remington ammunition each week, to smelt a Khartoum siege medal, and distributed it liberally among the defenders. He wrote to the sultan, the khedive, and the pope, asking them to raise funds for a Turkish force to take over the Sudan. He corresponded with the Mahdi's local supporters, sending gifts of soap with his letters, but without success. Above all, he repeatedly assured the people that troops were on their way.

Each week, the situation worsened. Further Mahdist bases mushroomed in the country around Khartoum, stringing together a net of camps and trenches that prevented Gordon from sending out foraging parties. The Mahdists wheeled up captured Egyptian artillery, and the sniper fire turned into a barrage. Colonel Stewart was wounded while firing a Krupps cannon from the palace roof. After a series of successful raiding parties along the Blue Nile, Gordon's ablest commander, Mohammed Ali Bey, was ambushed in the woods and killed with all his troops. On Gordon's next foray upriver, *Ansar* artillery nearly sank one of the steamers. The last escape route, south to the lakes, had closed. Gordon continued to send out optimistic messages, but from late July, he could no longer gather food from outside Khartoum, or delay the tightening of the siege. While Gordon doled out corn and biscuits, shortages of money and grain were exacerbated by hoarding and theft, and inflation ran at 3,000 percent.

On July 29, a lone messenger sneaked through the lines and delivered Gladstone's questionnaire. Gordon read with incredulity its request that he give his "intentions," and he replied with contempt. "I say I stay at Khartoum because Arabs have shut us up, and will not let us out . . . I fear it is too late. We must fight it out by our own means; if blessed by God, we shall succeed; if not His will, so be it."[34]

Gordon showed the dispatches to Stewart and Power. "All hope of relief by our Government is at an end," Power concluded, "so when our provisions (which we have at a stretch for two months) are eaten, we must fall. Nor is there any chance, with the soldiers we have and with the great crowd of women, children, etc., of our being able to cut our way through the Arabs."[35]

When Ramadan ended in late July, the Mahdi moved the main body of the *Ansar* toward Khartoum. As his followers left El Obeid, they burned their huts, faithful to the Mahdi's promise that their next home would be in Khartoum or Paradise. The sixty thousand warriors and their families carried no stores. Taking food and water from the villages in their path, they devastated the countryside; as the Mahdi promised, Allah had provided for his warriors. On the way, the French journalist Olivier Pain, who had converted to Islam in order to join the Mahdi, came down with fever. The Mahdi left him to die by the road. Reaching the Nile at Dueim, the Baggara massed awestruck on the banks of the first major river they had ever seen. When two of Gordon's steamers appeared on a reconnaissance, some Baggara jumped into the water to stop them with their bare hands, and were threshed beneath the steamers' paddles.

Realizing his predicament, Gordon decided to send Stewart, Power, and the French consul Herbin down the Nile on the steamer *Abbas*, with orders to force their way past Berber and report the situation at Khartoum from the telegraph station at Dongola. On September 9, Gordon said good-bye to Stewart and Power and watched the *Abbas*, escorted by the *Safia*, the *Mansura*, and two boatloads of heavily armed Greeks, sail away up the White Nile. They took with them a letter for Baring, Gordon's papers, and his cipher keys; either Gordon expected to be able to send few further messages, or he had now resigned himself to the fall of Khartoum.

"How many times have we written asking for reinforcements?" Gordon asked Baring bitterly. "While you are eating and drinking and sleeping on good beds, we and those with us, both soldiers and servants, are endeavouring to quell the movement of this false Mahdi. . . . You have neglected us, and lost time without doing any good. . . . Send troops as we have asked, without any delay."[36]

As rifle fire from the banks pinged off the steamers' homemade armor plate, Stewart's flotilla sped safely past Mahdist-held Berber. Approaching the Fifth Cataract, Stewart felt safe enough to send his escorts back to Khartoum. But below Abu Hamed the White Nile split into two channels, and Stewart picked the wrong one. The *Abbas* ran aground in the shallows. With no help available on the deserted river, Stewart, Power, and Herbin climbed into a dinghy and were about to go on alone when a man appeared on the bank wearing a government uniform and fez, offering to take them overland to Dongola by camel. They accompanied him to his house, and as they waited, a group of *Ansar* rushed in and hacked them to death.

On October 21, the first day of the Islamic new year, the Mahdi reached the *Ansar*'s camp before Omdurman. Gordon's cipher keys and private papers were waiting for him. They told the Mahdi everything: that the British government intended to cede the Sudan, that Gordon had gone against his orders, that the British had apparently abandoned him, and that he was trapped in Khartoum with unreliable troops and diminishing stocks of grain.

"We never miss any of your news, nor what is in your innermost thoughts," the Mahdi gloated to Gordon. "We have now understood it all."[37]

"POOR GORDON, his ammunition will soon be all expended," Garnet Wolseley predicted to Sir Samuel Baker. "He will have his throat cut or be made a prisoner by the Mahdi. I do not wish to share the responsibility of leaving Charley Gordon to his fate."[38]

Wolseley remembered Gordon every night in his prayers. All summer, he had lobbied Lord Hartington to give Gladstone an ultimatum, and to appoint him commander of a relief expedition. "My military experience," warned Wolseley, "tells me that in all such affairs, the worst course to pursue is to shirk the question, and to imagine you dispose of it by shutting your eyes and trying to ignore it or forget it."[39]

In the three months since the vote of censure, Gladstone had diverted his ministers with proposals for Egyptian finance, delayed a decision on grounds of insufficient information, and insisted that Gordon neither needed nor merited assistance. Lord Hartington believed that Gordon was in danger, he knew that a relief expedition would take at least three months to reach Khartoum, and he knew that as Secretary for War he bore the responsibility for Gordon's dispatch. But he did not dare confront Gladstone alone. It was not until the end of July 1884 that he found fellow members of the cabinet willing to "share the responsibility," and when he did, Gladstone fobbed him off with "five minutes at the fag-end" of a cabinet meeting.

"I cannot be responsible for the military policy under such conditions," Hartington told Granville, before giving Gladstone another two weeks.[40]

On the last day of July, with the summer recess imminent, Hartington threatened to resign if the government did not begin preparing an expedition. "It is a question of personal honour and good faith, and I do not see how I can yield upon it."[41]

Gladstone asked Hartington to be patient. The government already faced "a domestic crisis of the first class" in its Reform Bill, and "a foreign crisis of the first class" in its negotiations with France over the restructuring of the Egyptian debt. Could the Minister do "nothing to accelerate a Gordon crisis," at least until next week, when the Egyptian finance conference finished? Gladstone preferred to plan his crises ahead.

Granville, his ringmaster in the cabinet, negotiated a compromise. Just before the recess, the government voted three hundred thousand pounds for a "Gordon Relief Expedition." Confident that Hartington had been placated, Gladstone packed his summer reading, and Granville planned a seaside holiday to ease his gout.

Hartington had got his money, but he could not dispatch the expedition to Egypt. Gladstone insisted that any decision be put to a cabinet vote, so that his ministers might be "assured that they were not about to become unawares the slaves of Gordon's (probably) rebellious ideas." With the cabinet holidaying on country estates and the Riviera, there could be no vote before the autumn.[42]

"I despair of acquitting myself of the responsibility which will be placed on me by my colleagues and Parliament," Hartington complained, and again threatened to resign. Finally, Gladstone gave way, trimming a few hundred troops from Wolseley's force as he did so.[43]

On September 9, as Stewart and Power left Khartoum on the *Abbas*, HMS *Iris* delivered Lord Garnet Wolseley and seven thousand troops to Alexandria. The "usual crowd" were waiting on the dock, Wolesley noted in his diary: General Stephenson, "a real old man"; Khedive Tawfik, "cordial and affectionate"; and Nubar Pasha, "very Turkish in features, a cunning old fox."

With assistance from London, Wolseley and the Egyptian administrators managed to waste three precious weeks arguing about which route to take to Khartoum. First, Wolseley dismissed the overland route from Suakin to Berber. He insisted on reaching Berber via the White Nile, so he could use a detachment of Canadian *voyageurs,* veterans of his glorious Red River expedition. Then, although an advance party of cavalry had been sent ahead to Wadi Halfa ready for a dash to Dongola, and although native boats had been stockpiled at Dongola for the journey upriver, Wolseley insisted that when the water level dropped, the Nile would be too shallow for native boats. No forward move would be made until his *voyageurs* and four hundred specially commissioned flat-bottomed craft arrived with the main body of his force.[44]

The Canadians did not begin to arrive until October. Rather than hardened *voyageurs,* they turned out to be mercenary lumberjacks and adventurous storekeepers. By then, the Nile had begun to drop, making the Cataracts even harder to navigate. Meanwhile, Wolseley's chief of staff Sir Redvers Buller failed to organize coal for the Thomas Cook's steamers that would carry the expedition up to Wadi Halfa. Wolseley did not reach Wadi Halfa until September 30. On the same day, his advance guard under Sir Herbert Stewart entered Dongola. Yet instead of racing forward, Wolseley continued edging up the Nile, slowed by logistical errors and the disappointing performance of his *voyageurs,* who themselves had to be hauled through the Cataracts by thousands of press-ganged natives. After Wolseley reached Dongola on November 3, he waited there for a further three weeks, while downriver his *voyageurs* floundered with his supplies and reinforcements. "It is troubles of this sort that make men old before their time," he complained to Lady Louisa.[45]

Egotism and bungling aside, the most significant factor in Wolseley's slow progress was his inaccurate picture of the situation at Khartoum. Much of it derived from Gordon's letters. Surounded and unable to speak Arabic, Gordon picked through scraps of information from fugitives and Mahdist deserters. Selecting the most appealing material, he sent it upriver to Colonel Herbert Kitchener at ed-Debba, the terminus of the telegraph line. Kitchener worshipped Gordon and admired Wolseley. His telegrams from ed-Debba to Wolseley's headquarters emulated Gordon's nonchalance, while his messages from ed-Debba to Khartoum exaggerated Wolseley's progress.

As Gordon had sent away his cipher books with Stewart and Power, he had no way of reading Wolseley's messages warning that, contrary to Kitchener's messages, the relief expedition had fallen behind schedule. Gordon's strategic sense became highly distorted. By the end of October, false reports from fugitives had convinced him that British troops had been seen south of ed-Debba, and that northern Sudan was awash in Madhist forces. So he repeatedly warned Wolseley not to string out his forces as he advanced on Berber, in case of a Mahdist assault on his column, risking his couriers' lives in the process. "Gordon inundates us with telegrams without giving us any satisfactory intelligence," Wolseley complained.[46]

Gordon counted his supplies. "If they do not come before the 30th November, the game is up, and *Rule Britannia!*" On Kitchener's word, Gordon believed that Wolseley would arrive on November 15, two weeks before Khartoum's supplies ran out. Yet on November 4, with no troops in sight, Gordon extended his ability to resist the siege until mid-December, telling Wolseley, "We can hold out forty days with ease; after that it will be difficult."

Gordon still believed that the Mahdists would crumble at the first sight of British troops. He requested Wolseley to send an advance party from the expedition's forward depot at Um Bakul to Metemma, where they could meet Gordon's steamers and be ferried to Khartoum. This note reached Wolseley at Dongola on November 14. As the delays continued to multiply, Wolseley now expected to "shake hands with Gordon" around January 31. It was a race against time.[47]

"ONE TUMBLES AT 3AM into a troubled sleep; a drum beats—Tup! Tup! Tup! It comes into a dream, but after a few moments one becomes more awake, and it is revealed to the brain that *one is in Khartoum.* A hope arises it will go away. No, it goes on, and increases in intensity. The thought strikes one, 'Have they enough ammunition?'"[48]

Khartoum was now under constant fire, erratic but enervating. Gordon was now more worried by a revolt in the city than assault from outside. To boost morale, in daylight he paced the palace roof, telescope in hand. At night he sat by the open window of the palace, a lamp lit behind him to give a clear silhouette. He promised that a British column was on its way, shot off fireworks to celebrate victories over Mahdist scouts sent to probe his lines, and broke out rations when he sensed morale was falling.

His greatest problem was not ammunition, but food. While the Mahdi's men had exhausted their supply of looted Remington ammunition, and had taken to firing stones, Khartoum's foundry had turned out over 2 million bullets. But by early November 1884, stocks of grain and biscuits had run low. Gordon had to feed nine thousand soldiers, and a further thirty-five thousand citizens. A windfall of thirty-five cattle, captured after the Mahdists had driven them into the minefield in an attempt to detonate a path, made only a small difference. As food stocks fell and hunger increased, looting broke out. His Egyptian officers robbed their men of their grain, and the soldiers robbed women of their rations in the street.

Gordon also detected traitors in the camp. He caught Khartoum's civilian elite, the Qadi el-Islam and his circle, communicating with the Mahdi, and placed them all under house arrest. "I judge by the eye, by little signs, etc., for I do not know the language: but I cannot help thinking I am more often right than wrong in my suspicions. One comes on a group of clerks, heads all together, in the chief clerk's room; one sees disturbed countenances at once. I cannot help thinking, *You are concocting devilry!*, and I look out for some *tricks*."[49]

The last ranking European at Khartoum was the Austrian consul Martin Hansal, an alcoholic who lived with seven "female attendants." Gordon turned to his journal for solace. It became the repository of the details of the siege—the hours spent scanning the northern horizon for a smear of steamer smoke, the ceaseless patrolling of his lines and counting of his biscuit supplies, the mounting claustrophobia and filth in the streets, the crowds pulling at his sleeve begging for food—and the vent for his private suffering, the hidden fear and anger with which he faced death. In this memorial in the making, he blamed everyone but himself for his predicament, and for tying the fate of the forty-five thousand people at Khartoum to his selective interpretation of his orders.

"It is simply due to the indecisions of our Government," he insisted, adding that he felt "in honour bound to the people" of the town. He did not admit that he was bound to them not just by "six months' bothering warfare," but also by his repeated false claims that British troops were on their way.

If he had not stayed at Khartoum for his own honor, then he had stayed for the honor of Britain, a greater cause than that of the Liberal Party. In his journal, Gordon depicted himself as a martyr to Gladstone's foreign policy, and especially to Sir Evelyn Baring, who "had deigned to say that he would support me," and who, Gordon believed, had abandoned him at Khartoum for the sake of his career. Gordon did not know of Baring's efforts on his behalf.[50]

"I own to have been very insubordinate to Her Majesty's Government and its officials," he admitted, "but it is my nature and I cannot help it." Yet he refused to accept that the relief expedition came to save him only. "It has come to SAVE OUR NATIONAL HONOUR in extricating the garrisons, etc., from a position our action in Egypt has placed these garrisons. I was Relief Expedition No. 1. They are Relief Expedition No. 2. . . . We, the first and second expeditions are equally engaged for the honour of England . . . I am not the *rescued lamb,* and I will not be."[51]

Gordon prided himself on his composure before the garrison and populace, but they could see that since he had come to Khartoum, his hair had turned white. Increasing the psychological pressure, the Mahdi mobilized Gordon's old officers. Rudolf Slatin, who had exchanged command of the Darfur garrison for membership of Khalifa Abdullahi's bodyguard, wrote to Gordon, begging him to surrender and embrace Islam. Giuseppe Cuzzi, the ex-commander of the Berber garrison, now known as Mohammed Yusuf, crawled on hands and knees through the minefield to plead with Gordon.

Gordon refused to see him. Apostasy was no less disgraceful than suicide. He had decided to be a Christian martyr, and surrender his body to the torments of captivity. "I toss up in my mind whether, if the place is taken, to blow up the palace and all in it, or else to be taken and, with God's help, to maintain the faith and, if necessary, suffer for it (which is most probable). The blowing up of the palace is the simplest, while the other means long and weary suffering and humiliation of all sorts." Nevertheless, he chose it. "I think I shall elect for the last, not from fear of death, but because the former has the taint of suicide, as it can do no good to anyone and is, in a way, taking things out of God's hands."[52]

Everything was ready. Gordon had created his apotheosis. Now he faced the massed *Ansar* on the plain before Khartoum. On December 13, with artillery shells landing within fifty feet of his office in the west wing of the palace, he wrapped up his journals and entrusted them to a courier. "It is inexplicable, this delay." Calculating that Khartoum had a maximum of two weeks' food remaining, he wrote a final entry.[53]

"Now MARK THIS, if the Expeditionary Force, and I ask for no more than two hundred men, does not come in ten days, the town may fall; and I have done my best for the honour of my country. Good bye."

Signing it "C.G. Gordon," he added a last, bitter afterthought.

"You send me no information, though you have lots of money."[54]

AT DONGOLA ON the last day of 1884, Garnet Wolseley received a message from Gordon, written in tiny letters on a scrap of paper no bigger than a postage stamp.

"Khartoum all right. 14/12/84 C.G. Gordon."

But the courier also carried a verbal message for Wolseley. Khartoum was besieged on three fronts, fighting went on day and night, the defenders were starving at their posts, and the Mahdi controlled the approaches to Khartoum.

"Do not scatter your troops. Enemy are numerous. Bring plenty of troops if you can," Gordon urged. "We want you to come quickly."[55]

A second letter told Colonel Watson, "The game is up, and send Mrs. Watson, you and Graham my *adieux*. We may expect a catastrophe in the town on or after 10 days' time." Having blamed the cabinet, Baring, and Kitchener, Gordon now turned on his friend Wolseley. "This would not have happened (if it does happen) if our people had taken better precautions as to informing me of their movements, but this is spilt milk."[56]

Wolseley's "forward concentration" at Korti, scheduled for Christmas Day, had now been put back to January 22. Still struggling to gather his forces, and now realizing the urgency of Gordon's plight, Wolseley prepared to bypass Berber and send a "Desert Column" of fifteen hundred men on camels to Metemma. He had no idea what they might encounter as they crossed the desert. Wolseley then discovered that he possessed insufficient camels to reach Metemma in a single lift. He decided that General Sir Herbert Stewart would lead the Desert Column to Metemma in two stages. Adopting Gordon's advice, Wolseley told General Stewart that he was not to move on Khartoum until the main force had taken Berber.

On the afternoon of December 30, Colonel Kitchener and his Arab guides led General Stewart's advance party out of their camp at Korti and into the bare, scrubby desert. The shortage of camels obliged General Stewart to move slowly, ferrying the column's supplies up, establishing a temporary advance camp at Gakdul, and sending Kitchener and the supply train back to Korti. It was not until January 12 that General Sir Herbert Stewart, sixteen hundred men of the Camel Corps, and a further two hundred men from the Royal Sussex Regiment and the Naval Brigade reached Gakdul. By then, their laborious camel treks had alerted the Mahdi to their presence. As Stewart made south for Metemma, twelve thousand *Ansar* headed along the western bank of the White Nile to meet him.

The Mahdi hoped to defeat Khartoum through starvation. He wanted to take Gordon prisoner, as the trophy he could trade for recognition of his Sudanese empire. The advance of the Desert Column forced the Mahdi to fight, if only to delay its progress. His men had never faced British troops; Stewart, like Gordon and Wolseley, had never seen a Mahdist charge. On January 16, as Stewart reached a ridge overlooking the wells of Abu Klea, little more than twenty miles from Metemma, he saw "a long line of banners fluttering in the breeze and stretching right across the road."[57]

General Stewart halted his column and ordered them to prepare a *zariba* on a stony plateau. As *Ansar* scouts worked along Stewart's flanks and fired into the camp, the Camel Corps dug in for the night. Rising before dawn, they moved forward in a loose square, keeping *Ansar* raiding parties at bay, until they were less than a mile from the main *Ansar* force. At that moment, the *Ansar* began the charge, in three formations, each headed by a black or green flag. On the British left flank the Gardner machine gun operated by men from HMS *Alexandra* fired seventy rounds before jamming. The sailors were cut down as they ran for the square. As the British tightened their ranks and the Camel Corps dismounted to reinforce the line, the square could not open fire without hitting its own skirmishing parties, running back before the *Ansar*. "One poor fellow who lagged behind was caught and speared at once."[58]

Colonel Sir Charles Wilson, Stewart's intelligence officer, could not believe his eyes. The *Ansar* simply ran in close formation toward the British lines, in a human tide so densely packed that the rapid fire of Martini-Henry carbines appeared to have no effect. As a huge wall of dead bodies piled up in front of the square, the *Ansar* divided in two. Over five thousand warriors wheeled around the right side of the square, toward its rear.

"By Jove, they will be into the square!" Wilson realized. He watched a "fine old sheikh on horseback" leading the charge for the rear of the square, banner in one hand, the Mahdi's *ratib* in the other, chanting prayers as his horse breasted the line. As the sheikh planted his flag in the center of the square, he was shot from his saddle. The square filled with panicked British camels, *Ansar* horsemen, and a tidal wave of warriors that subsumed General Stewart and his horse. *Ansar* and Camel Corps fought hand to hand with spears, knives, and bayonets. To hold back the assault, the rear rank of the British soldiers at the front of the square turned round and directed their fire into the melée, forcing back the *Ansar* and killing many British troops. The *Ansar* withdrew, to cheers from the broken British. The bodies of over a thousand *Ansar* lay piled in and around the square, mingled with those of over seventy British officers and men. Colonel Frederick Burnaby, the popular cavalry officer whom Wolseley had picked to lead the steamer dash from Metemma to Khartoum, lay dead, a Mahdist spear through his throat.[59]

General Stewart spent a sleepless, frozen night in the desert, his officers huddled and shivering under a looted prayer blanket. He advanced late the next day, hoping to reach Metemma before dawn, but his exhausted camel drivers fell asleep in their saddles. Their mounts wandered loose, appearing "gaunt, spectre-like in the dim starlight" as the column became disordered.

Just after dawn, with the Nile in sight, the *Ansar* suddenly reappeared. Stewart was forced to regroup and dig in, two miles short of Metemma. By 0800, *Ansar* bullets "began to drop pretty freely into the square." The Camel Corps scrambled to tie down their camels and build parapets of saddles and store boxes. Hidden by long grass, the *Ansar* worked around the square, their enfilade fire hitting the defenseless soldiers. General Stewart was fatally wounded, his aide St. Leger Herbert shot through the head, and Cameron of the *Standard,* who had hidden himself among his camels, was killed as he rose to receive a box of sardines from his servant.

Stewart's second in command, Colonel Sir Charles Wilson, had never served in an active campaign. Realizing that his force would be destroyed if he did not move, Wilson left part of his force in the redoubt and formed the rest into a square under heavy fire, the men lying down for cover as they took up their places. Then he ordered a march to the Nile. "The men's faces were set in a determined way, and I knew they intended to drink from the Nile that night." Several were hit as soon as they stood up, one marine almost falling dead into Wilson's arms. Leaving their wounded where they fell, they edged forward. As they reached the last slope before the Nile, the *Ansar* stopped shooting, and hundreds of horsemen and spearmen came pouring down the hill. At three hundred yards, Wilson's bugler called "Commence firing," and the banners and the horsemen crashed into the grass fifty yards short of the square. The *Ansar* wavered, and then retreated, their charge broken.

Just before dusk, Wilson reached the "line of green vegetation" that hid the river. A tenth of his force had been killed. So many had been wounded that it was necessary to expand the redoubt to accommodate them. The survivors had barely slept or eaten in four days. Resting his force and burying the dead, Wilson waited two days before marching on Metemma. On January 21, as he skirmished with *Ansar* on the outskirts of the village, Wilson saw smoke trails on the river. Led by the *Bordein,* four battered boats appeared under Egyptian flags.[60]

"Gordon's steamers!" Wilson's men cried, running down to the river's edge.[61]

The Desert Column had linked up with the steamers, but Wolseley's plan had been ruined. Burnaby was dead. Stewart was dying. The Naval Brigade that was to have accompanied him to Khartoum had been decimated at Abu Klea, its commander, Lord Charles Beresford, so badly wounded that he could barely stand. Wilson's force was too battered to assault Metemma, and so drained that it had to spend three days organizing its withdrawal before he could board the *Bordein*.

The Mahdi's delaying tactic had worked. With word of his advance preceding him, on January 24, 1885, Sir Charles Wilson and a grand total of twenty-four soldiers donned the red uniforms that Wolseley thought would help them intimidate the Dervish horde and set sail for Khartoum.

MORE THAN FIVE WEEKS after Gordon had given Khartoum a life expectancy of ten days, the town still held out. By the end of December, the last cattle had been slaughtered and the soldiers' daily ration was down to eleven ounces of grain a day. So many civilians died in the streets that to avoid epidemic, Gordon promised extra rations to those who volunteered for burial parties. On January 6, 1885, most of the civilian population surrendered, walking over to the Mahdi, leaving only fourteen thousand within the town. On the twelfth, the outlying fort at Omdurman ran out of food and surrendered, its garrison joining the Jihadiya militia.

Gordon spent hours on the roof monitoring his defenses, the Mahdi's camp, and the northern horizon through his telescope. He stacked his reserves of ammunition in the Catholic church, rigging a mine so that it could be blown up if the town fell, and prepared a steamer on the quay by the palace so that the town notables could escape. He slept in the day so that he could patrol the lines at night, where sentries collapsed at their posts from hunger. The garrison ate rats, cats, dogs, donkeys, and goatskin water bags, with a bread made from a handful of flour mixed with palm tree hearts. The Khalifa Abdullahi wrote to Gordon, tormenting him, "There is no escape for you from death at our hands, and from death by starvation."[62]

The Mahdi wrote to him, too. Gordon had forced the Mahdi's hand at every stage. The Mahdi did not want to kill Gordon: He hoped to capture him and trade him with the British for Ahmed Urabi, carving the khedive's empire into two rebel states and breaking the Turkish hold over the Nile. Now the Mahdi made a final appeal for Gordon to surrender.[63]

"Having seen what you have seen, how long are you going to disbelieve us? We have been told by God's Apostle, may Allah's blessings and peace be upon him, of the imminent destruction of all those in Khartoum, save those who believe and surrender; them Allah will save. We do not wish you to perish with those doomed to perish because we have frequently heard good of you." Quoting the Koran, *Kill not your people, for surely Allah is merciful to thee*, the Mahdi almost begged Gordon not to force a final, futile battle. "We have repeatedly written to you urging you to return to your own country, where your virtue will achieve the highest honour. . . . If you accept our advice, you will be thereby blessed: but if you wish to rejoin the English we will send you to them without claiming a farthing. *Salaam aleikum.*"64

Still hoping that the steamers would return with Wolseley's advance guard, Gordon did not reply. On January 20, his hopes surged. Through his telescope, he observed crowds of grieving women in the Mahdi's camp. He deduced correctly that the Desert Column had defeated the *Ansar,* and must be at Metemma.

That night, the Mahdi held a war council. Despite over three hundred days' siege and months of constant warfare, Khartoum had refused to surrender. Now the British were on the Nile, and moving up from Dongola toward Berber. If the *Ansar* did not storm Khartoum soon, they would have to retreat to Kordofan, their ambitions for riches and glory crushed along with the Mahdi's messianic dream. A deserter from Gordon's troops had suggested a way into the town. At the western end of Hilmi Pasha's ditch and rampart, the White Nile had filled the ditch and then dried out as the water level had fallen. Both rampart and ditch had leveled into a soft bog, and many of the mines had been washed away. The garrison was too debilitated to repair the defenses.

On the morning of January 25, Gordon observed the *Ansar* moving to the riverbank. He ordered every man between the age of eight and eighty to man the defenses, but most of the inhabitants and soldiers were too weak and dazed with hunger to respond. He spent the day sitting at his desk, smoking. In the early evening, he heard three tremendous roars as the Mahdi's followers promised three times, "We swear allegiance to you unto death!"

"If Allah grants you the victory," the Mahdi ordered, "Gordon is not to be killed."

The *Ansar* repeated its oath, "We swear by Allah and his Prophet, and we swear by you, that we will not commit adultery, that we will not disobey your lawful commands, that we will not flee from the jihad."

The Mahdi pointed his sword toward Khartoum. *"Allahu akbar!"*65

At midnight, as Gordon fell into a shallow sleep of exhaustion, the first fighters of the *Ansar* edged into the wet mud at the edge of Khartoum's southern defenses. Just before dawn, forty thousand men deluged a single battalion of Egyptian soldiers. At the other end of the rampart, further massive charges melted Khartoum's defenses.

The *Ansar* now controlled the town. They killed thousands, dragging the exhausted citizens from their houses, shooting, clubbing, and stabbing them in the streets, raping the women, enslaving the children, torturing the wealthy for hidden gold. Gordon awoke to screams and gunfire, a wave of death rolling toward the palace. Axes hacked at the gate to the palace garden, and the *Ansar* poured into the courtyard below his office.

Taking up his revolver and rallying the palace guards, Gordon led the defense, firing from the windows of the upper story and working toward the top of the staircase leading down to the courtyard. He may have hoped to fight his way to the ammunition dump in the church, either to get more cartridges or to blow it up. The Dervishes charged up the stairs, but the defenders repulsed them at point-blank range. Rescuing a wounded bodyguard, Gordon was struck in the shoulder by a Mahdist spear, but he kept firing and repelled a second assault on the staircase. When his revolver was empty, he drew his sword and lunged forward.

In the courtyard below him a Sudanese jihadi took careful aim with his rifle and shot Gordon in the chest. The impact threw him backward against the wall. Gordon pulled himself onto his feet and again led the charge, pushing the Dervishes at swordpoint down the stairs, but as he stepped into the courtyard, a second spear struck his right side. Falling, Gordon disappeared into a swarm of Dervishes, their spearpoints flashing in the early morning sun.[66]

The rape, murder, and looting went on all day. By the time the Mahdi ordered a halt to the slaughter, hardly any adult males remained alive to be taken prisoner. The *Ansar* flogged suspected hoarders until the flesh hung in shreds from their bodies and crushed their skulls with vises made of twisted palm fibers. They strung men up by their thumbs and tortured women in their genitals. Consul Hansal's servants killed their master, dragged his corpse into the street, piled alcohol-soaked tobacco on top of him, and incinerated him before tipping the remains into the river. So many *Ansar* pressed forward to share in the killing of Gordon that his body became an unrecognizable pile of butchered flesh.

In the Mahdi's camp at Omdurman, a horseman rode up to Rudolf Slatin. Dismounting, he unwrapped a blood-soaked cloth. Inside was the severed head of Charles George Gordon, his blue eyes still open.

9

The New Caliphate
1885–89

Charles George Gordon immortalized.

*Those that make war against Allah and his apostle and spread dis-
order in the land shall be slain or crucified, or have their hands and
feet cut off on alternate sides, or be banished from the land.*

The Koran[1]

WILSON'S PARTY REACHED Khartoum two days late. As the
Bordein steamed past Tuti Island toward the landing stage, the
Ansar on the banks blasted it with rifles and government ar-
tillery.

"The bullets began to fly pretty quickly, tapping like hail against the ship's
sides, whilst the shells went screeching overhead or threw up jets of water in
the stream round us," Wilson recalled.

Gordon's palace appeared above the palms. Wilson looked for a red Egyptian flag. He saw only a smoldering ruin. With "a heavy feeling at the heart telling of some awful disaster," he ran in close to the bank, within sixty yards of the sand, before the "loud, rushing noise" of Krupps shells from Khartoum convinced him that the town had fallen. His last sight of Khartoum was of loinclothed gunners and a mass of *Ansar* waving their rifles over their heads in triumph, as bullets and shells churned the water white around the *Bordein*. "It seemed almost impossible that we should escape." On his return through the gauntlet, Wilson was hit above the knee, and his binoculars were shot from his hand.[2]

On the night of February 5, Wolseley cabled the War Office, "Khartoum is reported to have fallen." He could not confirm if Gordon was alive or dead, and asked for further instructions.

Fourteen hundred miles away, a messenger bearing a scribbled note in an unsealed envelope marked *Secret* woke Sir Robert Thompson, the permanent undersecretary for war, just after midnight. Thompson tried to prevent the news leaking before the government had settled on its response. After rousing Hartington's young secretary Reggie Brett, whose appearance on Gordon's doorstep in Southampton had precipitated Gordon's final journey to Khartoum, Thompson tried to find the government. But Parliament was in recess.

Gladstone was holidaying with Hartington at Holker Hall in Lancashire, one of Hartington's family estates, where the exhausted premier had recuperated through bracing walks and the occasional pheasant shoot. Brett and Thompson woke Gladstone's secretary Eddy Hamilton, and sent telegrams to Holker Hall and to the queen at Osborne Castle on the Isle of Wight. At 0300 they knocked on the door of Lord Granville's Mayfair mansion. They waited for half an hour in the hall before Granville's valet informed them, falsely, that His Lordship was out of town. By then, the messenger, who had been unable to resist an unsealed envelope marked *Secret*, had sold the story. The morning edition of the *Telegraph* broke the news.[3]

THE QUEEN ROSE EARLIEST. "Dreadful news after breakfast," Victoria wrote in her journal. "Khartoum fallen, Gordon's fate uncertain! All greatly distressed. It is too fearful."

Victoria felt that Gladstone had disgraced her and the nation. "The government is alone to blame, by refusing to send the expedition before it was too late." Casting grammar and security to the winds, she communicated her fury to Gladstone, Hartington, and Granville in unciphered telegrams, sharing her thoughts with every telegraph operator between the Isle of Wight and their destinations. "These news from Khartoum are frightful, and to think that all this might have been prevented and many precious lives saved by earlier action is too frightful."[4]

Up at Holker Hall, Lord Hartington had told his valet not to wake him before noon. The cable from London waited on a tray until Hartington came down for breakfast. As soon as he and Gladstone read it, they took the first train to London, collecting the queen's humiliating telegram en route.

"The circumstances are sad and trying," Gladstone admitted that night in his diary. "It is one of the least points about them, that they may put an end to this Government."[5]

"At Last!" *Punch* magazine had already prepared a celebratory cover, showing Gordon and his grateful soldiers rushing out of Khartoum to greet the redcoats on the steamers. Now a second cover was devised, with a grieving Britannia hiding her eyes from the sack of Khartoum, lamenting, "Too Late!"

A wave of sorrow, sentiment, guilt, and patriotism surged through the press, and met another wave of spontaneous public distress and outrage. The loss of Khartoum was a humiliation for British arms at the hands of "Dervish" savages; an embarrassment to ethnic dignity at the hands of half-naked "Fuzzy-Wuzzies"; a defeat for Free Trade; a disaster for the abolitionists; a hammer blow to Britain's imperial prestige.

"Our power in the East will be *ruined*," raged the queen, whose patriotism and pride in forward policy embodied the national mood. "We shall never be able to hold up our heads again." Although Wolseley could not confirm if Gordon was alive or dead, from the first the press and public assumed the worst. The blame settled on the government, and on Gladstone in particular.[6]

As the wave of contempt crashed onto Downing Street, Gladstone realized he must catch it before it washed away his ministry. At the next cabinet, the great anti-imperial campaigner announced that Britain must not ignore "the effect which the triumph of the Mahdi would have on our Mahometan subjects." With the survival of British India at stake, the cabinet decided it must avenge Gordon. It informed Garnet Wolseley that it had voted £2.75 million for the financing of an expanded, second Sudanese expedition for the following autumn.

Sure of his clear conscience, Gladstone then turned to a more pressing matter, the ongoing Great Power negotiations over Egypt's financial recovery. He had misread the intensity of the public's response. In the popular perception, a heartless government had abandoned Gordon to savages. On the evening of the eleventh, when the Gladstones went to the Criterion Theater—"*The Candidate,* capitally acted"—his fellow theatergoers hissed him in the street. The next morning, a rumor of Gordon's death reached London.[7]

"How shall I write to you, or how shall I attempt to express what I feel!" the queen wrote to Gordon's grieving sister Augusta. "To think of your dear, noble heroic brother, who served his country and his Queen so truly, so heroically, with a self-sacrifice so edifying to the world, not having been rescued; that the promises of support were not fulfilled—which I so frequently and constantly pressed on those who asked him to go—is to me *grief inexpressible!*"

Parliament voted twenty thousand pounds for Gordon's family and declared a day of national mourning. Tributes arrived from the emperor of China, and from Khedive Tawfik, whose eulogy elegantly skirted the darker truth of Gordon's motivations: "In his own death, Gordon has lost nothing, but has gained the glorious object he so fervently desired, to the attainment of which his life was so nobly devoted."

A barrage of anonymous hate mail descended on Downing Street. A popular joke inverted the initials of Gladstone's nickname from G.O.M. to M.O.G.—"Murderer of Gordon"—and a music hall song promised Gladstone that when he died, he would "sit in state on a red-hot plate between Pilate and Judas Iscariot." On February 12, the prime minister stayed in bed all day, "the disturbance, which has had so many forms, having at last taken the form of an overaction of the bowels."[8]

"IF ANYTHING CAN KILL old Gladstone, this news ought to."

Reading Gordon's journals in a fly-blown tent at Korti, Garnet Wolseley damned the prime minister. "He cannot, self-illusionist though he may be, disguise from himself the fact that he is directly responsible for the fall of Khartoum and all the bloodshed it entails: that it was owing to his influence, active measures for the relief of Gordon were not undertaken in time. Whilst Gordon was starving, this arrogant Minister who poses as a great Statesman, but without any just claim to be considered one, was discussing to himself whether Gordon was *hemmed in* or *surrounded,* and no one could persuade him that Khartoum was besieged or that Gordon in any danger. Never were the destinies of any great nation committed to a more incompetent pilot. . . . What an ending to all our labor, and all our bright hopes is this!!"⁹

Wolseley was disgusted by the government's new orders. Gladstone was prepared to waste men's lives to win votes. "Let all your soldiers, they say, grill for the summer in the Sudan, let many of them be killed and wounded, we care not, so long as the country will recognise that we have at last roused ourselves and adopted a spirited policy." If the government's original expectation of Wolseley's small force had been optimistic, their new orders courted disaster. The conquest of Khartoum had turned the Mahdi into "a great Military Power," and now all the Sudanese tribes must follow him or be destroyed: "He will be regarded as irresistible."

Like poor, murdered Gordon, Wolseley and his men would be sacrificed to satisfy the "fools and theoretical vestrymen" of the Liberal Party. Expanding the Sudanese war for domestic reasons seemed "a hideous mistake, the outcome of Mr. Gladstone's foolish policy in Egypt, beginning with that wicked, cruel and senseless bombardment of Alexandria." In scale and ambition, it would be "the most serious war we have undertaken since the idiotic Cabinet of 1854 declared war against Russia"—and Gladstone had served in that cabinet, too. Wolseley reckoned that the Mahdi could beat any army, British or Egyptian, simply by retreating into central Africa. "We shall have spent ten millions, and done nothing, and when we withdraw we shall very likely have a pack of yelping curs at our heels, take long shots at our retreating troops."¹⁰

Wolseley could hardly hold the line. The small British force had become stretched over harsh distances, and there was bad news on all fronts. By the Red Sea, General Graham had failed to break Osman Digna's grip on Suakin. On the Nile, Wolseley's main force was still caught in the Cataracts above Abu Hamed. After running aground both their steamers, Sir Charles Wilson and his party had to be rescued by the rest of the Desert Column, which staggered back to Korti leaving a trail of dead camels. On February 10, another delaying force of two thousand *Ansar* attacked a British column at Kirkeban. Although the British beat them off, they killed one of Wolseley's most able commanders, Major General William Earle, V.C.

Wolseley's expedition was falling apart. Sir Charles Wilson's nerves had "gone so completely from his experience of real war" that Wolseley expected nothing further from him. When Wolseley inspected the surviving members of Gordon's steamer crews, the possibility of augmenting his troops with Sudanese conscripts seemed absurd. He refused to believe that black Africans could be trained as British soldiers. "I never saw such a lot of men—a large proportion of them of the lowest type—many very little above the monkey in brain development." Ashamed of his inability to avenge Gordon, he saw no choice but to advise that British troops should withdraw from the entire Sudan and retrench at Wadi Halfa. If this was not done quickly, the Mahdi would push them out, a denouement with potentially fatal implications for the Wolseley career. "Oh, what a campaign of anxieties is this!"[11]

ON FEBRUARY 27, Gladstone escaped yet another vote of censure in the Commons. For three days, he defended the government's conduct with agonizing arguments built on erroneous reports from Garnet Wolseley. The circumstances of the fall of Khartoum still remained obscure, and Gordon's death had not been confirmed. Wolseley had forwarded an early rumor that the city had fallen not through assault, but treachery; other rumors suggested that Gordon had been taken prisoner. If the city had fallen to treachery, Gladstone argued, how could that be the fault of a government that had committed troops and money to defending it? If Gordon had been murdered, the government was determined to avenge him and save the Sudan, if not for Commerce and Christianity, then for Civilization. But, Gladstone insinuated, was it known for certain that Gordon, the best and toughest Sudanese hand of all, was actually dead?

Gladstone survived by fourteen votes. The public and political pressure of the last weeks had made him consider retirement again, but his digestion and his prospects both recovered swiftly. His second escape from censure over the Sudan persuaded him to persevere with his tormented coalition. "The final division in my mind turned the scale, so nicely was it balanced."

Gladstone knew little of "over-sea," but he had a lifetime's experience of Westminster. He knew that his promise to avenge Gordon would be tested against other, more demanding obligations. The international negotiations for a settlement of the Egyptian finances had not yet been resolved. At the other extremity of Britain's growing Islamic empire, a brewing frontier war in Afghanistan really did threaten India. The public would soon forget about Gordon and find a new focus for its unhealthy imperial obsession. When it did, the flexible consciences and pocketbooks of Gladstone's coalition would contract sharply. While Gladstone trumpeted promises of vengeance to Parliament, the nation, and Garnet Wolseley, what he wanted most of all was to be rid of the Sudan before the next election.

"The lowest of all the motives bearing on it," he admitted to Granville, "is that if we cannot kill the War in the Sudan, it will kill us, and not with an altogether clean death."

Gladstone searched for an exit strategy. Overruling Lord Granville, he accepted an offer from Wilfrid Blunt to sound out negotiations with the Mahdi via Jamal ed-Din al-Afghani.[12]

"This has been a day of consolation," Blunt wrote when he heard of the fall of Khartoum, "and I could not help singing all the way down in the train. Why had I so little faith?"

Blunt felt sure that Gordon had been taken alive. His cousin in the Foreign Office, Algernon "Button" Bourke, assured him that Gladstone would "treat with the Mahdi on almost any terms." Blunt found Afghani at the Hotel Wagram in Paris, triumphant: The Mahdi's victory had raised the price of peace, and that raised the prospect of returning Urabi to Egypt. Although Urabi was at Ceylon, the British authorities made no effort to monitor his mail or his visitors. Urabi had already agreed with Afghani's plan to divide the Egyptian empire between Urabi and the Mahdi. Blunt returned to London with Afghani's suggestion. Britain, he advised Gladstone, should send a negotiator to the Sudan.[13]

Gladstone was still calculating if the press and public would permit him this betrayal of Gordon's memory when his Sudanese position suddenly changed. At Suakin, General Graham finally defeated Osman Digna's rebels, securing the Red Sea approaches to the Suez Canal. In London, the Great Powers' negotiators assented to continued British supervision of Egypt's finances. With Britain's most important regional interests secure, Gladstone sensed an opportunity to shake off his Sudanese commitment. In early April, he played the financial card. Launching a second Sudanese expedition would cost £11.5 million, with more money required for an advance on Khartoum. Parliament had just funded an expedition to shore up the Afghan border against Russia and had reached the limit of its patriotism and its generosity. Just as Gladstone hoped, political and popular pressure for a renewed Sudanese campaign began to falter. The catastrophe at Khartoum was now a drama of public memory, not a current political issue.

On April 21, Wolseley received orders from Lord Hartington to withdraw to Wadi Halfa. There would be no second Sudanese campaign, and no chance for Wolseley to avenge Gordon and redeem his reputation. Britain would hold on to Suakin, but the rest of the Sudan would be surrendered to the Mahdi.

"Of all the miserable, foolish policies, this is the worst!" Wolseley suspected that the government intended to make him a scapegoat for the failed campaign and the withdrawal. The Wolseley brain preferred dividing the spoils to dividing the blame. It settled on two targets: Gladstone the Radical hypocrite, and Sir Charles Wilson, who, Wolseley now decided, had cost Gordon's life by wasting time at Metemma.

"Sir Charles Wilson is clearly responsible for all those delays but, poor devil, he had lost any nerve he had ever possessed," Wolseley wrote in his diary. He did not consider his own contributions to the fiasco: his insistence on advancing by the White Nile, the weeks lost to his Canadian *voyageurs,* the boats run aground, and the caution with which he had advanced on Berber. As he left the Sudan, Wolseley would fight two successful rearguard actions, one against the Mahdi, the other against the reputation of Sir Charles Wilson.[14]

Freed from its promise of action, the government aligned itself with the public's extravagant grief for Gordon. Packed services were held at Westminster Abbey and St. Paul's Cathedral, before a phalanx of mourners that included the Princess of Wales, the Duke of Cambridge, the Archbishop of Canterbury, and Lord Granville. Shelfloads of songs, poems, abolitionist polemics, and imperialist appeals sprouted on bookstalls. The poet William McGonagall beat his fellow bards to the obvious rhymes for "Khartoum," producing a dirge that fully justified his reputation as Britain's worst poet.

> *ALAS! Now o'er the civilised world there hangs a gloom*
> *For brave General Gordon, that was killed in Khartoum,*
> *He was a Christian hero, and a soldier of the Cross,*
> *And to England his death will be a very great loss.*

Like many of his contemporaries, McGonagall preferred to believe that Gordon had succumbed not to his own folly, but to treachery.

> *Yes, the black-hearted traitor opened the gates of Khartoum,*
> *And through that the Christian hero has met his doom,*
> *For when the gates were opened the Arabs rushed madly in,*
> *And foully murdered him while they laughingly did grin.*[15]

A series of Gordon Boys' Clubs opened for the encouragement of Gordonian tendencies among British youth. Spontaneous subscriptions poured in for memorials in stone and paint. The government engaged the admired Pre-Raphaelite sculptor Sir Hamo Thorneycroft to immortalize Gordon in bronze for Trafalgar Square. So many painters volunteered their speculations about Gordon's last moments that the Royal Academy held a special exhibition. William Joy, a remorseless melodramatist in oils popular for historical items like *Young Nelson and his Grandmother*, and *Flora MacDonald's Farewell to Bonnie Prince Charlie*, contributed a fantasia of Gordon's last moments that would become a defining image of the Victorian era, either in spite or because of its inaccuracy.

In *General Gordon's Last Stand*, a mass of spear-waving Dervishes crowd around the foot of the stairs in the palace courtyard, their freshly laundered white jibbas contrasting agreeably with their black faces. As the defense collapses, Gordon stands at the head of the stairs in his Royal Engineers uniform, its redness suggesting the blood that is about to be spilled. A giant Dervish mounts the stairs, and is about to throw a spear into Gordon's body at point-blank range. Although Gordon's revolver is cocked, he leaves it hanging limply at his side. His only attempt to defend himself is to raise his left arm across his body before, like Jesus, he is pierced on his right side. To the public who sanctified his memory, Gordon died like a Christian martyr.

Gladstone had escaped the Sudan, but he could not escape his own sacrifice. His coalition did not survive until the summer recess. On June 8, Parliament rejected his proposal to add a penny to beer and liquor taxes in order to fund the constant military involvements of empire. A cabinet exhausted by rivalry finally took the opportunity to resign, allowing Lord Salisbury to form a minority Conservative government.

Gladstone cleared out his office. In the bare room where he had sealed Gordon's fate, he knelt in prayer, "a moment to fall down and give thanks for the labors done, and the strength vouchsafed me there; and to pray for the Christlike mind."[16]

"KNOW THAT SHORTLY I shall come with the *Hizb Allah* to Egypt, for the affair of the Sudan is finished," the Mahdi announced in February 1885.

At Khartoum, the Mahdi planned the expansion of the new caliphate. He looked east to Christian Abyssinia, west to Morocco—from where admirers had written offering to join the revolution—and, above all, north to Egypt.

"We will be on hand for the sake of religion, to expel the enemies of Allah from the land of the Muslims and eradicate them to the last man if they do not surrender or turn to Allah," he warned Khedive Tawfik. Adopting Gordon's printing press, the Mahdi sent out hundreds of proclamations into the countryside. While he waited for the response, he indulged in the fruits of victory.[17]

In the hours after the fall of Khartoum, the *Ansar* had massacred, mutilated, and decapitated thousands of its inhabitants. They had enslaved thousands more, and had driven many out of the city and into the desert. Gordon's mutilated remains had been thrown down a well. After the slaughter, the Mahdi's three khalifas had rounded up the female survivors, brought them to his camp at Omdurman, and divided them into groups according to skin color. Penned up under the sun, many still spattered with the blood of their murdered husbands and sons, they had awaited their division among the *Ansar's* leaders.

The Mahdi chose first, taking all the girls of five years of age for future service in his harem. Then his three khalifas chose their concubines, followed by the rest of the *Ansar*. Those women who were not enslaved were left to starve. For weeks after the fall of Khartoum, women wandered naked through Omdurman's market, begging for food. Mothers who had given birth in the street lay dying with their babies.[18]

The Mahdi's emirs took the best gardens in Khartoum. Khalifa Abdullahi camped in the grounds of Gordon's palace; Khalifa Sharif in the Catholic Mission; and Khalifa Ali wad Helu took the house of Albert Marquet, a murdered merchant. The *Ansar* moved into the houses of the poorer Copts and Egyptians. Mirrors and fine china were destroyed with axes, cloth was hacked into squares to decorate jibbas, and gold and silver were stacked in the Mahdi's personal treasury.

Smashing up General Hicks's stables for materials, the Mahdi built two wooden houses, one for him and one for his harem. Publicly he continued to urge moderation on his followers, but in private he indulged in Turkish sensualities. The Mahdi developed a taste for Persian rugs. He dressed in fine linen shirts and an embroidered silk cap. After years of sleeping rough, he took to sleeping in a bed taken from the house of a Khartoum merchant. After the hunger, he treated himself to colossal feasts. He had always been heavy-set, and the splendor and the savories made him enormously fat.

He acquired so many concubines that they could no longer be crammed into their quarters and had to be accommodated in Gordon's palace. Occasionally he ventured into Khartoum for "pleasure and debauchery" in the palace of his enemies; as in the days of his youth, the largest building in Khartoum was again a seraglio. He received his inner circle reclining on a gold-brocaded pillow, while female attendants fanned him with ostrich feathers or massaged his feet, hands, and neck. When he washed, the dirty water was distributed among those fortunate enough to drink it for its magical powers; the palace eunuchs also sold small pouches of the earth on which he had walked. When he presented himself to the faithful at the mosque, he changed into his old jibba, waddling through the crowd as his eunuch attendants cleared a path with whips, and women fell to kiss his footsteps. When he returned to his hut, he took off his jibba.[19]

Outside the Mahdi's hut, a shanty town sprang up at Omdurman. In the heat of early summer, with unburied bodies still littering Khartoum and Omdurman, these ramshackle huts became a hive of disease. Typhus, dysentery, and smallpox broke out. On June 16, 1885, as Gladstone prepared to leave office, the Mahdi fell sick with a fever. His wives attempted to cure him with traditional medicine. They brought him gourds filled with liquid butter and a concoction of pomegranate skins. They cupped him with heated gazelle horns and slabs of iron. They injected his urine into his eyes, they wrote prayers on his stomach and hands, and they wrote koranic passages on a piece of paper, washing it off and giving the inky water to the Mahdi to drink. Nothing worked.

The Mahdi's aides summoned Hassan al-Zeki, an Egyptian doctor who had served in the Khartoum hospital under Gordon. Al-Zeki suspected typhus, caught from a flea on the plague of rats that had appeared in early summer. There was nothing he could do.[20]

Within days, the Mahdi's family and the khalifas gathered by his bed. Outside his hut, a crowd of anxious *Ansar* massed, waiting for the inevitable miracle. Inside, his inner circle watched his last hours. Mumbling and feverish, the prophet appointed Khalifa Abdullahi as his heir.

"La Illaha illallah, Mohammed rasul Allah," the Mahdi repeated several times. "There is no God but Allah, and Mohammed is his Messenger." Then he crossed his hands over his chest, stretched his limbs in a final convulsion, and died. He was forty-two.[21]

Beside the Mahdi's body, his inner circle knelt before Khalifa Abdullahi and acknowledged him as *Khalifat al-Mahdi*, the Mahdi's khalifa. As the corpse was washed, scented, and wrapped for burial, the news spread through Omdurman. The *Ansar* rallied in grief, unable to comprehend that their prophet had succumbed to mortal disease. Khalifa Abdullahi joined the Mahdi's family at the grave dug in the floor of his hut, as thousands pressed around its walls to throw in a handful of dirt.

Tears rolling from his eyes, Abdullahi left the hut. He ascended a temporary pulpit that he had ordered to be prepared outside the Mahdi's house.

"Friends of the Mahdi," he called to the sea of mourners, "Allah's will cannot be changed. The Mahdi has left us, and has entered into heaven, where everlasting joys await him. It is for us to obey his precepts, and to support one another, just as the stones and walls of a house go to make a building. . . . Never deviate from the path which he has shown you. You are the friends of the Mahdi, and I am his Khalifa. Swear that you will be faithful to me."[22]

So many *Ansar* queued to take the oath of allegiance that the ceremony went on through the night. Abdullahi al-Taishi, who could not read or write, now inherited the Mahdi's empire, supreme caliph of more than a million square miles, from Wadi Halfa in the north to the Gazelle River in the south, from the Saharan wastes in the west to the hills overlooking the deep blue waters of the Red Sea. Most of this territory was devastated. The Mahdi's revolution had destroyed the Sudanese economy, severed its communications, interrupted its agriculture, and massacred its government.

"Ed-din mansur," Abdullahi announced. "Religion is victorious."[23]

Then he turned on his allies. The Mahdi had built a coalition on the twin poles of his prophetic personality and a shared loathing of the Turkiyya. By August 1885, with the exception of a couple of starving garrisons in southern Sudan, his whole empire had been purged of Egyptian soldiers and Christian merchants. He had died at the moment of revolutionary success, when the next battle was the building of a state. As the leader of the Baggara, only Abdullahi had the military power to hold the coalition together. He had no other virtue. He commanded no support among the riverain tribes. Unlike his fellow khalifas, Mohammed Sharif and Ali wad Helu, he was not a member of the *Ashraf*. Nor, as an illiterate tribesman from the far west, could he pretend to be a prophet. The best he managed was an energetic propaganda campaign.

Abdullahi announced that an angel had visited him in a vision to confirm that God, the angel Gabriel, the Prophet, and the Mahdi all approved of him as "a guidance in the earth from east to west." It transpired that at the Mahdi's funeral, Abdullahi had unwittingly ingested a hair from the Mahdi's head. "The heart which this hair enters is safe from hypocrisy, and it enters it with a light. All this vision is caused by this hair." Presenting Abdullahi with "a long light in the shape of a rope," the angel passed on the Mahdi's wish that Abdullahi quarter it. To anoint himself and his followers as the Mahdi's true heirs, he must eat one slice, wipe his face with the second, imbue the Black Flag with the third, and scatter the last among the *Ansar* as they prayed. "Every rank that you command to its place shall be clothed by that light."

To complement his vision, Abdullahi compared himself to the Prophet Mohammed's heirs. "In his time, he conquered only Mecca and Khaybar; the rest of the conquest was by the hands of the Caliphs after him." The death of the Mahdi before the conquest of "Mecca, Constantinople and other cities" did not undermine the Mahdi's messiahship; it only passed the leadership of his jihad to his "successors and companions." Abdullahi's rivals cannot have failed to remember that the Prophet's heirs had soon fallen into schism and war.[24]

He dealt with the *Ashraf* first. Assisted by Khalifa Ali wad Helu, he disarmed the third khalifa, the Mahdi's cousin Muhammad Sharif. Abdullahi's brother Yacub collected all of Muhammad Sharif's soldiers, weapons, and stores, leaving him with a paltry bodyguard. Then, when another of the Mahdi's relatives, Mohammed Khalil Zughal, the governor of Darfur, came to Khartoum with an army—either to swear allegiance to Abdullahi or, more probably, to assist Muhammad Sharif—Abdullahi sent out his troops to head off the visitors and arrest Zughal. The new governor of Darfur was Abdullahi's young cousin Uthman wad Adam. Within a year, Abdullahi had displaced all but two of the Mahdi's provincial governors. Of the two, one was so far down the Gazelle River that he could not influence Omdurman politics; the other, Osman Digna, was too important an ally to disturb, as his tribesmen kept the British and Egyptians penned up at Suakin and Tokar.

Next, Abdullahi dealt with the few tribes who did not recognize his rule over the Sudan. The Kababish Arabs of northern Kordofan and Dongola had never acclaimed the Mahdi, and they had compounded this theological error by supplying the Gordon relief expedition with camels. In early 1887, Abdullahi captured a Kababish convoy and discovered two hundred Remington rifles and two hundred pounds in cash. He took this as a pretext for a campaign of genocide, displaying the head of their leader Sheikh Salih on the public scaffold at Omdurman. Then he massacred the Juhaina tribe on the western bank of the Blue Nile, whose fields produced most of Omdurman's grain. The head of their chief Yusuf al-Mardi joined that of Sheikh Salih. Their fields went unharvested.

In 1888, Abdullahi turned to distant Darfur. His imprisonment of Mohammed Khalil Zughal had tipped the province into open rebellion. An anti-Mahdist miracle worker, known as Abu Jummaiza from his habit of preaching under a wild fig tree, rallied a local coalition of Mahdi nostalgists and Darfur secessionists. In two years of brutal campaigning, Abu Jummaiza twice defeated Abdullahi's cousin Uthman wad Adam before, stricken by smallpox, he was unable to lead his followers at a climactic battle outside El Fasher. Fighting with only swords, spears, and knives, Uth-man wad Adam's *Ansar* drove the rebels from the battlefield and massacred as many men, women, and children as they could.

"The cavalry still continued pursuing till almost all were killed," he reported to Abdullahi. "They followed them even as far as the caves and forests, where they tried to conceal themselves, but they were all killed. Even those who transformed themselves into apes, wolves, dogs, and rabbits—for the natives of the western countries can be so transformed—were also all killed, even to the very last. The number of their dead was countless."[25]

To complete his control over his empire, Abdullahi engineered enormous population transfers. He invited his fellow Baggara into Omdurman. He established his supporters along the road to Kordofan, his escape route should he be overthrown at Khartoum. He displaced the unreliable riverain tribes north to Dongola, as the first line of defense against invasion from Egypt. He ordered the *Ansar* to leave the Turkish palaces of Khartoum and decreed that they resettle around his camp at Omdurman. Khartoum became a ghostly museum of its final moments. In the streets, grass grew around white skeletons, their wrists and ankles tied together, still lying where they had been dumped during the sack of the town. Buildings disintegrated as Abdullahi's followers ripped out fittings and smashed up brickwork for their projects.

The Mahdi had dreamed of a tribal confederacy in the service of Allah. It had degenerated from pious millennarianism to paranoid autocracy, and a politics of war and massacre. Abdullahi's campaigns of murder, expropriation, and population transfer followed years of chaos that had wrecked the Sudan's agriculture and economy. Its exports shrank to no more than smuggled slaves and gold. In 1887, the first of a series of poor Nile floods tipped Abdullahi's kingdom into massive famine. At the start of the revolution, the Sudan had contained about 8.5 million people. Eight years later, the pursuit of heaven on earth had killed more than half of them through war, disease, and starvation. Although Abdullahi's priority was to centralize power at Omdurman, his warriors needed grain, loot, and fresh slaves. He had no choice but to direct their energies outward. It was time to resume the jihad.

"The Prophet said to me, *You are permitted to raid the Abyssinians in their land.*" Overriding the Islamic tradition of not waging war on Christian Abyssinia, in April 1887 Abdullahi turned east. Like Khedive Ismail in the 1870s, he cloaked territorial greed with the pretext of avenging Abyssinian border raids. For nearly two years, Dervishes and Abyssinians clashed in battles of medieval crudity, hacking at each other with swords, knives, and lances, looting each other's baggage trains and enslaving camp followers. Beneath Abdullahi's gestures to jihad, the campaign was as naked in its violence and opportunism as a Turkish raid on the Gazelle River.

Finally, in March 1889, Abdullahi's general al-Zaki Tamal met King John of Abyssinia and his army at Gallabat on the Abyssinian-Sudanese border. It would be the last major battle to be fought almost exclusively with edged weapons. With appropriate chivalry, King John led the Abyssinian charge. For the first time the Dervishes faced their own tactic, the relentless human wave. But when John was mortally injured in the slashing melée and was carried back to his tent, his troops retreated with him. After the battle, the *Ansar* added the king's corpse to their mountain of booty. Naturally they sent his head back to Omdurman as an addition for Abdullahi's ghoulish collection. In 1889, the year the British army took delivery of Hiram Maxim's new machine gun, capable of firing five hundred rounds in a single minute, Khalifa Abdullahi reached his technological nadir of the Battle of Gallabat.[26]

When Abdullahi heard of his victory, he was overcome with joy. He distributed General al-Zaki's triumphant report from Gallabat throughout his kingdom. The unchallenged caliph of an uncharted expanse, Abdullahi had triumphed by destroying his subjects as he conquered them. The result was the disintegration of society. Communication with the outside world broke down, and the Sudan drifted into a waste of starvation and disease, a lost paradise of death.

The greatest prize still lay before him. In the early summer of 1889, Abdullahi's eye turned north to Egypt. He ordered his general at Dongola, Abd al-Rahman al-Nujumi, to advance on Wadi Halfa. Before al-Nujumi left Dongola, he burned down his house. The hour had come to fulfill the Mahdi's prophecy.

"GENERAL GORDON was sent to Khartoum not to act, but to report," Evelyn Baring explained. "General Gordon had failed to recognise the real facts in connection with the Sudan when he undertook his mission. After his arrival at Khartoum, he recognised them, but he could not enforce their recognition on Mr. Gladstone; the latter's blindness to facts, which were patent to all the world, eventually resulted in the death of General Gordon, of Colonel Stewart, and of many other brave men."[27]

Like Garnet Wolseley, Baring blamed his superiors and inferiors for the loss of Khartoum, and absolved himself. Unlike Wolseley, Baring was left to clear up the political debris. Britain had forced Egypt to retreat from the Sudan, yet Egypt still claimed the territory, and the Turkish sultan still claimed both Egypt and the Sudan. In March 1885, Gladstone had secured Egypt's debt repayments to its European creditors, but only by granting Bismarck's ambitious Germany a seat on the Commission of the Debt. This gave Germany an effective veto over the commission's future disposal of the Egyptian revenues, which might include funding the reconquest of the Sudan.

"Berlin, and not Cairo, is the real center of gravity of Egyptian affairs," Baring warned London.

Meanwhile, the Mahdi's sudden death had not altered the threat from the south. In 1885, Habib Anthony Salmone, a Syrian Christian who had volunteered to spy for Britain, infiltrated Jamal ed-Din al-Afghani's circle at Paris. Salmone reported that when the Nile fell to its lowest level that summer, the Mahdists planned to block it with a dam of boulders and destroy the Egyptian harvest, causing mass starvation. Baring was effectively defenseless. After Wolseley's withdrawal from the Sudan, only a skeletal force of inexperienced Egyptian troops held the line at Wadi Halfa, and Abd al-Rahman al-Nujumi's troops had filled the vacuum in Dongola. If Khalifa Abdullahi sent them further north, Egypt could not protect itself without foreign assistance. Worse, the only foreign assistance on offer was of the wrong kind.[28]

Gladstone had also shuffled out of office without settling the future of Egypt with Sultan Abdul Hamid II. In August 1885, the new prime minister, Lord Salisbury, dispatched Sir Henry Drummond Wolff to Constantinople to negotiate an Egyptian settlement. Within two months, the sultan signed an Anglo-Turkish Convention, setting out "the nature of the subjects which were to be discussed," and resolving the question of authority in Egypt: Pending the eventual exit of British troops and officials, Egypt was to be governed by a pair of British and Turkish commissioners.

Drummond Wolff believed that this twin-headed executive would help Egypt "in the elaboration of institutions which must combine both Eastern and Western elements." As it would be difficult "for English gentlemen, however able and conciliatory, to come to terms with races who had suffered so severely at our hands," the same went for the Sudan. Blithely dismissing the theological aspect of the Mahdi's revolt, Wolff reasoned that as Muslims, the Sudanese rebels recognized the sultan as their caliph. Therefore, Ottoman diplomacy was the best means of "tranquilising the Sudan by pacific means."[29]

"A delusion," Baring responded. The Mahdi, he said, had confounded Christians and Turks alike in one common anathema." The Ottoman Empire had been the Mahdi's nearest enemy, but not his only enemy.

Baring had survived the Mahdi's revolt, Gordon's defeat, the loss of the Sudan, and the fall of Gladstone's government. Now a few "imaginary facts evolved from the brains of Turkish diplomatists" threatened to return Egypt to the Turkiyya, and the Sudan, too. Apart from bringing catastrophe upon Egypt, this would mean the end of Baring's reign as the power behind the khedivial throne. The Gladstonian alternative, to dilute the sultan's ambition by sharing Egypt with the other European powers, had failed in the crisis of Urabi's revolt. To Baring, multilateralism and "Internationalism" meant "political egotism, a disregard of the rights of subject races and, in the case now under discussion, a decadence in the authority of that European Power on the maintenance of whose paramount influence the advance of true civilization in Egypt depends." What to do?[30]

Viewed from the consular villa, only one country could bring "true civilisation" to Egypt: "That Power is Great Britain." The Turks were incompetent, the French devious, and the Germans malevolent. Only Britain possessed the requisite integrity. Baring had always expected that Britain's economic and strategic investments in Egypt would necessitate a permanent British presence. With Khedive Tawfik in his pocket and British officers in the garrisons, he had planned Egypt's financial recovery, honoring its debts through high taxation and total fiscal transparency. He had forcefully suppressed any nationalist rumblings, even banning Wilfrid Blunt from entering the country, and had organized the training of a new Egyptian army, staffed by British officers and commanded by a new *sirdar*, Major General Francis Grenfell. This benign despotism had remarkable economic results. Although the Mahdi had deprived Egypt of its illicit Sudanese revenues, Egypt's economy underwent rapid paper growth. This allowed Baring to reduce Egypt's obligations to the bondholders and to plan for the day when British Egypt could fund its own reconquest of the Sudan.

Baring received little help from London. Between 1885 and 1887, the government changed four times. Lord Salisbury and the Conservatives had capitalized on Gladstone's Sudanese problems when they were in opposition, but in office they followed in Gladstone's Egyptian footsteps. At first, Salisbury refused to lead a minority government, until he was personally persuaded by Queen Victoria to do his patriotic duty. Beset by the Irish controversies that had undermined Gladstone, Salisbury's caretaker government lasted barely a year. In February 1886, Gladstone returned for a third ministry, but the Grand Old Man could do no better. Having allied with the Irish nationalists to bring down Salisbury, Gladstone then introduced a bill granting Home Rule to Ireland. The bill spilt the Liberal Party. In July 1887, Salisbury returned, and with a workable majority.

At the same time, negotiations crawled forward between Sir Henry Drummond Wolff and the Sultan's advisers. On May 22, 1887, Wolff finally presented London with a finished draft of the Anglo-Ottoman Convention. In Article V of the convention, Britain and Turkey agreed that within three years of the sultan's ratification of the treaty, Britain would withdraw its troops from Egypt. The withdrawal would not be unconditional. Britain reserved the right to cancel it if there was any "appearance of danger in the interior, or from without." And if "order and security" broke down in Egypt, both parties had the right to send in troops, singly or together. Still, it looked as if Baring might be toppled from his Egyptian throne—but then the sultan saved him.[31]

Abdul Hamid II distrusted foreigners in general, and his British friends in particular. His attempts to manipulate Great Power rivalries took unpredictable and erratic forms, partly because they were filtered through a swirl of advisers, each of whom backed a different Great Power. On May 26, 1887, Abdul Hamid II assured Sir William White, the British ambassador at Constantinople, that he was about to ratify the convention. A week later, the sultan's astrologer Abu al-Huda endorsed the opinions of the advocates of France and Russia. The sultan refused to sign the convention.

Sir Henry Drummond Wolff expected that a shift in planetary alignment would soon remind the sultan that Britain was his chief patron. Wolff hovered in Constantinople for two months, waiting for the sultan to relent, until a disgusted Lord Salisbury recalled him to London. When Abdul Hamid II realized that by refusing to assist Britain in its departure from Egypt, he had thrown away his best hope of regaining his prized province, he ordered his ambassador at London to renew the negotiations. Lord Salisbury turned him down.

"So long as the Sultan was so much under the influence of other advisors as to repudiate an agreement which he had himself so recently sanctioned, any fresh agreement would obviously be liable to meet the same fate," Salisbury told Abdul Hamid II. Just as he had in 1882, the sultan had bungled the chance to recover Egypt for the Ottoman Empire. Britain had done its best to leave Egypt. The sultan's folly had demonstrated that there was no alternative to extended occupation.[32]

Baring had prepared for that all along. Through the slow rotation of governments in London, and the elaborate dance between Sir Henry Drummond Wolff and the sultan's advisers in Constantinople, the consul had continued rebuilding Egypt on the assumption that Britain would stay there. In 1888, for the first time since the collapse of cotton prices in the mid-1860s, Baring recorded a small surplus in Egypt's accounts. Immediately, he created a reserve fund for "extraordinary expenditure."

He hoped to collect Egypt's budget surpluses, so that when the time came to retake the Sudan, Egypt could fund the invasion from its own savings. That way, he could bypass "Internationalism": the Commission of the Debt and the threat of a German veto. But the commissioners insisted that these revenues must also be subject to international division, and the Salisbury government assented, unwilling to risk confrontation over a hypothetical issue. Baring kept telling London that a British reconquest of the Sudan was strategically inevitable, and Salisbury agreed with his analysis. But so long as Britain had a choice, the government preferred not to fund an expensive and difficult war in the Sudan.

Meanwhile, Baring pared small slices from the Egyptian budget to fund the training of the Egyptian army, his only bulwark against the "barbarous tribes" beyond Wadi Halfa. Egypt's position had not worsened, but neither had it improved. Baring possessed excellent information about the entropic collapse of the khalifa's empire; Colonel Kitchener's intelligence aide Major Reginald Wingate had organized an efficient spy network in the Sudan. On the Red Sea, Kitchener had mobilized a coalition of disaffected tribes and pushed Osman Digna's raiders back into the hills. Yet Baring worried constantly about the sheer mass of Abdullahi's followers, the thinness of Egypt's defenses, and the untested nature of his new troops. To remind Baring of their unfinished business, Khalifa Abdullahi sent him abusive letters, threatening the slaughter of all infidels at Cairo.[33]

The Egyptian army had been trounced at Tel el-Kebir, dismantled after Urabi's revolt, reassembled for the Hicks expedition, and shamed in the flight from the Sudan. Baring rebuilt it from the bottom up. No slave raids filled its ranks, and no corrupt officers robbed their men. The recruits were trained by British officers and commanded by a mixture of British and Egyptians. By the summer of 1889, the Nile Frontier Force numbered ten battalions of Egyptian and six battalions of Sudanese infantry, eight cavalry squadrons, and eight companies of Camel Corps, all augmented by horse artillery, field guns, a battery of new Maxim machine guns, and transport and railway battalions.

In May 1889, Baring heard of General al-Nujumi's advance from Dongola. More than six thousand Dervish warriors, and a supporting column of women and children, were moving north along the Nile. As on previous Mahdist campaigns, al-Nujumi carried no provisions; he expected that Allah or the local peasants would provide food along the route. But bad harvests and a local population swollen by refugees meant that his army traveled hungry. The Dervish advance soon resembled a disordered retreat.

Within days, the *Ansar* had been reduced to eating powdered date stones and their own pack animals. To bypass Wadi Halfa and Egyptian gunboats on the Nile, al-Nujumi led his force into the desert toward Balaja. Again, he found no food or water along the route. When he attempted to fight a path back toward the river villages, Egyptian steamers landed troops and pushed him back. Many of his men collapsed from thirst in the desert, and many more deserted. His column left a trail of dying men, dead animals, and abandoned ammunition. When he camped at Balaja, al-Nujumi counted only three of his thirty-five artillerymen. Most of his bodyguards had abandoned him. Even his water-carrier had deserted.

Major General Grenfell led the new Nile Frontier Force south to meet the invaders. Hearing of al-Nujumi's plight, Grenfell offered terms.

"After me, thousands of English and Egyptian troops are about to arrive. I had in mind to wipe you out, and obliterate your traces, you and those who follow you, from the face of the earth in view of the barbarous deeds which your hands have committed." Grenfell reminded Al-Nujumi that he had nowhere to go. "You will find only English and Egyptian armies, long-trained and dreaming only of shedding the blood of their enemies. They await your coming, hour by hour, to drink your blood and send you to destruction." Grenfell begged him to spare the camp followers. "I call upon you to surrender, so that helpless women and children shall not die. If you surrender, your life and the lives of your commanders and the lives of all who are with you shall be preserved from evil."[34]

Al-Nujumi responded with fierce piety. "Our object is to come into the country and to compel all its people to enter the Faith. Do not be deceived by your soldiers, guns and rockets, or the quantity of your powder, which is void of God's help." He warned Grenfell to expect the fate of "Hicks, Gordon and their like," whose soldiers and weapons had proved worthless. "If you will profess Islam and surrender all your guns and weapons, you shall be saved and have the safe conduct of Allah, his Prophet, his Mahdi and his Khalifa."[35]

On August, 3, 1889, the armies met on the western bank of the White Nile, near the village of Toski. As more than three thousand of al-Nujumi's followers raced forward with the last of their strength, the Frontier Force formed into lines and began firing as if on the parade ground at Cairo. The new Maxim guns mowed down the fearless *Ansar* in heaps, their white jibbas piling up like fresh cotton. Al-Nujumi was shot three times, and as his guards ferried him from the battlefield on a camel, further Egyptian volleys killed his guards, the camel, al-Nujumi's five-year-old son, and the general, too.

As the survivors of al-Nujumi's wild charge melted back toward Dongola, thousands of starving camp followers surrendered. The khalifa's invasion of Egypt had dissolved on its first encounter with the new Egyptian army. More concerned with holding power at Omdurman than fulfilling the Mahdi's vision of permanent revolution, Abdullahi had dispatched an insufficient force to Egypt. He expected that they would face yet another terrified Egyptian motley. Instead, the *Ansar* had been slaughtered by well-drilled troops with the latest weaponry.

"It is my pleasant duty to bring to your notice the excellent condition of the Egyptian troops on the occasion of the action of Toski," Grenfell reported. "The conduct of the black troops has been tested on previous occasions, but the conduct of the purely Egyptian troops who were brought into close contact in line formation, with large numbers of Dervishes, was satisfactory."[36]

The rout at Toski demonstrated that properly trained and motivated troops could, with the help of improved machine guns, resist the *Ansar*'s onslaught. But by demonstrating that Egypt could be defended by native troops on a limited budget, it made the reconquest of the Sudan seem less urgent to the London government. So long as the Egyptian surplus was under the control of the Commission of the Debt, and Baring and the *sirdar* could guarantee the Suez Canal and the India Route, Salisbury would permit no military operations.

Baring had his own reasons for agreeing with Salisbury. Expanding the Egyptian army would raise "a whole crop of local and international difficulties" in the Egyptian finances. If Khedive Tawfik and his ministers were permitted to recover the Sudan unsupervised, Baring foresaw "the most serious risk" of a relapse into misgovernment. The desirable alternative, British troops, seemed remote. The abolitionist lobby's influence over Africa policy had declined with the deepening of Britain's economic and strategic involvement. Only a "small but influential section of public opinion" still advocated the conquest of the Sudan, and Baring was too clever to align himself with a minority. In 1886, he calculated that the Egyptian government would have to wait twenty-five years before it could finance an invasion of the Sudan without British funds and soldiers. The Sudan must wait, and Gordon's unquiet memory with it.[37]

From his plinth twenty-three feet above the swirling carriages of Trafalgar Square, a bronze Gordon looked down Whitehall toward Parliament. In a crumpled, beltless patrol jacket, carrying no weapon except his "Wand of Victory," Gordon gazed sightlessly toward the political heart of the empire, arms almost folded, his left foot resting on a broken cannon. His left hand holding a Bible, he raised his right to his chin as if reflecting on some distant, unattainable goal.

10

Gladstone's Egg
1889–96

The Third Marquess of Salisbury.

I had no difficulty in finding the Company's offices. It was the biggest thing in town, and everyone I met was full of it. They were going to run an over-sea empire, and make no end of coin by trade.

—Joseph Conrad, *Heart of Darkness*, 1899[1]

P RONE TO ILLNESS and privately tutored in an ancestral palace, Lord Robert Arthur Talbot Gascoyne-Cecil grew from a delicate, lonely second son into a large, awkward, and aimless young man. Withdrawn from Eton after being bullied, he scraped a Fourth Class degree in Mathematics from Christ Church, Oxford. He considered becoming an Anglican bishop, tinkered with his botanical collection, and became depressed. Alarmed by their pale, lonely son, his parents sent him on a tour of the empire. Fresh air and vigorous company, they hoped, would strengthen his physical and mental health.

The cure worked, though not quite as intended. The new Cecil had picked up a sense of humor among the gold diggers of South Africa, had filled out his frame with a subtropical diet, and had become an enthusiast for Britain's moral and economic mission in the world. Exercising his new confidence, he fell in love with Georgina Alderson, the daughter of a mere lawyer, and married her against his parents' wishes, supporting his household through political journalism. In 1866, following the death of his sickly elder brother, he entered Parliament as Viscount Cranborne, a self-styled "illiberal Tory."

Cranborne lowered himself into politics like a fastidious plumber entering a blocked drain, more from duty than desire. A political dynasty, the Cecils had served Britain for centuries. Lord Burghley, their founder, had been first minister to Elizabeth I, and his son Robert Cecil had performed the same service for James I. For the next two centuries, Cecils of varied intellect and competence had filled official positions, frequently with more loyalty than talent. Born at the end of an age of entitlement, Cranborne served in the era of a bloodless liberal revolution, in which electoral reform broadened the voting public. As secretary of state for India in Lord Derby's government, Cranborne resigned in protest against the Reform Act of 1867. Upon the death of his father in 1868, he escaped to the House of Lords as the third marquess of Salisbury. He would be the terminus of the line of ancient privilege, the last peer to serve as prime minister without abandoning his rank.

Tall and wide, weighing in at eighteen stone according to the scales on which the Prince of Wales weighed all his male guests at Sandringham, Salisbury had sad walrus eyes, a beard like the hedge marking an Englishman's private garden, a massive skull topped by a white cathedral dome of baldness, and a pained expression in which the sorrows of his early life were overlain by the sorrows of the waning of the aristocratic age.

"The classes that represent civilisation," Salisbury believed, "the holders of accumulated capital and accumulated thought, have a right to require securities to protect them from being overwhelmed by hordes who have neither knowledge to guide them, nor stake in the commonwealth to protect them."[2]

Salisbury detested populism, distrusted democracy, and despised atheism. He prized high principles, High Toryism, and High Anglicanism, and a sense of justice equal parts Whig and biblical. His domestic politics rested on the cusp between Tory libertarianism and its paternalistic ancestor, aristocratic diffidence. It was not the government's task to meddle with the economy or to regulate its subjects' access to alcohol or gambling. Yet even as he regretted the lost age of entitlement and privacy, he felt compelled by *noblesse oblige* and religious conscience to develop the reforms that dismembered the old world. It was Salisbury, not Gladstone, who established democratic county councils, extended free and compulsory education to all children, and forced employers to compensate injured workers. He did this not because he believed in mass democracy, but because he believed in the patrician's responsibility to care for the plebeian.

Wary of compliments, suspicious of praise, distrustful of civil servants, casual in dress to the point of shabbiness, happier in his private laboratory than on the hustings, Salisbury remained aloof from what Garnet Wolseley called the "dirty, dunghill sort of democratic wave" that washed through British politics in Gladstone's wake. Yet he thrice became prime minister. In a deferential age, Salisbury's distance from ordinary Britons, his enormous private wealth, and his blunt insistence on honesty in public life all recommended him to the horde of untrustworthy voters as a disinterested leader.[3]

As with many other Victorian misfits, the empire had been the making of him. He did his best to return the favor. In 1874, Salisbury returned to the India Office under Disraeli. At first, Salisbury suspected Disraeli as a Jewish parvenu: alluding to Dickens's *Oliver Twist,* he called Disraeli an "Artless Dodger." But soon their agreement over Britain's imperial destiny overrode Salisbury's distaste for Disraeli's populist maneuvers. In 1878, as Disraeli's foreign secretary, Salisbury negotiated the Treaty of Berlin, resolving the Russo-Turkish war in Britain's favor and creating a British blueprint for the resolution of the Eastern Question. After sheltering in the House of Lords for a further four years following Disraeli's death, in 1885 Salisbury, now fifty-five years old, descended to do his duty in the dunghill of the Commons as prime minister. Balancing his domestic duties with his true speciality, he doubled as foreign secretary.[4]

Characteristically, Salisbury's foreign policy rested on a single, clear idea: the principle that would become known as "splendid isolation." As Britain had the largest empire, the motives of the Great Powers could not be trusted. The inherited entanglement of the Concert of Europe offered Britain's Lilliputian rivals the chance to gang up on the British Gulliver, pinning him down with multilateral treaties. To divide, rule, and prosper, Britain should resolve disputes bilaterally. The decline of Britain's competitive edge made this more urgent than ever.[5]

By the 1880s, Britain sensed the loss of its industrial advantage. Exports of British technology had allowed its European competitors to develop potent industrial bases, notably in France and Germany. The rivals identified as the keys to Britain's power its empire, the source of raw materials and captive markets, and its navy, the controller of the sea routes. In Germany, Bismarck introduced a protectionism tinged with patriotic chauvinism and, like King Leopold II of Belgium, went looking for colonies in Africa. The French responded in kind.

"Colonies are for rich countries one of the most lucrative methods of investing capital," explained Jules Ferry, the architect of France's expanding empire. "France, which is glutted with capital and which has exported considerable quantities, has an interest in looking at this side of the colonial question."

This excited the ambitions of Italy, which as a new state desired the appurtenances of an older one, and of Portugal, an old state that already possessed a slumbering empire. Africa, with its combination of limitless raw materials, badly armed natives, and undefined spheres of influence, became the focus of the European charge for colonies or, as the new term had it, "Imperialism."[6]

In 1884, the Concert convened for its last significant performance, the Conference of Berlin. In the abused names of Christianity, Commerce, and Civilization, the European powers divided Africa into zones of interest. After several months of elaborate horse-trading, on February 26, 1885, the General Act of Berlin drew the starting lines of what would be known as the "Scramble for Africa," the race into the hinterland from the patchwork of ports and colonies that now lined the coasts of the continent.

Britain claimed the basin of the River Nile. France claimed the Chad River basin in the west. Germany claimed colonies on Africa's west and east coasts that overlooked Britain's longer India Route, via the Cape. Britain and Germany recognized Belgium's great diplomatic virtue—that it was not France—and granted King Leopold II a million square miles in the Congo. Further, thinner slices of the colonial pie went to Portugal, for having reached Africa first, and to Italy, for getting there last.

By regulating the Scramble, the conference, and especially Gladstone and Bismarck, aimed to prevent its volatile blend of greed and status from blowing back into Europe. In this they succeeded, but at a cost passed to the

Africans, whose representatives had not been invited to Berlin. Gladstone's last major contribution to international affairs laid the path for the greatest imperial expropriations in recorded history.

"The other powers are beginning a career of colonial aggrandisement," warned Lord Rosebery, a leading young Liberal who subscribed to "forward" policy. "We formerly did not have in our foreign affairs to trouble ourselves much with colonial questions, because we had a monopoly of colonies. That monopoly has ceased."

In contrast to the programs of the new empires, Britain already possessed a global empire, and largely by accident. Britain had established white dominions in South Africa, Australia, and New Zealand with little opposition from the European powers. Until the Indian Mutiny of 1857, London had delegated the running of India to the East India Company, which had ruled India as a private business. The Mutiny had obliged Britain to formalize its rule in India, but elsewhere, Britain continued to prefer informal influence and the persuasive powers of the Royal Navy. Colonies were expensive to run. In a peaceful system of Free Trade, the possession of colonies offered little advantage over the cheaper, indirect method: a "protectorate" supervised by some helpful local tyrant.

The two great exceptions were at either end of Africa. The Cape Colony and Egypt sat astride the best and second-best sea routes to India. Yet even in Egypt, Disraeli, Gladstone, and Salisbury all preferred informal control to annexing a key Ottoman province. Nevertheless, the rise of competing empires forced Britain, the unwitting leader of the charge, to follow its competitors into Africa.[7]

When Salisbury left the Foreign Office in 1880, Africa hardly figured in policy calculation. By his return in 1886, the Dark Continent had become the stage for a European struggle for resources and prestige. Like Gladstone before him, Salisbury's priority was to keep the peace in Europe, but without surrendering to the French. In 1887, Salisbury still distrusted Egypt as an "inconvenient" blend of European rivalries and domestic enthusiasm.

"I heartily wish we had never gone into Egypt," he admitted. "Had we not done so, we could snap our fingers at all the world. But the national, or acquisitional feeling has been aroused; it has tasted the fleshpots and it will not let them go." As for the Sudan, he resisted the "lunatics" who believed that "by some magic wave of the diplomatic wand, the Sudan can be turned into a second India." Annexation for its own sake or to avenge Gordon was Jingo cant, and Jingoism was the "bastard brother" of patriotism.

But when the sultan's trickery endangered the India Route, or when

Egypt became essential to Britain's dignity in Europe, there could be no backing down. The expanded strategic demands of the Scramble for Africa confirmed this judgment. Egypt became a cornerstone of Salisbury's African strategy. It was radical enough to oblige him to announce it indirectly—his parliamentary majority rested on the support of disaffected Liberals, and a public statement would antagonize the European powers. So he followed one of Britain's less grand African traditions, and floated his idea in the papers.[8]

In the summer of 1888, Salisbury invited to the Foreign Office Harry Johnston, thirty-year-old acting consul of Britain's Niger Coast Protectorate, and early example of the British species of imperialist. After examining Johnston on his policy in the Niger Delta, Salisbury invited him for the weekend to the Cecil seat, Hatfield House. As they strolled in the grounds after church on Sunday morning, Salisbury raised the imminent division of Africa.

"What a pity it is that no one could put the whole African question lucidly before the public," he mused. His eye settled momentarily on Johnston. "In some newspaper article, I mean."[9]

Johnson took the hint, supplying Salisbury with several drafts of an article. On August 22, 1888, the *Times* carried "Great Britain's Policy in Africa," by "An African Explorer."

"We are forced by German, French and Portuguese ambitions to extend our direct political influence over a large part of Africa," Johnston declared. Africa's material bounty made it the next New World, destined to be "exploited by the white races," but Britain risked losing its share of the market. Johnston offered two strategic options, both based upon British control of Egypt.

The first, "Niger-to-the-Nile," connected Egypt to expanded British territories in West Africa. Though this route was the shorter, it could only achieve contiguity in the unlikely event of France agreeing to swap its West African colonies in Dahomey and Ivory Coast for British Gambia. The second proposal was grander but more practicable: to connect the key territories of Egypt and South Africa by taking control of a three-thousand-mile swath in between. Britain could push north from South Africa into the unclaimed area known as "Zambezia"; negotiate a path through German East Africa to Lake Victoria and the sources of the Nile; and link up with a second drive up the Nile Valley toward Equatoria. Johnston called this scheme "Cape-to-Cairo." Unofficially, it became the strategic blueprint for Britain's African empire.[10]

"Africa is the subject which occupies the Foreign Office more than any other," Salisbury announced at the Guildhall in 1889.

That year, he removed from the walls of his suite in the Foreign Office the maps of Central Asia and the Balkans, the familiar backdrop of the Eastern Question. He repapered the room with new maps of Africa, and prepared to fill in the blanks.[11]

ACROSS THE RIVER from the ruins of Khartoum, Omdurman grew from a military camp to a new capital, its unplanned huddle of huts and alleys sprawling for six miles along the western bank of the White Nile.

Its three major roads began at the doorstep of the mosque. One ran west into the town's desert fringe, where the *Ansar* rallied after Friday prayers for a ritual parade to celebrate the revolution. The second ran south to the landing stage where military raiding parties departed to hunt grain and slaves in the south and west. The third, the *Darb al-Shuhada*, the Road of the Martyrs, ran north into the desert in the direction of Egypt. The institutional core of the Mahdist state coalesced around the mosque and its two neighbors, the Mahdi's tomb and the khalifa's house: the arsenal, the slave market, the treasury and the prison. Khartoum lay empty and smashed; only its dockyard still functioned, because it had proved impossible to relocate it. All life in the Sudan now centered upon Omdurman, and all life in Omdurman now centered on the Khalifa Abdullahi.

"The Mahdi is the representative of the Prophet Mohammed, and I am his successor," he explained. "Who, therefore, in the whole world holds so high a position as I?"[12]

At fifty, Abdullahi had grown sluggish in gait and grand in manner. He had replaced his sandals with soft leather socks and yellow shoes, and his old jibba with a new, patchless one in fine white cotton with a colored border. On his head was a silk skullcap from Mecca. A staff of twenty eunuchs and a dozen slave boys attended him; he preferred his body servants to be Abyssinian Christians or children because he believed they would be less likely to plot against him. When his attendants reached late puberty, they were drafted into the army, and new, young replacements selected. Mistakes were punished by flogging or chained starvation. He maintained a harem of hundreds of women, "from light brown to the deepest black," selected from every tribe in the Sudan, with expensive pale shades of foreigner, too. When he forced the sister of the late sultan of Darfur into his harem, she threw herself into the Nile. Limited to four wives by sharia, he simply divorced the

ones he tired of and married the ones he desired. The gold and silver jewelry that the Mahdi had banned and stockpiled in the treasury to finance
the jihad in Egypt gradually reappeared around the necks of Abdullahi's favorites. He developed a taste for Turkish and Egyptian dishes cooked by his
homesick new wives, and grew accordingly stout, his long face disappearing
in the pouches of fat that hung beneath his eyes.[13]

Planning a dynasty, he groomed his son Osman for the succession. When
Osman married, Abdullahi relaxed the Mahdi's ban on ostentatious festivities for an eight-day wedding feast to which he invited all Omdurman. Abdullahi attempted to provide Osman with the education he had never
received, but Osman had no appetite for the madrassa, preferring "nightly
orgies in his house." Abdullahi proceeded to govern without his son's help,
relying instead on his brothers Yacub and al-Sanussi Ahmed, and an expanding network of spies. Completely illiterate, he depended on two secretaries to read his letters and note his replies. When he conferred with his
chiefs, most of his orders came in the form of koranic recitation. He received
supplicants from a raised divan, lolling against a sheepskin pillow. They approached with eyes lowered, their hands crossed passively across their chests,
and they did not sit until he invited them. When they did they assumed the
prayer position, foreheads touching the dirt floor of the khalifial palace, the
first two-story building in Omdurman.[14]

Abdullahi did not like being looked at. Even a one-eyed Syrian who un-
knowingly directed his blind eye toward the khalifa was told never to come
near him again. The Mahdi had led a revolutionary rally at every Friday
prayers, but the khalifa hid from his subjects, using his brothers as deputies.
He ventured out under heavy guard only four times a year, for religious fes-
tivals, one hand holding a sword and the other a Hadendowa spear that he
used as a walking stick. Fearing his subjects and allies, he ruled by making
them fear him.

The Mahdi had been a scholar and the prophetic creator of a coalition,
but Abdullahi was neither. Having inherited the Mahdi's dream at its
apogee, between the delirium of conquest and the creation of a perfected
caliphate ruled by sharia justice, he had struggled to control his vast empire.
In three years, the Mahdi had taken the Sudan back four centuries. His revolt had demolished the Turkiyya's infrastructure along with its garrisons.
The Sudan had no telegraph lines, no regular steamer services, and no postal
service. Its civil servants had either fled or been murdered, its trade, agriculture, and pilgrim routes had been disrupted. The sultanates that once had

divided it into manageable tracts had folded into an empire that could not administrate them. Abdullahi inherited a medieval chaos.

He responded with the medieval answer. He turned the entire Sudan into a giant sultanate, a tribal dictatorship funded by war. Although the British at Cairo and Suakin continued to allow trade between the Sudan and the exterior, trade withered and little new money entered the country. All export commerce passed through the Beit al-Mal, but as the prime source of ivory, gum, ostrich feathers, and senna were the western districts most devastated by war, famine, and disease, supplies were short. The loot from Khartoum seeped away from the Beit al-Mal, squandered by Abdullahi on his favorites, or smuggled down to Egypt by his treasurer. The Sudan's currency declined in value: While the Mahdi's dollar of 1885 had been seven parts silver and one part copper, by 1895, the khalifa's dollar was two parts silver and five parts copper. The state ceased to exist as anything more than an extension of a tribal tyranny, and the Mahdi's jihad turned into an Afro-Arab imperialism. Abdullahi's genocidal campaigns against dissident Sudanese tribes, or his greedy rampage into Abyssinia, differed little in effect or motivation from the *ghazwas* of the Turkiyya.

The armies of Allah had depopulated the countryside and treated the farming population as a source of free food and fresh manpower. The 150,000 residents of Omdurman obtained most of their grain from the south. But by 1888, there were no reserves of grain at Omdurman, because Abdullahi's general al-Zaki Tamal had massacred the farmers in order to take control of their lands. When the rains failed in 1888, tribes across the Sudan suffered mass starvation. At night, jackals came into the villages and dragged half-dead people from their beds. Abdullahi issued orders for the centralization of all grain stocks at Omdurman. The entire population of the Nile Valley south of Berber either died in its homes or staggered to the capital.

If they survived the journey, they found that Abdullahi used food as a political weapon. Abdullahi's fellow Baggara had first access to any grain at discounted prices, and while an inflated market in looted grain ran in Omdurman throughout the famine, there was no food for the riverain tribes. People took the dried camel skins from the roofs of their shacks and roasted them, they made a kind of bread from powdered animal bones, and they died in the marketplace as they searched for scraps.

"As one walked along, one could count fifty dead bodies lying in the streets, and this quite irrespective of those who died in their own homes," wrote Father Joseph Ohrwalder, an Austrian missionary held in Omdurman. In the market, vendors stood over their goods with big sticks in their hands, beating back the walking, sunken-eyed skeletons. "Sometimes twenty or thirty of these miserable, starving people would join together and, regardless of the blows showered upon them, which covered their bodies with wounds and bruises, they would wildly attack the sellers, madly seize whatever they could lay their hands upon, and swallow it on the spot, begrimed with dust, and probably besmeared with their own blood."

Those fortunate enough to buy food used weapons to fight their way back home past gangs of starving vagrants. Cannibalism broke out. When soldiers broke into the home of one half-starved woman, they found that she had eaten all but "an ear and a piece of a leg" of her infant son. There were so many dead bodies that the khalifa ordered his men to simply tip them into the Nile or dump them in the desert to the north of the town, where the wind and sand polished their bones "like glass." The next harvest was better, but it attracted a plague of locusts. For the next four years, seasonal swarms ate everything in their path.[15]

The more Abdullahi favored his fellow Baggara, the more he alienated the *Ashraf* and the riverain tribes. The Mahdi's family had never accepted Abdullahi as their leader. In the famine, the Mahdi's widows had starved along with rural peasants. Abdullahi had already made the *Ashraf* junior partners to a dynastic union, marrying off his daughter to the Mahdi's son Mohammed. But when Mohammed attempted to strengthen his power base by marrying a cousin from the *Ashraf,* Abdullahi forbade the marriage.

In 1891, the *Ashraf* hatched a plot to overthrow Abdullahi. When he heard about it, his Jihadiya fought a gun battle in the streets of Omdurman with the *Ashraf*'s followers. The captured leaders of the revolt were shipped upriver in a Turkish steamer to Fashoda, where they were beaten to death with clubs and axes by al-Zaki Tamal and his men. Abdullahi kept the khalifa Mohammed al-Sharif in prison, in case he was needed for future military mobilization of the riverain tribes. After this purge, the *Ashraf* did not trouble Abdullahi again, but the conspiracy confirmed his paranoia that he faced revolt at any moment.

Abdullahi retreated further from his subjects. He built a long wall around his home and the houses of his brothers and bodyguards. His early propaganda of angelic interventions and endless jihad turned into an erratic stream of despotic pronouncements. He banned pilgrimage to Mecca: Now the only acceptable *haj* was to the Mahdi's tomb. He suspended almost all religious education: Only a minimal number of boys were trained as tax collectors and accountants in the treasury. He declared the Shaygia tribe to be outlaws and unleashed the Baggara on a four-day rampage of murder. He ordered all subjects to pray at Omdurman's central mosque, an order derived less from piety than from the desire to break up what he called "social life," the private gatherings at which his enemies might conspire. With man-power reduced by the famine, he banned the export of slaves. Only his pow-erful eastern ally Osman Digna dared to ignore this ordinance; Digna's long guerrilla campaign against the Red Sea ports had been waged with little other intent than to reopen the slave route to Jeddah.[16]

Hidden from the people and drip-fed with gossip and espionage, Abdul-lahi succumbed to fear and megalomania. He claimed that the domed shrine erected over the Mahdi's grave, designed by a government architect captured at Khartoum, and built from materials recycled from some of its grander mansions, had been his own work. On his occasional expeditions outside his compound, he rode in a carriage retrieved from Khartoum. In case he wanted to ride a horse, he kept a giant slave whose sole duty was to lift him in and out of the saddle.

The gallows, banned by the Mahdi as an un-Islamic symbol of the Turkiyya, returned to encourage the people's loyalty. When the Batahin tribe turned against him, Abdullahi ordered al-Zaki Tamal to bring as many of its members as he could to Omdurman. After dozens had died in captivity, the remaining seventy were brought for public execution. After the first eigh-teen had been dispatched and piled by the gallows, the rope broke. Abdul-lahi executed a further two dozen by beheading, then sent for the town butchers, ordering them to cut off the hands and feet of the remaining twenty-seven. "Soon there was a heap of these bleeding members, whilst the bodies of the poor Batahin lay writhing on the ground, beads of anguish pouring from their brows." Most of them bled to death where they lay, al-though a few survived to become beggars in the Omdurman marketplace.[17]

"I would not be too much impressed by what the soldiers tell you about the strategic importance of those places," Lord Salisbury told Sir Evelyn Baring in 1890. "It is their way. If they were allowed full scope, they would insist on the importance of garrisoning the Moon in order to protect us from Mars."[18]

Baring had not asked to advance up the Nile, only to expand the British foothold on the Red Sea coast by fifty miles, and secure Tokar. Salisbury granted him this adventure but, Scramble or no Scramble, he saw no urgency for further Sudanese expeditions. In Salisbury's opinion, Britain had acquired its empire because its governments had found themselves obliged to support their traders and missionaries with troops. He distrusted the specialists at the War Office, with their conviction that trade and evangelism were the forebears of war.

"When once you have permitted a military advance, the extent of that military advance scarcely remains within your own discretion," he warned Baring. "Step by step, the imperious exactions of military necessity will lead you on into the desert."

Salisbury would only heed these exactions if they led to raw materials and new customers, or if they kept them from foreign control. His policy was one of pre-emption, but as yet he had nothing to pre-empt. In the meantime, he rewarded Sir Evelyn Baring for his patience by ennobling him as Lord Cromer.

Nor did Salisbury see any domestic advantage in a Nile campaign. The public might be stirred by the acquisition of large tracts of desert, but Salisbury's party was still traumatized by Gordon's simultaneous assault on Khartoum and the Gladstone government. "They were so deeply impressed with the disasters of six years ago," he told Cromer, "and the apparently inexorable necessity which had driven them into situations where those disasters were inevitable, that they shrink instinctively from any proposal to advance into the Egyptian desert."[19]

The government already had wars to fund. In the early 1890s, Britain's expanding empire faced frontier disturbances from Afghanistan to Nigeria. Salisbury justified these small, expensive wars as "merely the surf that marks the edge of the advancing waves of civilisation." But he only fought them if they were obligatory. So long as he saw no "clear balance of undoubted advantage" in diverting forces and money to the Sudan, the Dervishes were safe in their brutal paradise. When Wilfrid Blunt called this policy "a Machiavellian one," he did not mean it as a compliment.[20]

Nonetheless, Salisbury's policy nearly succeeded. By trading cards of low value, he built up his winning Cape-to-Cairo hand. One by one, Portugal, Germany, Belgium, and Italy assented to his claim that Britain had inherited Turkey's rights in the Nile Valley, receiving in return British recognition of their claims. He bought off Bismarck by trading the British-held Baltic island of Heligoland for German claims to the Congo. He shunted the "tiresome little Power" Portugal out of the East African hinterland by ordering the fleet to coal up and prepare for war.[21]

Negotiations with Italy were trickier, not least because Britain's alliance with Italy underpinned Salisbury's Mediterranean policy. Back in February 1885, as the Egyptian garrison had withdrawn from the Red Sea port of Massowa, Gladstone had frustrated a suspected French intention to annex the port by inviting Italy to take it over until Egypt could recover it. Gradually the Italians expanded from the coast, fighting King John of Abyssinia to establish their first African colony, Eritrea.

In May 1889, after King John's death at the hands of the Mahdists at Gallabat, Italy signed a treaty with his rival, King Menelik of Shoa, and recognized him as emperor of Abyssinia. Menelik gave Italy a piece of the Abyssinian highlands, and the Italians gave him five thousand rifles, 2 million bullets and eighty thousand pounds in cash. Then the Italian premier Francesco Crispi turned on Menelik. Invoking the Berlin Act, Crispi announced that Italy had appointed itself protector over Abyssinia. Menelik pointed to the relevant clause of his treaty with the Italians, but as his Amharic translation differed from the Italian original, this did not help him.

As the Italians moved up the coast toward Suakin and inland toward the key town of Kassala, Sir Evelyn Baring rang the alarm. Clearly, Crispi would not settle for a temporary toehold on the coast. Italy threatened the Suakin-Berber road, and if took Kassala, it would also control the headwaters of the Atbara River, a major Nile tributary. When Baring met with Crispi in Naples, the Italian premier rejected Britain's claim to the Nile Valley.

This was why Salisbury allowed Baring to send Egyptian troops to take Tokar: If Britain did not get there first, then Italy would. Fortunately for Salisbury, in February 1891 Crispi's adventurous and expensive colonial policy brought about his fall from office. His successor, the Marquis di Rudini, backed down. That summer, Britain and Italy agreed that Tokar belonged to Egypt, that Egyptian and Italian troops would cooperate against Osman Digna, and that Italy could hold Kassala so long as the war against the Dervishes required it.

Salisbury's diplomacy turned the Scramble into an orderly takeover. But the premier who specialized in foreign policy had less feel for domestic affairs. Outflanked by Gladstone's promise of another Reform Act, and his accusation that the Conservatives intended to betray Free Trade and bring in protectionism, Salisbury failed to win the 1892 election outright. Although the Conservatives won the majority of the votes and a majority of English seats, they did not win a majority of Commons seats. Swayed by Gladstone's promise of another attempt at Home Rule, the Irish Nationalist MPs turned to the Liberal Party and formed a coalition government.

Eighty-two years of age, Gladstone returned for his fourth ministry in physical and mental decline. Already blind in his right eye, while campaigning at Chester he had been hit in his good eye by a "hard-baked little gingerbread" flung at two yards' range by "a middle-aged bony woman."

His sight never fully recovered. Within a year of the election, his vision had become so fogged that reading and writing were difficult. Instead of undoing Salisbury's foreign policy, he concentrated on holding together his narrow majority and pushing through Parliament the Home Rule Bill that he hoped would crown his career. He could not risk confrontation with his foreign secretary, Lord Rosebery. A "Liberal Imperialist" who had supported "forward" policy in Egypt in 1882, Rosebery now continued to advance Salisbury's African policy as though the government had never changed.[22]

As A YOUNG MAN, Rosebery had three ambitions: to marry an heiress, to own the horse that won the Derby, and to become prime minister. Like Gladstone and Salisbury a product of Eton and Christ Church, Oxford, Rosebery left Oxford without a degree after being forced to choose between his studies and his ownership of a racehorse. Like Salisbury, his early travels in Britain's white colonies made him a convinced imperialist. By his early thirties, he had married Hannah Rothschild and entered politics, collaborating with Gladstone on the Midlothian campaign. In the 1880s, as Gladstone's foreign policy failed, Rosebery became a potential Liberal leader: a Whiggish aristocratic by birth, an imperialist by choice, and one of the few Liberals of whom Queen Victoria approved.

He was also petulant, nervous, prone to outbursts of anger, and as a rumored bisexual, the subject of a whispering campaign by the Marquess of Queensberry, the hunter of Oscar Wilde. Gladstone thought Rosebery one of the most able men he had ever met, and one of the most honest, too, but quite lacking in common sense.

He also had no diplomatic experience. In Africa, Rosebery charged where Salisbury had tiptoed. Salisbury had approached the question of the Nile from the Mediterranean, but Rosebery worked from the other end of the river: If the security of Egypt rested ultimately on its water supply, then Britain must control Lake Victoria, the source of the White Nile. In turn, this required land access to the lake from the coast of Kenya. Facing Belgian and French expansion in the Congo, Rosebery judged that he must act immediately to secure the headwaters of the Nile. Without consulting Glad-

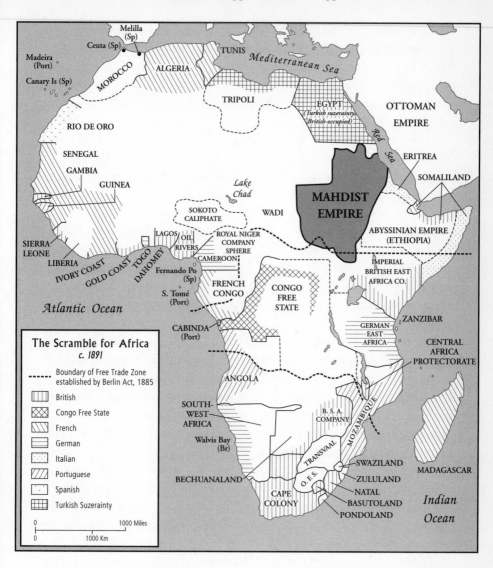

The Scramble for Africa
c. 1891

- - - - Boundary of Free Trade Zone
established by Berlin Act, 1885

|||| British

XXXX Congo Free State

\\\\ French

≡≡≡ German

∙∙∙∙ Italian

//// Portuguese

∙∙∙ Spanish

⊞⊞⊞ Turkish Suzerainty

```
0                    1000 Miles
├─────────────────────┤
0                    1000 Km
```

stone, he planned the immediate annexation of Uganda, the creation of a railway connecting it to the East African coast, and the expansion of British influence into the southern Sudan.

In Rosebery's plan, Gladstone recognized the hatching of the "African egg" that he had warned against, and the mutation of his party. He responded scathingly, "I thought it was a pleading from a Missionary society or from the Company, or should have thought so, but for the date from the Foreign Office."

Gladstone's perennial ally Sir William Harcourt joined in, calling it "Jingoism with a vengeance," and promising that he preferred to "die a thousand deaths, rather than have anything to do with it." Capitalizing on the split between ancient and modern Liberals, Salisbury weighed in, insisting he had always intended to annex Uganda when the time was right.[23]

Gladstone threatened to veto Rosebery's plan. Rosebery responded by offering to resign. To save the government and his Home Rule Bill, Gladstone backed down. In September 1892, he suggested a compromise: Pending a final decision, the government should temporarily subsidize the East Africa Company's operations in Uganda, while a commissioner went there to ascertain the situation. Rosebery accepted this and, like Gladstone, tried to create a situation that would force his opponent's hand. Rosebery won, and not just because the tide of political and public opinion had turned for Imperialism. While Gladstone invited the French ambassador for talks on a British withdrawal from Egypt, Lord Cromer issued a cry for help from the other end of the Nile.

That summer, Khedive Tawfik had died suddenly, less from illness than his doctors' ineptitude. Cromer expected Tawfik's eighteen-year-old son Abbas II to be as pliant as his father. Abbas, freshly graduated from an Austrian military school, resented Cromer's attempt to fit him with the short khedivial leash. Impertinently, the new khedive appointed nationalists as ministers. To Cromer, this smacked of Urabist anarchy. He requested the urgent reinforcement of the British garrison.

Gladstone replied that he preferred to "put a torch to Westminster Abbey" rather than to send more troops to Egypt. But his Home Rule Bill had just passed in the Commons, and he could not lose Rosebery now. Gladstone gave Cromer his troops, and Rosebery control over the government's Egyptian policy.

Gladstone's Egyptian tragedy of 1882 repeated itself as the farce of 1892. Though he could not create a policy, the old prime minister continued to stall Rosebery's plans for another year, even as the French press announced the departure of a Gallic expedition for central Africa. Once again, the Home Rule controversy broke the stalemate, and once again domestic divisions had crucial effects on foreign policy.

On September 9, 1893, the House of Lords rejected Gladstone's Home Rule Bill. Gladstone hung on for another six months. At one point, he took a month's holiday in Biarritz and forbade the cabinet from convening in his absence. But on March 3, physically exhausted, partially deaf, and mostly blind, he faced his final failure. He resigned, and retreated to the Lords.[24]

Gladstone wanted Sir William Harcourt to succeed him as prime minister, but Queen Victoria insisted upon Lord Rosebery. Two days into his premiership, Rosebery moved on Africa.

"The time has arrived when British policy [regarding] the Great Lakes, which form the sources of the Nile, must be defined," he told Cromer.

As British, French, and German plans converged on the center of Africa, the smallest of their competitors, Belgium, capitalized on the rising tension. Despite ruling a small European country better known for chocolate truffles than military prowess, King Leopold II had already secured in the Congo a gigantic colony the size of the Sudan. Using humanitarianism as a cover for exploitation, he instituted a regime of industrial deforestation and systematic slavery that enforced the benefits of the European way by chopping the hands off any Congolese who objected. Leopold now gained further leverage by offering Belgian support to both Britain and France, each of whom wanted to block the other's advance into central Africa. He obtained an agreement from Britain first: In May 1894, Rosebery agreed to lease to Belgium the left bank of the White Nile from Lake Albert to Fashoda for the rest of Leopold's lifetime.[25]

That month, Rosebery achieved his third ambition when his horse Ladas II won the Derby. He repeated this success in 1895 with Sir Visto, who romped home at a profitable nine to one. Rosebery's African gambles were less successful. The French would not allow little Belgium to stand in the way of French access to the lakes and the Nile. In July 1894, French negotiators forced the surrender of their Belgian counterparts "with the knife at their throats." Leopold signed a treaty with France, cropping back his new acquisition to a slim, rectangular slice of territory resting on the top left corner of Lake Victoria.

This wrecked Rosebery's Africa policy. He had jumped into central Africa, precipitated a further race for territory, antagonized the Powers, and indulged the Belgians, but had failed to secure the headwaters of the Nile. Instead of blocking the French advance, King Leopold's enclave could now become the stepping-stone that led the French to the source of the Nile. Britain and France were heading for a direct clash in Africa. Naturally, Rosebery blamed King Leopold.

"He is attempting to combine the position of a second-rate Power in Europe with a first-rate Power in Africa," Rosebery explained to Queen Victoria.[26]

In March 1895, Rosebery heard a rumor that the French were preparing an expedition to stake the *tricoleur* on the Upper Nile. He pressured his foreign secretary, Sir Edward Grey, to make a public statement that Britain regarded the entire Nile and all of its tributaries to be within its sphere of influence, and to threaten France with unspecified consequences if it interfered.

"The advance of a French expedition under secret instructions, right from the other side of Africa, into a territory over which our claims have been known for so long," Grey told the Commons, "would not be merely an inconsistent and unexpected act, but it must be perfectly well known to the French Government that it would be an unfriendly act."

The diplomats of the Quai d'Orsay had trouble finding a French synonym for "unfriendly," but they understood its sense. Britain was willing to fight for the Upper Nile.[27]

In June 1895, only weeks after Sir Visto's triumph in the Derby, Rosebery resigned. A politician with a brilliant future behind him, his nerves had shattered under the pressure. Taking office for the third time, Lord Salisbury attempted to rebuild his Africa policy like a chemist whose laboratory had been taken over by a promising but immature pupil. The worst of it was that the rumors of a French expedition were true.

"WE SHALL COUNTER the English dream expressed in the formula *Cape to Cairo*," declared the *colonialiste* Francis Deloncle. "We shall counter with the French dream, *From the Atlantic to the Red Sea*."[28]

Economics aside, France needed an empire. Defeated by Germany in 1871, pushed out of Egypt by Britain in 1881, domestically torn by the Dreyfus Affair of 1894, France could not afford defeat in the Scramble for Africa. It was a matter of prestige, as much as strategy. By late 1895, it was a matter of urgency, too. In French eyes, Britain had no legal right to foreclose the question of the Nile. Nor could it ignore international treaties and turn Egypt into a quasicolony.

In 1882, France had only accepted the British occupation of Egypt as a temporary measure. For more than a decade, British diplomats had assured their French counterparts of Britain's good intentions, securing French support for the Egyptian financial settlement of 1885 and the Drummond Wolff negotiations of 1887. Although the Egyptian economy had recovered, the British had tightened their grip, training native soldiers and claiming rights in the Nile Valley. Lord Cromer had turned Egypt into his private kingdom. As the French residents of Cairo said, it was no good having right on your side, if you did not have Lord Cromer, too. The British had jilted France, and now they wanted the Nile, too, from the Mediterranean to the middle of nowhere.

Rather than planning his departure, Lord Cromer now planned to dam the Upper Nile at Aswan. Although Cromer's priority was a year-round, stable flow of water to the Delta, security also figured in his calculations.

"If we settle at the headwaters of the Nile, we command Egypt," Sir Samuel Baker commented, "and a barrage at a low pass, where the Nile cuts through a rocky defile only eighty yards in width below the exit from the Albert Nyanza, would raise the level of the great reservoir of the Nile by fifty feet, and entirely control the water supply of Egypt."[29]

In 1885, Cromer had received Habib Anthony Salmone's intelligence from Paris that the Mahdi had contemplated blocking the Nile with boulders. In 1889, he had predicted that if European rivals approached the river carrying more than boulders, Britain would have to intervene to secure Egypt. In 1893, this specter appeared.

"I wish to re-open the question of Egypt," announced the French president Marie-Francois Carnot.

By the time Salisbury returned to office, France had initiated a covert policy to gain control of the White Nile above Khartoum. The threat of cutting Egypt's water supply could force the British from Egypt. The technical aspect of the French plan was supplied by one of Cromer's own employees. In January 1893, Victor Prompt, a French hydrologist employed in the Egyptian government, presented a lecture to the Egyptian Institute at Paris, entitled "Soudan Nilotique." Prompt suggested the abandoned Turkish outpost of Fashoda as the location for a dam. Closing the sluice gates in the summer would cause half the crops in the Delta to wither. And if the gates were suddenly thrown open, the resulting flood would destroy everything in its path.

In May 1893, President Carnot summoned to the Elysée Palace his colonial undersecretary Théophile Delcassé, Victor Prompt, and Colonel Parfait-Louis Monteil, a soldier-explorer lately returned from Lake Chad. Handing Monteil a copy of Prompt's lecture, Carnot told him that France needed a foothold on the Nile.

"*Il faut occuper Fashoda*," Carnot said.[30]

Monteil kicked his heels for a year. First he was delayed by French attempts to negotiate a path to the Nile via the chancellery at Brussels. Then he was blocked by Delcassé's cautious superior, Gabriel Hanotaux. Frustrated, Delcassé turned to other avenues for French expansion.

Delcassé contracted as a consultant the American mercenary Charles Chaillé-Long, veteran of Gordon's Equatoria mission and author of *Central Africa: Naked Truths About Naked People*. Like Lord Cromer, Chaillé-Long identified the hinterland of the Red Sea ports as the key to the Upper Nile. Much of it was controlled by Menelik, the "Lion of Abyssinia."

The French gave Menelik money, arms shipments, and a promise that the eastern bank of the White Nile would be his if he helped France take the western bank. Menelik duly renounced his treaty with Italy. He granted France permission to build a railway from Obock to the Abyssinian capital of Addis Ababa, and from there to the junction of the White Nile and the Gazelle River at Sobat. Next, Chaillé-Long and Monteil advised that Menelik should be pressured to invade the Sudan, with Chaillé-Long as unofficial military adviser.

The French colonialists now had to choose whether to advance from the Congo and ally with the Mahdists on the Gazelle River or to advance from Abyssinia and fight the Mahdists in eastern Sudan. Lord Rosebery provided the answer. The Anglo-Congolese Agreement threatened to exclude France from the western Nile basin. French attention turned away from Abyssinia and back to the Gazelle River. First France undermined the Anglo-Congolese treaty by forcing Belgium to scale back its claims, reopening a blank space on the map of the Gazelle River. Then France prepared a second expedition, under Captain Jean-Baptiste Marchand.

Wiry and tanned from the West African sun, with a sharp nose and a long jaw, Marchand had developed a private obsession with the French claim to the Nile. In the summer of 1895, he secured an interview with the skeptical Hanotaux. Sooner or later, Marchand said, an international conference would resolve the partition of the Nile basin. Given two hundred men and six hundred francs, Marchand promised he could cross from French West Africa to the Gazelle River, and stake the French claim that would ensure a seat at the conference table. His party could travel incognito, and would only raise the *tricoleur* if they bumped into a rival European party also engaged in violating the khedive and the sultan's rights.

Although the khalifa had recently chased a Belgian expedition from the Gazelle River, Marchand did not believe that the Mahdists presented any obstacle. Like many *colonialistes*, his distrust of Britain led him to conspiracy theories. As the *colonialiste* Francois Deloncle had told the French Chamber earlier that year, the Mahdist threat was a creation of "*l'intrigue Brittanique*," which had "created, sustained and fortified" the Mahdists, to keep France from its African inheritance.

Marchand made no mention of the White Nile, either, but Fashoda, the *colonialistes*' target, was also his ultimate destination. For the moment, Marchand restrained himself. His aim, he said, was "to force by pacific means" an international conference, at which "France's colonisation in Africa, currently so gravely threatened by English ambitions," might be secured.

"Is it not permissible to hope," Marchand asked, "that the question of the evacuation of Egypt will flow quite naturally from that of the Egyptian Sudan, and that it will impose itself with new urgency upon the conference's deliberations?"[31]

Hanotaux's wish to avoid conflict with Britain might have kept Marchand's speculations in the realm of hypothesis. But in October 1895, the government changed and Hanotaux, spurning a ministry in a Radical government whose proposals included the introduction of income tax, left office. His successor, Marcelin Berthelot, was a celebrated chemist and historian of alchemy, but no expert on Egypt. Guided by the zealots in the Quai d'Orsay, in November 1895 Berthelot approved *La Mission Marchand*.

"IT IS OBVIOUS," advised Lord Cromer, "that if any civilised power holds the waters of the Upper Nile, it may in the end be in a position to exercise a predominating influence on the future of Egypt. I cannot, therefore, help thinking that it will not be possible or desirable to maintain a purely passive attitude much longer."

In the view from Cairo, if Britain did not move upriver, it risked being pushed into the Mediterranean. "The only question, if this view be allowed to obtain, is, when and how we shall move forward?"

Cromer had already resigned himself to the likely outcome. "We must either yield to the French and make the best terms we can with them, which under the given conditions, must almost of necessity be very bad terms for us; or, if we take any decisive step on our own account, we risk a very serious quarrel with France. . . . The force of circumstances, much more than the faults of any ministry or of any individual, has driven us into a situation which renders war a not improbable solution of the whole mess."[32]

Rather than fund a war for the Sudan, Cromer wanted to use Egypt's savings to build a dam at Aswan. He recommended that Britain secure the Nile

Valley indirectly, by increasing its hold over the hinterland of the Red Sea ports. As for the sources of the Nile, Lord Salisbury had only just secured twenty thousand pounds from Parliament for the construction of the Uganda railway. Salisbury and Baring agreed that advancing up the Nile Valley, and fighting the khalifa, were not the best way to advance British interests. Yet in early 1896, that became their policy.

FIVE DAYS AFTER Marchand received his marching orders, King Menelik of Abyssinia used his new French rifles to devastate an Italian army in the hills above Adowa. Menelik's tribesmen killed more than six thousand of a ten-thousand-strong Italian brigade, castrating many of their Italian prisoners and mutilating their Askari militia by chopping off their right hands and left feet.

Menelik had aligned with all parties in the Scramble. He had taken modern rifles from Italy, France, and Russia. He had gained territory from British Somaliland by helping Britain against the khalifa. He had gained territory from French Somaliland by secretly consenting to the French railway linking Abyssinia with the Upper Nile. Even his breach with Italy would be temporary.

Menelik's slaughter of a modern European army had three consequences. The first was to collapse the Italian government. The second was to encourage Khalifa Abdullahi to lay siege to the Italians stranded in their fort at Kassala. The third was to tip Britain into the Sudan.

Desperate to avoid further colonial indignities, Italy asked Britain to use its Egyptian garrisons to relieve the pressure on Kassala. To do its ally a favor, Britain consented.

"The Italian ambassador has pressed me earnestly to take some steps against the Dervishes in favor of Kassala," Salisbury informed Cromer. "After consulting the military authorities, Her Majesty's Government are of opinion that the occupation of Dongola would be the most effective demonstration, and that the matter will be greatly in the interest of Egypt, and is a charge she may fairly be asked to bear. It will also tend to repel any disposition to attack Egypt which the recent victories of Africans over Europeans may have created among the Dervishes. Of course, it is intended to keep Dongola."[33]

At a stroke, Salisbury had broken the impasse of Egyptian policy and completed the eclipse of idealism by realism. Like Gladstone and Rosebery, Salisbury had been prepared to leave the Sudanese to starve until it suited him. The time, it seemed, had now come, and the Italian request was an ideal pretext. In a private letter the next day, he revealed his thinking. "We desired to kill two birds with one stone, and to use the same military effort to plant the foot of Egypt rather farther up the Nile."[34]

Salisbury did not want to annoy the French. In a message to Paris, he obfuscated his motives, and indicated that there would be no further advance.

"We have been applied to by the Egyptian Government to sanction a diversion in favour of Kassala against the Dervishes," he explained. "We have approved an advance of Egyptian troops as far as Dongola."[35]

Cromer feared losing Kassala to the Mahdists, but that did not mean he wanted to fight the eight thousand Dervishes at Dongola. Britain could just as easily support Italy by moving from Suakin up the Berber road. That would be cheaper, and "would give more effective help to the Italians." Taking Dongola would not make Egypt safer: As Gordon had warned a decade earlier, only "smashing" the Mahdists could do that. It would, however, be extremely expensive. "The Sudan is worth a good deal to Egypt, but it is not worth bankruptcy and extremely oppressive taxation."[36]

Having advised against the campaign, Cromer suggested where the five hundred thousand pounds needed to fund it might be found: the "extraordinary expenses" account where he had stored the Commission of the Debt's budget surpluses. Salisbury secured the assent of the Italian, Austrian, and German governments for this looting of the Egyptian treasury. But the French opposed him, from strategy if not probity, and they secured the support of the Russians.

Together, France and Russia pressured Sultan Abdul Hamid II to emit one of his periodic complaints about a European violation of his rights in Egypt. Adroitly, Cromer prevailed upon Khedive Abbas II to issue a letter to Constantinople, promising that Britain intended only to restore lost khedivial territories, and so was acting well within its treaty rights. Cromer was satisfied that the new khedive, who had begun his reign with rebellious postures, had reverted to type.

"His behaviour is fairly satisfactory," Cromer told Salisbury, "and I think with a very clear statement to the effect that we will guarantee him against any action from the Sultan, he may be kept straight for the time being."[37]

ON THE EVENING of March 12, 1896, Salisbury consulted with the cabinet and Lord Wolseley, and then cabled the Egyptian War Office at Cairo, ordering the advance on Dongola. Just after midnight, the message reached the Turf Club, where it was decoded by Lord Athlumney of the Coldstream Guards and Jimmy Watson of the Sixtieth Rifles, aide-de-camp to new *sirdar* Sir Herbert Kitchener. The *sirdar* had last been seen heading for a series of social engagements. It was three in the morning before Watson tracked him down to his official residence.

Kitchener awoke to the patter of stones on his bedroom window. Throwing it open, he saw the night watchman, and beside him Captain Watson, waving a piece of paper. Kitchener went down in his pajamas and read the cable by the light of the watchman's lamp. When Athlumney arrived, he found Kitchener, paper in one hand and lamp in the other, dancing a jig.

The years of waiting were over.[38]

11

The House of War
1896–99

Brigadier General Sir Herbert Horatio Kitchener.

Blood thought he knew the native mind;
He said you must be firm, but kind.
A mutiny resulted.
I shall never forget the way
That Blood stood upon this awful day,
Preserved us all from death.
He stood upon a little mound,
Cast his lethargic eyes around,
And said beneath his breath:
Whatever happens, we have got
The Maxim Gun, and they have not.

—Hilaire Belloc, *The Modern Traveller*, 1898

S TRAIGHT-BACKED, starchy, and over six feet tall, Sir Horatio Herbert Kitchener looked over the head of almost everyone he met. The
slight squint in his left eye, the frown with which he tried to mask it,
and the scar on his right jaw from a Mahdist bullet all gave an aggressive
cast to his mildest gaze. He exploited these accidents for effect and for cover,
like the ripe mustache that flowed over his wide mouth and implicitly stiff
upper lip. The *sirdar* liked his relationships distant and productive. He cultivated perfection, as if each order emerged from the flawless machinery of
his late Victorian mind.

"He has no age but the prime of life, no body but the one to carry his
mind, no face but one to keep his brain behind. The brain and the will are
the essence and the whole of the man, a brain and a will so perfect in their
workings that, in the face of extremest difficulty, they never seem to know
what trouble is," sang his camp follower, George Steevens of the *Daily Mail.*
"You feel that he ought to be patented and shown with pride at the Paris International Exhibition. British Empire, Exhibit No. 1, *hors concours,* the
Sudan Machine."[1]

The shy son of a lieutenant colonel in the Indian army who had retired
to a rundown Irish estate, at fourteen Kitchener lost his mother to tubercu-
losis. Weeks later, he entered the Royal Engineers' cadet school at Woolwich. The masks of military discipline and Christian fortitude soon overlaid
his natural shyness, and they became Kitchener's chief weapons in a long
frontier war against his emotions. In the summer of 1869, Cadet Sergeant
Kitchener met "Chinese" Gordon, the school's hero. Gordon's less celebrated brother Henry, then a senior officer in the Ordnance, regularly

hosted the school's commanders and their juvenile charges. Although Gordon never recalled their meeting, the young Kitchener cherished the memory, worshipping Gordon with "unbounded admiration."[2]

Kitchener followed Gordon's trajectory. At twenty-four, after failing to go "slaying niggers by the dozen" with Sir Garnet Wolseley in glamorous West Africa, he obtained a commission to the Holy Land. The new science of biblical archaeology required modern maps, so the Palestine Exploration Fund had engaged the Royal Engineers.

"What a glorious land this is, when one can see it through the spectacles of imagination," he confided to his sister Millie, "those grand old knights, so fierce in war, so gentle in religion."

Just as Kitchener's fluent Arabic rested on the foundation of the biblical Hebrew he had learned at Woolwich with an Evangelical friend, so his sense of Britain's imperial destiny rested on his Christianity. In 1876, back in London on a furlough from Palestine, he joined the Guild of the Holy Standard, an army brotherhood pledged to maintain its faith amid the profanity of the barracks and the temptations of the foreign posting. Kitchener swore to be "sober, upright and chaste," to avoid "immoral books," to pray regularly and receive Holy Communion at least three times a year, and to promote the religious and social welfare of his men and their families.[3]

When the Urabi revolt exploded in the summer of 1882, Kitchener was one of the few army officers fluent in Arabic. At the time he was at Cyprus on a second surveying expedition, and weak from malaria, but he hurried to Alexandria in civilian dress to offer his services. After watching the bombardment of Alexandria from the *Invincible,* Kitchener returned to Cyprus, unable to secure a permanent posting. When Hicks Pasha's expedition disappeared in Kordofan, Kitchener was in the Sinai Desert on another survey. Disguised as an Egyptian official, and calling himself Abdullah Bey, Kitchener rode two hundred miles by camel and secured a major's commission in the Egyptian army. For the next fifteen years, he devoted himself to British Egypt, until he succeeded Gordon as an icon of imperial morality.

Kitchener's great passion was his army career, and the stage was Egypt. Even his close brush with matrimony occurred within the narrow field of British society at Cairo. In the early 1880s, Kitchener had a chaste, unconsummated romance with Hermione Baker, daughter of Valentine Baker Pasha, the overseer of the new Egyptian *gendarmerie,* and niece of Sir Samuel Baker. Instead of marrying Kitchener to the British machinery in Egypt, the affair ended as a Victorian tragedy. In January 1885, when Kitchener was down in the desert at ed-Debba waiting for word from Gordon,

Hermione succumbed to typhoid. Valentine Baker Pasha gave Kitchener a gold locket containing a miniature of Hermione, which he wore under his shirt, as hidden as the rest of his passions. He continued to attend the balls and dinners that constituted the social round of expatriate Cairo, and to run the gauntlet of ambitious mothers and unmarried daughters, but Kitchener never again exposed his heart to outflanking by love, the great assassin.

He preferred the male society of the officers' mess, the Masonic lodge, and the military expedition. In the name of efficiency, he forced all new officers to promise not to marry or even get engaged for the first two years of their Egyptian service. He would not risk ridicule or weakness. Margot Tennant, an aristocratic tourist who met him at Cairo, observed, "Though a little underbred, he is not at all vulgar, and though arrogant, is not vain; but he is either way very stupid or very clever; and never gives himself away."[4]

For Kitchener, the deaths of his hero Gordon and his "dear friend" Colonel Stewart were both a national disgrace and a personal shame. Through the siege of Khartoum, Kitchener had been based in the desert at ed-Debba. Appointed special commissioner for the Arabs, he had gathered a force from the pro-Egyptian Ababdeh tribe, without whom communication in the Nile Valley would have been severed. Living and dressing like a desert Arab, Kitchener took a tribal oath of blood brotherhood with his hosts. As for Gordon before him, the experience of solitude, fraternity, and prayer in the desert increased his sense of isolation and destiny. At the same time, Kitchener had been implicated as both frustrated actor and helpless spectator in Gordon's slow martyrdom.

Kitchener had been Gordon's first and last point of contact, the link between Khartoum and Cairo, but had been powerless to help. Though he had warned, "If any harm befall Stewart, for every hair of his head I will have a life," he had been unable to assist Stewart's escape from Khartoum, unable to order Egyptian troops forward, and unable to convince Cairo of the true urgency of the situation.

Having failed to save Stewart's life, he had been devastated by the "dreadful" news of Gordon's death. "I can hardly realise it yet," he admitted to his father six weeks afterward. Gordon's death had "taken the heart and soul" out of the expedition, and it further cauterized Kitchener's heart against treacherous emotion, and its urgings toward misjudgment.[5]

In a final, ironic torment, it had been Kitchener's task to prepare the official report on Gordon's death. Interviewing witnesses, he had reconstructed his hero's last, desperate fight on the palace steps. Privately cultivating the flame of revenge, Kitchener drew rigorously professional lessons from the fiasco. He decided that Gordon had died not because he had been abandoned by civilian politicians, but because he had been let down by his fellow soldiers. Wolseley had thwarted the relief expedition through "mismanagement and mistakes." As he struggled anew against the twin evils of sentiment and bad logistics, for the next ten years Kitchener's upward progress became entwined with the project of avenging Gordon.[6]

Between 1886 and 1888, as governor-general of Suakin, he pushed Osman Digna's tribesmen back from the Red Sea coast. In one skirmish he caught a bullet in the face that, inaccessible to the surgeon's knife, eventually dropped into his throat and disappeared into his stomach. From 1889, as adjutant general at Cairo, he oversaw the training of the Egyptian and Sudanese peasants in the khedive's new army. At Toski, that army's first real victory over the Mahdists, he led the Egyptian cavalry.

He built an officer corps of skilled, motivated, and loyal leaders. They included Colonel Reginald Wingate, a brilliant intelligence officer whose sideline, popular histories of the Mahdist revolt, kept the outrage of British humanitarians on a slow simmer; Major General Archibald Hunter, a belligerent Scottish swashbuckler who kept an Abyssinian mistress at Shepheard's Hotel; and Gordon's nephew, Lieutenant Colonel William "Monkey" Gordon, who possessed the family traits of bright blue eyes and a taste for playing with high explosives. Kitchener appointed him director of stores.

In 1890, Kitchener, aged forty, became brigadier general and *sirdar.* His rise reflected his drive more than his charm. Lord Garnet Wolseley, who recognized ambition when he smelled it, admired Kitchener's competence as much as he disliked his insistence. Queen Victoria, the great armchair imperialist, succumbed to his graceless charm, its deficiency of social skill reflecting its proprietor's obsession for "the service." Lord Salisbury admired his soldierly directness and churchman's rectitude, the marks of utility and reliability. And Lord Cromer, who valued a well-balanced budget as much as he feared for the delicate Egyptian economy, cherished Kitchener's parsimonious way with military expenditure as much as he resented his constant urging toward conflict with the Dervishes. As British attention turned from the Suez Canal to the Nile Valley, Kitchener harnessed the policy drift to his campaign and waited for Lord Salisbury to return to power.

In March 1896, the rattle of stones on Kitchener's window summoned him from sleep to find a dream come true. He was returning to the Sudan, with an army at his back. Kitchener and Cromer sat up until dawn writing orders, so busily that they forgot to ask the khedive's permission to invade the Sudan. As Abbas II slept the sleep of the puppet at Abdin Palace, Kitchener roused his army. Within three days, it had left for Dongola, and four days after that, it had set up an advance camp at Akasha, nearly a hundred miles north of the Sudanese border. After two months, Kitchener had concentrated ten thousand troops south of Wadi Halfa, armed with artillery and machine guns, and wearing the new khaki camouflage that Queen Victoria so disliked.

In the first week of June, Kitchener's troops made their first contact with the Dervishes at the village of Farkah. Kitchener split his force into two columns. In a night march, one approached from the north and the other looped round from the south. At dawn on June 7, the two columns attacked the sleeping village simultaneously. They killed eight hundred Dervishes; many fled by swimming naked across the Nile. The road to Dongola, a further two hundred miles south, lay open. Hunter and Wingate advised a flying column for Dongola before the Dervishes could regroup, but Kitchener paused. He dragged his gunboats past the Second Cataract, stockpiled his supplies at Kosheh and, looking at his maps, planned his advance.

THE MODERN TRAVELER went by train. Wolseley's expedition had foundered because it had used the wrong transport. On the river, Wolseley had wasted time in the Cataracts, had struggled to find boats and sailors, and had placed his entire strategy at the mercy of the water level. On land, where he had used the old caravan route that ran haphazardly along the Nile, he had run out of camels. Although Kitchener intended to use the river from necessity and opportunity, he would not depend on it.

A railway would bypass all of these problems. As in India and the American West, every sleeper laid would be a step forward in creating a new infrastructure of control, forcibly drawing new lands and peoples into the shared modernity of speed and communications. Instead of laboring along the nine hundred miles of the curve of the Nile between Wadi Halfa and Berber, and hauling his force past three of the six Cataracts between Egypt and Khartoum, he would lay 400 miles of track, 230 of them cutting across the waterless Nubian Desert to Abu Hamed, just north of Berber.

Ignoring the experts who told him that the "Sudan Military Railway" was technically impossible, he engaged Percy Girouard, a French-Canadian sapper in the Royal Engineers whose previous experience included building the Canadian Pacific railway. Restricted by Cromer's budget, Kitchener rebuilt the first stretch of Ismail's railway by tracking down its looted parts. Sleepers had been used for the frames of native huts, the roof of a barracks at Wadi Halfa, and even a Dervish gallows. He worked through the summer heat, driving the Sudanese soldiers on in Arabic, personally supervising every stage, always calculating money saved and spent—he was proud to have reconstituted one ten-mile stretch for free—and seemingly impervious to the dysentery and cholera that, sweeping through the camp on the back of the burning south wind, killed ten times as many men as the Dervishes.

In August 1896, the railway reached Kosheh, bringing a battalion of British troops from the Staffordshire Regiment. Buoyed by the high Nile, four gunboats and three steam transports tied up by the camp. One, the *Zakir*, had been built in London to Kitchener's specifications, dragged up in sections, and rebuilt on the banks of the Nile. When the river started to drop in early September, Kitchener was forced to advance. After covering a hundred miles and passing the Third Cataract, Kitchener's scouts detected at the village of Karma an advance force of three thousand warriors under the khalifa's emir at Dongola, Mohammed Bishara.

On September 19, Kitchener moved on the village, to find that in the night Bishara's force had crossed the Nile and dug in on the opposite bank. Kitchener brought up his gunboats. In the duel that followed, Bishara was wounded, but two of Kitchener's gunboats were so badly damaged that to continue fighting would have risked their loss. Only a feint suggested by Lieutenant David Beatty, second in command of the *Zakir*, saved Kitchener from retreat. When the *Zakir* turned south toward Dongola, only thirty-five miles away, Bishara suspected that the British intended to cut him off. Under cover of night, the Dervishes withdrew.

Three days later, his whole army met the Dervishes on the plain outside Dongola. Still unsure of his native army, Kitchener stiffened the center of his formation with the Staffordshires and ordered them to swap their khaki jackets for redcoats, so that the enemy would understand that Gordon's avengers had come. As the gunboats opened up from the river and Kitchener's troops formed up, a wing of the Dervish army suddenly turned and left the battlefield. Kitchener and his officers suspected subterfuge, but the Dervish force disappeared into the desert. Already dispirited by the long famine, Bishara's emirs had refused his order to charge into the Egyptian guns. The remaining Dervish troops soon turned after them. Their flight was so wild that Kitchener's cavalry found in the desert small children abandoned in the route, and came back "laden with black and brown babies."[7]

After the collapse of Mahdist forces north of Dongola, Kitchener faced two obstacles: more than two hundred miles of baking desert, and a stack of superiors who did not want to spend British money on conquering the Sudan. France and Russia had spoiled Cromer's attempt to fund the war from Egypt's savings, forcing him to contemplate pausing at Dongola for as long as three years, while he found more funds. In London, the chancellor, Sir Michael Hicks Beach, did not intend to make up the difference. Kitchener went to Britain to personally extract half a million pounds from Hicks Beach and Salisbury, timing his assault on the Treasury to the short afternoon hours between lunch with the queen at Windsor and the departure of his train.

"His campaign against the Chancellor of the Exchequer was not the least of his triumphs," Salisbury told Cromer. "But his strategy is all of a piece. The position was carried by a forced march and a surprise."

In fact, the cabinet was motivated by news of another march. Captain Marchand, his ten French officers, and their two hundred Senegalese porters had struck out from Dakar, on the West African coast, for Fashoda and the White Nile.[8]

CROSSING THE DESERT with a railway proved harder than persuading the chancellor. The Military Railway's desert route contained no wells, but Kitchener remembered that one of his young sappers, Edward Cator, knew how to divine water. Marking two suitable spots on a map, Kitchener sent Cator and his divining stick out into the desert. To Cator's astonishment, he found water in both spots. "Kitchener's Luck" did not extend to Cator, who contracted typhoid on his adventure and died.

A few days later, when Kitchener reached for a whisky and soda, he swilled brackish water from seventy-two feet below the desert. With water for his workers, he knew he could build the railway. The laborers cost him nothing: he used soldiers and convicts. To save money, Percy Girouard borrowed steam locomotives from South Africa. Laying the tracks for "Cape to Cairo," Kitchener built his railway not to the Egyptian gauge, but to the South African.

From the turning of the first shovel at Wadi Halfa on New Year's Day, 1897, Kitchener supervised everything, driving himself to the breaking point. Sleeping four hours a night, at dawn he would visit the railhead in his dressing gown. If he found an idle locomotive, he personally drove it forward. If he came upon the assembly of a gunboat, he picked up a hammer and banged in rivets. The rate of accidents increased as the drive south intensified. Kitchener blamed his subordinates for the deaths. At one and a half miles per day, by mid-July 1897 the railway had snaked halfway to Abu Hamed. Kitchener was already looking ahead. While the railway worked its way across the desert, he planned to capture its terminus.

That summer, many of the riverain Jaalayin turned against the khalifa. At Metemma, Mahmoud Ahmed, the khalifa's nephew and most talented general, repressed a rebellion by massacring all the inhabitants, saving only the young girls for enslavement. The survivors, led by Sheikh Ibrahim Mohammed Farah, fled to Kitchener at Dongola, where they enlisted as irregulars, Kitchener's "Friendlies."

Kitchener ordered Sheikh Farah forward to take Berber before the khalifa could fortify it. Sheikh Farah procrastinated, claiming that the stars were not yet auspicious, until Kitchener informed him that they were. As the sheikh led his Friendlies into the desert for Berber, an Egyptian column under "Archie" Hunter made for Abu Hamed. Marching at night, and resting in the day without tents or shade, they covered 132 miles in just eight days, before storming Abu Hamed at dawn. In the first week of September, Hunter moved on to Berber, reopening the Suakin-Berber road.

Kitchener could not stop. The Military Railway had to be finished. At any moment, the money might run out. The khalifa might send the whole *Ansar* south, cutting Kitchener's supply line. The government might lose its nerve and prevent him from reaching Khartoum. It had already forced him to send men to relieve the Italians at Kassala. Only Lord Wolseley and the War Office supported Kitchener's repeated insistence that he needed at least a brigade of British troops. He responded to one request from Cairo that he cut back on expenses by cabling his resignation. Cromer ignored the resignation, but he relayed it to Salisbury, describing it as "the production of a sick man who has lost his nerve."[9]

Kitchener's passionless veneer finally cracked in the heat of the desert. "You have no idea what continual anxiety, worry, and strain I have through it all," he admitted to Clinton Dawkins, a friend in the Cairo government. "I do not think that I can stand much more, and I feel so completely done up that I can hardly go on, and wish I were dead. Before next years' work in the field begins, I must get some leave, or I shall break down."[10]

SITTING ON A CRATE of tinned beef and whisky, George W. Steevens of the *Daily Mail* watched "a swarm of Arabs," shoveling up sand to build an embankment. Behind him, a supply train rested on the rails. Fifty yards ahead of him, the embankment ended in an undisturbed dune, and the tiny figure of "a white man with a spirit-level." Seventy miles away, beyond the shimmering horizon, lay Berber and Kitchener's forward camp, and somewhere beyond that, the Dervish army.[11]

Through the 1890s, Steevens had recycled his newspaper reports into bestsellers like *With the Conquering Turk: Confessions of a Bashibazouk; The Tragedy of Dreyfus,* and, after a short trip to Chicago, *The Land of the Dollar.* Now he followed the big story to the Sudan.

At first, Kitchener had attempted to ban journalists from the front—they took up space that could be better used for supplies—but he had been unable to resist the pressure from London to relent. While Kitchener had been breaking down in the desert, Britain had celebrated Queen Victoria's Diamond Jubilee. Like the Great Exhibition of 1851, the Jubilee's rash of retrospectives and parades caused a sudden swelling of the national ego. If the journalists wanted to follow Kitchener, it was because their public wanted to read about him. Not a natural populist, Kitchener slowly grasped that journalists might be allies in his campaign for more men and money. He allowed them to join his camp but forbade them to join reconnaissance parties or to approach him directly. He also asked that they not stand in front of the firing lines during a battle, but he did not insist on it.

At Cairo, Steevens had bought "two horses and two nigger boys—one to look after the horses and one to look after me." Then he made his own way south to join the growing platoon of journalists embedded with Kitchener, "the man who has cut out his heart and made himself a machine to retake Khartoum." At Berber, he found that a Mahdist stronghold had turned into a British barrack town. Greek merchants had reappeared from Egypt, selling Turkish *mastik* liquor and Scottish whisky. British officers ate asparagus and oysters, their tables draped in linen napery, to the strains of "a full military orchestra wailing for the Swanee Ribber." The Greeks complained that Kitchener had bought every camel in the district, and had dismissed a deputation protesting this infringement of their supply chain.[12]

In the tent city south of Berber, Kitchener received no rest. In the first days of 1897, he heard that Mahmoud Ahmed and Osman Digna had massed twenty thousand *Ansar* south of Berber on the Atbara River. Alarmed, Kitchener requested a British brigade from Cairo. To his surprise, he received one, and the promise of another. Arriving before the railway was complete, the soldiers of the Warwicks, Lincolns, and Cameron Highlanders wore out their boots marching the last thirty miles to Berber. After securing new boots, Kitchener led his expanded force up the Nile.

In early March, he found the enemy. Overruling Osman Digna's idea that he outflank Kitchener, Mahmoud Ahmed had led the *Ansar* north along the Nile, head-on toward the invaders. When Kitchener's gunboats started to drop shells onto his column, Mahmoud realized Digna had been right. Turning away into the desert, he hit the dried-up Atbara forty miles above its junction with the Nile. When he found a pool of water in the riverbed, he camped there, ignoring Digna's requests that they withdraw up the river. Kitchener's cavalry found them dug in behind a *zariba* a thousand yards wide, with trenches, artillery, and ramparts of dried mud.

For three weeks, Kitchener could not decide what to do. Mahmoud had reversed the pattern of a Dervish charge on an Egyptian *zariba*. Kitchener's generals did not relish a frontal assault. If Kitchener marched his army forty miles into the desert, they would fight tired, and if they did not win the battle, they would be massacred as they retreated. His troops wilting in the heat, he wavered and consulted Cromer, who forwarded the question to London. Lord Wolseley bounced the dilemma back up the Nile.

On April 7, Kitchener finally decided to attack the next day, Good Friday. In his battle orders, he warned his troops that the Dervishes preferred death to surrender.

"The *Sirdar* is absolutely confident that every officer and man will do his duty. He only wishes to impress upon them two words: Remember Gordon. The enemy before them are Gordon's murderers."

General Gatacre, commander of Kitchener's British brigade, ordered his troops to file the tips of their ammunition to create dum-dum bullets.[13]

The army slept under a full moon in the desert. At one in the morning, with the moon down, a chain of whispers roused the men. Silently, their steps muffled by sand, they moved forward. At four they paused, some sleeping, some walking up and down to stay warm, speculating how they could surmount a *zariba* rumored to be twenty feet tall.

In a bunker inside the *zariba*, Mahmoud awoke to find a line of troops just under half a mile from his defenses. Expecting disaster, Osman Digna and his bodyguards promptly slipped away. At 0616, Kitchener's artillery launched a forty-five-minute barrage into Mahmoud's defenses, the rockets fizzing from their launchers as his new Maxim machine guns raked the *zariba*. The infantry waited, "a line of khaki and dark tartan blending to purple, of flashing bayonets at the slope, and set, two-month-bearded faces." At 0700, the bugles sounded the advance.

As the *Ansar* returned to their barricades and launched a maelstrom of Remington and elephant gun fire, all twelve battalions marched forward in perfect order. Halting at three hundred yards, they returned fire with tight volleys. For more than ten minutes, the two armies blasted at each other, with the Cameron Highlanders taking the brunt of the *Ansar*'s fire, before Kitchener at last ordered the advance again. The British marched forward to the wail of bagpipes, as the Egyptians and Sudanese charged the *zariba*.[14]

On the left flank, the impact of the Egyptian soldiers drove the defenders back into the riverbed, where they were slaughtered. On the right, the Sudanese troops, many of them sons of the garrisons driven from the Sudan by the Mahdi, set about their revenge. In the center, General Gatacre, leading the British brigade, was first to the *zariba*. As he pulled at the thorny barricade, a tall Dervish sprang from a trench with a spear.

"Give it him, my man," Gatacre shouted to Private Cross, who shot the Dervish, and bayoneted him where he fell.[15]

Crying "Remember Gordon," the Highlanders forced their way through the thorns to meet a maze of trenches, fire pits, and huts. Leading the charge, Captain Findlay, married for less than a month, killed two Dervishes with his sword before he was shot at point-blank range. One bullet grazed the cheek of Colonel Verner of the Lincolns; another took off his upper lip. With bullets flying from all sides, the Highlanders worked forward with rifle and bayonets, killing everyone in their path, including *Ansar* waving palm leaves in surrender. Many of the defenders had been tied to their posts to prevent them from fleeing. For more than an hour, the attackers hacked and blasted their way through Mahmoud's camp, until they reached a riverbed stacked with the bodies of escaping Dervishes cut down by the Sudanese troops.

"A very *Good* Friday," Kitchener called it. He had lost 93 killed and 493 wounded. His aide-de-camp Jimmy Watson counted more than 2,000 dead *Ansar* in the *zariba* alone, before nausea made him abandon the tally. Passing the corpse of a Dervish pinned to a tree by a rocket, Bennett Burleigh of the *Telegraph* saw the bodies of women and children in the carnage. When G. W. Steevens saw the work of Kitchener's "clean-jointed, well-oiled, smooth-running, clockwork-perfect masterpiece of a battle" close up, he was revolted: "Black spindle-legs curled up to meet red-gimleted black faces; donkeys headless and legless, or sieves of shrapnel; camels with necks writhed back onto their humps, rotting already in pools of blood and bile-yellow water; heads without faces, and faces without anything below; cobwebbed arms and legs; and black skins grilled to crackling on smouldering palm-leaf."[16]

A platoon from the Tenth Sudanese Battalion found Mahmoud hiding in his hut. After jabbing him in the thigh with a bayonet, they brought him to the *sirdar.*

"Are you the man Mahmoud?" Kitchener asked.

Almost as tall as Kitchener, Mahmoud looked the infidel in the eye. "Yes. I am Mahmoud, and I am the same as you."

"Why have you come to make war here?"

"I came because I was told—the same as you."[17]

Kitchener paraded Mahmoud through the streets of Berber, his hands bound.

AFTER SITTING OUT the summer in a shadeless camp, the military tortoise crawled up to Khartoum. Journalists, fashionable officers, and foreign attachés hared after it. His army bolstered by a second British brigade, Kitchener now commanded twenty thousand soldiers, eight thousand of them British.

Not all of them welcome. Kitchener had contrived to lose the Prince of Wales's application to join the force, but he had been obliged to admit to his ranks the queen's grandson Prince Christian Victor, and her Austrian in-law Prince Francis of Teck. He had also acquired a ragged platoon of fifteen journalists. Their ranks included G. A. Henty, the "Prince of Story-Tellers," reporting for the *Standard.* Henty specialized in historical novels that invariably introduced a pair of English adolescents to historical personages and lessons in Christian valor, in locations as various as sixteenth-century Holland (*By Pike and Dyke*), eighteenth-century India (*The Tiger of Mysore*), the American Civil War (*With Lee in Virginia*), and, to tragic and lucrative effect, 1885's *Dash For Khartoum.*[18]

Kitchener could tolerate a patriotic fantasist like Henty, but he drew the line at Winston Churchill. Although only twenty-three, Second Lieutenant Winston Spencer Churchill was already notorious in the army. Having taken part in an Indian campaign of imperial repression with the Fourth Hussars, he had parlayed his experiences into a popular book, *The Malakand Field Force.* A subaltern who criticized his superiors in print, and who appeared to be using the army as a stepping-stone to Parliament, could not expect Kitchener's favor. By Churchill's own admission, the terms "Medal-Hunter" and "Self-advertiser" attached themselves to him. Intensely ambitious, Churchill was "deeply anxious to share" in the imminent clash between *sirdar* and khalifa. From Bangalore in India, he had applied to join the Twenty-first Lancers, a recently formed cavalry unit. Despite the

War Office's approval of Churchill's commission, Kitchener turned him down.[19]

The son of the rebel Tory Randolph Churchill, Winston deployed his connections to thwart Kitchener. His mother, Lady Randolph Spencer-Churchill, née Jenny Jerome of Brooklyn, assisted him by launching a campaign of "pleasant luncheons and dinners" for influential politicians. Securing an interview with Lord Salisbury, to whom he had dedicated *The Malakand Field Force*, Churchill prompted Salisbury to make a personal appeal to Kitchener. Still Kitchener refused, claiming he already had sufficient officers. So Lady Churchill wheeled out the heavy artillery. After a dinner party conversation between her friend Lady Helier and Sir Evelyn Wood, the adjutant general, the War Office pulled rank on Kitchener. Two days later, Churchill received orders to proceed to the Abbasiyeh Barracks, Cairo.

"It is understood," the War Office informed him, "that you will proceed at your own expense, and that in the event of your being killed or wounded in the impending operations, or for any other reason, no charge of any kind will fall on British Army funds."[20]

Churchill had already made his customary private arrangements. Through a contemporary who happened to be the son of a newspaper proprietor, he had obtained a second commission, to report for the *Morning Post* at fifteen pounds an article. The night before he left, he picked up a third commission. After dinner, the president of the Society for Psychical Research made him promise to "communicate" from the other side, should anything unfortunate occur. The next morning, Churchill took the boat train for Marseilles. Six days later he was in Cairo.

"The movement of the regiment 1,400 miles into the heart of Africa was effected with the swiftness, smoothness and punctuality which in those days characterised all Kitchener's arrangements," Churchill recorded. "The journey was delightful."[21]

Two weeks of boats and trains were followed by a ten-day, two-hundred-mile march along the Nile to join Kitchener's column. Scouting ahead, Churchill turned back to see the army dwarfed by the desert. A thin khaki smear, three miles long, it disappeared into a mirage. In this "filmy world of uneven crystal," long streaks of glistening water seemed to cut across the knees and waists of the marching troops, and then suddenly receded, vanishing like the khalifa's horsemen, who hovered on the shimmering horizon.

Some of Kitchener's officers feared that the khalifa would fall back toward the equator and exhaust his pursuers. But Kitchener guessed that Abdullahi would never abandon his capital and the shrine of his mentor. He could not have known that one of Abdullahi's reasons for standing his ground was the promise of European support. Via Menelik of Abyssinia, the French government had sent him a flag, to be unfurled in case of emergency. In April 1898, an Abyssinian delegation had visited Omdurman, offering French protection and weapons. In honor of his guests, Abdullahi served alcohol and shot off fireworks, yet his apostasy did not extend to technical matters. Imitating the purism of the Mahdi, he spurned the chance to acquire infidel weaponry.[22]

By the last day of August 1898, Omdurman was only eighteen miles away. After laying 760 miles of railway and two thousand miles of telegraph cable, having dragged up eight gunboats, twenty thousand soldiers, and a horde of Sudanese camp followers, only a rolling brown plain separated Kitchener from the ruins of Khartoum.

THE NEXT MORNING, a patrol of lancers scouting six miles north of Omdurman noticed "a dark discoloration of the horizon." They took it for a forest of thorn bushes, but then it began to move. Abdullahi's *Ansar* was heading toward the advancing troops. Churchill's commander sent him racing back to Kitchener.[23]

Finding the *sirdar* on horseback with his staff, Churchill estimated that the khalifa could be little more than an hour away. Kitchener received him with a nod slight enough to acknowledge the report without acknowledging its bearer.

"Come along with us and have some lunch." One of the intelligence officers invited Churchill to a picnic. As he ate bully beef and mixed pickles and drank from "bottles of inviting appearance," Churchill tried to imagine the imminent battle: the howling Dervish charge, the hammer drill of the Maxim guns, the gouging spears and torn bodies. Death seemed "only a sporting element in a splendid game." That British soldiers might one day encounter an enemy also equipped with the "steel flail of artillery and machine-guns" seemed a distant improbability. After lunch, Kitchener's gunboats opened up, pouring the first of three hundred shells onto the defenseless civilians of Omdurman, and smashing the egg-shaped dome of the Mahdi's tomb.[24]

But the khalifa stopped short of contact. The armies dug in three miles apart, each in its *zariba*. Kitchener expected Abdullahi would attack at night, and he expected to lose. He ordered that if the Dervishes breached the British lines, they must be repelled only with lances and swords; random rifle fire would contribute to the chaos. To confuse Abdullahi, he sent out spies with word that the British also planned a night attack. Abdullahi believed them. Both armies passed a sleepless night, each waiting for the other's onslaught.

Sitting in the dust with his emirs, Khalifa Abdullahi presided over a bitter war council. He, Osman Digna, and Ibrahim al-Khalil, leader of the *mulazimin* bodyguard, all advocated a night attack.

"By Allah, these English. I have known them for fifteen years!" Digna burst out. "You cannot beat the English except by deceit."

"Let us attack in the morning after dawn prayers," the khalifa's son Uthman Sheikh al-Din interjected. "Let us not be like mice or foxes sneaking into their holes by day and peeping out at night." Sheikh al-Din's Army of the Dark Green Flag was the largest in the Mahdist alliance. It included the Baggara elite, and the Sudanese conscripts of the Jihadiya. Their Remingtons would be vital to a daylight battle, and to his share of the glory.

As the bickering developed into a shouting match, Khalifa Abdullahi decided. "The best course is what Allah chooses. We fight in the morning after prayers."

"The best course is what Allah chooses," Ibrahim al-Khalil echoed as he stood up and dusted himself off, "but there will be no victory."[25]

Abdullahi retired to plan his attack. Kitchener had camped with his back to the Nile and Omdurman to his left, his troops arranged in a semicircle. Abudullahi decided to mimic Kitchener's arrangement, spreading his armies out in a giant arc. Three hills stood between the desert and the Nile. On Abdullahi's right was Jebel Surgham, on his left the two hills of Karari. He decided to hold back most of his troops, and to maneuver them behind the hills as the battle developed. The khalifa and the 12,000 men of the Black Flag would wait behind Jebel Surgham. Ali wad Helu's 4,000 warriors of the Green Flag and Sheikh al-Din's 10,000 warriors of the Dark Green Flag would advance across the plain toward the Karari Hills.

Abdullahi chose Ibrahim al-Khalil's 4,000 elite guards and Uthman Azraq's 12,000 warriors as his first wave. From the slopes of Jebel Surgham, the British lines were less than two miles away. When the first wave crashed into the left and center of the British *zariba*, Ali wad Helu and Sheikh al-Din would charge on its right side. Then the Black Flag would emerge from behind Jebel Surgham and hit what remained of Kitchener's center.

The khalifa rested in a tent looted from King John of Abyssinia at the

Battle of Gallabat, its embroidered crosses replaced with koranic verses. The play of searchlights from the gunboats on the river kept him awake all night.

In the other *zariba,* Lieutenant Churchill also could not sleep. Taking a stroll by the Nile, he was hailed by two white-uniformed officers on a gunboat. One of them was David Beatty, whose quick thinking had saved Kitchener in the Dongola campaign. Amused to hear that the soldiers would not be able to use their rifles inside the *zariba,* Beatty offered Churchill a place on the gunboat if the worst happened. Then he slung a large bottle of champagne into the shallows. Churchill waded in up to his knees and retrieved the bottle from the mud. He and his fellow officers drank the champagne under the black desert sky. Seventeen years later, when Churchill was First Lord of the Admiralty during the First World War, he would appoint Beatty commander-in-chief of the navy.

Kitchener did not sleep, either. At 0430, with a full moon still in the sky, trumpets and fifes roused his troops. By dawn, the army was ready to move, and the lancers were scouting between the two camps.

Awestruck, Churchill saw the enemy appear with the rising sun, first as a shimmer in the hills, then as a series of glittering smudges, each composed of thousands of warriors. "The whole side of the hill seemed to move, and the sun, glinting on many hostile spear-points, spread a sparkling cloud." Color values shifted with daylight, and the *Ansar* clarified into a white band four miles wide and over forty thousand strong, speckled with red, green, black, and white banners that reminded him of "the Crusaders in the Bayeux Tapestry." As the lancers raced back to the British *zariba,* the hills thundered to the drums and the war cry, *La Illah illu'ah wa Mohammed rasul Allah!* [26]

IBRAHIM AL-KHALIL led his men up the last ridge between Kitchener and Omdurman in orderly files ten men deep. As they crested the rise, they saw the British *zariba* to their right and, to their left, a two-mile swath of Uthman Azraq's men. Then the world seemed to explode.

From the river, the gunboats opened up, their shells blasting spouts of red earth and shrapnel, and ripping holes in the ranks. Al-Khalil was blown from his saddle, and his horse almost decapitated by a splinter. Finding another mount, he ordered his men to close ranks. When the Maxim guns ahead of them crackled into fire, he began to charge.

It was a fatal error. Firing seven bullets per second, the Maxims worked back and forth across the Dervish lines. Al-Khalil was shot through the head and chest, his ranks shredded by the fire. As the Grenadier Guards joined in with their rapid-firing carbines, the slopes of Jebel Surgham became carpeted with smashed bodies.

In the center of the field, Uthman Azraq raised his rifle and fired a shot to launch the assault. Leading fifty cavalrymen and a hundred foot soldiers, he raced straight toward a battery of six Maxim guns. Eight thousand warriors followed them, whole families and tribes attacking as single units. As they charged, they compressed into a smaller and smaller target.

Kitchener ordered further cannon and Maxim guns to be brought up. Every second, a cannon shell landed on the charging warriors, blowing great gaps in the human tide. The Maxim guns hosed along the lines, killing men and horses, the wounded who staggered to their feet and pressed on, the flagbearers who tumbled forward with the momentum of the fanatic dead. When the Dervishes were 800 yards from the British lines, the Sudanese battalions opened up, and the battlefield disappeared under clouds of black powder smoke. Uthman Azraq fell 400 yards from the British line, shot through the thigh. As he struggled to his feet, the machine guns cut him down. The last fragments of his assault were blown to pieces 200 yards from the British guns.

"Cease fire! Please! Cease fire!" Kitchener shouted. "What a dreadful waste of ammunition!"[27]

It was a little past 0800. The smoke cleared to reveal a scene of slaughter. A medieval army had charged frontally into the guns of a modern one and had been annihilated before it could get within range. Piles of dead and dying Dervishes lay across the field like snowdrifts. Small groups of wounded staggered back as fifteen-pound artillery shells showered them with hot shrapnel. Al-Khalil's army had dissolved into a wreck of torn bodies and bloody jibbas. Most of Uthman Azraq's men had been massacred five hundred yards short of the British zariba. The rest now went to ground and began firing their rifles toward the zariba. In a more equal contest, they soon picked off two hundred of Kitchener's men.

The massacre of the first Dervish wave convinced Kitchener that he had already won the battle. He moved to take Omdurman before Abdullahi could retreat into the city and draw him into house-to-house fighting. He ordered the Twenty-first Lancers out of the zariba to reconnoiter the plain, and the rest of the army to follow them along the Nile to Omdurman.

In his haste, Kitchener exposed his flank. He also opened his rearmost troops, Sudanese riflemen under Brigadier General Hector MacDonald, to attack from two Mahdist armies.

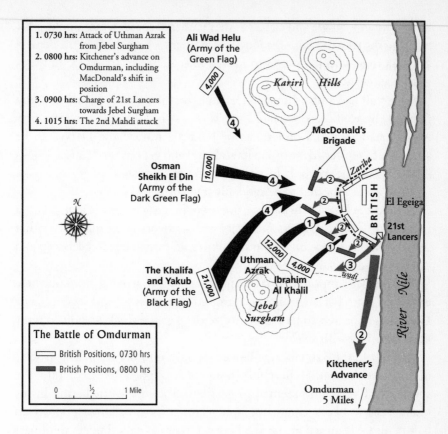

1. 0730 hrs: Attack of Uthman Azrak
   from Jebel Surgham
2. 0800 hrs: Kitchener's advance on
   Omdurman, including
   MacDonald's shift in
   position
3. 0900 hrs: Charge of 21st Lancers
   towards Jebel Surgham
4. 1015 hrs: The 2nd Mahdi attack

Ali Wad Helu
(Army of the
Green Flag)

Kariri   Hills

MacDonald's
Brigade

Osman
Sheikh El Din
(Army of the
Dark Green Flag)

Zariba

BRITISH

El Egeiga

21st
Lancers

The Khalifa
and Yakub
(Army of the
Black Flag)

Uthman
Azrak

Ibrahim
Al Khalil

*Jebel
Surgham*

wadi

River Nile

Kitchener's
Advance

Omdurman
5 Miles

The Battle of Omdurman

◻ British Positions, 0730 hrs

■ British Positions, 0800 hrs

0   ½   1 Mile

AT 0900, COLONEL MARTIN led the Twenty-first Lancers toward Jebel
Surgham. Behind him, Kitchener's whole force moved from behind its
zariba toward Omdurman. Although Martin had been ordered to reconnoiter, he wanted to win battle honors for his new regiment. When he spotted
a troop of thirty Dervish cavalry, "dark, cowled figures like monks on horseback," and about two hundred foot soldiers hiding in a shallow fold in the
ground, he ordered his four squadrons to draw their swords and lances and
prepare to charge. This recourse to premodern warfare was the last cavalry
charge in the history of the British army.[28]

"Of course, there would be a charge," thought Winston Churchill as they
formed up. "That was the one idea that had been in all minds since we had
started from Cairo."[29]

At three hundred yards, Churchill heard the trumpet call "Trot." The 320 horses began to jingle and clatter as they gathered speed, white smoke puffs marking the rifle fire from the long row of infantry crouching in the depression. As they wheeled round to form a line, "Charge" sounded, and they thundered forward.

Churchill had a bad shoulder. Deciding that if it came to hand-to-hand fighting, he would use a pistol instead of a sword, he had bought a new Mauser handgun in London. As he bounced toward the Dervishes, he struggled to replace his sword in its scabbard and get out the Mauser. Looking up, he saw he was only fifty yards from the Dervishes.

"The scene appeared to be suddenly transformed."[30]

Behind the Dervish firing line, over two thousand warriors loomed up, a mixture of Osman Digna's followers and survivors from the *Ansar*'s first wave. What had appeared to be a shallow fold turned out to be a deep and steep-sided dry wadi.

"Bright flags appeared as if by magic, and I saw arriving from nowhere emirs on horseback among and around the mass of the enemy. The Dervishes appeared to be ten or twelve deep at the thickest, a great, grey mass gleaming with steel."[31]

At full tilt, the 320 lancers plunged straight into the wadi. The ground disappeared beneath Churchill's pony as it slipped five feet into the spearmen. Everything seemed to go silent, the images flickering in his brain "exactly like a cinematograph picture." Two riflemen popped up before him. He aimed at the gap between them as their bullets went past his head. His pony scrambled up the other bank, trotting back onto the hard, crisp desert.

Suddenly a man appeared before him, diving to the ground as he drew a curved sword, ready to hamstring Churchill's pony. Twisting his pony aside, Churchill shot him at three yards. A second man jumped up, and Churchill shot him in the chest, so close that his pistol struck the man's sword. He fired again at an Arab horseman in a bright tunic and chain mail, but missed. The horseman turned away, and Churchill rejoined the rest of his unit.[32]

Fifty yards away, a morass of lancers and Dervishes fought hand to hand in the wadi. Churchill had been on the right flank, where the Dervish ranks had been thinner. In the center, the Second Squadron of Lancers under Churchill's friend Lieutenant Robert Grenfell had crashed into a mass of spearmen so thick that their charge had faltered. Men had been pulled from their horses and hacked to pieces. When Captain Fair's sword snapped against a Dervish blade, he threw the stump in his opponent's face. Grenfell lay dead, his skull split in half by a sword stroke as he scrambled up the wadi.

A "succession of ghastly apparitions" dribbled back from the melee, "horses spouting blood, struggling on three legs, men staggering on foot, men bleeding from terrible wounds, fish-hook spears stuck right through them, arms and faces cut to pieces, bowels protruding, men gasping, crying, collapsing, expiring." Lieutenant Nesham, slashed in the shoulder and right leg, emerged with his right hand almost severed by a sword stroke, his reins wrapped around his forearm. Sergeant Freeman tried to regroup the remains of the Second Squadron. "His face was cut to pieces, and as he called on his men to rally, the whole of his nose, cheeks and lips flapped amid red bubbles." Somehow, Colonel Martin had ridden through the melee without drawing his sword, and without a scratch. In two minutes, a third of his men had been killed or wounded. It was then that the colonel remembered that his chivalrous lancers also carried carbines.

Churchill's hearing returned to the crackle of Martini-Henry fire. Within twenty minutes, the wadi was clear of Dervishes.[33]

As the leading brigades raced for the honor of being first into Omdurman, Brigadier General Hector MacDonald and the First Egyptian Brigade fell a mile behind the advance. At the same time, the khalifa's Army of the Black Flag emerged from behind Jebel Surgham, and the two armies of the Green Flags converged on MacDonald's rear. The son of a Scottish crofter who had risen to the ranks as an imperial campaigner, "Old Mac" rode along the lines, roaring at his Egyptian soldiers when they wavered. A pony messenger raced off in search of Kitchener and reinforcements.

Kitchener had glory on his mind. "Can't he see we're marching on Omdurman?" he complained. "Tell him to follow on."[34]

Then he reconsidered. Wheeling west, away from the river, he swung around in time to shelter MacDonald's left flank from the onslaught of the twelve thousand warriors under the Black Flag.

"Macdonald is in for a terrible time." Bennet Burleigh of the *Telegraph* observed the charge from the eastern slope of Jebel Surgham. "Will any get out of it alive?"[35]

MacDonald ignored Major General Archie Hunter's order that he withdraw. He knew that to do so would be to crumple in the face of the Mahdist charge, exposing his men to slaughter. "Old Mac" had personally trained his four battalions of Sudanese riflemen. When the Black Flag's runners poured out from behind Jebel Surgham, his soldiers held their line, the Egyptians maintaining crisp volleys, the Sudanese firing at will. This bought time for reinforcements to arrive on MacDonald's left flank. When the cannon and Maxims opened up, they caught the khalifa's attack in crossfire. Two hundred yards short of MacDonald's riflemen, the attack faltered, the tide of screaming warriors ebbing in chaos.

As it did, the Armies of the Green Flag attacked from the north. MacDonald swung the Eleventh Sudanese Battalion around in time to face the onslaught head-on. The Dervishes poured past the Eleventh's flank and into the seam between the Eleventh and Ninth battalions. For a moment, the path lay open for them to wheel around and encircle MacDonald's brigade, but the Second Egyptian Battalion ran up at the double and broke the Dervish charge at point-blank range.

The bravery of MacDonald and his men had saved Kitchener's army. They had broken Abdullahi's. Thousands of Dervishes, the flower of the Mahdi's jihad, lay dead or dying all around his lines. The khalifa fled for Kordofan.

"A good dusting," pronounced Kitchener as he closed his field glasses. It was 1130. In four hours, the Mahdi's dream had been ground beneath the murderous juggernaut of the Sudan Machine. Under the Khalifa's captured Black Flag, Kitchener led the Sudanese brigade into Omdurman.[36]

The city stank. The khalifa's army had used it as a vast latrine, and Kitchener's bombardment had strewn the smashed streets with the swelling bodies of donkeys, men, women, and children. Kitchener rode up to the square outside the mosque, littered with abandoned copies of the Koran, and then to the Mahdi's tomb, its sepulcher covered in debris from its smashed dome. In the khalifa's house, he found Gordon's telescope. In the prison, he found the khalifa's European prisoners. Returning to his tent at dusk, Kitchener reclined on a camp bed, dictating telegrams by the light of a journalist's matches to Colonel Wingate, who scribbled as he lay on the ground. Outside the tent, an armorer sawed at the European prisoners' chains.

"I thank the Lord of Hosts for giving us victory at so small a cost in our dead and wounded," Kitchener reflected, and fell asleep.[37]

THE NEXT DAY, he visited the ruins of Khartoum. Exploring the remains of Gordon's palace, he paused at the staircase where Gordon had been hacked to death. He spent the rest of the day drafting a memorial service.

The next morning, his gunboats ferried detachments from each regiment up to the landing stage by the palace.

Two flagpoles had been raised on the ruins. When Kitchener raised his hand, a giant Union Jack unfurled. On the *Melik,* "Monkey" Gordon fired a salute of live ammunition in Uncle Charley's memory. Kitchener raised his hand again. A smaller Egyptian flag appeared, the shells moaned southward over the water, and the band played the Khedivial Hymn. Kitchener called for three cheers for the queen and three for the khedive, and then General Wauchope of the British division called for three more for Kitchener.

"Lord, who shall dwell in thy tabernacle?" the Anglican chaplain recited the Fifteenth Psalm. "Who shall rest upon thy holy hill? He that walketh uprightly, and worketh righteousness, and speaketh the truth in his heart."

To a muffled drum roll, the pipers played a Highland lament for Gordon, and then the band of the Eleventh Sudanese played his favorite hymn, "Abide With Me." By the end of the service, many of the British officers were sobbing. Great, round tears poured silently down Kitchener's sun-burned cheeks. Too upset to speak, he signaled Archie Hunter to dismiss the parade.

"Tell some stonemason," Winston Churchill wrote home, "to bring his hammer and chisel, and cut on the pedestal of Gordon's statue in Trafalgar Square the significant, the sinister, yet the not unsatisfactory word, *Avenged.*"[38]

YET THE EXTENT of the revenge troubled even Churchill. In a mostly lop-sided slaughter, Kitchener had overseen the killing of over ten thousand Dervishes. Hundreds more had been killed in Omdurman the night after the battle, when the Sudanese troops had exacted their own revenge on the Mahdists. Thousands of wounded were left to die on the sunbaked plain outside the city. Three days after the battle, Churchill rode back onto the field to see what remained of the "valiant warriors of a false faith and a fallen domination."[39]

"All was filthy corruption." Dead Dervishes lay every three yards, dis-membered and contorted, their corpses swollen to twice their size. In some places, the bodies piled two or three high like lumber. The hot wind was thick with the smell of decaying flesh. After the battle, many of the wounded had fought to the last, rising up to spear and stab medical order-lies and souvenir hunters, but others still clung to life, crawling and dragging themselves to the Nile for water. Churchill found a warrior, one foot blown off, who had covered a mile in three days, and had two miles to go. Another, with both legs shattered, dragged himself along in sitting position. More lay face down in the shallows. Churchill felt Kitchener should have sent out either "a large bucket of clear, cool water" to the wounded, or "a nameless man with a revolver and a big bag of cartridges."[40]

Kitchener's abandonment of the Dervish wounded gave rise to a story that he had ordered their killing. The Liberal opposition in London amplified this rumor until it assumed the dimensions of popular legend. Kitchener insisted that his priority had been the welfare of his own wounded, and that he had engaged the Mahdi's old physician Hassan al-Zeki to set up a hospital for the estimated sixteen thousand wounded Dervishes. But the stigma adhered. His methods had been brutal. In Britain, even imperialists wondered if Kitchener, by waging total war on savages, had himself become a barbarian.

His campaign was not yet over. Before leaving England, Kitchener had been given a secret set of orders, written in Salisbury's hand and sewn into a jacket. Now he opened them. He was to sail seven hundred miles into the far south and complete the conquest of the Upper Nile by forcing the French interlopers from Fashoda without starting a war.

"No corpses," Salisbury requested.[41]

ON JULY 10, 1898, while Kitchener had geared up for his final advance on Omdurman, Captain Marchand's party had reached Fashoda after a two-year odyssey through forest and swamp. Renaming the site Fort Saint-Louis, they ran up the *tricoleur,* built some mud ramparts, and planted a vegetable garden. The local Mahdists did not seem to be aware of the grand French scheme for an anti-British alliance on the Nile. They attacked Marchand's fort, and though he repulsed them, he knew they would be back. On September 17, he heard that a Dervish army was on its way with five gunboats. The French took to their trenches and prepared to fight to the death.

The first gunboat appeared the next morning. Impeccably turned out in the red fez and khaki uniform of the Egyptian army, two Sudanese soldiers stepped ashore. Saluting crisply in the Kitchener style, they gave the astonished Marchand a letter from their commander.

Marchand read that Kitchener, having retaken Khartoum, had come to reclaim the rest of the khedive's empire. The British general appeared later that morning, the *Dal* puffing round a bend in the river at the head of three more gunboats. Anchoring offshore, Kitchener's men trained their rifles on the French garrison.

Bearing a large *tricoleur,* Marchand rowed out to the *Dal* to parley. Neither wanted war, but neither felt able to back down. The two soldiers agreed that they could not honorably resolve their countries' dispute in a marsh at the wrong end of the Nile, and to refer the matter back to the politicians. Kitchener did not insist that Marchand lower the *tricoleur* from over the fort, and Marchand allowed Kitchener to run a Union Jack up a nearby tree. Even more generously, he humored Kitchener's mangled French and agreed to toast their meeting with the awful British drink, warm whisky and soda. The champagne came out later, along with fresh vegetables from the garden.

The next day, Kitchener steamed off. Leaving six hundred Sudanese soldiers next to the fort, he planted another pair of British and Egyptian flags at the junction of the Sobat and the White Nile, trumping Marchand's claim to a site near the headwaters on Lake Victoria. The French bluff had been called. Marchand's government had no way of reinforcing his position; in fact, it was falling apart. From newspapers that Kitchener's party had left behind at Fashoda, Marchand discovered that the Dreyfus Affair had reached a crisis point. Digesting the news, Marchand and his officers cried silently by the Nile. The French government blustered, but when Salisbury threatened to run out the fleet, they climbed down.

On December 4, 1898, Marchand received orders to leave. Spurning Kitchener's offer of free passage down the Nile, he prepared to complete his crossing of the African continent by heading for the Red Sea via Abyssinia. Always ambitious, the French expedition had ended in fiasco. As the French flag came down, one of the African soldiers asked the expedition's doctor why, having come so far, they were leaving so soon.

"*Le blanc ne sait pas,*" replied Doctor Emily. "The white man does not know."[42]

"SIR HERBERT KITCHENER, the *Sirdar* of the Egyptian Army and the Commander of the Sudan Expeditionary Force, has become the hero of the hour," the *Sketch* announced, describing the victor of the Omdurman as "another example of the successful mingling of the Saxon and the Celt."[43]

Kitchener sailed back to glory and controversy. Queen Victoria nominated him for a peerage. The crowd that welcomed Lord Kitchener of Khartoum off the boat at Dover was the largest the port had ever seen. But a second scandal further soured his triumph, suggesting that in the days after the conquest of Omdurman, Kitchener's self-control had given way to unbridled vengeance.

Four days after the battle, "Monkey" Gordon laid a trail of gun cotton around the Mahdi's tomb and blew the last resting place of his uncle's tormentor to pieces. Kitchener claimed that the building, damaged in the shelling of Khartoum, was structurally unsound. His real motivation was to prevent the largest building in Omdurman from becoming a shrine to Mahdism.

He had no excuse for what happened to its contents. "Monkey" Gordon's demolition party tipped the Mahdi's bones into the Nile by night, and one of them detached the Mahdi's shapely skull. When Kitchener returned from Fashoda, his acolytes presented it to him as a trophy.

The *sirdar* did not know what to do with it. Perhaps, a wag suggested, he might use it as an inkpot? Or a drinking sconce? While Kitchener decided, he stored it in an old kerosene tin.

When this story leaked out, it triggered widespread revulsion, and not only among Salisbury's parliamentary rivals. Churchill thought it "a wicked act, of which the true Christian, no less than the philosopher, must express his abhorrence." Salisbury's government promised that a White Paper would inquire into how such an abomination had occurred.[44]

Queen Victoria wrote to Kitchener, registering her disgust at "the destruction of the poor body of a man who, whether he was very bad and cruel, after all was a *man* of certain importance." Icily, she upbraided him, "It savours too much of the Middle Ages not to allow his remains to be buried in private in some spot where it would not be considered as of any importance politically or an object of superstition. The graves of our people have been respected, and those of her foes should, in her opinion, be also."[45]

"When I returned from Fashoda, the Mahdi's skull in a box was brought to me," Kitchener protested, "and I did not know what to do with it."[46]

He wondered if the Royal College of Surgeons, who already possessed a section of Napoleon's intestine, might be interested in it. By then, the Mahdi's skull had reached Egypt, one item among the hoard of souvenirs that Kitchener had stashed in a Cairo warehouse. Kitchener suggested it be interred in a military cemetery at Cairo. Lord Cromer hustled it back to Wadi Halfa as quickly as possible. Finally, the skull was buried secretly in an unmarked grave in the Muslim cemetery on the edge of the desert.

The White Paper was a whitewash, the uproar faded, and the newspapers moved on to new outrages in other remote districts of empire. In South Africa, a new war against the Boers was beginning.

"How strange and varied are the diversions of an imperial people," Churchill marveled. "It is like a pantomime scene at Drury Lane. These extraordinary foreign figures, each with his complete set of crimes, horrible customs and 'minor peculiarities,' march one by one from the dark wings of Barbarism up to the bright footlights of Civilisation."

Whatever his revulsion at Kitchener's methods, Churchill believed the struggle and slaughter had been worthwhile. In the new graveyard at Omdurman, rough piles of red stones and white crosses marked the resting places of the soldiers who had "paid the bill for all the fun and glory." But they would not be the only monument to Gordon's crusade and Kitchener's conquest.

"The destruction of a state of society which had long been an anachronism—an insult as well as a danger to civilisation; the liberation of the great waterway; perhaps the founding of an African India; certainly the settlement of a long account; these are cenotaphs which will excite the interest and the wonder of a not ungrateful posterity."[47]

The triumph of Omdurman had been bought so cheaply that the affair of the Mahdi's skull seemed a minor blemish on Kitchener's crown. Mahdism, the specter that had threatened the British Empire, had been annihilated, and cheaply. As Kitchener boasted, he had conquered the Sudan for only £2,354,000, a third of the expense of Wolseley's failed relief expedition. Thanks to Lord Cromer's budgeting of the Egyptian accounts, the British taxpayer would be asked to cover only £800,000 of the bill. Britain had acquired over a million square miles of Africa, and over two million Muslims, at bargain rates: two pounds, six shillings, and sixpence per square mile, and one pound, three shillings, and threepence a head. No less economically, Salisbury now imposed an "Anglo-Egyptian Condominium" upon his new subjects.

For the first time in history, the Nile was open from source to Delta. From Alexandria to Lake Victoria, the great and ancient river, and the millions who depended on it, were British possessions. A war begun at the turn of a new Islamic century had ended on the cusp of a new Christian century. Its extension of Kitchener's methods and technology would render him as quaint as the last charge of the Twenty-first Lancers. At Omdurman, Kitchener's machine guns and artillery killed more than ten thousand Dervishes in a single morning. In July 1916, over nineteen thousand British soldiers would die on the first day of the Battle of the Somme.

ON THE FINAL DAY of the nineteenth century, Wilfrid Blunt sat at his desk in his house outside Alexandria and composed an epitaph.

"I bid good-bye to the old century, may it rest in peace as it has lived in war. Of the new century, I prophesy nothing except that it will see the decline of the British Empire. Other worse empires will rise perhaps in its place, but I shall not live to see the day. It all seems a very little matter here in Egypt, with the pyramids watching us as they watched Joseph, when, as a young man four thousand years ago, perhaps in this very garden, he walked and gazed at the sunset behind them, wondering about the future just as I did this evening.

"And so, poor wicked Nineteenth Century, farewell!"[48]

Cairo, 1899

The Sirdar's escort, Khartoum.

We took our chanst among the Khyber 'ills,
The Boers knocked us silly at a mile,
The Burman gave us Irriwaddy chills,
An' a Zulu impi *dished us up in style:*
But all we ever got from such as they
Was pop to what the Fuzzy made us swaller;
We 'eld our own, the papers say,
But man for man the Fuzzy knocked us 'oller.
Then 'ere's to you, Fuzzy-Wuzzy, an' the missus and the kid;
Our orders was to break you, an' of course we went an' did.
We sloshed you with Martinis, an' it wasn't 'ardly fair;
But for all the odds agin' you, Fuzzy-Wuz, you broke the square.

—Rudyard Kipling, *Fuzzy-Wuzzy (Soudan Expeditionary Force)*, 1890[1]

A FTER HIS EXPULSION from Egypt, **Khedive Ismail** attempted to retire at Naples. He left in disgust; after one of his wives eloped with a barber, the prefect of police refused to return her to the harem. Ismail floated around the capitals and spa hotels of Europe, searching for the support that might return him to Egypt and the cure that might ease the ache in his liver. In 1877, against the advice of his friends, he accepted Sultan Abdul Hamid II's offer of a palace at Constantinople.

Half-guest, half-prisoner, Ismail joined the Ottoman menagerie of broken-down causes. Isolated from society, pining for the spa at Carlsbad whose waters had always cured him, and fearful of assassination by his host, he spent the rest of his life in a gilded cage on the Bosphorus. He died on March 2, 1895, just as his old French allies reignited his dream of an equatorial empire. He finally returned to Egypt in a coffin. "The winding-up of the estate," admitted a friend from his wild ride in Egypt, "proved to be a very complicated matter." Visionary and fraudster, the prince whom Lord Cromer called "the great high priest of Sham" was the first great kleptocrat of modern African history.[2]

Ismail's trio of accomplices drifted into retirement. After resigning in protest at Gladstone's plan to force Egypt to abandon the Sudan, **Sharif Pasha** never returned to office; he died at Graz, Austria, in 1887. In 1893, Lord Cromer and Abbas II agreed on **Riaz Pasha** as a compromise prime minister, but he retired the following year due to ill health; he died in 1911. In 1895, **Nubar Pasha** was pensioned off after fifty years' service to Egypt, the foreign powers, and his own pocket. The negotiator of the Suez Canal, and thrice a prime minister, in 1898 he died at Paris.

Khedive Abbas II declared his full support for the Anglo-Egyptian Condominium in the Sudan. As the junior partner, he stood to gain from the British program of justice systems, education, irrigation, and tax remission. Meanwhile, he resumed his polite struggle against Lord Cromer, aligning with the nationalists in the hope of recovering his independence. An enthusiastic breeder of cattle and horses, Abbas II also had numerous children, but none succeeded him. In 1914, Turkey entered the First World War on the side of Germany and the Austro-Hungarian Empire. Herbert Asquith's Liberal government completed Gladstone's work, declaring Egypt a British protectorate and deposing Abbas II. Retired in Switzerland, Abbas II wrote his own version of events, *The Anglo-Egyptian Settlement*. In 1944, the last khedive died as he had lived, neutral and rich.

In 1903, **Ahmed Urabi** returned to Egypt after twenty years' exile at Ceylon. A small crowd gathered at Cairo station, some to cheer and some to hiss. Eight years later, he died of cancer, addled by senility and ignored by Cromer's Egypt. **Toulba Pasha,** who led the defense of Alexandria against Admiral Sir Beauchamp Seymour, had sickened in Ceylon; in 1899, his jailers returned him to Cairo to minimize a popular response to his death. When no response transpired, the British allowed Urabi's master **Mahmoud Sami al-Barudi** to return home.

In 1907, **Jamal ed-Din al-Afghani** died from cancer of the jaw while a "guest" of Sultan Abdul Hamid II. His small circle of admirers alleged that the sultan's doctor had injected poison into his chin. Although his death was barely noted at the time, his pan-Islamic apologetics and anti-Western spleen made him the founding ideologue of Islamism. Afghani's protégé Rashid Rida inspired Hassan al-Bana to found the Muslim Brotherhood in Egypt; members of that organization have included the Islamist theoretician Sayyid Qtub and Ayman al-Zawahiri, who, after rising to leadership of Egyptian Islamic Jihad, became Osama bin Laden's deputy.

Of the rebels of 1881, only **Sheikh Mohammed Abdu** prospered. The failure of Afghani's revolutionary vision turned Abdu toward reform. In 1899, Lord Cromer appointed Abdu the grand mufti of Egypt, the chief Muslim authority of a Christian occupation. Abdu and his neighbor **Wilfrid Scawen Blunt**—their gardens backed onto each other—worked on a memoir of the thwarted Urabi revolution and their dashed hopes for an Islamic reformation. On July 11, 1905, the anniversary of the bombardment of Alexandria, Abdu died. Blunt completed their work, *Secret History of the Occupation of Egypt*, a candid, entertaining, and frequently unreliable account of the Urabi revolution.

Although Blunt persevered with his radically anti-imperial politics, he had shed his romantic illusions about Islam. In 1897, traveling in the Western Desert of Egypt, he was robbed, beaten, and abducted by Senussi tribesmen. This revelation convinced him that a purist revision of Islam would end not in authenticity, but "mere madness."

"I had made myself a romance about these reformers, but it has no substantial basis," he admitted. "The less religion in the world, perhaps, after all, the better." More successfully, the six Arabian mares that he and Lady Anne brought back from Egypt in 1878 became the basis for the Crabbet Stud, one of the most successful bloodlines in European and American horseracing.[3]

On May 19, 1898, **William Gladstone** died in bed, sparing himself the spectacle of Kitchener's triumph at Khartoum. After Gordon's death and Gladstone's departure from office, **Lord Granville** retired from politics; he died in 1891. **Sir Charles Dilke** lost his parliamentary seat to a divorce scandal, and **Lord Hartington** crossed the floor to support Lord Salisbury's Conservative government from the back benches. In 1902, **Evelyn Baring, Lord Cromer,** presided over the opening of a dam at Aswan, ending the Delta farmers' millennial dependency on the Nile flood. He retired four years later; Sir Eldon Gorst succeeded him as virtual ruler of Egypt. **Lord Salisbury** left office in 1902, exhausted and heartbroken by his wife's death.

In 1895, **Viscount Garnet Wolseley** finally displaced the "great German sausage" the duke of Cambridge as commander-in-chief of the British army; on his death in 1913, his daughter Frances inherited his viscountcy. Gordon admirer **Reggie Brett,** later Viscount Esher, became an influential Liberal politician, the governor of Windsor Castle, and a successful historian. In 1912 **W. T. Stead,** one of the greatest of Victorian journalists, followed the big story to the end and went down with the *Titanic.* The following year, **Major General Hector MacDonald** shot himself in a Paris hotel room after being accused as an active homosexual. Afterward, it emerged that he had a wife and son, but had kept them secret; Kitchener tended to promote only unmarried officers.

Kitchener's conquest of the Sudan brought the imperialists' "Cape to Cairo" dream closer to realization. No obstacle seemed too great, and certainly not the militia of Boer farmers who objected to the northward expansion of British South Africa. A year after smashing Mahdism at Omdurman, the British army went to war again. This time, the enemy were white guerrillas armed with German-made Mauser rifles. Among the casualties was **G. W. Steevens,** who, having turned his Sudanese experiences into another bestseller, *With Kitchener to Khartum,* died of enteric fever at the siege of Ladysmith.

If Kitchener's triumph had inflated the imperial conceit to its fullest, then the Boer War pricked that delusion. In Britain, blame for the Boers' humiliating successes settled on **General Sir Redvers Buller, V.C.,** whose logistical errors had handicapped the Gordon relief expedition. **Lord Kitchener** took over the campaign. He forced the Boers to terms by waging total war against their families and farms, his methods including the imprisonment of civilians in "concentration camps."

In 1904, France and Britain agreed to the Entente Cordiale, settling centuries of hostility. Ten years later, the rivals of Fashoda allied with Russia against Germany, Austria-Hungary, and Turkey. The rising generation of 1898 became the presiding generation of 1914 and the "Great War For Civilization."

Lieutenant **David Beatty** became a vice-admiral, a commander in the war's great naval clash at Jutland. **Kitchener,** now an earl, became secretary of state for war. Against the cabinet's opinion, he warned that the long-awaited European war would last three years, require mass mobilization, and exact huge casualties. The resulting recruitment poster, in which Kitchener pointed at the viewer's eye and fixed him with a fiery stare, became one of the twentieth century's most enduring images. The slaughter of the army that he recruited became a byword in futility. In 1916, en route to Russia on a diplomatic mission, Kitchener drowned with all hands when HMS *Hampshire* struck a German mine off the north of Scotland.

Just as Kitchener had suspected, **Winston Churchill** used his soldiering and journalism as a springboard into Parliament. The bumptious second lieutenant rose to First Lord of the Admiralty. In 1915, Churchill attempted to knock Ottoman Turkey out of the war by an amphibious landing at Gallipoli. The operation failed, thousands of soldiers died, and Churchill resigned. Back in favor after the war, he helped draw the map of a new Middle East. An enthusiast of empire, he hoped that Britain would emerge from the Second World War as an imperial power. Instead, in the 1950s Churchill became the empire's accidental undertaker. His death in 1965 marked its symbolic terminus.

WILFRID BLUNT'S VISION of Arab nations emerging under Anglo-French supervision came true; though not, as he had envisioned, around an Arab caliphate. Instead it happened via the imperialism he detested. The Ottoman Empire collapsed in 1917; after the Great War, the British and French carved its Arab territories into modern states in the making. In 1924, Turkey's secular nationalist ruler Kemal Ataturk suspended the caliphate. The restoration of *al-Khalifa* is a key Islamist ambition.

After the First World War, Britain took Germany's African colonies as a peace dividend. But economic constraints meant that "Cape to Cairo" remained only a line on a map. After the Second World War, Britain contended not only with its worsening economic position, but also with rising African and Arab nationalism. In 1952, Ahmed Urabi's ghost returned to Egypt. Once again, a group of radical army colonels raised a nationalist revolt against Britain, France, and their Egyptian puppets.

This time, it worked. Led by Gamal Abdel Nasser, the Free Officers Movement overthrew the British puppet King Farouk. In 1956, President Nasser announced his intention to nationalize the Suez Canal—in order, he claimed, to fund the construction of a new Aswan dam. Britain and France conspired with Israel to secure the Canal and overthrow the rebels. American pressure forced their armies out of Egypt. Seventy-four years after Gladstone had promised a British withdrawal from Egypt, it finally occurred. The age of colonial powers had given way to the age of superpowers. At Port Said, a mob toppled the giant statue of Ferdinand de Lesseps with high explosives.

Nasser led Egypt into a dead end of pan-Arab militancy and Soviet sponsorship. After the revolution, the cosmopolitan strollers no longer filled the Ezbekiyyeh Gardens. The traces of Khedive Ismail's brave new Cairo crumbled. In 1971, Ismail's wooden Opera House burned down, taking with it the original costumes, scenery, and score of Verdi's *Aida*. The Abdin Palace became a museum. Ismail's gardens at Giza became a public zoo, and his Giza hunting lodge became the Mena House Hotel, site of the first Egyptian-Israeli peace talks. In 1999, property developers tore down the Mattatias building, in whose café Jamal ed-Din al-Afghani and Mohammed Abdu had dreamed of revolution.

General Gordon's star rose and fell with the empire he loved and hated. After 1918, public cynicism about Britain's leaders and their motives found glib expression in Lytton Strachey's *Eminent Victorians*. One of the icons whose clay feet were exposed was Gordon, characterized by Strachey as an imbalanced alcoholic. As empire passed out of fashion, Gordon's statue was moved from Trafalgar Square to a public garden next to the Thames.

IN 1899, BRITISH TROOPS hunted down **Khalifa Abdullahi** and the last of his followers in the woods two hundred miles south of Khartoum. Cornered, Abdullahi and his emirs laid out their rugs and weapons and sat down to wait for the Maxim bullets. Abdullahi was shot three times in the chest, one bullet through the heart. Once again, **Osman Digna** survived by slipping away at the last moment. He got as far as the Red Sea coast before, betrayed as he took a boat for Arabia, he was taken prisoner. The British imprisoned Abdullahi's surviving emirs at Rosetta on the Nile Delta. Many of them died there, allegedly from neglect. The dead included **Mahmoud Ahmed,** Kitchener's opponent at Atbara.

After the battle, the Mahdi's nephew **Mohammed Sharif Pasha** returned to Aba Island. When the British heard a rumor that he intended to stir up a new revolt, troops surrounded his house and killed him. The same year, the British allowed the archslaver and erstwhile pasha **Zubair Rahmat** to return to the Sudan. In 1913, Zubair dictated his autobiography to the British civil servant H. C. Jackson, who reported the "tottering and uxorious old Arab" to be fond of "the delights and dalliances of Cairo," but otherwise a "venerable, courteous old gentleman." Zubair died peacefully in 1913. A major thoroughfare in modern Khartoum bears his name, honoring the slaver who hunted his fellow Sudanese, and who might, but for the humanitarian lobby in London, have saved Gordon's life.[4]

HAVING CONQUERED THE SUDAN with the barbarous tools of modern war, for the next fifty-seven years Britain ruled it in enlightened selfishness. Contrary to imperial logic, the Sudan absorbed more resources than it produced. The Mahdi's jihad had caused the deaths of millions from war, starvation, and disease. Some parts of the Sudan had been entirely depopulated. The surviving tribes were as divided by the Mahdi's legacy as they had been united by his rule.

Britain built a new capital at Khartoum, its avenues laid out according to Lord Kitchener's sketch. To render the Sudan independent from Egypt, British administrators constructed a new Red Sea outlet, Port Sudan; Suakin, its Egyptian neighbor, promptly decayed. The British also organized modern systems of law, transport, and communications. By 1911, revenue had increased seventeenfold. By the 1920s, aggressive policing of Sudan's southern and western borders had, for the first time in Sudanese history, virtually stopped the slave trade that had once consumed millions.

Yet the underlying religious and tribal divisions of Sudan endured: northern Arab Muslims against southern Christians or animist Africans; settled riverain tribes against desert nomads. These divisions were not healed by the pragmatic British policy of installing the Mahdi's heirs as their proxies. Under the Mahdi's posthumous son Said Abd al-Rahman, his family aligned with the British to become the Sudan's leading political dynasty. Meanwhile, Egyptian politics continued to spill over into Sudan. In 1924, Egyptian nationalists assassinated Sir Lee Stack, governor-general of the Sudan, in a Cairo street.

In 1956, when the British left Egypt, they left Sudan, too. The new Sudanese government sent back the statues of Gordon and Kitchener to England. Gordon's took up residence in the grounds of the Gordon Boys' School in Woking, Surrey. The **khalifa's house** at Omdurman became a national monument, replete with carriage. The **Mahdi's tomb** was rebuilt with a shiny silver dome. Lovingly maintained, it became an international pilgrimage site. Outside Omdurman, the memorial to the Twenty-first Lancers killed in the wadi by Jebel Sarghum was fenced off to protect it from stones thrown by local patriots.

Within two years of the British withdrawal, Sudan fissured into tribal and religious violence. Following a military coup in 1958, all power passed to the northern Arab tribes. When they reneged on their promise to grant federal rights to the southern tribes, the southerners began what would become the world's longest-running civil war. Sudan became a Soviet client, and large parts of the Omdurman battlefield became a military base stocked with Russian radar equipment. By the late 1960s, aided by transfers of Soviet weapons from Nasser's Egypt, the northern armies had killed over half a million southern civilians and displaced hundreds of thousands more. In 1983, President Jaffar Nimeiri announced the imposition of traditional Islamic punishments and made Sudan the first Sunni sharia state. In 1985, Nimeiri executed Mahmoud Mohammed Taha, a prominent advocate of Islamic reform, for apostasy. Later that year, the Mahdi's grandson Saddiq al-Mahdi overthrew Nimeiri. But in 1986, al-Mahdi was himself overthrown by the National Islamic Front, led by Omar Hassan al-Bashir and Hassan al-Turabi.

With the withdrawal of Soviet aid after 1989, Sudan collapsed into a failed state. Cited by the State Department as a sponsor of terrorism, its only exports became refugees, slaves, and radical Islam, its only imports the grain from the United States and United Nations that prevented widespread famine. In the early 1990s, Osama bin Laden arrived as a guest of the government. The Egyptian government alleged that he imported hundreds of *mujahideen* from Afghanistan and intrigued with the banned Egyptian Muslim Brotherhood.

"The rubbish of the media and the embassies," bin Laden insisted to Robert Fisk of the London *Independent*. "I am a construction engineer and an agriculturist."[5]

As proof, bin Laden pointed to the new road he had built, connecting Khartoum to Port Sudan. Fisk's article appeared under the headline *Anti-Soviet warrior puts his army on the road to peace*.

In 1998, when President al-Bashir wanted America to lift its sanctions against Sudan, he expelled bin Laden and his followers. Among the engineers and agriculturists who left with him for Afghanistan were Ayman al-Zawahiri, suspected to be the chief planner of the 9/11 attacks, and Wadih el-Hage, later imprisoned for life for his role in the 1998 bombing of American embassies in Tanzania and Kenya.

The Clinton administration responded to the embassy bombings with gunboat diplomacy, launching Tomahawk missiles against suspected terrorist sites in Afghanistan and Sudan. The administration claimed that its single Sudanese target, the al-Shifa chemical plant in Khartoum, had been used to produce a precursor of VX gas. The al-Bashir regime claimed otherwise.

In 2000, another extensive drought brought foreign aid workers back into Sudan. That year, government fighter jets dropped mustard gas on Christian rebels in the south. Dependent on foreign aid, al-Bashir endorsed a peace plan. Revisiting Gordon's proposal of 1884, the plan offered autonomy for southern Sudan. Given that oil fields had lately been discovered in the south, few believed al-Bashir.

As the negotiations edged forward, the National Islamic Front continued to wage war on its own subjects. Its weapons included mustard gas, forced conversion, and systematic murder, rape, and slavery. In the western province of Darfur, *Janjaweed* militias, covertly supported by the government, initiated a campaign of ethnic cleansing and indiscriminate killing. On its southern border, Sudan supported the Lord's Resistance Army, a brutal Ugandan militia that enslaved children as soldiers.

In May 2004, Sudan was re-elected to the U.N.'s Human Rights Commission. Two weeks later, an American-led Security Council resolution condemned the Sudanese government for the Darfur crisis. That July, the U.S. Congress voted to define the Darfur war as genocide. In September 2004, Secretary of State Colin Powell endorsed this analysis. Human rights groups, modern heirs of the nineteenth-century "humanitarians," were crucial in mobilizing their government.

To ease the pressure, President al-Bashir signed a cease-fire agreement that no one expected him to honor. He began negotiating a power-sharing agreement with the Darfur rebels and consented to the presence of African Union peacekeepers. These gestures unlocked a quarter of a billion dollars in aid money. NATO helped airlift supplies and African Union troops into Darfur. A new Western involvement in Sudan had begun. As in the nineteenth century, it started with a humanitarian impulse.

The U.N. Security Council had promised action if the al-Bashir regime reneged on its promises. Meanwhile, an international consortium of countries developed the Sudanese oil fields. China, a major investor, warned that it would use its veto to block a punitive Security Council resolution.

Today, the price of a child slave in Sudan is thirty-five dollars.

Glossary

Ansar	The koranic word for the "followers" of the Prophet Mohammed, used for the Mahdi's army.
Aswan	Egyptian (later British) military camp on the Egyptian-Sudanese border.
Asyut	The terminus of the Forty Days' Road, just south of the Egyptian-Sudanese border.
Baggara	Fierce cattle-herding nomads from southwestern Sudan.
Bastinado	A common and often crippling punishment in Egypt and the Sudan: The offender was placed in the stocks, and the soles of his feet beaten to a pulp with wooden rods.
Beit al-Mal	Treasury.
Berber	Dongola market town on the road between the Nile Valley and the Red Sea ports.
Bilad al-Sudan	Traditional Arab name for the Sudan: "The Land of the Blacks."
Chamber of Notables	The sham parliament devised by Khedive Ismail.
Copts	Indigenous, Arabic-speaking Egyptian Christians.
Corvée	System of forced labor used by the pashas and khedives to build public works cheaply.

Dar al-Harb	The House of War: territory into which *Dar al-Islam* might legitimately expand through military conquest.
Dar al-Islam	The House of Islam: territory controlled by or previously controlled by Islamic rulers. (see: *Dar al-Harb*)
Dongola	A northern Sudanese province.
El Fasher	A market town in Darfur; nexus of the White Nile slave trade and source of the Forty Days' Road.
Equatoria	The southernmost sector of the Egyptian empire in the Sudan.
Faranji	Arabic term for European Christians, dating from the Crusades and derived from "Franks."
Fashoda	Egyptian military camp on the upper White Nile.
Fellahin (sing. *Fellah*)	(Ar.) Egyptian peasants.
Forty Days' Road	The historic desert route of trading caravans, running from El Fasher in Darfur to Asyut in southern Egypt.
Ghazwa	A slave raid; from the term used to describe the Prophet Mohammed's early battles.
Gondokoro	*Aka* Ismailia: an Egyptian fort in Equatoria.
India Route	British shorthand for the sea routes to India: sailing down the Atlantic coast of Africa, round the Cape of Good Hope and up into the Indian Ocean; or by the shorter route, via the Suez Canal and the Red Sea.
Ismailia	A new city on the Suez Canal; a European suburb at Cairo; the alternative name for Gondokoro.

Jazira	The area south of Khartoum, between the forks of the Blue Nile and the White.
Khalifa	(Ar.) caliph; denoting the sultan of Turkey; or one of the Mahdi's deputies.
Kordofan	A district in southwest Sudan.
Kourbash	A long, hippo-hide whip used by the Turkiyya.
Mahdi (al-Mahdi al-Muntazar)	"The Redeemer" ("The Expected Redeemer"): the Islamic messiah.
Massowa	A port on the Red Sea.
Mogren e-Bahur	"Mouth of the streams," Lake No, where the streams of the Upper Nile unite.
Ottoman Turks	The House of Osman, rulers of the Turkish Empire.
Overland Route	The British term for the land-based alternative to a sea route to India: overland via Ottoman Syria, Turkey, and Persia.
Red Sea ports	Suakin, Massowa.
Sennar	A key market town for the Blue Nile slave trade.
Sharia	The Islamic law code.
Shendi	Town on the Nile between Atbara and Khartoum.
Shilluk	Tribe in southwestern Sudan.
Suakin	A Red Sea port.
Sublime Porte	An honorific title for the sultan, derived from the building that housed his foreign ministry.
Sudd	A mass of floating vegetation that frequently blocked the Nile.

Sufism	An Islamic mystical tradition, its cults central to Sudanese Islam.
Three Cs	Christianity, Commerce, and Civilization.
Turkiyya	The Sudanese name for the Egyptian empire in the Sudan.
Wadi Halfa	The last Egyptian site before the Sudanese border.
Zariba	A temporary palisade made of stacked-up acacia thorn bushes; also an encampment surrounded by such a palisade.

Notes

⁂

Abbreviations Used in the Notes

Add. Ms.	Additional manuscripts
BL	British Library
BM	British Museum
FO	Foreign Office papers, PRO
NRO	National Record Office, Cairo
PRO	Public Record Office, London
SAD	Sudan Archive, Durham University
SNR	*Sudan Notes & Records*
SOAS	School of African & Oriental Studies, London University

Prologue: Port Said, 1869

1. "We are capable": Queen Victoria, April 29, 1851, J. Morris, 196.
2. "God's diplomacy": Richard Cobden, cit. J. A. Hobson, *Richard Cobden: The International Man* (London: Fisher & Unwin, 1919), 246. Figures for industrialization: Hobsbawm, 50.
3. In 1869, Britain and India exchanged 480,000 telegrams; in Porter (ed.), 251.
4. Opening ceremony of the Suez Canal: Z. Karabell, *Parting the Desert: The Creation of the Suez Canal* (London: John Murray, 2003), 252–55.
5. "incessantly": H. P. Measor, *A Tour in Egypt, Arabia Petraea and the Holy Land in the Years 1841–2* (London: Rivington, 1844), 119; see Fahmy, K., *All the Pasha's Men: Mehmed Ali, his Army and the Making of Modern Egypt* (Cairo: American University in Cairo, 2002), 4–8.
6. "notoriously addicted": British Consul Charles Murray to Lord Palmerston, No. 30, July 6, 1848 (FO78/757). "execrable," "servants," "a moron," and "Several have it": *Flaubert in Egypt: A Sensibility on Tour,* trans. and ed. F. Steegmuller (Little, Brown: Boston, 1972), 82 (January 15, 1850), and 65 (December 22, 1849).
7. Mehmet Said Pasha trembling: Malortie, 69, n.310. "He openly confessed he could not control it."
8. "small people": Palmerston to the Commons, August 23, 1860, *Hansard's Parliamentary Debates* (IIIrd Series, London: Cornelius Buck, 1860), vol. 160, 1724. "mutton chops": Palmerston to Cowley, ambassador at Paris, November 25, 1859, E. Ashley,

The Life and Correspondence of Henry John Temple, Viscount Palmerston (2 vol.; London; Bentley & Son, 1879), II, 124. "founded" and "the future": Palmerston, Minute on de Redcliffe to Clarendon, February 22, 1855 (FO78/1156).

9. Livingstone's sales figures: Jeal, 163.

1: Ismail's Dream

1. "Meanwhile it is singular": Carlyle, *History of the French Revolution* (London: Chapman & Hall, 1837), I, ii, 38.

2. Description of Ismail's reception room: McCoan, 91.

3. Ismail's physical appearance: Elbert E. Farman (U.S. consul at Cairo 1876–81, later the American representative on the Mixed Courts), *Egypt and its Betrayal* (New York: Grafton, 1908), 9; see also [Edwin] de Leon (American consul-general at Alexandria, 1853–61), 97.

4. Ismail's daily routine: McCoan, 91. His constitutional and the quality of his cellar: de Leon, 100 and 188; McCoan, 20.

5. "fat and clumsy": McCoan, 18. Dicey supplies a subsequently popular alternative version, in which an English train driver drove off the tracks onto the barges at high speed. Nubar Pasha's account matches that of McCoan.

6. Ismail's finances in 1863: Malortie, 71, n.326.

7. "Gentlemen": Ismail, January 18, 1863, in McCoan, 22–23.

8. "the price of cotton": D. Landes, 240. "began to buy their own": "The peasantry of Egypt, who suddenly gained extraordinary sums of money for their cotton during the American Civil War, spent some of their profits in the purchase of slaves to help them in the cultivation of their lands"; and, "Nearly all of the slaves who had applied at Mansura for their emancipation were agricultural, not domestic": Consul Reade to Stanley, Alexandria, August 9, 1876 (FO141/63).

9. Ismailia quarter: de Leon, 33.

10. "Shades of the Pharaohs!": McCoan, 48. The *Levant Herald* was printed at Constantinople.

11. "a thrifty, saving landlord": M. Bell, *Khedives and Pashas: Sketches of Contemporary Egyptian Rulers & Statesmen, by One Who Knows Them Well* (London: Sampson & Low, 1884), 71.

12. The Agricultural Society and the Egyptian Steam Navigation Company: Douin, G., *Histoire du Règne du Khédive Ismail* (3 vol.; Rome: Stampata, 1933–38), I, 241–47 and 250–57.

13. "I am more *canaliste*": Ismail to the French consul, January 1863, in C. W. Hallberg, *The Suez Canal: Its History & Diplomatic Importance* (New York: Columbia University Press, 1931), 375.

14. "to buy his liberty": The Civil Tribunal of the Seine ruled in the case of Nubar Pasha versus the Canal Company on February 28, 1864.

15. "a capital for his colony": See R. C. Stevenson, "Old Khartoum, 1821–85," in *SNR*, XLVII (1966), 1–38.

16. "the cattle-herding Baggara": Estimated slave-holding among the Baggara, 40 percent; among riverain agriculturalists, 25 percent; in towns, 20 percent. Figures from P. F. M. McLoughlin, "Economic Development & the Heritage of Slavery in the Sudan Republic," in *Africa*, XXXII (1962), 355–89. "At Berber or Shendi": Jean-Louis Burckhardt, *Travels in Nubia* (London: John Murray, 1819), 343–44.

17. "lined on either side": Sir H. H. Johnston, *Pioneers in West Africa* (London: Blackie & Son, 1912), 90.
18. "said to excel," and Mehmet Ali's gift: Burckhardt, 329–30.
19. "ten to twelve years": McCoan, 324. Burckhardt estimated that "five or six years are sufficient to destroy a generation of slaves" (*Travels*, 341–42).
20. "Three thousand survived": Henry Salt (re Sudanese conscripts in Upper Egypt, 1822–23) to the Foreign Office, February 8, 1824 (FO78/126).
21. "trickle of European adventurers": At his death in 1871, the Maltese Andrea Debono left £12,150. Alexandre Vaudey began as secretary to Clot Bey in 1837–39. Returning to Europe, he got accredited as Sardinia's vice-consul and came back to Khartoum with his nephews Ambroise and Jules Poncet. He got funds from Joyce Thurburn & Co. and, via the efforts of the Sardinian ambassador at London, a letter of credit from Lord Palmerston. Bruno Rollet arrived in 1831 in service of a French slaver and launched his own venture in 1839, also funded by Joyce Thurburn & Co. (For Vaudey and Rollet's funding, see Thurburn to Murray, April 15, 1841, FO141/19.) John Petherick, a Welsh mining engineer, was sent by Mehmet Ali to investigate the rumored gold mines of Kordofan and entered the gum trade. In 1850 he became Britain's vice-consul at Khartoum, with permission to travel three months a year for trading. In mid-1851 he entered the ivory trade, and in 1856 was in the Bahr al-Ghazal with Bruno Rollet when slaving expanded in that district. In 1859 he was given full consular powers; the consulate was abolished in 1864.
22. "In 1851" and "in 1863": Petherick to Bruce, May 12, 1856 (FO141/320); Joyce to the Egyptian Trading Co., November 10, 1864 (FO84/1246).
23. "hostile tribes": Joyce to the Egyptian Trading Co., November 10, 1864 (FO84/1246).
24. "his desire": Colquhoun to Russell, June 4, 1865; Petherick to Colquhoun, March 17, 1865 (FO78/2253); Green to Malmesbury, December 31, 1858 (FO84/1060). "Said treated himself": M. F. Shukry, *Khedive Ismail and Slavery in the Sudan* (Cairo: Libraire de la Renaissance d'Egypte, 1938), 95, 99, 118.
25. "two of the Khartoum consuls": Petherick described his and Rollet's 1856 exploration of the Gazelle River area in a letter to Bruce, December 5, 1860 (FO141/30). They were preceded in 1854 by a Khartoum-based "Egyptian" called Habashi; this surname ("Abyssinian") was often given to the progeny of an Egyptian master and an Abyssinian slave.
26. "turbulent and warlike tribes": Petherick to Russell, May 5, 1860 (FO78/1542). "a report from the Austrian": Report of Dr. Josef Natterer, Austrian consular agent at Khartoum, to his consul-general at Cairo, April 5, 1860, enclosed in Colquhoun to Russell, May 29, 1860 (FO84/1120). "Mr Petherick has a wild Arab sort of manner": Russell's drafts 1 and 2, April 2, 1861, and letter of April 16, 1861, enclosed in Petherick to Russell, London, March 29, 1861 (FO78/1612).
27. "beautiful sheet": J. H. Speke, *Journal of the Discovery of the Source of the Nile* (1864; New York: Harper & Bros., 1868), 202. "sea of quicksilver": Sir S. Baker, *The Albert Nyanza, Great Basin of the Nile* (2 vol.; Philadelphia: Lippincott & Co., 1866), 308.
28. "large sums from European banks": Ismail's borrowing in the 1860s, his revenue in 1868, and the cost of the collapse of the Agricultural Society and the steamers, then known as the Khedivial Mail Line: Malortie, 134, 140–41.
29. "a transection of Egyptian society": List of slaves freed by Consul Reade, June 26, 1866–June 19, 1868 (FO84/1290). "indentured to their own government": *Fellahin* slave purchases decribed in Reade to Stanley, August 9, 1876 (FO141/63). "Ismail

personally held": Rogers to Clarendon, November 24, 1869 (FO84/1305). "A decade after" and "a matter": Stanton to Clarendon, May 9, 1866 (FO84/1260).

30. "absolute and supreme power": Ismail's *firman* of May 1869, backdated to April 1, 1869, because Baker wanted to be paid from the date he accepted the commission; T. D. Murray and A. S. White, *Sir Samuel Baker: A Memoir* (London: Macmillan & Co., 1895), 149.

31. "In the end": Baker, *Ismailia* (2 vol., London: Macmillan, 1874), II, 513.

32. "I was most thoroughly": Ibid., 482.

33. "The first thing": Baker to the mayor and Corporation of Brighton at a banquet given in his honor, January 1874; cit. M. Brander, *The Perfect Victorian Hero: Samuel White Baker* (Edinburgh: Mainstream, 1982), 175.

2: The Engineer: 1873–79

1. "I will take": Gordon to Augusta, Le Havre, May 18, 1881, *Letters to his Sister*, 222.

2. "What eyes they were!": Arthur Stannard, a civilian employee of the Royal Engineers at Gravesend: "Gordon at Gravesend: A Personal Reminiscence," in *The Nineteenth Century*, XVII, April 1885, 714.

3. "No such thing as chance": Gordon to Augusta, Gravesend, October 19, 1866, *Letters to his Sister*, 7.

4. "I do not think," "an atrocious fib," and "Our wounded": Trench, 19 and 17.

5. "Is this all": Gordon to E. A. Maund, as recounted in January 1884 on the day he left for Khartoum, in Maund to Augusta, January 30, 1888, *Letters to his Sister*, 302. "to be too closely": Gordon to the Reverend R.H. Barnes, Jaffa, September 26, 1883, Barnes Mss., Boston (Mass.) Public Library, f.2r.

6. "Whosoever confesseth": I John IV: 15.

7. "Something broke in my heart": Gordon to Barnes, op.cit., f2r. "the great secret": Gordon to Augusta, Gravesend, July 31, 1867, *Letters to his Sister*, 18.

8. "You see a new boy, don't you?": Trench, 58. "There were boys running about": O. Freese, *More About Gordon, by One Who Knew Him Well* (London: Richard Bentley, 1894), 37. "Great blessings": Trench, 62.

9. "The creature is in bondage": Gordon to Augusta, Mauritius, February 18, 1882, *Letters to his Sister*, 253. *"A Problem in Greek Ethics"*: A pioneering, discreetly apologetic study of ancient Greek pederasty and the utility of "inversion" to an imperial culture, written by J. A. Symons in 1873 and published privately in 1883. "homosexuality": A term that arrived in English in 1892 via C. B. Chaddock's translation of Krafft-Ebbing's *Psycopathia Sexualis*. Its earliest recorded use dates from 1869, in a German pamphlet by Karl Maria Kertbeny against the Prussian sodomy laws, published anonymously. "Do not disgrace the throne" (Jeremiah, XIV: 21): Gordon to Augusta, Kokstadt (the Cape), July 2, 1882, *Letters to his Sister*, 269.

10. "I wished I was a eunuch": Gordon to Barnes, Jaffa, September 26, 1883, Barnes Mss., Boston (MA) Public Library, Mss. Eng. 450 (21). "I never had": Gordon to Barnes, Jaffa, October 13, 1883, Barnes Mss., Boston (MA) Public Library, Mss. Eng. 450 (33). "We are so": Gordon to Augusta, Gravesend, June 12, 1866, *Letters to his Sister*, 3. "The world": Gordon to Augusta, from a series of tracts from 1870 to 1871, *Letters to his Sister*, 66.

11. "May Heaven's high": Jeal, 356.

12. "The lesson": Ismail's instructions to Gordon, February 16, 1874, in Gordon, *Central*

Africa, xxxii; see also BM Add. Ms. 51296, f.272, undated; Stanton to Granville, February 21, 1874 (FO78/2342).

13. "Greek or Hebrew": Gordon to Augusta, Cairo, February 14, 1874, *Central Africa,* 2. "the rottenness of Egypt": Gordon to Augusta, Suakin, February 26, 1874, *Central Africa,* 4. "quite innocent": Gordon to Augusta, Cairo, February 14, 1874, *Central Africa,* 1. "You have no idea": Gordon to Augusta, Cairo, February 18, 1874, *Central Africa,* 3.

14. "My object": Gordon to Augusta, Tultcha, November 17, 1874, *Letters to his Sister,* 91.

15. "When that man comes into the room": Ismail, cit. Landes, 20.

16. "The Khedive is an honest fellow": Gordon to the Reverend Horace Waller, Cairo, February 14, 1874, cit. Allen, 13. "I wear Engineer": Gordon to Augusta, Suakin, February 26, 1874, *Central Africa,* 2.

17. "African chief's palace" and "silver bullets": Dr. G. Schweinfurt, *The Heart of Africa: Three Years' Travels & Adventures in the Unexplored Regions of Central Africa, from 1868 to 1871* (2 vol., London: Sampson, Low, 1873), I, 383, and II, 325. His full name was Zubair Rahmatallah Mansur.

18. "re-establish" and "secure": Stanton to Derby, December 18, 1875 (FO78/2404). "retain her": Ismail, in Stanton to Derby, December 29, 1875 (FO78/2404).

19. "he borrowed £7 million" and "huge loan from Henry": Malortie, 134. "when revenue was £7.3 million": From the 1873 budget, enclosed in Rogers to Vivian, October 5, 1873 (FO141/82). "amount to be repaid": Marlowe, 174.

20. *"Muqabala":* Marlowe, 173.

21. "The *kourbash":* L. D. Gordon, *Letters from Egypt, 1863–65* (London: R.B. Johnson, 1875), 208–09.

22. "at intervals": Between Sobat and Lado, January 29, 1875, *Central Africa,* 67.

23. "I never in the course of my life": Gordon to Augusta, Fatiko, January 3, 1876, *Letters to his Sister,* 116. "The fact is": South of Bedden, July 15, 1875, *Central Africa,* 93.

24. "pestiferous": Between Lado and Sobat, January 26, 1875, when he was bitten twice by a scorpion hidden in the folds of his mosquito net, *Central Africa,* 66. "rank jungle-grass": Dufilé, October 17, 1875, *Central Africa,* 133.

25. "No steamer as yet": Lado, June 25, 1875, *Central Africa,* 84. "'horrid climate'": Mugi, September 9, 1875, *Central Africa,* 119. "most ordinary": Bedden, July 15, 1875, *Central Africa,* 92.

26. "fearful mysteries": Near Bedden, July 15, 1875, *Central Africa,* 93.

27. "IT IS ALL OVER!": Dufilé, October 17, 1875, *Central Africa,* 131.

28. "mosquitoes": Dufilé, February 10, 1876, *Central Africa,* 155.

29. "What right have I?": South of Bedden, July 15, 1875, *Central Africa,* 93.

30. "Oh! I am sick of these people": Rageef, April 10, 1875, *Central Africa,* 80. "Poor sheath! It is much worn": Dufilé, February 16, 1876, *Central Africa,* 156.

31. "You are a barnacle to the world": Gordon to Augusta, Fatiko, January 3, 1876, *Letters to his Sister,* 119.

32. "All we want": Palmerston, rejecting the chance to annex Abyssinia, in a Minute on Plowden to the Foreign Office, August 28, 1847 (FO1/4).

33. "a comfortable": Disraeli, at Crystal Palace, June 1872, cit. Sir E. Clarke, *Benjamin Disraeli: The Romance of a Great Career, 1804–1881* (London: John Murray, 1926), 207–08. "I am the blank": Morris, 385.

34. "some competent": Stanton to Lord Derby, January 4, 1876 (FO78/2404).

35. "Egypt is well": The Cave Report, cit. McCoan, 402.

36. "would repudiate": Goschen, cit. Derby to Vivian, December 12, 1876 (FO78/2499).

37. "Sadyk Pasha": *Moniteur Egyptien,* November 15, 1876; cit. de Leon, 111.
38. "What an affair!": Gordon to Augusta, Esneh, south of Thebes, November 29, 1876, *Central Africa,* 200.
39. "his murderers' thumbs": McCoan, 198.

3: God's Diplomacy: 1879–81

1. "Religion is the Mainstay": al-Afghani, *The Truth about the Neicheri Sect, and an Explanation of the Neicheris* (1880–1881), trans. Keddie, in Keddie, *An Islamic Response to Imperialism,* 132. As Afghani explains (ibid., 133), a *neicheri* is to be understood as synonymous with the French *naturaliste* and English *materialist.*
2. "tea, coffee, tobacco, and the odd brandy": Salim Rufa'il Jirjis al-Anhuri, *Sihr Harut* (*Harut's Magic;* Damascus, 1885), 179 and 185, cit. Kedourie, 18.
3. "an assumed identity": Keddie, 5–7. Much of our information about Afghani's early life comes from a Foreign Office investigation of his origins (FO60/594).
4. "Owing to his preoccupation": Rashid Rida, *Tarikh,* I, 72, cit. Kedourie, 8. "cut the organ": Muhammad al-Makhzumi, *Khatirat Jamal al-Din al-Afghani* (*Reminiscences of Jamal al-Din al-Afghani;* Beirut: 1931), 110–11; cit. Kedourie, 9.
5. "the sciences of the Franks," "complete votary," and Abdu's attitudes and hair: Abdu's contemporary, the sheikh Mustafa Abd al-Raziq, in a 1922 lecture reported in *Al-Manar,* XXIII (1922), 526–27; cit. Kedourie, 12 and 15, n.44. "You have made us": Abdu to Afghani from Beirut, early 1880s, in Afshar & Mahdavi, *Documents,* plates 134–37, trans. and cit. Kedourie, 10.
6. "the government allocated nine thousand pounds": Enclosed in Rogers to Vivian, October 5, 1873 (FO141/82).
7. "I used to see them": Sharubim, *al-Kafi* (1898–1900), IV, 258–59, cit. Cole, *Colonialism and Revolution,* 125.
8. "iron-fisted" and "great diversity": Cromer, *Modern Egypt,* I, 38.
9. "I have a strong": Salisbury to Consul Vivian, July 17, 1878 (FO78/1951).
10. "political ignorance": Abdu, *The Grand Mufti's Remarks* (on Arabi's *Autobiography*), Blunt, *Secret History,* App. I, 489.
11. "an Italian," "stockpiled," and "clever attempts": Vivian to Derby, No. 7, October 20, 1876 (FO141/100). "A Sufi from Mecca": Vivian to Derby, No. 100, April 19, 1877 (FO141/106). "Sheikh Ahmed": Vivian to Derby, No. 186, June 21, 1877 (FO141/106). The telegram (FO141/111) was translated by "Acting Vice-Consul" Raphael Borg, a Maltese of British citizenship, prominent in the Star of the East lodge that elected al-Afghani as its leader.
12. "I wish": Gordon to Augusta, Shaka, September 17, 1877, *Letters to his Sister,* 150. "your affectionate": Ismail to Gordon, cit. Allen, 108.
13. "Either give me": Gordon to Augusta, February 11, 1877, reporting the events of the previous day, *Central Africa,* 210.
14. "the suppression": Ismail to Gordon, February 17, 1877, cit. Sir H. W. Gordon, *Events in the Life of Charles George Gordon* (London: Kegan, Paul & Trench, 1886), 106–07.
15. "Here slavery": Gordon to Augusta, Khartoum, May 4, 1877, *Central Africa,* 229 and 225. "If the liberation" and "It is rather amusing": Gordon to Augusta, Shaka, April 20, 1879, *Central Africa,* 351.
16. "a grand uniform": Gordon to Augusta, Khartoum, January 9, 1879, *Central Africa,* 334. "cut the divans": Gordon to Augusta, Khartoum, May 4, 1877, *Central Africa,* 230.

17. "With the help": Gordon to Augusta, Khartoum, May 4, 1877, *Central Africa*, 230. "The people": Gordon to Augusta, Khartoum, May 18, 1877, *Central Africa*, 231.

18. "torrid wastes": Gordon to Augusta, Umchanga, June 15, 1877, *Central Africa*, 236. "a single, dirty": Gordon to Augusta, Dara, August 31, 1877, *Central Africa*, 270–71.

19. The multiple sackings of May 1878: Gordon, *Central Africa*, 314.

20. "furtive, polecat": Gordon to Augusta, Keren, March 25, 1877, *Central Africa*, 218. "mutilating," "daily deadly blows," and "Government of Terror": Gordon to Augusta, Khartoum, August 8, 1878, *Central Africa*, 319.

21. "Consider the effect": Gordon to Augusta, Khartoum, May 4, 1877, *Central Africa*, 225.

22. "I look upon": Gordon to Augusta, Massowa, January 5, 1878, *Letters to his Sister*, 176. "His Highness": Khartoum, January 24, 1879, Gordon, *Central Africa*, 335. "hermaphrodite": Gordon's memo at Shaka, April 24, 1879, *Central Africa*, App. B, 438–39. "God or Baal": Gordon to Augusta, Lado, June 27, 1875, *Letters to his Sister*, 100.

23. "The only thing": Between Umchanga and Toaschia, June 16, 1879, *Central Africa*, 366.

24. "I wish": Gordon to Augusta, Khartoum, August 8, 1878, *Central Africa*, 319.

25. "The long crucifixion": Edowa, March 31, 1879, *Central Africa*, 347. "A rush of blood": Khartoum, November 15, 1878, *Central Africa*, 324.

26. "I have brought it": Gordon to Augusta, Red Sea, September 6, 1879, *Letters to his Sister*, 202.

27. "There is no deliverance": Afghani, cit. E. Kedourie, *Politics in the Middle East* (New York: Oxford University Press, 1992), 274.

28. "I strongly approved": *The Grand Mufti's Remarks on Arabi's Autobiography*, Blunt, *Secret History*, App. I, 489.

29. "If a philosopher": Mustafa Abd al-Raziq, *Muhammad Abduh* (Cairo, 1946), 74–75; cit. Kedourie, 14–15.

30. "The first book," "disastrous," "in a fearful," and "After this": *Arabi's Autobiography*, in Blunt, *Secret History*, App. I, 482.

31. "I admire the khedive": Gordon, Shaka, April 25, 1877, *Central Africa*, 352.

32. "Death to the dogs": Vivian to Salisbury, No. 57, February 20, 1879 (FO141/125).

33. "If you are": Vivian to Salisbury, No. 57, February 20, 1879 (FO141/125).

34. "The Khedive alone": Ibid.

35. "My family": Ismail, cit. Crabitès, *Ismail*, 278.

36. "This is a grave": Salisbury to Lascelles, April 25, 1879 (FO141/123).

37. "Bismarck weighed in": Blunt, *Secret History*, 65. "officially to abdicate": Salisbury to Lascelles, June 19, 1879, cit. Cromer, *Modern Egypt*, I, 135.

38. "It has been proved": Cromer, *Modern Egypt*, I, 140.

4: The Redeemer: 1881–82

1. Legends of the Mahdi's childhood: Beshir, M. O. Beshir, "Abdel Rahman ibn Hussein el-Jabri and His Book, *History of the Mahdi*," *SNR*, XL (1963), 136–39.

2. "The governor": Mehmet Ali told Hafiz Ibrahim Effendi to stop using the garrison doctor to amputate the feet and ears of convicted criminals, and bastinado them instead. See Hill, *Egypt in the Sudan*, 36, 41, and 44.

3. "the single cloud": Beshir, 136–39.

4. "How he fasted!": Bermann, 116–17.
5. "This is the hour": Mahdi, October 9, 1880, cit. Abu-Salim, I, 67, trans. Nicoll, 54.
6. "You show the truth": Nur al-Daim, cit. Holt, *Mahdist State*, 48; Slatin, 125.
7. "After midnight": Yusuf Mikhail; cit. Holt, 63–67. The Mahdi's pledge: "We pledge our allegiance to Allah, his Prophet and to you that we will [uphold] the Unity of Allah and will not set up associates to him. We will not steal, commit adultery, make slanderous allegations or disobey your command to do what is good and honorable. We pledge our allegiance to you to renounce and forsake the world, to be content with what lies with Allah and the Hereafter, and not to shirk from jihad." From M. Mahmoud, "Sufism and Islamism in the Sudan," in *African Islam and Islam in Africa*, ed. D. Westerlund and E. E. Rosander (London: Hurst, 1997), 162–92; 175.
8. "Lights, good omens": Mahdi, between October 5 and November 4, 1880, cit. Abu-Salim, I, 67, trans. Nicoll, 54.
9. "revolution": Afghani, in the second installment of the French socialist Ernest Vauquelin's series *Souvenirs de la Revolution d'Egypte*, published in *L'Intransigeant*, August 3, 1882, cit. Kedourie, 29–30. "young thugs" and "the ruin": *The Pyramids*, August 28, 1879, cit. M. Subaih, *Muhammad Abduh* (Cairo, 1944), 55–77, trans. Kedourie, 31.
10. "a firing squad": William Dye, *Moslem Egypt and Christian Abyssinia, or, Military Service under the Khedive, in his Provinces and Beyond their Borders, as Experienced by the American Staff* (New York: Atkin & Prout, 1880), 483.
11. "Your petition": Riaz Pasha, cit. Blunt, *Secret History*, 136.
12. "We were on our guard": Urabi, *Kashf al-Sitar* (Cairo, 1953), 157, cit. Schölch, *Egypt for the Egyptians*, 140.
13. "I am empty": Mahdi, quoted by Abd al-Rahman Birra, Aba Island, January 2003, cit. Nicoll, 63.
14. Characteristics of the Mahdi: Shaked, 57; Nicoll, 60.
15. "At length I plucked": Abdullahi to Slatin, cit. Slatin, 126–30.
16. "I was awake": Mahdi, May 12, 1883, cit. Abu-Salim, I, 334–39, trans. Nicoll, 65.
17. "I must reveal": Mahdi to Mohammed Rauf Pasha, cit. Abu-Salim, I, 94–95, trans. Nicoll, 71–72.
18. "I began" and "sympathies": Blunt, *Secret History*, 1 and 7.
19. "a moral" and "infecting": Ibid., 28. "to champion": Ibid., 7.
20. "the patriotic idea" and "cosmopolitan finance": Blunt, *Gordon at Khartoum*, ix. "Semitic influence": Ibid., x. "too powerful": Blunt, *Secret History*, 21.
21. "I knew that": Ibid., 83. "Philo-Asiatics": Ibid., 89.
22. "the Caliphal question": Ibid., 87. "I am full": Ibid., 89.
23. "a little house" to "more spiritual": Ibid., 105–06. "wild man": Ibid., 100.
24. "bondage," "the freeing," "religious reformation," "better elements," and "In God's name": Ibid., 121–22.
25. "A foreign occupation": *Further Account by Sheikh Mohammed Abdu*, in Blunt, *Secret History*, App. I, 493.
26. "the Colonels overruled": At a meeting on September 8, 1881, Schölch, *Egypt for the Egyptians*, 160–61.
27. "Now is your moment" to "We are not slaves": Blunt, *Secret History*, 150.
28. "The Egyptians": Sharif to Blunt, ibid., 196.
29. "Perhaps you might": Currie to Blunt, mid-November 1881, ibid., 158.
30. "We have won": Urabi to Blunt, December 6, 1881, ibid., 170–71.
31. "certain": Ibid., 173.

32. "composed a program": The *Programme of the National Party of Egypt, forwarded by Mr. Blunt to Mr. Gladstone, December 20, 1881* is in Blunt, *Secret History*, App. V, 556–59. On December 18, 1881, Blunt, "in conjunction with Sheikh Mohammed Abdu and others of the civilian leaders," and with Sabunji as their scribe, drew up "a manifesto." Abdu gained the "adhesion" of Mahmud Sami al-Barudi, the minister for war, and the "approval" of Urabi, before Blunt, "with Malet's knowledge," forwarded it to Gladstone on December 20 (Blunt, *Secret History*, 173).

33. "It will be": Granville to Gladstone, September 9, 1881, Gladstone, *Political Correspondence*, I, 290, it. 527.

5: Egypt for the Egyptians! 1882

1. "It has been": Gladstone to Sir Francis Doyle, cit. Matthew, 257. "hopelessly" and "a sophisticated": M. R. D. Foot, Introduction to Gladstone, *Midlothian Speeches*, 11.

2. "the operations," "the amity," and "lusts": Gladstone to the Political Economy Club in 1876, at a dinner marking the centenary of Adam Smith's *Wealth of Nations*, cit. Matthew, 272. "public law": Gladstone, Third Midlothian Speech, in *Midlothian Speeches*, 128.

3. "noble": Gladstone, Diary, December 29, 1876, *Diaries*, IX, 181.

4. "like a deluge": Bulgarian Horrors, *The Fortnightly Review*, September 5, 1876. "Jingoes": George Russell, nephew of Lord Russell (the foreign secretary who gave John Petherick his guns, later Whig prime minister), cit. Granville to Gladstone, February 20, 1880, in Gladstone, *Political Correspondence*, I, 114, it. 175 and n.3 (BM Add. Ms. 44172, f.16).

5. "highest grounds" and "gratuitous": First Midlothian Speech, Gladstone, *Midlothian Speeches*, 35. "pernicious" and "cruel": Second Midlothian Speech, *Midlothian Speeches*, 92–93. "hoodwinking," "theatrical," "monstrous," and "A little": Glasgow speech, *Midlothian Speeches*, 196–97.

6. "Do not suffer": Second Midlothian Speech, *Midlothian Speeches*, 94.

7. "Modern times": Third Midlothian Speech, *Midlothian Speeches*, 128. "equal rights" and "always": Ibid., 115–16.

8. "Our first sight": Gladstone, "Aggression on Egypt," in *The Nineteenth Century* (August 1877), II, 149.

9. "radically," "susceptibilities," and "the ends": Ibid., 149.

10. Gladstone's holding in Egyptian Tribute Loan Stock: Matthew, 287; figures taken from the *Approximate Annual Sketch of Property* compiled by Gladstone every December.

11. "We shall" and "I am not": Granville to Gladstone, December 5, 1881, Gladstone, *Political Correspondence*, I, 320, it. 588 (BM Add. Ms. 44173, f.249). "dawdling": Blunt, *Secret History*, 78.

12. "information": Gladstone to Granville, September 13, 1881, *Political Correspondence*, I, 291, it. 529 (PRO 30/29/124).

13. "order": Gambetta's foreign minister Jules Barthélemy de St. Hilaire to Granville, shortly after the September 1881 mutiny, cit. Cromer, *Modern Egypt*, I, 214.

14. "They will propose": Granville to Gladstone, December 5, 1881, Gladstone, *Political Correspondence*, I, 320, it. 588 (BM Add. Ms. 44173, f.249).

15. "very idea": Gladstone to Granville, January 4, 1882, Gladstone, *Political Correspondence*, I, 326–27, it. 599 (PRO 30/29/125).

16. "Anglo-French": Ibid. "the bondholders": Granville to Malet, quoting Gladstone, No. 8., January 11, 1881 (FO78/3446).
17. "They will take": Malet, cit. Blunt, *Secret History*, 188.
18. "It is the language": Blunt, *Secret History*, 189.
19. "What a blunder!" ("Quelle boulette!"): Sharif Pasha, cit. Schölch, *Egypt for the Egyptians*, 203.
20. "I have offered": Ibid., 196.
21. "For many days": Blunt, *Secret History*, 190.
22. Al-Barudi's reading: Schölch, 352, n.98.
23. "Smouldering fires": *Pall Mall Gazette*, March 1882, cit. Blunt, *Secret History*, 255.
24. "It would be" and "The house": De Freycinet and Colvin, April 20, 1882, cit. Cromer, I, 255.
25. "The Sultan": Gladstone to Granville, April 5, 1882, *Political Correspondence*, I, 354, it. 665 (PRO 30/29/125).
26. "The Swell": Sir Garnet Wolseley to Lady Louisa Wolseley, August 17, 1882, in Wolseley, *Letters*, 72.
27. "Do not fear": Blunt to Urabi, May 31, 1882, following assurances from Eddy Hamilton—"He promised me there would be no landing of troops or intervention at all"—cit. Blunt, *Secret History*, 296.
28. "fighting": Sheikh Assad's report to the Sultan, in Documents Pertaining to the Yildiz Collection of the Basbanlik Arşivi in P. M. Holt (ed.), *Political & Social Change in Modern Egypt* (Curzon: London, 1968), 55.
29. "Dervish is a man": John Morley, *Pall Mall Gazette*, June 15, 1882.
30. "Allah give victory": Blunt, *Secret History*, 306.
31. "preparing," "other," and "Islamic": Dufferin to Granville, July 10, 1882, in D. Gillard (ed.), *British Documents on Foreign Affairs: Reports & Papers from the Foreign Office Confidential Print, Part 1: From the mid-Nineteenth Century to the First World War, Series B: The Near & Middle East, 1856–1914*, Vol. IX (London: HMSO, 1984–85), 62, Doc. 50.
32. The Urabist oath: Kedourie, 35. Malet, 346ff, describes the Powers' attempt to exile Urabi.
33. "He shall be cast": Sheikh Ullaish's *fatwa*, cit. Broadley, 176.
34. "Admiral wants": Granville to Gladstone, 4:00 P.M., May 30, 1882, *Political Correspondence*, I, 376, it. 720, n.5 (PRO 30/29/125). "thrown off": Gladstone to Granville, June 2, 1882, Gladstone, *Political Correspondence*, I, 378, it. 723 (PRO 30/29/125).
35. "Everything": Blunt, June 1, 1882, *Secret History*, 296.
36. "Intelligence": *Times*, August 23, 1881.
37. Rauf dismissed al-Daim's warning: Slatin, 135.
38. "despondent": Giegler, 177.
39. "The Prophet" and "After the collection": Mahdi, cit. Abu-Salim, I, 288–89, trans. Nicoll, 88–89.
40. "I seek refuge," "He gives life," and "There is neither": *Ratib al-Imam al-Mahdi (The Mahdi's Ratib)*, Sudan Archive at Durham University, it. 97/1, f. 9, trans. Nicoll, 86.
41. "ultimate" and "the attainment": Shaked, 87. "a permanent": Shaked, 90.
42. "a dog": R. S. Kramer, 145–8.
43. "unless," "even," "immodestly," and "obscenity": R. S. Kramer, 145. "wailing": Ibid., 147. "confined": Ibid., 148. "let her wage": Ibid., 145.

44. "idle yarns" and "a burning": M. I. Abu-Salim and K. Vikor, "The Man who Believed in the Mahdi," in *Sudanic Africa,* 2 (1991), 29–52.

45. Rauf's request for reinforcements, December 17, 1881: Shibeika, *Independent Sudan,* 59. "a false prophet": M. Safon, in Cookson to Malet, No. 149, December 13, 1881, enclosed in Philip to Cookson, December 6, 1881 (FO141/149). Overthrow of prokhedive rector: Malet to Granville, No. 350, November 17, 1881 (FO141/144); No. 377, December 12, 1881.

46. "almost naked": Slatin, 143. "My progress": Mahdi to al-Shallali, cit. Abu-Salim, I, 121–28, trans. Holt, *Mahdist State,* 78–88.

47. Schuster's expedition: Schuster took the first photograph of an Eclipse Comet on May 17, 1882, at Sohag, sixty miles south of Asyut. A German-born Jew, Schuster led the Royal Society's 1875 expedition to observe a total eclipse in Siam (Thailand). In 1882 Schuster was Professor of Applied Mathematics at Manchester University, and from 1888, Professor of Physics. He was knighted in 1920.

48. Origins of the Alexandria Riot: *Declaration of Mr. John Ninet* (a Swiss supporter of Urabi), in Blunt, *Secret History,* App. II, 533. The cheese knife was attached to a table by a long string. "These particulars I had the next day from a Christian policeman who was present."

49. The riot at Alexandria: C. Royle, 44–55.

50. "Butchered": Salisbury, cit. C. Royle, 59.

51. "I am afraid": Hartington to Granville, June 19, 1882 (PRO 30/29/132).

52. "a military" and "bankruptcy": J. Chamberlain, *A Political Memoir, 1880–1892* (ed. C. D. Howard; London: Batchworth, 1953), 71.

53. Suez Canal traffic: Hobsbawm, 58; C. Newbury, "Great Britain & the Partition of Africa, 1870–1914," in Porter (ed.), *Oxford History of the British Empire, III,* 626–27.

54. Dervish's pension offer: Zubair Pasha to Blunt, over breakfast on December 22, 1888, cit. Blunt, *Secret History,* 320n. The French pension offer: Blunt's cousin Algernon "Button" Bourke, then on the *Times,* told Blunt on June 13, 1882, that "the Rothschilds" had offered Urabi £4,000 a year for life if he left Egypt. Urabi denied this to Blunt and recalled only a French offer contingent upon his going into exile at Paris (*Secret History,* 334n).

55. "Use will be made": Urabi, July 2, 1882, in Blunt, *Secret History,* 371–72. The letter was translated and forwarded to Blunt by Jean Sabunji; on July 17 (ibid., 374) Blunt sent it on to Gladstone and the Prince of Wales—against the advice of Lord de la Warr (ibid., 370).

56. "Egypt's Europeans": Cromer, *Modern Egypt,* I, 288–89. "no party": Gladstone to Granville, July 4, 1882, Gladstone *Political Correspondence,* I, 385, it. 739 (PRO 30/29/29A). "My brain": Gladstone, Diary, July 5, 1882, after long debates on the Irish Crimes & Arrears Bill and an "Anxious Cabinet behind the [Speaker's] chair," *Diaries,* X, 292. "an act," "the whole," and "improbable": Gladstone to Granville, July 5, 1882, Gladstone, *Political Correspondence,* I, 386, it. 741 (PRO 30/29/29A).

57. "It was heavy": Israel Harding, interviewed for "Sailor V.C.'s," *Strand Magazine,* October 12, 1896.

58. Description of the bombardment of July 11, 1882: Royle, 60–85.

59. Description of the riot of July 11, 1882: Royle, 98–106. Damages in the riot: The International Commission of Indemnities awarded compensation of £4,341,011 (FF106,820,236) for houses, furniture, and merchandise lost. The figure excluded claims for cash, jewelry, and artworks (Royle, 102n).

60. "The fire" and "made": Gladstone to Granville, July 13, 1882, Gladstone, *Political Correspondence*, I, 394, it. 757 (PRO 30/29/126).
61. "Instructions": Cabinet Minutes, July 31, 1882, cit. Matthew, 374.

6: The Wind and the Whirlwind: 1883

1. "I have always": Wolseley to Lady Louisa Wolseley, September 28, 1882, Wosleley *Letters*, 82–83.
2. "My eyes fill" and Wolseley on the *Calabria:* Wolseley to Lady Louisa, August 2, 1882, *Letters*, 69–70.
3. "every work" and "beg": Wolseley, *Story*, I, 8.
4. "The Man": Title of Spy's 1874 cartoon.
5. "I am the very": W. S. Gilbert's lyric to Gilbert and Sullivan's "I Am the Very Model of a Modern Major-General," from *The Pirates of Penzance* (1879), Act I, No. xiii.
6. "Great German": Wolseley, cit. Pakenham, 87. "Grand Key": Wolseley, *In Relief of Gordon*, ed. Preston, xvi.
7. "I long": Wolseley to Lady Louisa, September 7, 1882, *Letters*, 75.
8. *"Truly Allah"*: Koran, IX; 111. Urabi declared martial law on July 11. He deposed Tawfik on July 17.
9. "What say you": The question (*istifham*) to the al-Azhar clerics that led to their *fatwa* against Tawfik, cit. Broadley, 175.
10. Meeting of seventy notables, July 17: Schölch, *Egypt for the Egyptians*, 263–64.
11. Tawfik sacked Urabi on July 20.
12. "Egyptian" and "Islamic-Ottoman": Urabi's second meeting at the Interior Ministry, July 29, cit. Schölch, *Egypt for Egyptians*, 270–71 and 262.
13. Mahdist handbook: Expounding "how the Muslim community should behave towards non-Muslims, especially those invading their territory, and the justification for that outlook according to the *sharia*" (M. I. Waley, "Islamic Manuscripts in the British Royal Collection: A Concise Catalogue," in *Manuscripts of the Middle East*, VI (Leiden: Brill, 1994), 8. "Much of the time: Blunt, *Secret History*, 395. Urabi's landholdings: Having inherited 8.5 *feddans* from his father, Urabi bought 560 more as he rose to power (Blunt, *Secret History*, App. I, 481), and acquired a further 810 *faddans* in July 1882 (Schölch, *Egypt for Egyptians!*, 282).
14. "criminal": Wolseley to Louisa, September 10, 1882, *Letters*, 76.
15. "Take no action": De Lesseps to Urabi, August 20, 1882, cit. Blunt, *Secret History*, 398.
16. "Sincere": C. Royle, 143.
17. Urabi's order that Hilmi not obey Tawfik: Cit. A.-M. Omar, *The Soudan Question Based on British Documents* (Cairo: Misr, 1952), 3. Tawfik's contrary order: "The Khedive . . . used to write to the Governor not to mind about the Mahdi's progress, so as to increase the embarrassment" (Ahmed Rifaat Bey, cit. Blunt, *Secret History*, App. II, 503).
18. "maintain": Urabi to the khedive, June 18, 1882, cit. Shibeika, *Independent Sudan*, 60.
19. Hilmi's laughter: Giegler, 208. Blood money: J. J. Leverson, *Insurrection of the False Prophet, 1881–83* (4 vol., Cairo: War Office, 1883–84); I, 8. Letter bomb: Hilmi to Tawfik, July 12, 1882, cit. Shibeika, 61.
20. *Message on the Mahdi* was by Sheikh Shakir al-Ghazzi, mufti of the Khartoum Court of Appeal. *General Advice . . .* was by Sheikh Ahmad al-Azhari, mufti of western Sudan. A third text, *Guide for Him who Seeks Guidance on the Mahdi and the false*

Mahdi, was by Sheikh Mohammed al-Darir, whose appointment had been personally endorsed by the sultan.

21. "Our refuge": Holt, *Mahdist State*, 108–09.

22. "We killed" and "nothing": Yusif Mikhail, *Mazkarat Yusif Mikhail* (London: Dar al-Nusairi, 1998), 45–46, trans. Holt, 117–19.

23. "I have resolved": Wolseley to Louisa, September 7, 1882, *Letters*, 75.

24. "a new thing": Wolseley to Louisa, September 14, 1882, *Letters*, 78.

25. "Note the time": Wolseley, the night of September 12/13, 1882, cit. Sir H. McCalmont, *Memoirs of Major-General Sir Hugh McCalmont* (ed. Major-General Sir C. E. Callwell; London: Hutchinson, 1924), 218–19.

26. "Anything": Sir W. Butler, *An Autobiography* (ed. E. Butler; London: Constable, 1911), 232 and (re killing) 237.

27. "What a change!": Wolseley to Louisa, September 15, 1882, *Letters*, 79.

28. "charming": Wolseley to Louisa, September 15, 1882, *Letters*, 80. "tears": Malet to Granville, October 1, 1882 (PRO 30/29/160).

29. "very nervous": Wolseley to Louisa, September 14, 1882, *Letters*, 78. "Seymour": Wolseley to Louisa, September 15, 1882, Wolseley Papers (Hove), WP11/17i/2.

30. "Wolseley in Cairo": Gladstone's Diary, September 15, 1882, *Diaries*, X, 331. "fresh great": *Economist*, September 16, 1882. "a vote": Lawson, cit. C. Royle, 191n.

31. "whirlpool" and "If Garnet's": Lady Wolseley to Mrs. (later Viscountess) Goschen, cit. Arthur and Maurice, *Wolseley*, 162.

32. "The difficulty": Granville to Gladstone, October 2, 1882, Gladstone, *Political Correspondence*, I, 439, it. 855 (BM Add. Ms. 44174).

33. "The parties": Gladstone to Granville, October 3, 1882, *Political Corrrespondence*, I, 440, it. 857 (PRO 30/29/126). "only local alternative": Wolseley to Louisa, September 14, 1882, *Letters*, 79. "plant": Gladstone's Diary, November 15, 1883, *Diaries*, XI, 59. "bid a long": Gladstone, "Aggression on Egypt," in *The Nineteenth Century* (August 1877), II, 161.

34. Sixty-six protestations between 1882 and 1922: A. J. P. Taylor, *The Struggle for Mastery in Europe, 1848–1918* (New York: Oxford University Press, 1954; 1971), 90.

35. "Although": Granville, cit. Cromer, *Modern Egypt*, I, 340.

36. "For some time": Dufferin, cit. J. C. Hurewitz, *The Middle East & North Africa in World Politics* (New Haven: Yale, 1975–79; 2nd ed.), I, 191–94; Karsh, 66.

37. "The Egyptians": Riaz Pasha, cit. Beamon to Blunt, *Secret History*, 459.

38. "stirring up" and other charges: Royle, 200. Spitting eunuchs: Blunt, *Secret History*, 459.

39. "African Garibaldi": C. Royle, 202.

40. Departure of Urabi for Ceylon: Malet to Granville, No. 58, December 27, 1882 (FO78/3455). "Egyptians": Matthew, 389n. Gladstone's stock in the 1871 issue was worth £17,100 before the invasion of Egypt, and £24,600 just after it (ibid., 387).

41. Siege of El Obeid: Ohrwalder, 52–53.

42. "smugglers": Ibid., 55.

43. Sack of El Obeid: Ibid., 56–59; Leverson, I, 14.

44. "As you have": Abu-Salim, V, 458, trans. Holt, *Mahdist State*, 112.

45. "I have been": Mahdi, "to all his beloved, the believers," cit. Wingate, *Mahdiism and the Egyptian Sudan*, 92–93.

46. "It is no part": Gladstone, Diary, November 2, 1882; Diaries, X, 360.

47. Wilson's memo, and Lutfi Pasha's request: Enclosed in Malet to Granville, No. 659, October 2, 1882 (FO78/3442). "a constant drain": Dufferin to Granville, No. 6, No-

vember 18, 1882 (FO78/3454). "without aid": Malet to Granville, No. 788, November 4, 1882 (FO78/3443).

48. Hicks's selection: H. Keown-Boyd, *A Good Dusting: A Centenary Review of the Sudan Campaigns, 1883–99* (London: Secker & Warburg, 1986), 10.

49. "anxious," "overwhelmed," "some wonderful," "£10,000," and "the inevitable": Hicks to Sophia Hicks, *Road to Shaykan,* 12, 11, 25, 5.

50. "I have never": Hicks, in Colborne, 81. "Here I have": Hicks, 30–31.

51. "Who would": Ibid.

52. "It is simply": Ibid., 22. "dolts and fools": Ibid., 37. "Walker": Ibid., 45. "using inflammatory": Ibid., 78.

53. "I cannot": Ibid., 21–22.

54. "It would be": Giegler, 216.

55. Guards tied up at night: National Record Office, Cairo, CAIRINT 3/9/197 (Intelligence Department, Anglo-Egyptian Interior Ministry) 3/9/197, ff. 4–9, *Ms. of Muhammad Nur Barudi* (Hicks's assistant cook), cit. Nicoll, 152.

56. "In Kingdom": O'Donovan, cit. Farquhar; Slatin, 242.

57. "All around": Muhammad Bey's slave boy, SAD, 643/4. This account paraphrased in C. Royle, 247–49. See Abbas Bey, "The Diary of Abbas Bey," in *SNR* XXIII (1952), 179–96.

58. "These are bad": Major Arthur Herlth, cit. Ohrwalder, 86.

59. *"Allahu"*: Holt, *Mahdist State,* 141.

60. "terrible and sudden": Muhammed Bey, SAD, 643/4. See also Gulla, Sheikh A., "The Defeat of Hicks Pasha," in *SNR* VIII (1925), 119–24.

61. "We are about": Gladstone at Guildhall, November 9, 1883, cit. Allen, 183.

7: The Unrolling of the Scroll: 1884

1. "The dawdling policy": Cromer, *Modern Egypt,* I, 393n.

2. "The origin": Ibid., I, 11. "military" to "Equatorial": Ibid., 388n.

3. "The Avenger": Schölch, *Egypt for Egyptians,* 303–04.

4. "separate": Baring to Granville, November 22, 1883 (PRO 30/29/161). "a serious": Baring to Granville, No. 547, November 24, 1883 (FO78/3559).

5. "till the danger" and "our engaging": Gladstone to Granville, November 23, 1883, *Political Correspondence,* II, 114, it. 1148 (PRO 30/29/127).

6. Sharif Pasha's plan: Baring to Granville, No. 43, September 28, 1883 (FO78/3557).

7. "Very ticklish": Granville to Gladstone, November 27, 1883, Gladstone, *Political Correspondence,* II, 117, it. 1153 (BM Add. Ms. 44176, f.10).

8. "The Egyptian government": Baring to Granville, No. 559, November 26, 1883 (FO78/3559).

9. "Khartoum is": Memo from Wolseley, enclosed in Hartington to Gladstone, November 23, 1883 (PRO 30/29/133).

10. "We are resting": Granville to Baring, December 7, 1883 (PRO 30/29/199).

11. "Hicks' army": Colborne, 287.

12. Survivor reaches Khartoum: December 17, 1883, reported by Frank Power in the *Times,* December 18, 1883.

13. "more definite" and "without any": Baring to Granville, December 10, 1883, cit. Cromer, *Modern Egypt,* I, 379. "absolutely": Baring to Granville, No. 597, December 12, 1883 (FO78/3560). Khartoum untenable: "The only way of saving what remains

is to attempt a general retreat on Berber; this is the real state of affairs here, and I beg you to impress it on His Highness the Khedive," Colonel de Coetlegon, another of Hicks's officers to survive after being invalided back to Khartoum, in Coetlegon to Wood, November 25, 1883, enclosed in Baring to Granville, No. 560, November 26, 1883 (FO78/3559).

14. "If the whole": Baring to Granville, November 22, 1883 (PRO 30/29/161).
15. "the burden," "of doubtful," and "abandon": Granville to Baring, December 13, 1883 (PRO 30/29/199).
16. "the very strongest": Baring to Granville, December 17, 1883, PRO 30/29/161. "an increase"; Baring to Granville, No. 615, December 16, 1883 (FO78/3560).
17. "We have thousands": Sharif Pasha, *The Standard,* January 11, 1884.
18. "He is in very good": Baring to Granville, January 8, 1882 (PRO 30/29/162).
19. Nubar's orders of January 16–18, 1884: Enclosed in Baring to Granville, No. 79, January 19, 1884 (FO78/3665).
20. "The Egyptian government": Baring to Granville, No. 44, January 16, 1884 (FO78/3665).
21. "He has always": Sir Harry Verney to Granville, November 17, 1882 (PRO 30/29/168).
22. "His name alone": (Col. Bevan Edwards) and "If the Mahdi" (Sir Andrew Clarke): To Granville, cit. S. Childers, *The Life & Correspondence of the Rt. Hon. Hugh C.E. Childers, 1827–96* (2 vol.; London: John Murray, 1901), I, 176.
23. "Do you see": Granville to Gladstone, November 27, 1883, Gladstone *Political Correspondence,* II, 116, it. 1152 (BM Add. Ms. 44176, f.8).
24. "I can quite": Gladstone to Granville, November 29, 1883, ibid., II, 117, it. 1156 (BM Add. Ms. 44547, f.3).
25. "It is odd": Gordon to Augusta, Lausanne, March 18, 1880, *Letters to his Sister,* 206.
26. "The grandest Englishman": Caption to Ape cartoon "The Ever-Victorious Army," *Vanity Fair,* February 19, 1881. "I nearly burst": Gordon to Augusta, Bombay, June 19, 1880, *Letters,* 208. "I strike": Gordon to Augusta, Port Louis (Mauritius), June 24, 1881, ibid., 227.
27. "Unrolling of the Scroll": Twywell, June 24, 1881, ibid., 213. "the Garden of Eden": Trench, 171–72.
28. "All events": Gordon to Augusta, SS *Quetta,* January 5, 1883, *Letters,* 285.
29. "I foresaw": Jerusalem, February 28, 1883, ibid., 304. "I feel for": Gordon to Miss Felkin, December 1883 (Gordon Boys' School Mss., Woking), cit. Trench, 196. "in the suppression": Gordon to Augusta, Jerusalem, February 28, 1883, *Letters,* 304. "Tell him": Gordon, according to his nephew Colonel Louis Gordon, cit. Allen, 167–68.
30. "at its head": Gordon to the Anti-Slavery Society, January 5, 1884, cit. Allen, 212.
31. "I hate the idea": Wolseley to Gordon, January 4, 1884, BM Add. Ms. 52388, cit. Nutting, 226.
32. "You have 6,000 men in Khartoum": *Pall Mall Gazette,* January 9, 1885.
33. "We cannot send": *Pall Mall Gazette,* January 9, 1885.
34. "No effort": *Morning Advertiser,* January 11, 1885.
35. "a grave mischief" and "bastinadoed *fellahin*": Gladstone to Granville, Hawarden, January 6, 1884, Gladstone *Political Correspondence,* II, 145, it. 1208. "a few years," "confidence," and "The sultan's whole": Gladstone to Granville, Hawarden, January 11, 1884, ibid., II, 147, it. 1211. "I care more": Gladstone to Granville, Hawarden, January 7, 1884, ibid., II, 145, it. 1209.

36. "inquire into conditions": Arthur and Maurice, 173–74. "If Gordon says he believes": Granville to Gladstone, Foreign Office, January 14, 1884, Gladstone, *Political Correspondence,* II, 149, it. 1214.

37. "While his opinion on the Soudan": Gladstone to Granville, Hawarden, January 16, 1884, ibid., II, 150, it. 1216.

38. "Do you ever tell a lie?": Holland, I, 417. Allen (228) assumes this was merely Gordon's reflection on his own experience as an aide. Holland, unsurprisingly, implies intent to fool the ministers.

39. "want you to understand" to "Yes": Gordon at the War Office, January 18, 1885, from Gordon to Reverend R. H. Barnes, January 22, 1885 (BM Add. Ms. 51298), cit. R. H. Barnes and C. E. Brown, *C.G. Gordon, A Sketch with Facsimile Letters* (London: Macmillan, 1885), 102–03, which uses "orders" for "ideas."

40. "Does not believe": Northbrook to Baring, evening of January 18, 1885, cit. Cromer, *Modern Egypt,* I, 429. Dilke's account: L. S. Gwynn and G. M. Tuckwell, *Life of Sir Charles Dilke,* (2 vol.; London: Macmillan, 1917), II, 29.

41. "report on," "consider," "the possible," and "Colonel Gordon": Granville to Baring, War Office, January 18, 1885 (FO78/3696).

42. Hartington's report: Hartington to Gladstone, January 18 and 19, 1885 (PRO30/29/128). "Northbrook, Harrington" and "very pleasing": Granville to Gladstone, Foreign Office, January 18, 1884, Gladstone, *Political Correspondence,* II, 151, it.1217.

43. Gladstone's day: *Diaries,* XI, 102.

44. Gordon's telegrams of the night of January 18: Gordon to Granville, January 19, 1884 (FO78/3696).

45. "At Last!": *Pall Mall Gazette,* January 19, 1885.

46. "Are you sure we did not commit": Granville, cit. Trench, 207. "Gordon's mission": Gladstone, *Diaries,* XI, 103.

47. "would in no time eat up": Gordon's memo to Baring, SS *Tanjore,* January 22, 1884 (FO78/3696). "a mere figurehead" and "to advance": Lieutenant General Sir G. Graham, *Last Words with Gordon* (London: Chapman & Hall, 1887), 4.

48. "trouble": Baring to Granville, January 19, 1884 (PRO 30/29/162).

49. "What a curious creature": Baring to Granville, January 28, 1884 (PRO 30/29/162). "a few months," "confederation," and "with the least": Baring to Gordon, enclosed in Baring to Granville, January 25, 1884 (FO78/3666); see also Cromer, *Modern Egypt,* I, 444–46.

50. "mystic" and "The Mahdi's": Wingate Mss., SAD 245/3.

51. "slave for life": Wingate Mss., SAD 245/3.

52. "Zubair's appointment": *Times,* December 1, 1883.

53. "desirable to interfere": Granville's minute on a memo from the British and Foreign Anti-Slavery Society, December 4, 1883 (FO78/4194).

54. "I leave for Sudan tonight": Gordon to Augusta, January 28, 1884, *Letters,* 374.

55. "supported": Rev. A. H. Sayce, *Reminiscences* (London: Macmillan), 229–30. "I have always contemplated": Baring to Granville, March 9, 1884 (FO78/3665).

56. "deluge": *Last Words,* Graham, 28.

57. "rather wild": Baring to Granville, February 4, 1884 (PRO 30/29/162).

58. "As you are aware": Stewart's diary, enclosed in Baring to Granville, February 11, 1884 (FO78/3667, No.171).

59. "violent and protracted," "prestige," "evacuation," and "the only": Gordon to Baring, No. 225, February 8, enclosed in Baring to Granville, February 25, 1884 (FO78/3667).

60. "Know, respected sir": Gordon to the Mahdi, February 11, 1884, cit. Abu-Salim, II, 244–45.

61. "pondered all night," "the Pandora," "the divorce," and "No": Stewart's diary, enclosed in Baring to Granville, No. 171, February 11, 1884 (FO78/3667).

62. "I have come here alone": Stewart's diary, enclosed in Baring to Granville, No. 296, March 11, 1884 (FO78/3668).

63. "the white element": Stewart, diary enclosed in Baring to Granville, No. 296, March 11, 1884 (FO78/3668).

64. "I am watching": Gordon, enclosed in Baring to Granville, No. 237, February 27, 1884 (FO78/3667).

65. "Pray do not consider": Gordon to Baring, March 3, 1884, enclosed in Baring to Granville, No. 254, March 3, 1884 (FO78/3667).

66. "When evacuation": Gordon to Baring, February 26, 1884, enclosed in Baring to Granville, No. 240, February 28, 1884 (FO78/3667).

67. "More like": Granville to Gladstone, February 6, 1884, Gladstone, *Political Correspondence*, II, 154, it. 1226, n.1.

68. "more formal": Kimberley to Granville, February 9, 1884 (PRO 30/29/136). Granville replied, "I do not know how our present hold is to be strengthened." "must be struck": Victoria to Gladstone, February 9, 1884, Buckle (ed.), III, 477.

69. "Another element of trouble": Gladstone to Granville, February 10, 1884, *Political Correspondence*, II, 156, it. 1231, Add. Ms. 44176, f.134.

70. "double purpose" and "a simple service": Gladstone, February 12, 1884, *Hansard's Parliamentary Debates* (IIIrd series; London: Cornelius Buck, 1884), vol. 284, cols. 724 and 726–27.

71. "a degradation": C. H. Allen to Granville, March 10, 1884 (FO78/4194). "For generations": William Forster to the Commons, March 10, 1884, *Hansard,* III, vol. 285, col. 1073. "Oriental crackers": Granville's note on Gladstone to Granville, February 27, 1884 (PRO 30/29/144).

72. "Public opinion": Granville to Baring, No. 109, February 23, 1884 (FO78/4194).

73. "Englishmen": *Newcastle Chronicle,* March 7, 1884.

74. "This may well be the last": Gordon to Augusta, Khartoum, March 11, 1884, *Letters,* 381.

8: Armies of God: 1885

1. *The Ballad of East & West: Ballads & Barrack Room Ballads* (London: Macmillan, 1899), 3–11.

2. *The Indissoluble Bond: Al-Urwah al-Wutka,* in French *Le Lien Indissoluble.* "the Root": Afghani, "The Neicheri [Materialists] in India" (1881), pub. in *The Indissoluble Bond,* August 28, 1884, trans. Keddie, *Islamic Response,* 133.

3. "bales," "remotest corners," and "the spirit": Afghani to Rochefort, cit. H. Rochefort, *Les aventures de ma vie* (4 vol.; Paris: Paul Dupont, 1896), IV, 346. "England believes": Ibid., IV, 345.

4. "somewhat Europeanised": Blunt, *Gordon,* 208. "all nations" and "In truth": Answer of Jamal ed-Din to Ernest Renan, *Journal des Debats,* May 18, 1883, trans. Keddie, *Islamic Response,* 182.

5. "very curious," "humanitarian," and "attachment": Blunt, March 27, 1884, *Gordon,* 208–09. For several possible reasons, including his unwillingness to explicitly associ-

ate Afghani with a modish and mildly ridiculous cult, Blunt does not name the "Russian lady" as Madame Blavatsky. Her companions were Colonel H. S. Alcott, founder of the Theosophical Society, and two Bengali Hindu adepts on their way to study for the Bar at London. Blavatsky and Alcott came to Europe to meet with their London and Paris lodges and to lobby the British Foreign Office for religious rights for Ceylonese Hindus.

6. "He is the forerunner": Blunt, *Gordon,* 208. "a caravan," "secret letters," and "my old pupil": Rochefort, IV, 347.
7. "the champion of the Mohammedans": Blunt, March 30, 1884, *Gordon,* 211. "mediator" and "treaty": Blunt, April 23, 1884, ibid., 223. "opportunely" and "the pacification": Blunt to Gladstone, April 23, 1884, ibid., 583–84.
8. "If all": *Pall Mall Gazette,* April 24, 1884.
9. "a somewhat decayed blood" and "a thousand sportsmen": Blunt, April 29 and 18, 1884, *Gordon,* 231 and 221.
10. "The enemy": Gordon to Henry Gordon, March 15, 1884, cit. Nutting, 254.
11. "I am not a trickster": Ohrwalder, 98; Abu-Salim, II, 254.
12. "a filthy": Allen, 320. "I cannot have": Wingate, 115.
13. "The town": Gordon to Baring, March 31, 1884, cit. Allen, 321.
14. "trumpery": Gordon to Baring, received April 9, 1884, cit. Cromer, *Modern Egypt,* I, 549.
15. "some 500": Gordon to Baker, April 18, 1884, cit. Nutting, 255.
16. "I consider": Gordon to Baring, April 18, 1884 (FO78/3761).
17. "You know" and "Messieurs": Frank Power, January 2, 1884, Power, 70.
18. "General Gordon": Gladstone, April 3, 1884, *Hansard* (III), vol. 282, col. 1151.
19. "I have from the first": Gladstone to Hamilton, April 9, 1884, cit. Hamilton, II, 566. "one who bore": Gladstone, memo by Hamilton, BM Add. Ms. 56452.
20. Cuzzi's telegrams: Allen, 321. "The question": Baring to Granville, No. 350, March 24, 1884 (FO78/3669).
21. "These officers": Baring to Granville, No. 362, March 26, 1884 (FO78/3669).
22. "You shot," "actual," "plans," and "wishes": Granville to Baring, No. 191, March 28, 1884 (PRO 30/29/200).
23. "Gordon is our officer": Hartington to Granville, February 6, 1884 (PRO 30/29/134). "The first thing" and "some sort of independent": Hartington to Granville, April 16, 1884 (PRO 30/ 29/134). Wolseley's memo to Granville, March 22, 1884, and Wilson's memo, March 28, 1884, both PRO 30/29/170.
24. "in the last": Gladstone to Hartington, April 13, 1884, BM Add. Ms. 44547. "hemmed in," "surrounded," "bodies," and "more or less": Gladstone to the Commons, April 21, 1884, *Hansard* (III), vol. 283, col. 138. "If Berber": Gladstone to the Commons, April 23, 1884, *Hansard* (III), vol. 283, col. 476.
25. "more as a man": Blunt, May 13, 1884; Gordon, 240.
26. "It meant a war": vote of censure debate, May 12, 1884, *Hansard* (III), vol. 288, col. 55.
27. "You will incur": Ibid., col. 65.
28. "What does he mean" and "What is the answer": Ibid., col. 65.
29. "solemn covenant," "reasonable assurance," and "resources": Ibid., col. 73. "It may" and "treasure": Ibid., col. 71. "British and Christian": Ibid., 70.
30. "I believe": Ibid., 216.
31. "grudge": Ibid., col. 235.
32. "aggressive" and "measures": Granville to Egerton, No. 266, May 17, 1884 (FO78/3663).

33. "We are all": Gordon to Baring, July 13, 1884 (received at Cairo August 28, 1884), Cromer, *Modern Egypt*, I, 578.
34. "I say": Gordon to Baring, cit. Cromer, *Modern Egypt*, I, 578, and Allen, 360. The questionnaire, dispatched from London on April 23, 1884, reached Khartoum on July 29; Gordon's reply reached Cairo on September 18.
35. "All hope": Power to Moberley Bell, July 31, 1884, *Power*, 111.
36. "How many": Gordon to Baring, September 9, 1884, cit. Trench, 262, and Nutting, 271. This did not reach Cairo until November.
37. "We never": Mahdi to Gordon, October 22, 1884, cit. Gordon (ed. Habe) *Journals at Khartoum*, 522–30.
38. "Poor Gordon": Wolseley to Baker, July 26, 1884, cit. Sir R. Wingate, "Sir Samuel Baker's Papers," in *Quarterly Review*, CCCV (1967), 295–308, 303.
39. "My military": Wolseley to Hartington, July 23, 1884, cit. Holland, I, p. 468.
40. "share the responsibility": Gladstone to Hartington, August 19, 1884, BM Add. Ms. 44147. "five minutes" and "I cannot be responsible": Hartington, memo to Granville, July 15, 1884, BM Add. Ms. 44147, f.87.
41. "It is a question of personal honour": Hartington to Granville, July 31, 1884, BM Add. Ms. 44147, f.91.
42. "a domestic," "a foreign," and "a Gordon": Gladstone to Granville, August 1, 1884, Gladstone, *Political Correspondence*, II (BM Add. Ms. 44177, f.6). "assured": Gladstone to Hartington, August 19, 1884, BM Add. Ms. 44147.
43. "I despair": Hartington to Gladstone, August 22, 1884, BM Add. Ms. 44147.
44. "usual crowd," "a real old man," "cordial and affectionate," and "very Turkish": Wolseley's diary, September 9 and 10, 1884, Wolseley, *In Relief of Gordon*, 11, 13, and 14.
45. "It is troubles": Wolseley to Lady Wolseley, November 25, 1884, *Letters*, 132.
46. "Gordon inundates": Wolseley, September 19, 1884, Wolseley, *In Relief*, 18.
47. "If they do not": Gordon, October 23, 1884, *Journals*, 212. "shake hands": Wolseley to Lady Louisa, September 13, 1884, *Letters*, 119.
48. "One tumbles": Gordon, November 12, 1884, *Journals*, 292.
49. "I judge": October 5, ibid., 144.
50. "It is simply," "in honour," and "six months": Ibid., 139. "had deigned to say": September 19, 1884, ibid., 50.
51. "I own": Ibid., 54. "It has come": September 24, ibid., 86–87.
52. "I toss": September 14, 1884, ibid., 28–29.
53. "It is inexplicable": December 13, 1884, ibid., 364.
54. "Now MARK" and "You send": December 14, 1884, ibid., 365.
55. "Khartoum": Gordon to Wolseley, December 14, 1884, in Wolseley to Baring, December 31, 1884, enclosed in Baring to Granville, No. 1, January 1, 1885 (FO78/3799).
56. "The game is up": Gordon to Watson, December 14, 1884, enclosed in Baring to Granville, No. 182, February 25, 1885 (FO78/3801).
57. "a long line": Wilson, 19–20.
58. "One poor": Ibid., 27–28.
59. "By Jove" and "fine old": Ibid., 28.
60. "The men's": Ibid., 71.
61. "Gordon's steamers": Allen, 418.
62. "There is no escape": Abdullahi to Gordon, December 7 or 8, 1884; Gordon, *Journals at Khartoum*, App. AB, 476.
63. The Mahdi wished to trade Gordon for Urabi: Slatin, 344.
64. "Having seen": The Mahdi (via Abdel Rahman al-Mahdi) to Gordon, January 12,

1885, cit. Al-Mahdi, A., "Correspondence (inc. Arabic text and trans.) on the Mahdi's last letter to Gordon," in *SNR* XXIV (1941), 231–32.

65. "We swear": B. Bedri, *Memoirs of Babikr Bedri* (2 vol., ed. and trans. Y. Bedri and P. Hogg; London: Ithaca Press, 1969, 1980), 28–29.

66. The circumstances of Gordon's death remain controversial. The first printed account, that of Bordeni Bey, who was not an eyewitness, was the least reliable. Cemented in the public imagination by William Joy's painting, *General Gordon's Last Stand*, it was endorsed in F. R. Wingate's *Mahdiism & the Egyptian Sudan* (London: Frank Cass, 1891), 163–72. But two other accounts indicate that Gordon, true to character and intention, went down fighting, probably en route to the ammunition store. Kitchener's investigation of 1885 found only one witness, a palace servant who reported that Gordon was shot while leading a party toward the house of Austrian consul Martin Hansal, which lay near the ammunition dump. Gordon's bodyguard Khalil Agha Orphali corroborated this account; Orphali, the wounded man Gordon rescued from the palace steps, claimed to have been next to Gordon as they fought their way into the courtyard (SAD, 439/637/2). See Trench, 290–91; J. A. Reid, "The Death of Gordon: An Eyewitness Account," in *SNR*, XX (1937), 172–73.

9: The New Caliphate: 1885–89

1. "Those that have": The Koran, 5:31.
2. "The bullets": Wilson, 170. "heavy feeling": Ibid., 179. "loud, rushing": Ibid., 174. "It seemed": Ibid., 175.
3. "Khartoum is reported": Wolseley to Hartington, No. 44, February 4, 1885 (PRO WO/33/34/II/224).
4. "Dreadful news": Victoria, February 5, 1885, Buckle (ed.), III, 597. "These news": Victoria to Gladstone, February 5, 1885, ibid., 598.
5. "The circumstances": February 5, 1885, Gladstone, *Diaries*, XI, 289.
6. "Our power": Victoria to Sir Henry Ponsonby, February 5, 1885, Buckle (ed.), III, 598.
7. "the effect": Gladstone to Eddy Hamilton, February 7, 1885, Hamilton, II, 790. *"The Candidate"*: Gladstone, February 10, 1885, *Diaries,* XI, 293.
8. "How shall": Queen Victoria to Augusta Gordon, February 11, 1885, cit. Blunt, Gordon, 204–05. "In his own death": Tawfik to Sir Henry Gordon, cit. Nutting, 314. "sit in state": B. Farwell, *Prisoners of the Mahdi* (London: Longmans, 1967), 100. "the disturbance": Gladstone, February 12, 1885, *Diaries,* XI, 295.
9. "If anything": February 4, 1885, Wolseley, *In Relief,* 135.
10. "Let all" and "He will": February 6, 1885, ibid., 138. "fools": February 4, 1885, ibid., 135. "a hideous," "the most serious," and "We shall": February 24, 1885, ibid., 153.
11. "gone so completely" and "Oh!": February 11 and 14, 1885, ibid., 141 and 145. "I never saw": March 1, 1885, ibid., 159.
12. "The final": Gladstone, February 27, 1885, *Diaries,* XI, 301. "The lowest": Gladstone to Granville, April 1, 1885, cit. Gladstone, *Political Correspondence,* II, p. 354, it. 1616 (PRO 30/29/129).
13. "This has been": Blunt, *Gordon,* 373. "treat": Ibid., 384.
14. "Sir Charles": March 11, 1885, Wolseley, *In Relief,* 164.
15. William McGonagall, "General Gordon, the Hero of Khartoum," in *Poetic Gems from the Works of William McGonagall* (1890; London: Duckworth, 1954), 167–69.

16. "a moment": Gladstone, June 25, 1885, *Diaries*, XI, 368.
17. "Know that": Mahdi to the people of Fez, May 8, 1885, cit. Abu-Salim, IV, 481–88. "We will": Mahdi to Tawfik, trans. P. M. Holt, "The Sudanese *Mahdia* and the Outside World: 1881–89," in *Bulletin SOAS*, XXI (1958), vol.1, 281.
18. Division of slaves: Ohrwalder, 164–65.
19. Mahdi's decline: Ibid., 181–83.
20. Mahdi's treatment: Bermann, 290–91.
21. The Mahdi's death: Slatin, 370.
22. "Friends of the Mahdi": Ibid., 371–72.
23. *"Ed-din"*: Khalifa, cit. Ohrwalder, 187.
24. "a guidance," "a long light," and "Every rank": "Manshur al-Sha'ra" ("The Proclamation of the Hair"), in *Ms. Abd al-Rahman al-Nujumi* (SOAS, London: photographed material from Sudanese State Archives, Box 9, File 11) ff.96–98, trans. Holt, *Mahdist State*, 123–24. "in his time," "Mecca," and "successors": Abdullahi, cit. and trans. Nicoll, 233.
25. "The cavalry": Uthman wad Adam, February 1889, cit. Wingate, *Mahdiism & the Egyptian Sudan*, 457.
26. "The Prophet": Abdullahi in a vision published January 6, 1888, trans. Holt, *Mahdist State*, 133.
27. "General Gordon": Cromer, *Modern Egypt*, II, 369.
28. "Berlin": Baring to Rosebery, No. 48, February 9, 1886 (FO633/6).
29. "the nature": Cromer, *Modern Egypt*, II, 373. "in the elaboration" and "for English": Ibid., 373–74. "tranquilising": Ibid., 61.
30. "A delusion" and "the Mahdi": Ibid., 374. "Internationalism": Ibid., 442.
31. "appearance": Ibid., 376–77.
32. "So long": Salisbury to the sultan, ibid., 380.
33. "extraordinary expenditure": Ibid., 449. "barbarous": Baring to Salisbury, No. 318, October 9, 1888 (FO78/4147).
34. "After me": Grenfell's letter to al-Nujumi, trans. Holt, *Mahdist State*, 161.
35. "Our object": Ibid., 162.
36. "It is my": Grenfell to G.O.C. Egypt, enclosed in Clarke to Salisbury, No. 331, August 26, 1889 (FO78/4242).
37. "a whole crop" and "the most serious": Baring to Salisbury, No. 101, December 11, 1889 (FO78/4243). "small but influential" and the 1886 prediction: Cromer, *Modern Egypt*, II, 80 and 81.

10: Gladstone's Egg : 1889–96

1. "I had no": Joseph Conrad, *Heart of Darkness* (1899; London: Everyman, 1993), 12.
2. "The classes": Salisbury, *Bentley's Quarterly Review*, 1869, cit. Roberts, 295.
3. "dirty, dunghill": Wolseley to Lady Louisa, Dongola, November 24, 1884, Wolseley, *In Relief*, 31.
4. "Artless Dodger": Title of a Salisbury article in the *Saturday Review*; Roberts, 199.
5. "splendid isolation": Joseph Chamberlain, quoted by the *Times*, January 22, 1896.
6. "France": Ferry, cit. W. L. Langer, *The Diplomacy of Imperialism, 1890–1902* (New York: Knopf, 1935), I, 74.
7. "The other powers": Rosebery, ibid.
8. "inconvenient" and "I heartily": Salisbury to Scott, May 4, 1887, cit. Lady G. Cecil,

Life of Robert, Marquis of Salisbury (London: Hodder & Stoughton, 1924), IV, 43. "lunatics": Salisbury to the earl of Lytton, December 1888, cit. Roberts, 530. "bastard": Salisbury, cit. Roberts, 518.

9. "What a pity": Sir H. Johnston, *The Story of My Life* (London: Chatto & Windus, 1923), 221.
10. "Great Britain's Policy": *Times*, August 22, 1888.
11. "Africa": Salisbury, cit. Lady G. Cecil, *Salisbury*, II, 254.
12. "The Mahdi is the representative": Slatin, 516.
13. "from light brown to deepest black": Ibid., 521.
14. "nightly orgies": Ibid., 520. Abdullahi's slaves: Ibid., 525.
15. "As one walked": Ohrwalder, 308–09. "an ear": Ibid., 312. "like glass": Ibid., 313.
16. "social life": Slatin, 526.
17. Massacre of the Batahin: Ohrwalder, 335–37.
18. "I would not": Salisbury to Baring, cit. Cromer, *Modern Egypt*, II, 75.
19. "When once" and "They were": Salisbury to Baring, March 28, 1890, ibid., 75–76n.
20. "merely the surf": Salisbury at the Mansion House, November 1888, cit. W. S. Churchill, *The Story of the Malakand Field Force* (London: Longmans, Green, 1901), title page. "a Machiavellian": Blunt, *Gordon*, 505.
21. "tiresome little Power": Salisbury to Lord Harrowby, 1889, cit. Roberts, 520.
22. "hard-baked" and "middle-aged": Gladstone, June 25, 1892, *Diaries*, XI, 36.
23. "I thought": Gladstone to Rosebery, September 17, 1892, cit. R. R. James, *Rosebery: A Biography of Archibald Philip, 5th Earl of Rosebery* (London: Weidenfeld & Nicholson, 1963), 262. "Jingoism": Sir William Harcourt to Rosebery, September 23, 1892, cit. A. G. Gardiner, *Life of Sir William Harcourt* (London: Constable, 1923), II, 193–95.
24. "put a torch": Gladstone, cit. James, 279–80.
25. "The time has arrived": Rosebery to J. R. Rodd, ex-consul at Zanzibar, later Cromer's assistant at Cairo, March 5, 1894 (FO10/625).
26. "knife": E. C. H. Phipps to Lord Kimberley, No. 24, August 9, 1894 (FO10/618). "He is attempting": Rosebery to Queen Victoria, August 15, 1894, Buckle (ed.), II, 420.
27. "The advance": *Hansard's Parliamentary Debates* (IV series; London: Eyre & Spottiswoode, 1894), vol. 32, col. 405–06.
28. "We shall counter": Francis Deloncle, cit. C. Michel, *Mission de Bonchamps: Vers Fachoda à la Rencontre de la Mission Marchand* (Paris: Plon, 1905), 5.
29. "If we settle": Sir Samuel Baker, May 1893, Langer, I, 127.
30. "*Il faut*": Carnot to Monteil, *Souvenirs Vécus: Quelques Feuillets de l'Histoire Coloniale* (Paris: Société d'Editions Géographiques; Maritimes et Coloniale, 1924), 65–68. V. Prompt, "Soudan Nilotique," in *Bulletin de l'Institut Egyptien*, III, iv (1893), 71–116.
31. "*l'intrigue*" and "created": Deloncle to the Chamber, February 28, 1895, cit. Sanderson, *Upper Nile*, 272n. "to force," "France's," and "Is it not": Marchand, November 10, 1895, *Documents Diplomatiques Français, 1871–1914* (First Series; Paris: Alfred Costes, 1951), vol. XII, no. 192, 280 (*Note du Capitaine Marchand*).
32. "It is obvious": Cromer to Rosebery, Rosebery, April 1895, cit. H. Temperley and L. M. Penson, *Foundations of British Foreign Policy from Pitt to Salisbury, or, Documents Old & New* (Cambridge: Cambridge University Press, 1938), 504–05.
33. "The Italian": Salisbury to Cromer, No. 17, March 12, 1896 (FO78/4863).
34. "We desired": Salisbury to Cromer, March 13, 1896, cit. marquess of Zetland, *Lord Cromer: Being the Authorised Life of Evelyn Baring* (London: Hodder & Stoughton, 1932), 223.

35. "We have been": Salisbury to Dufferin, No. 130, March 12, 1896 (FO78/4893).
36. "Would give": Cromer to Salisbury, No. 1, January 13, 1896 (FO78/4986). "The Sudan is worth": Temperley and Penson, loc. cit.
37. "His behaviour": Cromer to Salisbury, No. 69, March 28, 1896 (FO78/4863).
38. Kitchener dancing: Arthur, *Life*, I, 187.

11: The House of War: 1896–99

1. "He has no age": Steevens, 45–46.
2. "unbounded": Kitchener to Augusta Gordon, October 16, 1885, BL Add. Ms. 51300, f. 156.
3. "slaying niggers": Kitchener to Millie Kitchener, December 3, 1873 (Parker Papers, private collection), Pollock, 29. "What a glorious": Kitchener to Millie, March 7, 1875 (Parker Papers), ibid., 34. "sober": Undated article (c. 1910) by Reverend F. Penny, from the Archives of the Guild of St. Helena, ibid., 37.
4. "Though a little": Margot Asquith, *More Memories* (London: Cassell, 1933), 122.
5. "dear friend": Kitchener to his father, May 14, 1884 (Parker Papers), Pollock, 87. "If any harm": Arthur, I, 88. "I can hardly" and "taken the heart": Kitchener, March 17, 1885, ibid., I, 105.
6. "mismanagement": Kitchener to E. A. Floyer, March 17, 1885, Royal Engineers Archives, Chatham, file 5001.4/3 (ES41).
7. "laden with black": "An Officer" (H. L. Pritchard), *The Sudan Campaign, 1886–1899* (London: Chapman & Hall, 1899), 70.
8. "His campaign": Salisbury to Cromer, November 27, 1896, Salisbury Papers (Hatfield House), 109, Magnus, 107.
9. "the production": Cromer to Salisbury, Salisbury Papers (Hatfield House), 110, ibid., 114.
10. "You have no idea": Kitchener to Clinton Dawkins, October 6, 1897, Arthur, I, 217.
11. "a swarm": Steevens, 31. "a white": Ibid., 30.
12. "two horses": Ibid., 32. "the man": Ibid., 52. "a full military": Ibid., 86.
13. "The *Sirdar*": C. Repington, *Vestigia* (London: Constable, 1919), 33.
14. "a line": Steevens, 145.
15. "Give it him": Burleigh, *Sirdar*, 235.
16. "A very": Repington, 166. "clean-jointed" and "Black spindle": Steevens, 151.
17. "Are you": Ibid., 153.
18. "a pair of English lads": Henty, *The Dash for Khartoum* (1885).
19. "Medal-Hunter": Churchill, *My Early Life*, 177. "deeply": Ibid., 176.
20. "It is understood": Ibid., 182.
21. "The movement": Ibid., 183.
22. "filmy world": Ibid., 186. The French flag: Holt, *Mahdist State*, 209.
23. "a dark": Churchill, *My Early Life*, 189.
24. "Come along" and "many bottles": Ibid., 192–93. "only a sporting" and "steel flail": Ibid., 195.
25. "By Allah": Digna, according to the accounts of Sheikh Amin Ahmad Sharfi, nephew of Amhad Abdel Karim, who attended the council as an emir of the Red Flag, and the emirs Yunus al Dikaim and Ismail Ahmad, via Said Musa Yacub, the Khalifa's nephew; Zilfu, 152.
26. "The whole": Churchill, *The River War*, II, 87. "Crusaders": Churchill, dispatch of

September 6, 1898, Churchill, *Winston's Wars*, 105.

27. "Cease fire!": E. W. C. Sandes, *The Royal Engineers in Egypt & the Sudan* (Chatham: Institute of Royal Engineers), 264.
28. "dark, cowled": Churchill, *My Early Life*, 201.
29. "Of course": Ibid., 203.
30. "The scene": Ibid., 205.
31. "Bright flags": Ibid.
32. "exactly like": Churchill, *River War*, II, 142.
33. "succession": Churchill, *My Early Life*, 208. "His face": Churchill, dispatch of September 6, 1898, Churchill, *Winston's Wars*, 111.
34. "Can't he": Sandes, 268.
35. "MacDonald": Burleigh, *Khartoum Campaign*, 285.
36. "A good dusting": Churchill, *River War*, II, 162.
37. "I thank": Magnus, 133.
38. "Tell some": Churchill, dispatch of September 9, 1898, Churchill, *Winston's Wars*, 123.
39. "valiant warriors": Churchill, dispatch of September 10, 1898, ibid., 128.
40. "All was filthy," "a large bucket," and "a nameless man": Churchill, dispatch of September 10, 1898, ibid., 127.
41. "No corpses": Salisbury to Kitchener, D. Bates, *The Fashoda Incident of 1898: Encounter on the Nile* (Oxford: Oxford University Press, 1984), 140.
42. "Le blanc": Emily, 226.
43. "Sir Herbert" and "another example": *The Sketch*, September 7, 1898.
44. "a wicked act": Churchill, *River War*, II, 214.
45. "the destruction" and "It savours": Victoria to Kitchener, March 24, 1899, Buckle (ed.), III, 353–54.
46. "When I returned": Kitchener to Victoria, ibid., 352–53.
47. "How strange" and "It is like": Churchill, dispatch of September 12, 1898, Churchill, *Winston's Wars*, 139 and 140. "paid the bill" and "The destruction": Ibid., 122.
48. "I bid good-bye": W. S. Blunt, *My Diaries: 1888–1914* (2 vol., New York: Alfred A. Knopf, 1921), I, 380.

Epilogue: Cairo, 1899

1. *Fuzzy-Wuzzy*: Published in the *Scots Observer*, March 15, 1890, collected in *Departmental Ditties, Barrack Room Ballads & Other Verse* (New York: U.S. Book Co., 1890), 63–66. The British soldiers nicknamed the Hadendowa of the Red Sea hills "Fuzzy-Wuzzies" for their hairstyles.
2. "The winding-up of the estate": Dicey, 225. "the great high priest": Cromer, *Modern Egypt*, II, 443.
3. "I had made": Blunt, *My Diaries: 1888–1914* (2 vol.; New York: Alfred A. Knopf, (1921), I, 340.
4. "tottering," "fond," and "courteous": Jackson's introduction to Zubeir Pasha, *Black Ivory, or, The Story of Zubeir Pasha, Slaver & Sultan, as Told by Himself* (trans. and ed. H. C. Jackson; Khartoum: Sudan Press, 1913), 1.
5. "The rubbish": Osama bin Laden to Robert Fisk, *Independent*, December 6, 1996.

Bibliography

Abdu, Cheikh M. *Rissalat al-Tawhid: Expose de la Religion Musulmane,* trans. B. Michel and M. A. Razik (Paris: Librairie Orientaliste Paul Geuthner, 1925).

Abu-Salim, M. I., ed. *Kitab sa'adat al-mustahdi bi-sirat al-Imam al-Mahdi* (6 vol.; Oxford: Oxford University Press, 1972).

Adams, C. C. *Islam & Modernism in Egypt: A Study of the Modern Reform Movement Inaugurated by Muhammad Abduh* (London: Oxford University Press, 1933; reprinted as *Orientalism: Early Sources: Vol. X,* London: Routledge, 2000).

Ahmed, J. M. *The Intellectual Origins of Egyptian Nationalism* (London: Oxford University Press Middle Eastern Monographs, 1960).

Al-Afghani, J. ed-D. *Documents Concernant Seyyed Jamal-al-Din Afghani,* ed. I. Afshar, I. and A. Mahdavi (Teheran: Teheran University Publication No. 841, 1963).

Ali, A. I. M. *The British, the Slave Trade & Slavery in the Sudan, 1820–1881* (Khartoum: Khartoum University Press, 1972).

Allen, B. M. *Gordon & the Sudan* (London: Macmillan, 1931).

Anti-Slavery Jubilee: Meeting of the British & Foreign Anti-Slavery Society in the Guildhall of the City of London, Under the Presidency of H.R.H. the Prince of Wales (Pamphlet reprinted from *The Anti-Slavery Reporter,* 1884; British Library BL 8156.cc.6/3).

Arthur, Sir G. *The Life of Lord Kitchener* (3 vols.; New York: Macmillan, 1920).

Arthur, Sr. G., and Maurice, Major General Sir F. *The Life of Lord Wolseley* (London: William Heinemann, 1924).

Baker, F. *Morning Star: Florence Baker's Diary of the Expedition to Put Down the Slave Trade on the Nile, 1870–73,* ed. A. Baker (London: William Kimber, 1972).

Baker, Sir S. "The Soudan & its Future," *The Contemporary Review,* XLV (January 1884), 64–80.

Berlioux, E. F. *The Slave Trade in Africa in 1872, Principally Carried on for the Supply of Turkey, Egypt, Persia and Zanzibar* (London: Edward Marsh, 1872).

Bermann, R. *The Mahdi of Allah: The Story of the Dervish Mohammed Ahmed* (New York: Macmillan, 1932).

Blunt, W. S. *Secret History of the British Occupation of Egypt: Being a Personal Narrative of Events* (London: Unwin, 1907).

Blunt, W. S. *Gordon at Khartoum: Being a Personal Narrative of Events in Continuation of "A Secret History"* (London: Stephen Swift, 1911).

Broadley, A. M. *How We Defended Arabi & His Friends: A Story of Egypt & the Egyptians* (London: Chapman & Hall, 1884).

Buckle, G., ed. *The Letters of Queen Victoria* (3 vol.; London: John Murray, 1928).

Burleigh, B. *Khartoum Campaign* (London: Chapman & Hall, 1899).

Burleigh, B. *Sirdar & Khalifa, or, The Reconquest of the Sudan* (London: Chapman & Hall, 1898).

Cave, S. "The Financial Condition of Egypt" ["The Cave Report"], in *Parliamentary Papers* LXXXIII (London: HMSO, 1876).

Chaillé-Long, C. *The Three Prophets: Chinese Gordon, Mohammed-Ahmed (El Maahdi), Arabi Pasha* (New York: Appleton & Co., 1884).

Churchill, W. S. *My Early Life: A Roving Commission* (London: Thornton Butterworth, 1930).

Churchill, W. S. *The River War: An Historical Account of the Reconquest of the Sudan* (2 vol., ed. Col. F. Rhodes, D.S.O., London, New York & Bombay: Longmans, Green & Co., 1899).

Churchill, W. S. *Young Winston's Wars: The Original Despatches of Winston S. Churchill, War Correspondent, 1897–1900,* ed. F. Woods (London: Leo Cooper, 1972).

Colborne, Col. J. *With Hicks Pasha in the Soudan: Being an Account of the Senaar Campaign in 1882* (London: Smith, Elder & Co., 1884).

Cole, J. R. I. *Colonialism & Revolution in the Middle East: Social & Cultural Origins of Egypt's Urabi Movement* (Princeton: Princeton University Press, 1993).

Cole, J. R. I. "New Perspectives on Sayyid Jamal al-Din al-Afghani in Egypt," in *Iran and Beyond: Essays in Middle Eastern History in Honor of Nikki R. Keddie,* eds., Mathee, R., and Baron, B. (Costa Meza: Mazda, 2000), 13–35.

Colomb, Captain, R.N., *Slave-Catching in the Indian Ocean: A Record of Naval Experiences* (London: Longmans, Green & Co., 1873).

Colvin, Sir A. *The Making of Modern Egypt* (London: Seeley, 1906).

Cooper, J. *The Lost Continent, or Slavery and the Slave Trade in Africa* (London: Longmans, 1875).

Crabitès, P. *Gordon, the Sudan and Slavery* (London: Routledge, 1933).

Crabitès, P. *Ismail: The Maligned Khedive* (London: Routledge, 1933).

Cromer, Earl of (Sir Evelyn Baring). *Abbas II* (London: Macmillan, 1951).

Cromer, Earl of (Sir Evelyn Baring). *Modern Egypt* (2 vol., London: Macmillan, 1908).

Curtin, Philip D. *The Image of Africa, Vol. I: British Ideas and Action, 1780–1850* (Wisconsin: University of Wisconsin Press, 1964, 1973).

Daly, M. W. *Empire on the Nile: The Anglo-Egyptian Sudan, 1898–1934* (Cambridge: Cambridge University Press, 1991).

Daly, M. W. *Imperial Sudan: The Anglo-Egyptian Condominium, 1934–56* (Cambridge: Cambridge University Press, 1991).

Dicey, E. *The Story of the Khediviate* (London: Rivingtons, 1902).

Dujarric, G. *L'Etat Mahdiste du Soudan* (Paris: Librairie Orientale et Americaine, 1901).

Elton (Lord) G. *General Gordon* (London: Collins, 1954).

Emily, Dr. J. *Mission Marchand: Journal de Route du Dr. J. Emily* (Paris: Librairie Hachette, 1913).

Ewald, J. *Soldiers, Traders & Slaves: State Formation & Economic Transformation in the Greater Nile Valley, 1700–1885* (Wisconsin: Wisconsin University Press, 1990).

Farwell, B. *Queen Victoria's Little Wars* (London: Allen Lane, 1973).

Ganem, H. "Europe's Stake in the Soudan," in *The Fortnightly Review,* CCIX (May 1884), 645–54.

Gessi, R. *Seven Years in the Soudan: Being a Record of Explorations, Adventures & Campaigns Against the Arab Slave Hunters,* trans. L. Wolffsohn and B. Woodward (London, Sampson, Low, Marston & Co., 1892).

Giegler, C. C. *The Sudan Memories of Carl Christian Giegler Pasha, 1873–83,* ed. R. Hill (Oxford: Oxford University Press, 1984).

Giffin, M. B. *Fashoda: The Incident and Its Diplomatic Setting* (Chicago: University of Chicago, Press, 1930).

Gladstone, W. E. *The Gladstone Diaries with Cabinet Minutes & Personal Correspondence, Vols. IX: January 1875–December 1880; X: January 1881–June 1883; XI: July 1883–December 1886,* ed. H. C. G. Matthew (Oxford: Clarendon, 1986, 1986, 1990).

Gladstone, W. E. *Midlothian Speeches, 1879,* ed. M. R. D. Foot (New York: Leicester University Press, 1971).

Gladstone, W. E. *Political Correspondence of Mr. Gladstone & Lord Granville, 1876–1886, Vol. I: 1876–82; Vol. 2: 1883–6,* ed. A. Ramm (Oxford: Oxford University Press, 1962).

Gleichen, Lieutenant Colonel Count, ed. *The Anglo-Egyptian Sudan, a Compendium Prepared by Officers of the Sudan Government, Vol. I* (London; HMSO, Harrison & Sons, 1905).

Gordon, C. G. *Colonel Gordon in Central Africa, 1874–1879,* ed. G. B. Hill (London: Thomas de la Rue, 1881).

Gordon, C. G. *The Journals of Major-General C.G. Gordon at Khartoum,* ed. E. Hake (Boston: Houghton, Mifflin & Co., 1885).

Gordon, C. G. *Letters to his Sister* (London: Macmillan, 1888).

Gray, R. *History of the Southern Sudan, 1839–1899* (London: Oxford University Press, 1961).

Hamilton, Sir E. *The Diaries of Sir Edward Hamilton* (2 vol.; Oxford: Oxford University Press, 1972).

Harrington, P., and Sharf, F., eds. *Omdurman 1898: The Eye-Witnesses Speak* (London: Greenhill, 1998).

Harrison, R. T. *Gladstone's Imperialism in Egypt: Techniques of Domination* (Westport: Greenwood, 1995).

Hasan, Y. F. *The Arabs & the Sudan from the 7th Century to the Early 16th Century* (Edinburgh: Edinburgh University Press, 1967).

Hicks Pasha, Gen. Sir W. *The Road to Shaykan: Letters of General Sir Williams Hicks Pasha, Written During the Sennar & Kordofan Campaigns, 1883,* ed. M. W. Daly (Durham: Durham University Centre for Middle Eastern & Islamic Studies, 1983).

Hill, R. *Egypt in the Sudan, 1820–1881* (London: Oxford University Press, 1959).

Hill, R. L. *A Biographical Dictionary of the Sudan* (2nd ed., London: 1957).

Hobsbawm, E. *The Age of Capital* (London: Weidenfeld & Nicolson, 1975; 1995).

Holland, B. H. *The Life of Spencer Cavendish, 8th Duke of Devonshire* (2 vol.; London: Longmans, Green, 1911).

Holt, P. M. *The Mahdist State in the Sudan, 1881–1898: A Study of Its Origins, Development and Overthrow* (Oxford: Clarendon Press, 1958).

Holt, P. M. "The Place in History of the Sudanese Mahdia," in *SNR,* XL (1959), 107–12.

Hunter, F. *Egypt Under the Khedives, 1805–1879: From Household Government to Bureaucracy* (Pittsburgh: Pittsburgh University Press, 1984).

Jackson, H. C. *Osman Digna* (London: Methuen, 1926).

Jeal, T. *Livingstone* (London: Heinemann, 1973).

Karrar, A. S. *The Sufi Brotherhoods in the Sudan* (London: Hurst, 1992).

Karsh, E., and Karsh, I. *Empires of the Sand: The Struggle for Mastery in the Middle East, 1789–1923* (Cambridge: Harvard University Press, 1999).

Keddie, N. R. *An Islamic Response to Imperialism: Political & Religious Writings of Sayyid Jamal ad-Din al-Afghani* (Berkeley: University of California Press, 1968; 1983).

Keddie, N. R. *Sayyid Jamal ad-Din al-Afghani: A Political Biography* (Berkeley: University of California Press, 1972).

Kedourie, E. *Afghani and Abdu: An Essay on Religious Unbelief & Political Activism in Modern Islam* (1966; London: Frank Cass, 1997).

Kramer, M. "Pen and Purse: Sabunji and Blunt," in *The Islamic World From Classical to Modern Times: Essays in Honor of Bernard Lewis,* eds. C. E. Bosworth et al. (Princeton: Darwin, 1989), 771–80.

Kramer, R. S. *Holy City on the Nile: Omdurman, 1885–1898* (Unpublished Ph.D. dissertation; Northwestern University, Evanston, Illinois, 1991).

Laffin, J. *The Arabs as Master Slavers* (Englewood: SBS, 1982).

Landes, D. *Bankers & Pashas: International Finance & Economic Imperialism in Egypt* (London: Heinemann, 1957).

Leon, E. de. *Egypt Under Its Khedives: Or, The Old House of Bondage Under New Masters* (London: Sampson, Low, 1881).

Lewis, B. *Race & Slavery in the Middle East: An Historical Enquiry* (Oxford: Oxford University Press, 1990).

Lewis, D. L. *The Race to Fashoda: European Colonialism & African Resistance in the Scramble for Africa* (London: Bloomsbury, 1998).

Madden, R. R. *Egypt & Mohammed Ali: Illustrative of the Condition of His Slaves and Subjects* (London: Hamilton, Adams & Co. 1841).

Magnus, P. *Kitchener: Portrait of an Imperialist* (London: John Murray, 1958; Arrow, 1961).

Malet, Sir E. *Egypt 1879–83* (London: John Murray, 1909).

Malortie, Baron de. *Egypt: Native Rulers & Foreign Interference* (London: William Ridgway, 1882).

Marlowe, J. *Spoiling the Egyptians* (London: Andre Deutsch, 1974).

Matthew, H. C. G. *Gladstone, 1809–1898* (2 vol., 1986 and 1995; single-volume edition, Oxford: Oxford University Press, 1997).

McCoan, J. C. *Egypt Under Ismail* (London: Chapman & Hall, 1889).

Mengin, F. Histoire. *Somaire de l'Egypte sous le Gouvernement de Mohamed Aly* (2 vol., Paris, 1839).

Meredith, J., ed. *Omdurman Diaries, 1898: Eyewitness Accounts of the Legendary Campaign* (London: Leo Cooper, 1998).

Michel, C. *Vers Fachoda: À la Rencontre de la Mission Marchand* (Paris: Librairie Plon, 1909).

Mofawi, Reda. *Slavery, Slave Trade & Abolition Attempts in Egypt & the Sudan, 1820–1882* (Lund: Studies in International History, 1982).

Moorehead, Alan. *The White Nile* (London: Hamish Hamilton, 1960).

Moorehead, Alan. *The Blue Nile* (London: Hamish Hamilton, 1962).

Morris, J. *Heaven's Command: An Imperial Progress* (London: Faber & Faber, 1973).

Neufeld, C. *A Prisoner of the Khaleefa: Twelve Years' Captivity at Omdurman* (London: Chapman & Hall, 1899).

Nicoll, F. *The Sword of the Prophet: The Mahdi of Sudan & the Death of General Gordon* (Stroud: Sutton, 2004).

Nutting, Anthony. *Gordon: Martyr and Misfit* (London: Constable, 1966).

O'Fahey, R. S. *Sufism in Suspense: The Mahdi and the Sufis*, in *Islamic Mysticism Contested*, ed. F. de Jong and Berndt Radtke (Leiden: Brill: 1999), 267–82.

Ohrwalder, Fr. J. *Ten Years' Captivity in the Mahdi's Camp, 1882–92, from the Original Manuscripts of Father Joseph Ohrwalder, late Priest of the Austrian Mission Station at Delen in Kordofan, by Major F. R. Wingate* (London: Sampson Low, Marston & Co., 1892).

Pakenham, Thomas. *The Scramble for Africa, 1876–1912* (London, Weidenfeld & Nicolson, 1991).

Pollock, J. C. *Kitchener, comprising The Road to Omdurman & The Saviour of the Nation* (London: Constable, 2001).

Porter, A., ed. *The Oxford History of the British Empire, Volume III: The 19th Century* (Oxford: Oxford University Press, 1998).

Power, F. *Letters from Khartoum: Written During the Siege* (London: Sampson, Low, 1885).

Ratib al-Imam al-Mahdi (The Mahdi's Ratib), SAD 97/1.

Roberts, A. *Salisbury: Victorian Titan* (London: Weidenfeld & Nicolson, 1999).

Robinson, R., and Gallagher, J. *Africa & the Victorians: The Official Mind of Imperialism* (London: Macmillan, 1961).

Robson, B. *Fuzzy Wuzzy: The Campaigns in the Eastern Sudan, 1884–85* (Tunbridge Wells: Spellmount, 1993).

Royle, C. *The Egyptian Campaigns, 1882–1885* (London: Hurst & Blackett, 1900).

Royle, T. *The Kitchener Enigma* (London: Michael Joseph, 1985).

Russell, H., and Gattie, W. *The Ruin of the Soudan: Cause Effect, and Remedy* (London: Low, Marston, 1892).

Sanderson, G. N. *England, Europe & the Upper Nile, 1882–1899* (Edinburgh: Edinburgh University Press, 1965).

Sanderson, G. N. "Conflict & Co-operation between Ethiopia & the Mahdist State, 1884–98," *Sudan Notes & Records*, L (1969), 84–90.

Schölch, A. *Egypt for the Egyptians!: The Socio-political Crisis in Egypt, 1878–82* (London: Ithaca, 1981).

Schölch, A., "The 'Men on the Spot' and the English Occupation of Egypt in 1882," in *Historical Journal*, XIX (1976), 773–85.

Segal, Ronald. *Islam's Black Slaves: The History of Africa's Other Black Diaspora* (London: Atlantic, 2001).

Shaked, H. *The Life of the Sudanese Mahdi: A Historical Study of Kitab sa'adat al-mustahdi bi-sirat al-Imam al-Mahdi by Ismail din Abd-al-Gadir* (New Jersey: Transaction, 1978).

Shibeika, M. *British Policy in the Sudan, 1882–1902* (London: Oxford University Press, 1952).

Shibeika, M. *The Independent Sudan* (New York: Peller & Sons, 1959).

Shukry, M. F. *Equatoria under Egyptian Rule: The Unpublished Correspondence of C. G. Gordon with Khedive Ismail during the Years 1874–1876* (Cairo: 1953).

Slatin, R. C. *Fire & Sword in the Sudan: A Personal Narrative of Fighting & Serving the Dervishes, 1879–95* (London: Edward Arnold, 1892, 1896).

Spiers, E., ed. *Sudan: The Reconquest Reappraised* (London: Frank Cass, 1998).

Stanley, Henry M. *Address Before the Anti-Slavery Society at Manchester, October 23rd, 1884* (BL 10097.m.12/1).

Steevens, G. W. *With Kitchener to Khartoum* (London: Blackwood, 1898).

Stevenson, R. C. "Old Khartoum, 1821–85," in *SNR*, XLVII (1966), 1–38.

Strage, Mark. *Cape to Cairo* (London: Jonathan Cape, 1973).

Taylor, B. *A Journey to Central Africa* (New York: Sampson, Low, 1854).

Theobald, A. B. *The Mahdiya: A History of the Anglo-Egyptian Sudan, 1881–1899* (London: Longman, Green & Co., 1951).

Trench, C. C. *The Road to Khartoum: A Life of General Charles Gordon* (New York: Norton, 1979).

Trimingham, J. S. *Islam in the Sudan* (London, Frank Cass, 1965).

Warburg, G. *Islam, Sectarianism & Politics in Sudan since the Mahdiya* (London: Hurst, 2003).

Wilkinson-Latham, R. *The Sudan Campaigns, 1881–98* (London: Osprey, 1976).

Wilson, Col. Sir C. W. *From Korti to Khartoum: A Journal of the Desert March from Lorti to Gubat, and of the Ascent of the Nile in General Gordon's Steamers* (London: Blackwood, 1886).

Wingate, Major F. R. *Mahdiism and the Egyptian Sudan: Being an Account of the Rise & Progress of Mahdiism & of the Subsequent Events in the Sudan to the Present Time* (London: Macmillan, 1891).

Wingate, Colonel F. R. "Note on the Dervish Wounded at Omdurman," in *Parliamentary Blue Books: Egypt*, I (London, HMSO, 1899).

Wingate, R. *Wingate of the Sudan: The Life & Times of General Sir Reginald Wingate, Maker of the Anglo-Egyptian Sudan* (London: John Murray, 1955).

Wolseley, Field-Marshal Viscount G. *In Relief of Gordon: Lord Wolseley's Campaign Journal of the Khartoum Relief Expedition, 1884–85*, ed. A. Preston (London: Hutchinson, 1967).

Wolseley, Field-Marshal Viscount G. *The Story of a Soldier's Life* (2 vol., London: Ernest Russell, 1903).

Wolseley, Field-Marshal Viscount G., and Wolseley, Lady Louisa Erskine. *The Letters of Lord & Lady Wolseley, 1870–1911*, ed. Sir G. Arthur (London: William Heinemann, 1922).

Ziegler, P. *Omdurman* (London: Fredrick Warne, 1980).

Zilfu, I. H. *Karari: The Sudanese Account of the Battle of Omdurman* (London: Frederick Warne, 1980).

Zubair Pasha, R. *Black Ivory, or, The Story of Zubeir Pasha, Slaver & Sultan, as Told by Himself*, ed. H. C. Jackson (Khartoum: Sudan Press, 1913).

Acknowledgments

———— ⌀⌀ ————

THIS STORY OF THREE EMPIRES was developed by two agents: Lizzy Kremer at David Higham Associates in London and George Lucas of Inkwell Management in New York. It was improved beyond recognition by a remarkable editor, Bruce Nichols at Free Press. Overall supervision came from the wonderful Maja Löfdahl, lover, friend, and editor, too.

Much of my research was carried out in the Rare Books & Music and Manuscripts Room of the British Library, the London Library, and the Public Record Office, London. The staffs of all three were as helpful as ever.

I benefited from the expert opinions of Professor Michael Reimer of the American University at Cairo; Professor Ehud Toledano of Tel Aviv University; Professor Emad Hemal of Suez University; Dr. C. David Laney of the South African Astronomical Observatory; and the philatelist Kevin Burrell.

M. Didier Hirsch checked my French translations, and Natasha Green helped with illustrations. Alex Britell of Harvard University was a patient and ingenious research assistant.

I am especially indebted to Fergus Nicoll. Apart from writing the first modern biography of the Mahdi—*The Sword of the Prophet*, a book abundant in information and interpretation—he also gave freely of his time and knowledge.

Index

————— ⟋⟍ —————

Page numbers in *italics* refer to illustrations and maps.

About the Author

DOMINIC GREEN studied English Literature at Oxford
and pursued a dual career as writer and jazz guitarist
before returning to academia at Harvard.
He lives in Cambridge, Massachusetts.